GAME DESIGN:
A PRACTICAL APPROACH

GAME DESIGN:
A PRACTICAL APPROACH

PAUL SCHUYTEMA

CHARLES RIVER MEDIA
Boston, Massachusetts

Cover Design: Tyler Creative
Cover Image: Austin Brooks
Technical Editor: Rafael Chandler

CHARLES RIVER MEDIA
25 Thomson Place
Boston, Massachusetts 02210
617-757-7900
617-757-7969 (FAX)
crm.info@thomson.com
www.charlesriver.com

This book is printed on acid-free paper.

Paul Schuytema. *Game Design: A Practical Approach.*
ISBN: 1-58450-471-4

Library of Congress Cataloging-in-Publication Data
Schuytema, Paul.
  Game design : a practical approach / Paul Schuytema.
     p. cm.
  Includes index.
  ISBN 1-58450-471-4 (pbk. with cd-rom : alk. paper)
  1. Computer games--Programming. I. Title.
  QA76.76.C672S38 2006
  794.8'1526--dc22
                              2006019629

Printed in the United States of America
06 7 6 5 4 3 2 First Edition

To Mary and the girls, who always remind me
that the trickiest but most rewarding game design of all is life.

—Paul Schuytema

Contents

Foreword

Game design is an interesting mixture of art and science, and only recently has the science part gotten more of the focus it deserves. Everyone has ideas for making a game they would love to play more than anything else; everyone has revolutionary ideas that will change the face of gaming as we know it; and everyone thinks that because they have these ideas, they're fit to be a game designer. They're wrong. It takes far more than a great idea to be a game designer. Although one amazingly great idea can get you halfway there, the rest is where the sweat and hard work come in: writing your design document properly and working hard with a development team to see your ideas come to fruition.

This book is just what you need to help you reach your goal. The guidance Paul offers you is the result of many years of hard work in the real world of game development; believe me, I've known Paul for a long time. New designers, pay close attention to the details here; they will really make a difference in the quality of your work. More often than not your development team coworkers and engine technology will dictate the course of your game and not the other way around —it's working with these fluid parameters efficiently that will bring you a great development experience and hopefully a great game.

Always remember: the journey is the reward.

John Romero

Preface

GAME DEVELOPMENT: A PRACTICAL APPROACH

Game development is an exciting process—there is nothing more satisfying than to create an interactive play experience that can provide hours of enjoyment for a player. Working to design a play experience that you create yourself or an entire development team creates is a thrilling, yet very difficult, endeavor.

Designers have many places to go to learn their craft, but often this learning is trial and error and experienced on the job. Very little foundational information exists documenting the skills and roles of a game designer at work. It is the goal of this book to provide those foundations—the skills needed to succeed and perform as a game designer in the professional world.

AUDIENCE

This book is aimed at three primary audiences:

Designer-to-be: The meat and potatoes of this book is aimed at aspiring designers—those who know games, have been playing games for years, and would like to learn more about the craft of designing games. The book assumes knowledge of the medium of interactive games, but not of game design itself.

Game designer: This book will also prove useful to a working game designer. The game design atoms provide some vital touch points on various aspects of "in the trenches" game design, and the sidebars from some of our top designers provide some very real and practical wisdom.

The development hobbyist: The games industry has inspired an army of weekend hobbyists who enjoy learning more about games and game development by working on their own projects. This book provides a framework upon which a hobbyist can begin prototyping gameplay and dynamics right away, using the Lua language and the included game engine "sandbox."

IN THIS BOOK

In this book, you will find an introduction to the craft of game design, starting with an exploration of just what a game and game design are. From there, the book explores the skills a designer needs to bring to bear on a game design and then dives into the very practical nuts and bolts of a number of vital game design topics.

The book starts you at square one and takes you on a journey of discovery as we get deep into the work of game design. Along the way, we'll learn the scripting language Lua and explore a sample game that will allow us to test and explore the game design concepts we discuss. The book is divided into three major parts:

Part I: Part I is an introduction to game design and the skills an individual needs to think and perform like a game designer.

Part II: Part II is an exploration of the more abstract concepts of game design, from sensory reaction, to game stimulus, to challenge, to emotion in games.

Part III: Part III is a detailed exploration of key design topics, with game design "atoms" and actual examples delivered through the included 2D game engine and the Lua scripting language.

ON THE CD-ROM

The CD-ROM that accompanies this book provides a host of useful materials that will extend your understanding of game design even further. On it, you will find:

- *Eye Opener,* the "demo game" we explore in Part III
- A complete 2D game engine and all support Lua scripts
- Game examples that go beyond those found in the text of the book, to allow hobbyists to go even further
- Example game design and pitch documents
- A command-line Lua interpreter (the application and documentation)
- A custom Lua-enhanced shareware version of the Zeus program editor
- A basic Lua scripting style guide

Acknowledgments

This book wouldn't have been possible without the fine scripting work of Nick Carlson, who worked with me on the sample game and the various examples in the book—he's been Johnny Olson to my Clark Kent for the last two books! In addition, a huge thank you goes out to Austin Brooks, for the awesome comic art in the *Eye Opener* game.

I want to send out a huge thanks to the Game Designer's Workshop—their mentorship has meant so very much to me over the years. To the working designers who have contributed to this book: I am humbled by your wisdom and willingness to help. And thanks to John Romero for penning the introduction for this book—his wide breadth and depth of design experience never ceases to amaze me.

I would be remiss if I didn't thank the technical editor, Rafael Chandler, for excellent additions to the context of the book (as a writer, sometimes I can't see the forest for the trees) and to Beth, the copy editor who makes me look like a better writer than I am. Finally, thanks to the rest of the Charles River Media team (especially Lance Morganelli!) and the entire production team for helping to create a project I am very proud of. A special thanks goes out to Jenifer Niles, who was patient almost to the point of breaking, but who also allowed me to write a book I've been dreaming about for years—you are the best!

Part

I

Introduction to Game Design

A re you ready to get started? Before we dive in, we need to build a firm foundation upon which to grow, and that's what we'll be doing here.

We're going to make some assumptions before we get started. We're going to assume that you already play many games, and have a solid understanding of what today's games and some of the classics of the past are like. We're also going to assume that you've already done some thinking, brainstorming, or experimenting with game design or game ideas.

In this introduction, we cover the basics of game design, what a game designer does, and what homework you can expect to do to ready yourself for the tasks ahead. Then, we dive into the primary tool of the trade: the game design document. We then provide a quick overview of the game environment you'll be working in within this book, so you'll be able to study, deconstruct, and enhance our examples throughout the book.

Time to sharpen your pencils and get out that notebook, and ask our first all-important question: what is game design?

1 What Is Game Design?

If you were a builder you would expect to arrive at a job site and find all the materials you need: the wood, the plumbing fixtures, the shingles, the boxes of nails, the joists, bags of dry cement, heating ducts, bags of insulation, etc. so you could build your client's dream house. With all the materials you need, where would you begin? Odds are, you'd probably stand there and scratch your head. You have the raw materials, but you have no idea what to do with them. You have no plan. To even start your task, you need a blueprint—the plan for the dream house that allows you to take the component materials and assemble them into a complete structure (Figure 1.1).

The simplest answer to the question, "What is game design?" is this: a game design is a blueprint for a game. A designer is the person charged with creating that blueprint, and out of that blueprint, given the right mix of talent and effort, a game will emerge.

FOUNDATIONS

Let's begin at the beginning, with the most basic of all game design questions: *just what is a game*? When you train yourself to think as a game designer, you had better have a clear idea of what you're talking about. Is a game a process or a result? Is a game active or passive? Is a game a story? Is a game a simulation? Is a game always fun?

FIGURE 1.1   Here are all the components to build a house, but where do you begin? What's your plan?

Try something for a few moments—put down this book and fire up a game you have been playing recently—either on your computer or your favorite console. Enter the game and play for five minutes—no more and no less. Now, grab a sheet of paper and come back to the book.

First, write down a short description of your game experience. It might read something like this:

> *My level-seven barbarian appeared on the spawn point and I selected my two-handed broadsword. I heard the door ahead of me creaking open, so I walked forward. In a few seconds, two giant spiders jumped out of the open door and closed on me. Moving backward, I swung my sword back and forth, green ooze spraying everywhere. The first spider fell and I jumped forward, somersaulting and coming down on top of the second spider with my sword in the middle of its abdomen—the spider exploded in a shower of green and red goo. I sheathed my sword and stepped over the fallen arachnids, picking up 250 gold pieces and a plain platinum ring. In the distance, I heard a howl...*

Now, think back and write down just what you did, as a human being in the real world, during those moments of gameplay. Remember, you were just sitting at your desk or in front of your console game system. It might be something like this:

> *I tapped the Start button to select inventory, used my thumb to select the two-handed broadsword, and tapped the triangle button to re-enter the game. I moved the left analog stick to the left with my thumb. I then jammed the stick right to backpedal and hammered the X button with my right thumb over and over again. Next, I tapped the triangle button and held it, then released and*

quickly tapped the X button twice. I then used the left analog stick to move my character left and right over the spawned treasure to pick it up.

Finally, take a few minutes to jot down the messages the game presented to you and the decisions you made based on those messages. A message is some sort of information the game delivers to you as a player: it may be a sound or something you see on screen. Your exercise might look something like this:

Game Message	Decision
Spawned into a dark, creepy dungeon.	Armed avatar with two-handed sword.
Sound of door creaking open.	Move forward, alert, sword at the ready.
Two spiders lunging for attack.	Since I can't kill both by standing there (not without taking a ton of damage), I backpedal and swing my sword to kill the first spider.
First spider dies.	I know that the odds are now in my favor, so I tap a special kill move to leap at the second spider and kill it.
The sound of coins falling and a pile of gold and a ring icon appear where the spiders were.	I walk my character over the treasure icons to collect them.

Take a moment to look over what you have written down. Each of these little paragraphs is a different representation of the same game experience, and in a way, each reflects a different key aspect of what makes the play experience so fun and engaging. Do any of these representations of your gameplay experience give us more insight than the others as to what a game might be?

What Is a Game?

By now, your mind might be churning a bit and we'll bet that you might say that a game is a process that leads to a result—that is, you do something, and then something happens, like you win or lose. Of course, "do something" can be very complicated— consider the game of *Monopoly*®, for example (Figure 1.2). A player's "do something" realm comprises rolling dice, moving along the board, picking up cards, buying property, purchasing buildings, collecting rents, mortgaging property to the bank, and so on—so many processes to lead all the players to a single result: who has the most money?

FIGURE 1.2 The game of *Monopoly* engages the player through many activities and decisions.

As computer gamers, we've seen amazingly simple games, like *Tetris* and *Bejeweled*. We've also seen games of amazing complexity, such as modern-era flight simulators or a massive-multiplayer game like *Star Wars Galaxies*™. Each of these games presents a player with a series of challenges as the play progresses and a goal in mind, whether it is victory in a scenario, accumulation of money, reaching the next level, beating the ultimate boss, or achieving a high score.

Let's begin with a simple definition of what a game might be: a game is a series of processes that takes a player to a result.

If we think of our previous gameplay narrative, we fit this definition quite nicely. Think for a moment about other games you've played—do they fit within the scope of this definition? Odds are, the answer is yes, but so do many other things in life—following a Yahoo!® map to find a friend's house, going to the grocery story, or practicing a new song on the guitar. All of those fall neatly within the definition we've come up with, but clearly aren't games. It seems like we are on the right track, but we're missing a key point that makes an activity a game. Take a moment, look through our threesome of game experiences, and see if you can locate a clue in there.

Let's turn for a moment to one of our veteran designers, Sid Meier. Sid has crafted such classic games as *Pirates!*®, *Railroad Tycoon*™, and *Civilization*®. Sid has a very simple definition of what a game is: a game is a series of interesting decisions.

With this nugget, we are on to something. Look at the decision table shown previously. Consider the last entry where we pick up the gold. We receive the information that treasure is available (both visually and aurally) and decide to move our barbarian avatar over the objects to pick up the treasure. This is a very clear decision, but is it interesting? Not in the slightest. Imagine an entire game made up of this kind of decision—it's quite easy to do. Visualize the classic *PacMan*® for a moment and think of playing it without the ghosts who wander through the maze—you are free to wander through the maze and chomp through powerups until you win the level. Would you call that a game?

However, look at our previous example and consider the decision we make when the two spiders jump out and attack us. We know we are too weak to take them both head-on, so we backpedal and swing while we retreat, to destroy one spider and shift the scales of power in our direction. Is that an interesting decision? Absolutely. Imagine a game with those types of decisions—it would be like . . . well, like *PacMan* intact. We decide on which row of dots to chomp based on where the ghosts are and if they are in a danger state to us. The data comes in quickly, it's 100% visual, and informs us to make each jerk of the joystick. Of course, we can make a poor decision and run right into a ghost, or those two spiders, but that's still interesting.

However, using the rubric of "interesting decisions," we have reached into a core element in the definition of a game. But, think for a moment about all the games you've played—and those that have given you the most richly rewarding experiences. There is more there than just decisions. There is the context of the game, be it football or raiding the Mummy-King's lair. There is the mood and tone of the game, from the humor of a *Leisure Suit Larry*™ game to the cold, naked fear of a *Resident Evil*® game. There is also the skill aspect of a game—you need to spend time to master body punches in *Fight Night*, and it takes a lot of practice to land a simulated plane on an aircraft carrier. All of these aspects of the experience are vital and all contribute to what we think of as an "electronic game."

With these factors in mind, let's postulate a slightly more robust definition for an interactive, electronic game.

A game is a play activity comprised of a series of actions and decisions, constrained by rules and the game world, moving toward an end condition. The rules and the game world are delivered by electronic media and controlled by a digital program. The rules and game world exist to provide a framework and context for a player's actions. The rules also exist to create interesting situations to challenge and oppose the player. The player's actions, his decisions, choices, and chances, really, his journey, all comprise the "soul of play." It is the richness of context, the challenge, excitement, and fun of a player's journey, and not simply the attainment of the end condition, that determines the success of the game.

While this may seem a rather academic definition, it's quite useful. Read it through and compare this definition against some of the most fun games you've played and against the least fun—how does it hold up?

If you look at the last sentence of the definition, it illuminates the importance of the "journey." This can't be over-stressed in the slightest, since this journey is what we also call the "gameplay." Gameplay is what happens between the bookends of the start and finish of a game—from the time you learn your goals until you reach your victory or loss at the end. It is the challenges along this journey of gameplay, and the macro- and micro-victories a player will achieve, that will create a compelling and exciting play experience.

The Concept of Fun

If we consider an experience that fits within the scope of the previous definition, we clearly have a game on our hands. Does this mean that a game will necessarily be fun? Certainly not. While we can work to nail down a very useable definition of a game, things aren't nearly as easy when it comes to fun—because so much of our sense of "fun" is based on who we are.

From a philosophical vantage point, here are four components to an experience of fun: receptiveness, expectations, your subjective likes, and "ingredient X."

First, before you can experience a truly fun play experience, you need to be tuned in to receive it. That means that you know something is coming and you're ready to go. If you're not in the receiving mood, nothing will seem like fun to you. If you've had a bad day or are distracted, a potentially fun experience can be nothing more than an annoyance. You have to be receptive to fun to enjoy an experience. There are times when you may be more receptive to a book or a movie or another noninteractive experience. And there will be times when you pick up a game controller, power up your console, and are ready for a game experience—you are prepared to be receptive.

Once you're ready to receive a play experience, your interpretation of that experience is governed by your expectations. For an experience to be satisfying, it has to meet or exceed your standing expectations. In everything we do, we have expectations, and those expectations are grown out of some kind of knowledge of that experience (either firsthand or secondhand). If you're given a chance to participate in an experience wholly without reference and expectations, you probably won't enjoy it (familiarity is necessary for it to be processed by your brain).

If you are excited about the thrilling expectations of water skiing, only to discover that the experience doesn't create a sensation of speed and excitement but makes you nauseous, then your expectations are not met and you won't have any fun. Think about when you were a kid—how you loved to spin—on tire swings, merry-go-rounds, and your Dad's office chair. Spinning was preceded by an expectation of the dizzy sensation, and when that sensation occurred, it was a blast. Now think of that same sensation as an adult—some still enjoy that feeling of disorientation, but most adults are rather violently opposed to feeling dizzy—the expectation of the experience is negative and spinning is not fun at all (Figure 1.3).

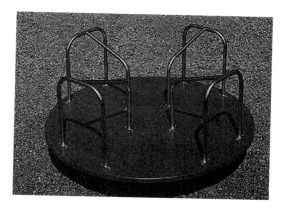

FIGURE 1.3   A merry-go-round may be a blast for a child, but how fun is it for an adult to feel dizzy?

The third component is your own subjective quirks—consider it an amendment to cultural expectations. Some people like the "whoopee" feeling of a roller coaster, while others don't. Some people love the music of the Grateful Dead, while others don't. Some people like action games like *Medal of Honor*™, while others prefer a game like *Myst*® or *Bejeweled*. If you have a subjective leaning one way or the other, it will color your expectations and your impressions of value and coolness.

Entire volumes could be written about the origin of our subjective likes and dislikes—they are born of our experiences and the positive and negative associations we have with those experiences. We refer to these as quirks because our internal associations aren't often 100% rational. We may fear or deeply dislike entering a hospital, even though we know it is a place for healing. Some experience in the past with a loss of a loved one or a personal illness can color our interpretations of the experience.

Conversely, the music of a certain band you love might not be the most skilled—the melodies may be derivative and the lyrics rather simplistic and sentimental. However, perhaps you were jamming to that music the moment you met your future spouse or the moment you scratched off the winning numbers on your lotto ticket. The positive context forever linked a strong positive feeling with that music, even though the music itself was rather passive in the original experience.

Now on to the meat of the matter: ingredient X. It's that elusive "something extra" that transforms an experience from one of interest to one of fun and joy—*but first*, we need to have already satisfied everything else—we are ready to receive, it has lived up to or surpassed our expectations, it plays into our honeycomb of subjective likes and positive experience, and so on.

So, what is ingredient X? It's a combination of things: surprise, coincidence, flashes of genius, extreme emotion, and transientness. For us, the easiest way to think about an experience that is truly fun is this: it's a moment when your expectations are not just surpassed, but shattered in new and unexpected ways, and also it's a moment that has that flavor of a "fleeting moment in time"—it happens for an instant and you know it can't be duplicated (that's very important).

Think of a moment during a gaming experience when you snatched victory from the jaws of defeat. Your focus was intense, the game was meeting your expectations, the play was challenging, and your avatar was struggling to survive until you reached the next save point. At that moment, you are having a great gameplay experience, and as a designer, this is the state you hope to achieve for the players for 70–80% of their playing time (it's not an easy task, but it's possible). But then, near death, just about ready to lose the game, you come through with an amazing combination of luck and skill and destroy the final enemy as you launch your way through the exit of the level. Panting and sweating slightly, you lean back and let out a sigh. Now *that* was fun!

In the medium of game creation, we can capture fun in two areas: in the general flow of the game experience and in the individual moments of a certain player's unique experience during a playing session. As designers, we strive to create a game experience that creates an overarching feeling of fun for our players, *and* we work to create gameplay situations that provide those unrepeatable moments of fun. More often than not, those gameplay moments will be centered on the mini-victories a player experiences during his or her journey toward the meta victory condition of the game.

GAME DESIGN

Earlier, we explored some core foundations to give us a platform from which to work. We learned that the decisions we make during a game are the most essential elements of a game, but it is when they are blended with an interesting context, directed toward a goal, and constrained by rules that we then have a game on our hands.

We also explored the idea of fun from a player's point of view. One lesson to remember is that no matter how excellent a game you create, it won't be fun for everyone—players come into a game experience with their own baggage, and you, as a designer, have to accept that.

We also touched on the idea of game design being a blueprint for a game not yet created, and it's from this concept that we'll now work forward.

Expanding the Blueprint Analogy

In the introduction of this chapter, we likened game design to a blueprint—we may have raw materials and skilled technicians to build a house, but without a plan, work can't proceed with any real direction. Imagine a team of builders trying to just "wing it" on the job site and build a house. The builders may all have their areas of expertise, from roofing to plumbing to framing, but without a plan, who does what first? Can the roofer begin his job before the framer has built the walls? Can the plumber rough-in the water lines without knowing where the bathroom is or where the kitchen will be?

True, the team can talk together and decide some basic things. They can agree on a 30×40 foot house and then allow the concrete man to lead them in helping to pour and smooth the foundation. The framer can then take over and can decide that the walls are to be nine feet tall and instruct the rest of the team to help. Going forward in this way will eventually get a house built, but there will be times that the lack of a plan will call for reworking a section of the house—and a structure built on-the-fly and not fulfilling some sort of plan won't end up as a unified whole when it is complete (and probably won't meet the local zoning codes!).

While this process seems like a crazy way to build a house, especially if you are the one forking over the $50 per hour for the contractors, it is precisely how early game development occurred.

A handful of years ago, you could just roll up your sleeves, head down to the basement, flare up your 486, and dive into creating your own game. Think of the creative freedom—you are in charge of the look, the sound, the interface, and the graphics—every aspect of the game. Pound away on weekends and at night, and in three to four months you might actually have a game. And, if the stars aligned properly—if you intuited the right blend of risk and reward and blended in some originality—then you may actually have created a game experience of lasting value (Figure 1.4).

But think of the flip side—working forward on a game in your basement with just yourself or a small team, but no plan in place. You have some ideas and you've created some prototypes, but that's it—now you are diving ahead full force on creating a game without a plan or a schedule. More often than not, you run into dead end after dead end—you discover that your control idea needs seven buttons and a mouse and you realize that humans have fewer fingers than that. You make

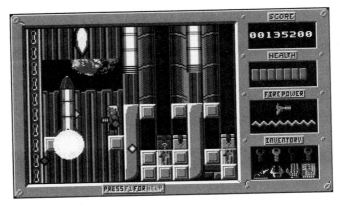

FIGURE 1.4   The original *Duke Nukem* is an example of the small studio model of the early 1990s. Used with permission. Copyright Apogee Software 1991.

a game that's so hard it's no fun to play. Or you try to throw in so many eye-catching goodies that your game plays more like a PowerPoint® presentation than a real-time game.

Working on your own nickel, on weekends and evenings without a publisher breathing down your neck—this type of trial and error development can work and can be quite rewarding. However, it can, more often than not, lead to a disjointed game of low quality. And if you are working for a publisher, this planless approach is a recipe for certain failure.

Fast forward to 2006—spend any more than a few minutes with a cutting-edge game, and you'll become instantly aware that this is no longer weekend fare. Like a blockbuster movie, games now require a massive team of specialists, from artificial intelligence programming to tool development, to particle effects to texture compression. In this modern-era realm of high-tech development, where game budgets can easily and regularly top $10 million, development without a plan is commercial suicide.

Modern-era games rely on game design "blueprints" (called design documents), often created by teams of designers, to guide the development of the game from start to finish—to be the plan for the professionals.

The Game Development Cycle

Each game goes through multiple stages, but generally, there are three major periods in each development cycle: pre-production, production, and post-production. During each stage, the role of a designer is crucial to getting the game done on time.

During pre-production, the entire development team is creating a concept for a game, and actual creation of assets hasn't really started yet. This is a time for discussion, brainstorming, and the evaluation of competitors' games. The designer's role is to brainstorm and develop concepts, including those that are handed down by management or the publisher. In many cases, the core idea is developed by someone other than the designers on a project; rather than create an idea from scratch, the design team must find a way to make the sequel or movie tie-in feel fresh and exciting. Designers also spend time during pre-production working with programmers on the scripting tools; to execute new features, the designers will need improvements to the scripting program, if not a new one altogether. Getting resources for these changes will be difficult once production begins, so pre-production is a valuable time for such meetings. During this period, designers are also writing different design documents, which are then submitted for approval. Some of the documents are short overviews that paint concepts with broad strokes; others are lengthy and technical, and serve as blueprints for other members of the development team. These documents are the foundation for the larger game design document that will guide the production process.

During production, the game is being built. Artists are creating character models and levels, and programmers are writing and revising the code base. Marketing has begun developing an advertising strategy, and testing has begun to evaluate the game with each new build. Designers are scripting gameplay, evaluating it for fun, and working closely with art and programming to make sure the game's functionality is consistent with the design documents. This is crucial, because the testing department will be using those documents as their standard during the testing process. During production, designers also continue to refine design documents, based on testing feedback and directives from both producers and managers. For example, during a game's production, a rival company may release a game boasting a new feature. To counter this, it may be decided that a new feature needs to be added to remain competitive, which will require the design team to return to the drawing board. This "arms race" of features can add a great deal to a designer's workload during production.

The post-production cycle, which begins once the game has been released, may include designing additional content for download, creating content for patches that continue the process of balancing gameplay, or evaluating a game's reception with an eye toward future sequels or expansion packs.

The structure of a development team varies from company to company, and even within different projects at a given company. However, certain roles are generally universal, and a typical game development team features the following: managers, producers, artists, programmers, testers, and designers. Usually, managers typically handle the operation of the company: finances, director-level decision-making, and determining the scope of each project. Producers are project managers who keep the development team going through hire-and-fire, scheduling, and team meetings. Artists create the visual assets in a game, typically with programs like 3D Studio Max™, Maya™, or Photoshop®. Programmers create the code base for a game, and build or modify the game engine and scripting tools. Testers check the game for bugs, and report any defects found.

Designers play a number of roles, and there is typically a hierarchy of designers on a project. The Lead Designer manages the other designers, and reports to a producer. The Lead Designer's job is to manage the documentation of the game's design, and to manage the core vision of that design. Sometimes, that core design vision has been created by someone else, and the Lead's job is merely to protect the integrity of that idea throughout the development process. The Lead Designer maintains a schedule for designers on the project, works out issues in the Leads Meeting, and delegates design tasks to the other designers.

Designers perform a number of different tasks through the stages of a game's development. For example, a Designer writes core design documents that outline a game's features. A Designer also plays other companies' games and writes competitive analyses. Other tasks include developing gameplay concepts, creating scenarios, and creating prototypes of gameplay.

Scripters use the scripting tools to implement game design. A Designer writes a document outlining the placement of enemies on a map; the Scripter places those enemy characters in the game and assigns them behaviors. This process can take months, and generally requires a great deal of iterative refinement as the game gets closer to completion.

Other designers on a team may include a Scenario Designer (also sometimes called a Writer or Story Designer), whose focus is the game's storyline and dialogue. The Multiplayer Designer is responsible for the online or offline multiplayer features.

Art or Craft?

For years, a sideline debate has raged in the games industry. Are games art? Are games capable of making you cry? Can a game be held up with other great works of art, from paintings (Mona Lisa), to books (The Great Gatsby), to poems (Ode on a Grecian Urn), to films (The Seventh Seal)?

Answering this question is beyond the scope of this book, and it's irrelevant in our context of studying game design, but it does point us to a similar but more interesting question: is game design art or craft? Both require skill, but art is often defined as a piece of work that elicits an emotional response in the participant and causes him or her to see or experience the world in a new way.

While we may be able to achieve this for a game as a whole, it really isn't the forte of the game design blueprint. A game design is not an end to itself, but a tool that enables a team of skilled individuals to create a game. The game design requires great skill from the game designer (or team of designers)—it requires wisdom (of games and human perception), creativity, understanding, and intense visualization skills, since a game design is a model of a game that has not yet been created. A game designer must be able to create that model in his mind and on paper in order to create a design. And that is an act of serious, skilled craft.

It is the basic learning of this craft that will guide our learning throughout this book. We will work to grow and foster the skills you need to act as a designer to craft a compelling, clear, and useful game—and the game you create may just be the game that emerges and stands alone as a work of art.

Introduction to the Design Document

Later in this book, we'll dive into the nuts and bolts of the design document, but we'll touch upon it quickly here. A game design is a blueprint for a game. If we think of an actual blueprint, it is a series of large pieces of paper with architectural drawings, from floor plans to elevations to isometric views, of a building or structure. That plan is augmented with notes—from electrical capacities to load-bearing information to general color and style notes. This blueprint is the work of an architect.

A game design document is a document that uses words, tables, and diagrams to explain the workings of a game, from the back-story of the game's fictional world, to the layout of buttons on an interface, to the way in which an archer fares against a swordsman.

A blueprint can have multiple audiences: the new homeowner and the banker who will finance the project, to name a few. However, the primary audience is the construction team: they will use the blueprint to direct their work to create the structure.

The same is true for a game design document. The audience can be a publisher who may be interested in finding the game, or a voice actor who wants to understand the context for the character he will provide the voice-overs for. However, the primary audience for a game design document is the game development team: the programmers, artists, and level designers who will create the game and take it from concept (the document) to reality (the CD-ROM you buy in the store).

SUMMARY

In this chapter, we explored some foundational concepts to begin our journey. Our goal is to learn the basic skills and concepts of game design. By using the analogy of the blueprint, we explored what a game design is—a plan for the creation of a game. We also worked to understand what a game itself is, and how we might think about fun in a more analytical way than we are used to.

This foundation will serve us well as we move forward. In the next chapter, we will explore the actual role and job of a game designer within the context of a game development project—to give us a better understanding of the skills we need to foster in ourselves in our quest to design fun and addictive games.

CHAPTER EXERCISES

1. Take a favorite game and write a short narrative of an exciting few moments of gameplay. Then, break the narrative into a chart of triggers and decisions—which decisions were the most interesting?
2. Think about all the interactive games you have played—what are the common threads? Write a short but workable definition of an interactive game and see how it holds up to group discussion.

2 What Does a Game Designer Do?

In This Chapter

- Your Dream Job
- The Roles of a Designer at the Start of a Project
- The Roles of a Designer once the Design is Complete

First thing in the morning you are shown to your desk, just down the hall from the game room and the fridge stocked with Mountain Dew®. You settle yourself down into your Herman Miller® knock-off chair and survey the desktop. You have a computer, a legal pad, a soup can full of sharpened pencils, and a small egg of Silly Putty®. Welcome to day one at your dream job!

You continue to survey your desk as you boot up your computer and you spy a small Post-It® note that simply says "Design Kasbah of Pain." You've been brought in to design a new action adventure console game—you impressed the team with your knowledge of the genre and your understanding of the true player experience. They took a chance on you because of the confidence and knowledge you exuded during the interview. And now you are here, working full time in a job you've been dreaming about for years. And you have a killer game to design. So what do you do? (Figure 2.1.)

WEAR MANY HATS

No matter how specialized a designer you are, you will be expected to wear many hats in your roles as a game designer. You are hired to be a creative thinker, a communicator, a writer, a cheerleader, a technician, an oracle, a fount of new ideas, and a game player.

FIGURE 2.1   No matter how well you prepare, at some point you'll hit crunch time and will have to burn the midnight oil!

A game designer, no matter what his or her role, bridges the development process from idea to implementation. It is the designer's core job to determine what a game, or portion of the game should do and then document that behavior so it can be created by the development team.

Sometimes, a designer will work alone, but more often he or she will be part of a design team (the ever-increasing scope of today's games mandates this). No matter if you are a lone wolf or part of a team, you will find yourself drawing upon many of the same skills and performing the same tasks across the board. In the pages that follow, we'll explore some of the roles you'll most likely face in your career as a designer.

Writing

Wearing the hat of a writer is essential. True, in many larger games, a designer will work hand in hand with a professional writer on such things as backstory, exposition, plot, and dialogue, but that still doesn't get the designer off the hook for doing a ton of writing along the way.

Since the designer is charged with visualizing and then describing the game to the team's developers, there must be some tool used to present that visualization, and that's where writing comes in.

The primary blueprint for a game is dispersed to the team through the medium of the design document (we'll talk in depth about this document in Chapter 5).

While a design document may use tables, charts, and graphs, its primary means of communication is language. It is meant to be a formal description of all game systems and interactions, and to date, other than the game itself, no medium is better suited for explanation than the written word. And writing all that design down is perhaps the primary job of the game designer.

So, how long is a design document? It varies from game to game, but as you sharpen your pencils and grab another heavily caffeinated soda, you should be prepared to write quite a bit. On the short end, a design document may be 20 pages or less, but that's generally for a game that is very narrow in scale and scope. It's quite typical for a design document to be 100+ pages in length, and remember, that's in its finished state. The designer will have to write, revise, and rewrite many times until the document is ready for the rest of the team.

Listening

One of the most important aspects of a game designer's day-to-day roles is that of listener. While many think of a designer as an explainer, a designer must also be able to listen and learn from skilled team members. An experienced designer can be the most senior member on the team, while a green designer might be the newest—yet both share the distinction of being the least skilled members on the team when it comes to the technical skills required to facilitate the creation of a game.

As a designer, you don't need to know how to program rendering pipelines or kinematic animation linkages, but you do need to know what those technologies are, and most importantly, you need to know their limits and opportunities and what role the various technologies will take in the game. Your programmers know, so you, as a designer, need to talk with them, ask them questions, and learn from them. Remember that the technical team may not be the best at explaining technical concepts. Your job is to ask the right questions so you can learn the most essential concepts.

As a listener, you will be learning about the technology upon which your game will be developed—its limitations and its opportunities. You will also be listening to team members to hear their ideas—don't for a moment fall into the trap of thinking you are the sole source of great ideas of the game. Your team members can come up with great ideas that can make the game better—you just need to be able to listen. Your job is to refine and polish the ideas into moments of great gameplay—and it really doesn't matter where the idea comes from.

Cheerleading

As a designer, you will often find yourself in the role of cheerleader. I hope not the perky type with pom-poms, but rather as an articulate champion for ideas, concepts, and technologies that will make your game a better playing experience.

There will unquestionably be times when an essential feature or component of the game is threatened with being cut or some bad idea is inexplicably moving its way up the priority queue. It's your job to champion the good ideas, whether they come from you or from your lead programmer or a junior texture artist. As a designer, you need to understand the context of a feature, in terms of the cost to implement that feature (how many programmers will the feature take or how much new art—you don't need to know the nuts and bolts—that's for your producer, but you need to have an understanding of the impact). If the costs of a feature are manageable and the impact on the overall game is significant, it's your job as a game designer to fight for the idea—for the good of the game. Your job is not to whine, scream, or rant, but to think of yourself as an articulate debater—your job is to explain the real costs and the real benefits, probably to the producer of the game, but maybe to the technical or art team as well, and be prepared to back up your position and field questions. As a cheerleader, you are the champion for the future player's experience, and it's your responsibility to carry that flag through the duration of the project.

Stewardship of Ideas

Game designers are often thought of as the "idea folks" on a team, sometimes with pride and sometimes with jealousy. Odds are a game that is designed with only the ideas of a designer will be destined to fail. A designer needs to be able to be open to new ideas from the development team, and understand how those ideas can impact, both positively and negatively, the game experience and the game development process.

When listening to ideas from other team members, a designer should not just listen to the idea itself, but to the context from which the person is presenting the idea. No one wants to present a dumb idea (but it certainly does happen), but if an idea doesn't make sense, a mature designer will know how to talk with the person to understand what he or she was getting at with the idea and why it seemed like a worthy feature. The same can be said about team members who feel that a given feature of a game should be cut. Rather than suffering a bruised ego, the designer should seek to understand why an existing feature seems like a bad idea to the individual.

The designer may also have to do some digging, via back-and-forth conversation, to be able to extract the idea. Once the designer has a clear idea of the core and context of the new idea, the designer must understand how it could fit into the fabric of the game, and what the ramifications would be, both for the player experience and for the developer.

Designers spend a lot of their time thinking up their own design ideas, and talking to development team members, both formally and informally, to mine the best ideas. Formal sessions may be brainstorming meetings or productions meetings, and informal ideas may be shared over a quick game of pinball or a lunch of double-sized burritos.

HEDONISTIC BRAINSTORMING

Noah Falstein

One of my favorite anecdotes about the glorious life of a game designer goes back to my days at Lucasfilm Games. There were many memorable projects and people there, but one stands out for "most hedonistic brainstorming session." In the days before the World Wide Web, there were online communities like GEnie, CompuServe®, and Prodigy. And Prodigy was originally called Trintex. A group of about five of us at Lucasfilm was recruited by Trintex to spend two days brainstorming a game concept. The idea was an online *Star Wars* universe game with a million players—sounds familiar now of course, but this was around 1987! We spent two days blue-sky brainstorming about how such a game might be structured, what people would do in it, and how it might be implemented. The location for these brainstorming meetings was the Sonoma Mission Inn and Spa, a luxurious resort in California's Wine Country. We had gourmet meals at their award-winning restaurant, even held one session in the outdoor Jacuzzi.

One evening I was scheduled to do an online interview/chat on GEnie about a game I had recently released, PHM Pegasus™. I was the very first person to bring a computer to the hotel and ask to connect its modem through their phone lines—they had to send someone over to figure out what needed to be done. But then I had my Commodore 64 and 300-baud modem running, and addressed the group while sipping a Cabernet from a complimentary bottle the Inn had supplied. Sadly, this did not become the accepted method of brainstorming in the industry, but I'll always treasure it as an example of how when it was good, it was very, very good . . .

Creating New Ideas

One of the most obvious roles for a game designer is to be the "ideasmith" for a game. Even before prototyping, even before visualizing anything, a designer must come up with a plethora of ideas for a particular game or portion of a game. Those ideas don't come from a vacuum—they are born out of the context of a game (e.g., a Mississippi Riverboat first-person RPG), the designer's own experiences (in both gaming and life), the ideas of the team, and the limitations of the technology (the game must run on an Apple 2E).

Thinking through the new ideas that will become the atoms of a game is a fast process for some and a slow process for others. It may be collaborative or it may be solitary. The designer may come up with his best ideas sitting in front of his computer, or the muse may touch him when he's out on a brisk walk.

No matter how the ideas come, idea generation is one of the central duties of a game designer, and when someone who doesn't know that much about game design and development thinks about a designer, he or she often thinks of someone just coming up with ideas.

Of course, veteran designers know the old Edison adage: 1% inspiration and 99% perspiration. The ideas are the easy part—sculpting them into a design and then seeing that design through to a finished game are the real challenges.

HOW MUCH FREEDOM?

 Designer: Paul Schuytema

There really aren't any industry standards as far as how much information you'll be given before you are asked to dive in and design all or part of a game. In my career, I've seen both extremes. When I began my job at 3D Realms in Garland, Texas, I experienced the "tons of freedom" extreme. I was told that I would be helping them to make a first person shooter, that character was essential, and the character they wanted had a few traits and a last name. That was it. It was up to me to craft a design from within a virtual vacuum. At times, working without constraints can be even more difficult that working with constraints.

$\rightarrow$

On the opposite end of the spectrum were some Mahjongg games we created for eGames. The rules of the games are pretty much set, and the feature-list came from the publisher in the form of a bullet-point document that explained exactly what must be in the game. What we received from them was a high-level design of the game already—and my task as a designer was to nail down the details so the player experience was as fun as possible.

Visualization

It's hard to say, with any degree of certainty, what the most important aspect of the designer's job is. Certainly, one of the most essential tasks is the act of visualizing gameplay. Often, when a designer begins, he has nothing but some rough requirements, and he must make the first steps in turning ideas and requirements into some sort of documentation of how the game will play. This is a two-step process of visualization and documentation.

The process of visualization can take many forms: it can be purely a mental activity, not unlike daydreaming, or it can be a more formalized approach using tabletop miniatures, paper and pencil, or other tools.

Visualizing gameplay requires designers to clearly understand the context of the game they are trying to create, the audience they are trying to reach, and the types of games that have come before. When visualizing, the designer will try to put himself in the player's experience and will try to imagine, in as much detail as possible, what the player will see, hear, and do during the game. Of course, the designer will also have the understanding of what is going on under the surface. If the designer is visualizing a medieval RTS game, he may imagine the player taking a small squad of archers out to explore a forest path, when they are set upon by Celtic swordsmen.

The designer is working to imagine what the player is seeing and doing: how does the player interact with the screen? How does he know the status of his troops (health, etc.)? How can the player know what effect his troops are having on the swordsmen? How does the player beat a hasty retreat?

At the same time, the designer also understands that archers are faster than the swordsmen are, and they have less than half the hit points. They understand the speed of the attack, how they move in formation, and how they respond to way-point orders.

Putting this all together, the designer works to visualize the experience with the goal of getting an understanding of how the play of the game will proceed. At this point in the process, the specific numbers don't matter—it's more the feel and flow of play.

Once the player has visualized the game experience (more often than not, this is done in small bite sized sections), he must then be able to document that experience on paper (or on a computer screen, which is far more likely these days). This act of deconstruction will allow him to make that first vital step from idea to plan—by documenting, in an organized way, what the experience is like, he provides the first foundation from which a designer will document a more formalized plan for the design of that section of the game.

Prototyping

One key component of a game designer's job is to prototype a play experience. A prototype is a working approximation of what the final product might be. Programming teams often prototype the technical aspects of a game to see what the performance might be like given certain system requirements. They may populate a landscape with hundreds of copies of a test model to see how many units can be displayed on screen at once. They may test particle effects or other rendering effects so they have a sense of what the best engineering approaches will be when they are writing their production code. (Figure 2.2.)

FIGURE 2.2   A screen shot from a prototype test for a game that eventually became Infogrames' *Castles & Catapults.*

Similarly, the game designer will prototype examples of play to test the dynamics of the game before committing them to the game design document. For a game designer, prototyping means making a functional portion of the game so he can test the play dynamics. There are many ways to prototype a sliver of gameplay, but the common thread is to use an approach that enables the designer to create the game-play himself so he can test it out or try it with other members of the development or design team. Some prototyping approaches are

- Using a spreadsheet like Excel® to create a numbers game
- Creating a modified tabletop or board game to model gameplay
- Using cards to model gameplay
- Using a scripting language to prototype gameplay on the computer

Scripting

Once the game concept has been established, and the documents have been written, the scripting process can begin. Think of scripting as the photography of a feature film. Once the cast has been assembled, the crew has been hired, and the set has been constructed, the process of filming can begin. The camera operator will need instructions from a director, who'll be using a movie script as his guide, and the scenes will have been laid out in storyboards beforehand. All major decisions will have been made, and the only remaining step will be the recording of the action. The same applies to games.

Scripting is a process of controlling specific events in your game, and is typically executed in the form of a scripting language, a code that's entered into the scripting tool by a member of the design team. This script is not the same as the engine code that constitutes the game's executable; instead, the game script can be modified and run without having to recompile. This makes it easy to change events, altering the player experience on a small scale. The artificial intelligence that governs enemy behavior is part of the code base, but the fact that this particular bad guy is holding a rifle and shooting from a rooftop is something the designer has scripted.

When the core gameplay decisions have been made, and the artists have created the character models, levels, and other assets, then the scripter can place objects in the game world and assign them characteristics and behavior patterns. Using a scripting tool, also known as an editor, the scripter chooses objects and characters from a menu system and gives them purpose. The editor can be as simple as a series of drop-down menus, requiring no programming experience at all, or it can be complex enough to require the scripter to master a scripting language such as Lua.

Some companies license a game engine, such as Unreal, which comes with an editor (known as UnrealEd). Other companies build their own engines and editors, which means that scripters from different companies will employ completely different skill-sets in their day-to-day work. However, in any case, the scripter's job is to take the building blocks that have been created, along with the directions described in the design documents, and create a gameplay experience that satisfies the Lead Designer's requirements.

In any case, during the scripting process the design department will work closely with programming to ensure the editor delivers the necessary functionality. For example, it may be discovered that the scripters need to be able to copy and paste data in the editor, functionality that doesn't currently exist. After a meeting between design and programming, that capability may (or may not) be added to the editor, depending on time constraints and manpower.

ONCE THE DESIGN IS DONE

While the lion's share of a designer's job at the start of the project may be the creation of the design document (and all the tasks that must precede that action), what does a designer do once the design document is completed?

The first response to that question is the simple fact that a design document is never completed. It is an organic plan that will change over time as new ideas emerge, as schedule limitations force the cutting of features, as technological limitations are discovered, or opportunities are unearthed.

No longer does a design document exist as a printout of 100+ pages of a Microsoft® Word document sitting on a designer's shelf. More often than not, the document exists in some dynamic form, be it a Web page, a shared Word document, or a Wiki site.

However, once the document is done enough so that full-scale development can commence, the designer will no longer spend all of his time writing or maintaining that document. So what does he do?

Depending on the project, there are many tasks for the designer to do during the development of a game, including

- Maintaining and revising the living design document
- Writing dialogue and in-game text or collaborating with the team writer
- Implementing scenarios or missions
- Testing the game (or working with focus groups)

The Living Design

As mentioned previously, the design for a game is a living thing—it is not a finished and bound document set on a shelf to gather dust. One of the primary goals of a designer is to create as comprehensive an initial design as possible, since it is the blueprint the development team will follow as work on the game begins.

As development continues, there will certainly be changes that will affect the game. The publisher may require schedule changes, certain features may take longer than expected, mandating the removal of other features to keep the game on schedule. On rare occasions, progress may be such that there is time enough to incorporate some features that weren't part of the original specification.

As a designer, one key aspect of your job will be to keep track of the progress of the game in various areas (not as a scheduler, which is the job of the producer) to see any red flags as soon as they pop up. The sooner you can see a landmine in the development of a game, the better innovative solution you can find.

Often, designers work in small teams, each with responsibility over a certain aspect of the game. Even if you are not responsible for the entire design, you still need to keep an eye on the larger landscape of the game to see how progress is going, and regularly communicate with the other designers to see if any changes in their areas of the game will affect your portion of the game.

When changes arise, the designer must revise, edit, or augment the game design document to reflect the new reality, but at the same time keep a careful eye on the continuity of the game to make sure any changes make sense in the flow of the game in general.

Several years ago, changing a design document meant editing a document file and then printing new versions for the team. More and more, design teams are now taking a paperless approach to the design document and have the design living on an intranet either as a Web page or a dynamic Wiki (Figure 2.3).

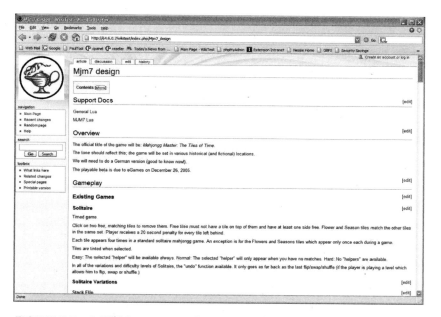

FIGURE 2.3   A Wiki is a great tool to support dynamic game design documents. Here, we see a design document on a Wiki powered by MediaWiki (*www.mediawiki.org*), the software that runs the Wikipedia.

Designers, who communicate most of the time via the written word, have long ago learned that, try as they might to get the team involved, the entire design team often does not read the design document. It's essential for the team to read the entire design at the outset of the project, but as changes occur during development, team members are less concerned with the larger project and more concerned with their own responsibilities.

With this in mind, the designer must make sure that changes in the design are clearly marked, so a team member can quickly see what's new and what's changed without having to read through the entire document (this is where a Wiki can be a great tool).

Writing the Content

The initial design for a game rarely includes all needed text and dialogue. The design is meant to be a blueprint to get the development team up and running and the specifics of the text are not often nailed down at that early point. Therefore, designers often spend considerable amounts of time early in the development of a game, once the design has moved into the development stage, working on dialogue, backstory writing, cinematic scripting, and other in-game text.

Years ago, it was almost a given that a designer was also the head writer for a game. Designers are, by their nature, very good at communicating with the written and spoken word, and understand all aspects of the game, so it was natural that the duty would fall to the designer.

As the production values of a game increase, and the player's expectations for a deep and satisfying game experience also grow, development teams often enlist the work of a professional writer to handle the game writing that directly relates to character, plot, and the like. Just because a game designer is very good at writing, and is very creative, does not mean that a designer understands all aspects (or even some aspects!) of character development, theme development, or plot and pacing. A great designer may be a terrible dialogue writer, and designers should embrace the opportunity to work with professional writers.

This collaboration may begin early in the design process, when the writer and the designer work together to craft the plot and flow of the game, with the writer making sure the story is exciting, meaningful, and fulfilling, and the designer making sure the story fits within the limits of the game and serves the target game experience well.

Once the game is in development, dialogue, NPC interactions, and text exposition will be written. This will be handled either by the designer or by the writer in collaboration with the designer and the producer. Cinematic sequences are also often scripted once full development starts (the sequences were probably quick-scripted for the initial design). This process is often handled by the designer, the writer, and the art lead, as each brings his or her own expertise to the table and understands the limits and the opportunities of his or her own medium.

However the process is handled, a designer will generally always have some role in content writing and creation early on in the development process.

Scenarios, Levels, and Missions

Depending on what type of game you are working on, you may be called upon to design scenarios, levels, or missions for the game. These "micro games" are where the rubber meets the road in game design. A standard design document is a blueprint for a game, while a mission, scenario, or level is an instance of play within that game.

A game generally follows an arc through the play experience, building in challenge and excitement until the game reaches some climax where the player either wins or loses. Along the way, games often consist of a sequence of scenarios, missions, or levels that provide the arena for the gameplay. These game components are often created by the designer (many games have specialized designers who do this as their primary job).

These game components are often created with custom-made tools that allow a designer to create a dynamic game experience within the technology of the game. The designer will need to know the context for a particular mission or level, understand how to use the tools, and be very attentive to the player's experience.

Level and scenario design generally comes on line once a game's basic technology and tools are in place, since it's rather pointless to create a mission that can't actually be played or experienced.

Since the designer is communicating directly with the player (rather than with the development team, as with the design document), the designer needs to have an understanding of how to use the tools and technology to create a challenging game experience.

Ideally, a designer will be able to create a mission or level and test it out without requiring the intervention of the technical or art team. (Figure 2.4.)

In larger games, a design team may be charged with creating the levels and missions for a game, and at times, level design may be more on the designer's plate or more on the artist's side of the plate (for architectural complex environments).

For levels that require a high degree of technical or artistic implementation, a designer may be teamed up with another developer to create these game atoms.

If the game uses these types of game structures, the latter half of the development process will be filled with this type of dynamic design and creation.

Game Testing

Most professional game development cycles include time near the end, once the game reaches beta stage (when it is first functionally complete), for testing. Testing can be done in house by the developer, or by the publisher or by a third party. The

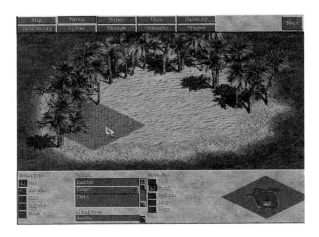

FIGURE 2.4   In games like *Age of Empires II*®, a designer is responsible for crafting the scenarios using a custom-made scenario creation tool. Used with permission. Copyright Microsoft Corporation 1999.

purpose of testing is, first and foremost, to make sure the game experience is error free. Beyond that, testing makes sure the difficulty curve matches the intended audience, performance is acceptable, and so on.

Generally, the designer isn't in the trenches during this eleventh-hour testing, but all through the game development process, one of a designer's most vital roles is to test the game. The designer will test the game as a whole, or focus just on the parts of the game he is responsible for, but this early, ongoing testing is vital for the success of the game project.

During this pre-beta testing, the designer is making sure game systems work as they were designed, and, more importantly, if the game systems were designed so the experience is fun and rewarding.

The nuts and bolts, under-the-hood testing is the realm of the designer, and during this process, the designer often revises the initial design as testing and playing the game reveals errors or behaviors that are not desired. Perhaps the archers are too weak, or a particular weapon is too powerful—all of these are discovered in testing and refined by the designer along the way.

Sometimes, a designer may be so engrossed in the minutia of the game that he or she loses critical perspective of the player experience (after all, if you are playing the same game day after day, you'll lose some perspective as well).

Often, larger budget games will employ a testing service early in the development of the game to test out such things as general gameplay, interface, and player interest. Often, the designer is intensely involved in this focus group testing as potential players put the game through its paces without the designer looking over their shoulder, but rather watching the responses on tape or through a one-way mirror. This process can shed light on areas of the game that may seem obvious to the team, but not obvious to the player.

THE GAME IS TOO HARD

When we were working on our *Combat*™ game for Infogrames™, we were very proud of the flow of the levels and how the game created a single, satisfying experience. The game featured two primary designers and two additional level designers, and during the level design portion of development, the designers would continually test each other's levels and offer suggestions for improvement.

On this project, we had a workable level editor and a playable game up very, very quickly, so it allowed us to play the game constantly, over and over again, all throughout the development process. When we handed the game over to the publisher for beta testing, we gave them a game that had already been play tested for months and very nicely balanced (Figure 2.5).

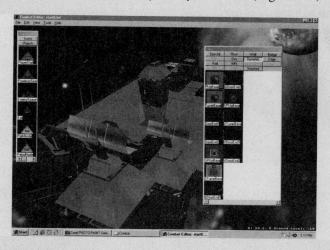

FIGURE 2.5   The *Combat* level editor in action.

We were very jazzed to hear from our testing lead that the testers really loved the game and were having a ball playing it. Not too many errors were discovered, so we started to feel smug that we had created an excellent game, right out of the gates.

→

Then we started to get disturbing reports back from the testers. Levels couldn't be completed—there was no way to advance. Time after time, a tester would hit a wall and couldn't get any further. We would explain "Oh, that's easy . . . just get hit by a shell so you are catapulted up on top of the wall and then ride the wall over the door," or "Just back your hover tank off the topmost part of the level and you'll fall back on a ledge that will take you around the corner," or "move backward and side strafe the assassin robots until you get to the platform."

We were explaining things that seemed so obvious to us . . . but then it hit us all at once—we've been playing this game nonstop for months and we know how to control our tanks perfectly—we know how the world dynamics work, and we know all the behaviors of the computer-controlled enemies. And we worked very hard to make our levels challenging for each other.

In the process, we made the levels far, far too hard for our intended audience. The game was solid, but it was several orders of magnitude too difficult. It took a team of external testers, who were approaching the game as players would, to discover this—we would have never done so on our own.

SUMMARY

In this chapter, you started your first day on the job as a game designer. As you settled into your desk, you asked yourself the rather obvious question: so what do I do? We explored the various roles and tasks game designers undertake during the development of the game, from writing down the initial design to the myriad of jobs and revisions during the development of the game.

During the entire process, the designer strives to keep the player experience at the forefront and to keep a consistent vision of the game, always remembering that no matter what changes occur in the design during the evolution of the game, the vision should stay on track and the goal of creating a fun, addictive game experience for the player is the overarching target.

In the next chapter, we'll give you a glimpse into what core knowledge you should have at the ready when you begin your career as a game developer. What skills should you possess? What reading is essential? What homework do you need to do to prepare yourself for this challenging and fulfilling career?

CHAPTER EXERCISES

1. Give yourself 10 minutes and write down as many new, original, and wacky ideas for a game concept as you can think of. Share your list with others to see how many ideas are actually new—you'll be surprised how few truly original ideas are out there!

2. Using only a spreadsheet program or a deck of regular playing cards (your choice), prototype a conflict between a small cabal of magicians and a squad of swordsmen and archers.

3. Writing in short phrases (often called pseudo-code), write out the step-by-step decisions that a computer card player would need to make when playing a game of Blackjack.

3 Design Boot Camp: Doing Your Homework

In This Chapter

- Gathering Information
- Reporting Information

In the last chapter, you imagined yourself on the first day of your new job and learned some of the tasks and roles you'll be undertaking from day to day. Now, we'll turn our attention to getting you ready for that job. You have a lot to learn before you can jump into the trenches and be an effective and professional game designer.

Later, we'll be addressing some of the unique concepts and knowledge you'll need to have a handle on in order to design effective games, but that knowledge must be built upon a foundation. Therefore, we'll start building the foundation boot camp style. When you enter military boot camp, you don't start learning military tactics and marksmanship—you begin with the foundations, and that's what we'll do here.

Before you are ready to dive in and design, you need to prime the pump a bit and learn some basic skills and do some essential homework. Working as a game designer is a modern-era "Renaissance Man" type of job—your skills and knowledge must be varied, but we have to start somewhere. Let's dive in and begin.

GATHERING INFORMATION

Your first step as a designer is to be effective in gathering information. Being a game designer means creating new gameplay experience from your existing pool of knowledge. To be effective, you'll need a substantial pool of knowledge to draw from, and that means getting very good at receiving information.

You may be asked to design a game set in the Civil War or an RPG set in Victorian England. To create a play experience that feels like it fits into the context of the game world, you'll need to know about that game world in depth. Odds are, you won't be able to do that off the top of your head—you'll have to gather some information and do some serious research.

Listening

Let's start with the most basic of skills: listening. In the last chapter, we talked about the importance of listening. Your team is going to tell you very important things during the course of your work as a designer and you need to hear what they are saying. They may be sharing ideas with you, they may be explaining technology, or they may be warning you of an upcoming red flag. You need to listen and you need to be able to remember and use what you hear.

You may be creating a chariot racing game, but your tech leads tells you that due to the target system specs and the overhead of the rendering pipeline, no chariot can have more than two horses—that's vital information you need to hear. You don't want to come to the next team meeting and propose an eight-horse chariot drag race, do you?

How good of a listener are you? Most of us take good listening for granted—it's not something we work at or pay much attention to. Does your spouse or significant other say to you, "You are such a good listener?" or does he say, "You never hear what I'm saying!"?

In the games industry, much of your reputation, at least to your team, as a designer, will stem from your ability to attentively listen to what others are saying. Listening earns respect, but it also garners you essential knowledge to do your job more effectively. You've certainly heard the old adage: "Seek first to understand…"

One of the first things you need to do is to practice listening. To practice effectively, you need to listen to something challenging. Television, radio, and normal conversation are generally too stripped down to present much of a challenge. If you enjoy politics, turn to C-Span and listen to debates or hearings. If you enjoy drama, track down some "Golden Age of Radio" serials and listen to those. If you enjoy comedy, track down some of the early work by the Firesign Theatre on CD. All of these will provide you with some interesting and challenging practice to get your mind used to hearing, remembering, and processing complex aural communication.

IN COLD BLOOD

When Truman Capote set out to write the true crime book, *In Cold Blood*, he knew he would have to interview many people associated with the brutal murders. In his first pass, he would have those who he wanted to interview come to a hotel room, and he was ready with tape recorder, typewriter, and yellow legal pad. He would ask questions and get responses, but he started to notice that the interviewees were giving rather bland, uninteresting responses. They were just answering the questions and nothing more. Perhaps the tape recorder and typewriter intimidated them. For his second pass, Capote practiced being a very good listener. Now, when the subjects sat down, there was no recorder, no typewriter, and no yellow pad, just a man engaging them in conversation. Capote would listen carefully to what they were saying, and strived to remember nearly everything. Then, the moment the subject left, he would pull out his typewriter and transcribe what he remembered. By using a trained listening skill, he was able to break down communication boundaries and get far more information from his subjects.

Growing Your Vocabulary

It is also essential to have a strong and deep vocabulary to listen effectively. Your attention will be derailed if you are hit with a word you don't understand, and you'll miss the meaning of the word, and additional content as you are struggling to determine what was just said.

There are courses and books on growing your vocabulary, and those can be very helpful, but you can also make vocabulary growth part of your everyday life. Of course, as a designer, you are expected to read, so take advantage of the additional benefit of growing your vocabulary as you read and learn. Keep a dictionary handy so that when you run across a word you don't know, look it up right away, and spend a few moments working to really understand and remember the word.

You can also create some exercises for yourself, such as spending some time to learn a group of synonyms. Grab a thesaurus, pick a word, look at all the related words, and spend some time looking up and learning their meanings and how the meanings are similar and yet distinct and different.

Listening Skills

To listen effectively, you need to be ready to listen. This may sound obvious, but it really isn't. You need to be able to focus your concentration on what another is saying and be ready to listen to his words, not be formulating your next response or thinking about something else. You should probably also have some type of note-taking widget with you, and in this case, a small pad of paper is just about the best thing going. A laptop pulls your attention away from the conversation and into the mechanics of the device.

When you listen, concentrate on what the speaker is saying, and pay attention to the key points or ideas the speaker is working to convey. When you take notes, don't try to transcribe the conversation, but use your own internal shorthand (you know, those scribbles no one but you can read). When you are finished, go back to your notes and flesh out the details (or transcribe them into your computer), so you can use them later, once the memory of the conversation is finished.

When you are listening to speakers, let them see that you are engaged. Look at them, react to their statements, but be passive rather than aggressive—when you are in "listening mode" your goal is to learn, not to usurp or direct the conversation. Ask relevant questions. Be attentive.

Also, and this is key, don't be judgmental when you are listening. You may not agree with what a speaker is saying, but hold your judgment back until he is finished and you have truly understood what has been said.

As a game designer, your goal is to create the blueprint for an exciting game, and you are going to need input to make the plan as solid as possible. You are not an island, but rather a causeway for ideas, and listening is one of your most essential tools.

Note Taking

While you may think school is over now that you are working as a game designer, it's actually just beginning. One of the most rewarding aspects of a career in game design is that you are also embarking on a journey of continuous learning. Continuous learning also means that you need to take good notes.

Ask yourself, when you were in school, did you take good notes? Did you use the notes you took? Nearly everyone has his own unique style (or lack of style) when it comes to note taking. Some approaches are loose and "from the hip," while others can be so formal that they end up like outlines for a textbook.

Many techniques and many excellent books out there can walk you through your note-taking process, so we won't dive in too deeply, but we will spend some time on some key issues that are essential in your role as game designer.

The first is your choice of tools—some prefer pencil and paper while others prefer a laptop. It really doesn't matter what your note-taking tool is—what matters is that you have it always at the ready, and that using the tool does not pull your attention away from what you are supposed to be paying attention to.

Using a stylus on a PDA may be great to jot down a quick URL you need to check out, but for taking notes during a lecture on the history of Egypt, it's just not the right tool. You'll be spending your time wrestling with the technology to document the experience rather than simply getting it down. Often, the same is true with laptops—banging on a keyboard may be disruptive, and nothing puts a barrier between you and a speaker like the wall of the laptop screen. Of course, in a large lecture hall with dozens of folks on their computers, it may be perfectly acceptable.

While we don't profess to be Luddites at all, we find it hard to beat those medium-sized composition notebooks for note taking. Pair that with a felt-tip pen or roller-ball pen (easy on your fingers—remember, since you are now typing on your keyboard most of the day, your writing muscles are getting weaker) and you have a portable, battery-free system to record your thoughts. Composition notebooks are also great because you can stick them up on a shelf like a small book and the pages are all firmly bound together. Personally, we prefer the type with graph paper rather than rules pages, because we also tend to sketch and doodle with our notes (Figure 3.1).

FIGURE 3.1   Old-time composition notebooks
can be the best tools for effective note taking.

With a note-taking tool at the ready, you next need to think about how you take notes. The purpose of note taking is to document knowledge that you will need later but you don't have the time or the ability to commit to permanent memory at the moment. The bottom line is that notes are meant to be referenced later. That means, first and foremost, they must be somewhat legible—at least so you can read them yourself several months down the road. They are also meant to document concepts so you can glean the knowledge later.

Just jotting down headings or a keyword here or there might be fine if you are going to transcribe your knowledge in the next day or so (when the keywords will help you jog your memory), but ideally, you'll want notes that will stand the test of time. That means that you'll want to organize your notes in a meaningful way and jot down enough detail so you can reconstitute most of the knowledge no matter when you refer to your notes.

Since you are going to be using your notes yourself, don't stress things out too much. There is no need to over-think how you outline or indent or how many useless doodles you put on a page. Just allow yourself to be focused and think clearly, and catch key topics and document them with facts or information as best you can.

MIND MAPPING

There is a very visual style of note taking called "Mind Mapping" or "Radial Thinking," and it's a very useful tool for game designers. A Mind Map is basically an organized, hierarchical doodle. The approach has been around informally for hundreds years, but it was formalized by the British thinker Tony Buzan (who has written many, many books on the subject).

The basic idea is built around documenting notes concerning a central topic. You jot the topic down in the center of a page and then surround that topic with other subtopics that pop into your head. You continue, drawing lines like the branches of a tree, to connect topics and subtopics together, as you flesh out your Mind Map. Since the approach is visual, it's great to do with colored markers or pens (Figure 3.2).

Mind Mapping is a great tool for brainstorming a topic and allowing you to see an issue from many different angles and contexts. It's very useful when a designer is sitting down and beginning to work through a complex design problem (or is just jotting down first notes for a game design).

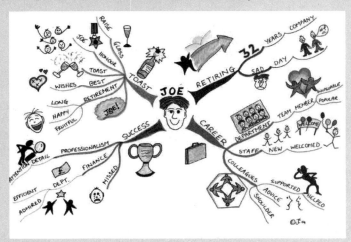

FIGURE 3.2   An example of a "mind map"—a graphical way to organize your thoughts and take effective notes.

Research

There are plenty of times when you will attend a meeting or a lecture that will provide you with vital information you need to do your job better. Listening effectively and taking good notes will allow you to absorb and retain that information. There are times, though, when you are totally on your own. Some days, you'll really need to know what the effects of boiling oil poured from the ramparts are, and you won't have anyone nearby who knows. For those times, you'll need to develop good research skills.

It wasn't too many years ago that good research skills meant the ability to use a library card catalog and periodical reference effectively. Now, while those skills are still important, we really need to be able to search effectively on the computer.

When we need to dive into the archives, whether real or digital, we generally have need of two types of knowledge: general and specific. As game designers, our work will carry us across many fields of knowledge, from *Texas Hold 'Em* betting strategies to the history of medieval castle building. At times, we just need to know something very general and simple, such as what are the Seven Wonders of the Ancient World (can you name them?)? At other times, we may need to track down some more specific and esoteric information, such as why do elite counterterrorist groups train using a "double tap" approach to pulling the trigger (hint: it has to do with "temporary cavitation").

As game designers, the majority of our first pass research is done at our desks, using our computer. Often, we can track down the information we need right from there. If not, then we can generally find our information through a giant online bookseller such as Amazon™. Wander into any veteran designer's office and you are bound to see an eclectic collection of reference books.

As designers just starting out, how do we dive into research effectively? Truly, research is a skill that grows over time, as you find more and more avenues for information that fit your sensibilities, but we'll begin with a few points. Let's start at the beginning.

Your first stop on any research safari should be the WikiPedia (*www.wikipedia.org*). This collaborative online encyclopedia boasts nearly a million articles, all hyperlinked together. A simple search in WikiPedia will generally get you all the top-level information you need, and drilling down through the links will provide an amazing amount of depth (Figure 3.3).

Two important words of warning: the WikiPedia is not a "professional" encyclopedia—it is written by hobbyists, and while some articles may be accurate, others may not—think of it as a great starting point, but not as the end-all resource. Second, encyclopedias, by their very nature, are only brief overviews of a topic. You can glean top-level information from them, but not the depth you'll often need.

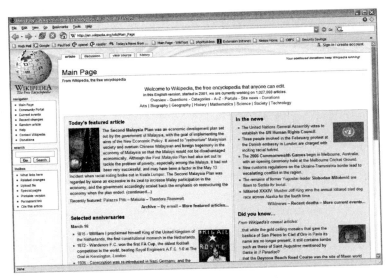

FIGURE 3.3   Wikipedia is a great first stop when researching nearly any topic.
Used with permission. Wikipedia® is a registered trademark of the Wikimedia Foundation, Inc.

Once you hit WikiPedia, your next step is one of the search engines, like Google™ or Yahoo!™. The trick to using search engines is to use just keywords that are relevant and likely to be found close together (and are dependant on each other). Doing a search on "red car" won't get you far, because those common words can appear on pages that have nothing to do with red cars, and you'll have to sort through endless pages that aren't relevant. Refining the search to something like "candy apple Ford Mustang" will let you zero in on your target information even further.

When you are doing Web searches, remember that there are countless commerce sites out there trying to sell things to you, and there are small armies of folks employed to have those sites hit high on nearly any search you make, so you'll probably have to wade through some eCommerce sites before you can get to some meaty information.

Another great source of off-the-beaten path information is group forums, such as Usenet. Groups bring together like-minded people for discussion of everything from alpacas to running Linux on an iPod. Using a tool like Google's™ Group search, you can often find very, very precise information (in fact, we'll bet that many of the artists and programmers on your team already use Google Groups to find technical answers to code and art problems). To search group postings (which often contain thousands of posts on a specific subject), you'll want to be even more specific with your search terms and make sure you search on word clusters that are relevant to your topic.

Your next attack areas are the online book superstores (like Amazon.com®) or perhaps a local mega-bookstore such as Borders® or Barnes & Noble. Nothing beats a book for long-term reference, and searching online can take you down many interesting paths into books you had no idea existed. Going to a bookstore in person is also great to make sure a volume has enough information to justify the purchase (this is especially true of youth reference books).

THE WONDER OF CHILDREN'S BOOKS

One "secret" that many professional designers will admit is that some of the best research material out there comes in the form of kids books and especially teen reference books.

Sure, there may be dozens of scholarly and historical books on medieval castles, but how many of them will provide you with insights that will actually help you design your game? On the other hand, there are dozens of kid's books about castles and medieval life, filled with photos and drawings, that give you a "short attention span" glimpse into the daily lives of knights, kings, and servants. Those books will get your creative gears turning.

While a giant online retailer like Amazon is great to find specific and hard-to-find books, it's not really your best source for children's reference books. You'll be far better served by making a trek to one of the giant bookstores like Barnes & Noble or Borders and hanging out in the children's section and seeing what they have. As a designer, you'll know what will be helpful when you see it.

One of the best series of books for game designers is the children's "Eyewitness" topical encyclopedia by Dorling Kindersley. The encyclopedia is made up of dozens and dozens of excellent books on specific subjects, from Early Humans to Medieval Life. Photos dominate the pages and the text is short and sweet—not enough for in-depth learning, but perfect for sparking the imagination of a game designer.

Your best sources of in-depth detail about esoteric subjects are professional and academic journals devoted to the particular field you are researching. Often, these sources won't provide the imagination-stimulating pictures of a good reference book or Web site, but they'll more than make up for that shortcoming with precise and accurate detail. If you want to know about "permanent and temporary cavitation," consult the *Journal of Wound Ballistics*.

The problem with professional journals is that it's often hard to find out what journals actually exist—it's sort of an old-boys club, since most journals are meant for a very closed audience. Your best bet is to contact experts in the field and ask them if any professional publications deal with their work. Alternatively, you can try to track down professional organizations and contact them to see if they have a journal or know of any that service their field.

Reading

As a game designer, you need to be well read and you need to be able to read effectively. You'll need to pack your brain with some deep knowledge before you ever dive into your first design document. You will also need to know how to read quickly and effectively, so you can expand your knowledge arsenal—this, in turn, will give you the raw material to be even more creative in your day-to-day efforts.

Reading Effectively

How effective of a reader are you? Do you plow through books with ease, or do you take weeks to get through a book? How much do you remember two weeks after you finish a book? An effective reader can read quickly and remember what was read—a skill you'll need nearly every day in your job as a game designer.

If you aren't already an effective reader, how do you get better? Like any skill, practice is the key, but some simple techniques can drastically improve your reading speed and ability.

The average reader takes in about 250 words every minute, but most of this time our mind is idling. Our brain prefers to process information much more quickly, and one of the Catch-22s of slower reading is that your mind will actually wander more and you'll retain less of what you read. Your goal is focus—to engage your mind fully in the act of reading and to train your senses so you provide input to your brain at a pace that won't allow it to wander too far.

There are many things we do to put the brakes on our reading speed. We subvocalize words. We either mouth the words we're reading or at least partially engage our tongue in forming the words, even if our lips are closed. It's natural for us to equate the idea that we have to speak words we read or write in order to hear them in our mind. Our mind really doesn't need us to subvocalize—it's more of a habit than any cognitive adaptation—so that's one thing to work on: simply read and detach your speaking circuits from your reading circuits. With practice and awareness, you can do this easily.

We also tend to allow our mind to wander when we are reading. Consider your reading effectiveness when you read at a table in one of those in-store cafés in a large bookstore, and then compare that with how effectively you read when sitting on a plane. In one environment (the café), you have movement all around you to catch your eyes, conversations at every table, interesting looking people wandering around, and the sound of milk being steamed for the endless lattes they serve—a very distracting environment, indeed. On the plane, the sound is just the engine—

everyone is sitting and there isn't anything interesting at all happening except in your book. If you are like most, you'll notice that your in-flight reading effectiveness is quite good.

The bottom line is that you need to pay attention to what you are reading, and that may mean reading in a controlled environment if you can't effectively block out the world around.

The skill that will most improve your reading speed it to increase the number of words you take in with a single mental "gulp." Generally, if we aren't paying attention, we gobble up a single word at a time, but this is idle speed for our brain. Our brain can process information much faster than that. Here's where practice really counts. You'll want to train your eyes and your sensory muscles to take in four to eight words in a single input thought. How do you do that? You begin by using a visual guide—your finger works perfectly. Use your finger to scan under the line you are reading at a steady pace. Never stop your finger moving on a page, and don't allow yourself to re-read anything—just keep going forward (Figure 3.4).

FIGURE 3.4 Use your finger as an eye-guide to speed your vision across the page.

Try this for several days and you'll notice that you'll easily start taking in maybe two words at a time with no sweat. When you are comfortable with that, speed up your finger and you'll notice your input will grow and expand. Your ability is only limited by your willingness to stick with it, practice, and keep pushing yourself. At the maximum level, a human can take in an entire line of text in a single glance, and at that rate, you can read between 1,000 to 1,500 words per minute. This is probably faster than you need and it takes quite a bit of time and practice to get there. However, in three or four weeks you can easily be taking in four words in a "gulp" and reading at around 500 words per minute, which allows you to be very effective in a short period of time.

The next skill is remembering what you read. If you read many different books, they can tend to blur together. To commit what you read to memory—especially in the nonfiction books you'll be reading to enhance your knowledge base—you'll want to turn to note taking. The most effective and fun way to document what you read is to give yourself time to read—say, 30 minutes. Then, give yourself five minutes or so to create a mind-map page of notes on what you read. This "ritual" will have the double effect of helping to burn what you just read into your mind even further and to create a shorthand reference page for use later. Do this for several years and you'll have a notebook or two of very useful reference notes that will serve you well for years to come.

What to Read

Once you are deep into your job as a game designer, you'll easily be able to direct your own reading list. If you are working on a medieval RTS, you'll seek out books on medieval history and tactics. If you are working on a gangland urban simulation, you'll seek out books on urban combat and gang psychology. However, what should you read before you land that first job?

Being a game designer is, in some ways, striving to be a modern renaissance person. You'll want to have knowledge across a broad range of topics. Being well read can be a real advantage, but where should you start? Several areas will provide you with a great knowledge foundation upon which to build:

The history of the games industry: To make the best games in the future, you need to know what has gone before. Seek out history books on the industry to learn about the early days so you can understand today's games in their proper context.

Writing: You'll use writing as your primary communication medium almost every day. Read examples of great writing and seek out books on the craft of writing and journalism to further hone your skills with the written word.

Game how-to books: Each year, the library of game how-to books grows, and there are excellent volumes across all disciplines. How-to books are great first steps for a game designer to learn some basic technology understanding as well.

Psychology: As a game designer, your job is to create an experience for your player. To control the fun and enjoyment of that experience as much as possible, you'll need to know how the mind works during periods of problem solving, play, and stress. Learning about psychology, of individuals and social groups, will pay off in improved understanding of game design approaches that will produce the most effect in your players.

Marketing: Even game designers need to know something about marketing. Often, you'll hear about the tension between marketing "suits" and game developers, but at the end of the day, everyone wants the same thing: to sell large quantities of very fun games to game players. Understanding what's effective and what's not in the realm of marketing will help you understand how your game and its features fit into a marketing campaign.

Professional magazines and Web sites: Professional magazines, such as *Game Developer* (*www.gdmag.com*), are great tools to keep up with the latest tools and techniques in the industry. There are also great news and resources sites out there, such as Gamasutra (*www.gamasutra.com*), which is geared to the professional game developer. Other sites, such as Blues News (*www.bluesnews.com*), focus on the industry from a fan and player perspective. Build yourself a good set of bookmarks of the sites that can keep you informed from week to week.

ON THE CD

You'll find a short bibliography and reading list on the CD-ROM that accompanies this book to get you started. The selection of books is part of a comprehensive list put together by many, many professional designers. These titles will help you get a start—from there, let your own context and interests guide you forward.

Playing

To design fun, addictive games, you have to play games—many games. You will need to play games across the board, from the best to the worst (sometimes, you'll learn more about the right way to do something by seeing it done horribly wrong first). You'll also need to play across platforms, from Web games to cell phone games to console games, no matter what your medium might be.

WHAT INSPIRED YOU TO MAKE GAMES?

Game designer: Noah Falstein

I was a friend of the great game designer Dan Bunten (M.U.L.E., Seven Cities of Gold) both before and after he had a sex change and became Dani Bunten Berry. But this story was when she was a he, so to prevent confusion (the language isn't really built to handle pronouns in this case), I'll refer to Dan as a male.

→

We were at one of the early CGDC conferences before it became the GDC. There were just a few hundred people at the conference then—only 180 at the first one I went to—and it was much more intimate. There were half-hour breaks between the sessions for networking, and often a conversation started in a break ended up taking up the next few hours. One such talk was among a group of us—I remember Dan was there, and I think perhaps Chris Crawford and Will Wright as well. We were talking about enjoying making games, and Dan, rather passionately, announced that he'd figured out what had prompted him to do it in the first place. He told us that when he was growing up, one of the only times his whole family was together and cooperating happily was while playing board games. He thought that a big part of why he liked to make games, and multiplayer family games in particular (like M.U.L.E, but his Robot Rascals game was a four-player classic as well), was a subconscious desire to recapture that feeling, or perhaps a conscious one to provide it for others.

That really hit home for me, literally. I didn't have as turbulent a family life as Dan described, but I treasured the times we spent playing games, too, and began to make my own board games while still in elementary school. The pleasure of playing a good game is a special thing. I do get a wonderful sense of exhilaration when I think about all the millions of hours of enjoyment people have had playing games I designed. Sometimes, when I worry about whether this job is too frivolous at heart, I think about that, and it keeps me going!

You'll want to play games from a number of different contexts, to make sure you are well rounded:

Today's Hot Games: You'll want to make sure you play the best games that are currently on the market, to understand what gameplay trends are hot, what genres are active, and what the state of the art for design and technology currently is.

Games across genres: You'll want to play games across multiple genres, so you understand what they are, even if they aren't your favorite. Play casual games, play FPS games, RTS games, tycoon games, MMOs—look for the best representation of each genre and play it until you understand how it fits the genre and how it expands the boundaries of that genre.

Play bad games: You don't have to play bad games for too long, but make sure you read the review magazines and take some time to look into the real dogs of any given month. Bad games often can teach more than good games, and don't be too smug—as a game designer, odds are at least one of your projects will end up in the $4.95 discount barrel (the ignoble end for many a bad game).

Play the best games ever: Take time to track down the best games ever created, even if the technology or design now seems old and out of date. Games like *NetHack* and *Scorched Earth* may seem dated today, but the play is still addictive, and their core mechanics influenced hundreds of games that came after.

Games you would never play: If you are addicted to WWII shooters, you may never even give a *Barbie*® game or a game about horse jumping a second look, but as a professional game designer, you'll never know what you will be asked to create. You'll need to understand games that appeal to all audiences—since you may not always be designing the games you want to play. However, even if you are designing a game you would never play yourself, you are still expected to do the best design job possible.

Don't just play electronic games: Games have been part of our human culture for thousands of years, but there have only been electronic games for a few decades. Get to know the real roots of great games. Play cards. Play chess. Play *Scrabble*® and *Monopoly*. Also, take some time to look at some of the best modern board games out there. There is a play dynamic and social aspect of board games that is still elusive to electronic game designers—study how the game plays and perhaps you can help to carry some of that magic to the interactive medium.

ON THE CD

You'll find a list of what the author considers some of the best games ever on the companion CD-ROM—it provides a great starting point for checking out some of the best games created in our electronic and interactive medium. It's a great place to start experiencing the best of what has come before.

Technology

Do you need to know how to program to be an effective game designer? Absolutely not! However, you can't live in a technology vacuum—part of your responsibility is to understand the technology your technical team is using, so you can effectively understand their problems, issues, and opportunities.

Many beginning game designers already have a rough understanding of technology from playing games and following the industry or their favorite game development studios, but don't think this cursory understanding is enough. You need to have a firm grasp on what's going on under the hood so you can effectively communicate, and design within technical limitations.

So, how do you build up some technical knowledge? For detailed knowledge, your technical team is your best source of information, but you want to have some foundational knowledge so you can understand what they are talking about and can grasp the concepts they are telling you.

Often, the best way to do this is to dive into some technology yourself and work on a small sample game or mod, so you can understand, from a working point of view, just what's going on. A great place to start is working with a flexible technology like the Unreal engine, which allows you to create environments and work with scripts and rudimentary programming. Building a level, even if it's not the greatest in the world, will give you insight as to how the various components of technology fit together (Figure 3.5).

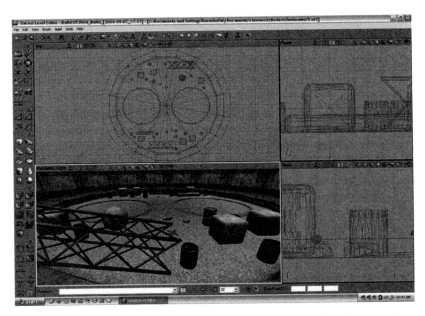

FIGURE 3.5 Creating a level in something like the Unreal engine can be a great way to get a handle on all the technologies that come together to create a game experience.

After working on some modes of an existing game, spending some time looking over some technical books—at least on a surface level—will give you further insight.

Today's games are systems build upon a myriad of smaller subsystems, from rendering to network code, and you need to know how they fit and work together to understand what your limitations are as a designer.

The following aspects of game technology are probably components of the games you'll be designing—work to get a decent level of understanding of each.

Rendering: Rendering is the technology that draws objects to the screen, be they sprites (2D objects) or 3D models.

System architecture: The lowest level components (and the most distant to the designer) often control access to system memory, texture loading, caching of assets, and interaction with any operating system functions.

Scripting: Many of today's games use scripting languages between the low-level functioning of the game and the mission or level designer.

Networking: This system will coordinate connection between multiple systems and the passing and processing of messages between the systems.

Sound and music: This system will control audio output, from managing the sound files to streaming the audio data to mixing multiple channels or 3D sound effects in real time.

Core game code: This is the catch-all term to cover all aspects of game-specific rule coding, from artificial intelligence to game cycling, events, and clock management.

Animation/character system: This will generally handle all character animation, path finding, and other components required in controlling characters.

User interface: This system will display interfaces, collect user input, and coordinate the passing of the input to the appropriate game systems.

World system: This system will handle the data needed to draw the game world, be it a 3D level-based environment or a rolling isometric terrain.

Database system: This system will control and manage all game data, whether runtime data or saved games. This may be low-level custom code, it may use a database engine or format (such as XML), or be handled via a scripting language.

Professional Organizations

Professional organizations and conferences are a great place to learn more about the game development industry and the craft of game design. They are also great places to network with other developers, and to begin your job search.

The granddaddy of them all is the Game Developer's Conference (*www.gdconf.com*), which happens every spring on the west coast. This conference brings together hundreds of teaching sessions with a professional expo and a job fair. If you are serious about breaking into the industry, attending this is a must. They even have a great intern program that will allow you to volunteer at the conference in exchange for attending the various workshops.

One of the most active professional groups is the International Game Developer's Association (*www.igda.org*). The IGDA has been around for years and has great programs for those looking to break into the industry, and special interest groups on many, many aspects of the game development field. The IGDA is represented by many regional groups that often hold regular meetings. These groups are great ways to regularly network with other professionals working in your region (Figure 3.6).

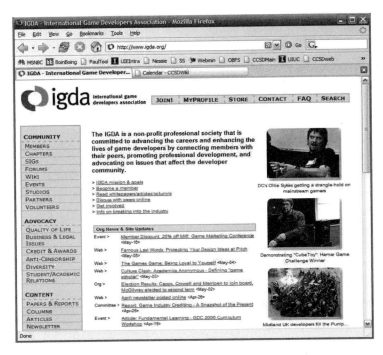

FIGURE 3.6   The IGDA Web site is a great resource to learn more about the games industry and to network with other professional game developers. Used with permission. Copyright IGDA 2006.

REPORTING INFORMATION

Your next meta-task as a game designer is to report on the information you've gathered and created in your own mind. In the previous pages, we explored many ways to get information into your brain. Now, we'll explore some time exploring how to get that information out into the world—on paper, on the computer screen, or in a meeting.

Talking

There are going to be countless times during your career as a game designer that you are going to need to communicate your ideas, not through the written word, but through conversations, meetings, and presentations. A game designer simply can't avoid that fact, so it's a good idea to get comfortable with speaking clearly and persuasively.

You may have to give a presentation on a game's design to the producer or publisher, report on design progress for a team meeting, or explain a concept or an idea over lunch to members of your team—no mater what the venue, there are a few tricks to speaking effectively.

The first thing to know is that it's not a bad thing to present your ideas to a group, and your team or your producer will not be judging you as a person by your ideas. You don't need to be afraid to communicate your ideas, good or bad. A dialogue of ideas is one of the crucibles of great design, and you need to be at the forefront of that dialogue.

When you are in the role of presenter, either for a pitch meeting or team meeting, it's good to remember that you are a professional doing your job. Even if you work in a studio that allows you to wear a Felix the Cat T-shirt and flip-flops, at the team meeting you are a professional, and you should act no differently than if you were wearing a suit and tie.

The first step is to have a clear idea of what you are going to present—spend some time beforehand laying out your notes and the key points of your presentation. Generally, you don't want to be reading from a piece of paper, a laptop, or a PowerPoint™ slide—you want to use notes or that slide to be the anchor that helps you guide and organize your presentation.

When you speak, speak clearly, and control your pacing. You don't want to be unnaturally slow, but most people tend to speed up when they are nervous or excited. Just keep the pacing normal and conversational and do your best to avoid peppering your words with "ums" and "ahs" . . . better to just have a short pause than an "um."

You also want to appear confident. Don't overdo it, but be relaxed and use confident and engaged body language: lean forward, don't slouch back in your chair (often, you'll be giving these presentations around a conference table), don't fidget, and sit or stand with good posture. Make eye contact with your audience and go ahead and move your hands a bit (but don't gesture too wildly).

When it's time to field questions, use your new listening skills to hear the question fully. It's okay to pause to formulate an answer, and more importantly, it's okay to say, "I don't know" if you don't have an answer.

Writing

Writing, like speaking, is a skill that many take for granted, and yet, writing well is one of the most challenging and difficult tasks for a game designer. Your primary and permanent means of communication for your game design will be the written word. You may be able to explain things well in a meeting or presentation, but later, it will be your written design that the team, the publisher, and your producer will refer to. For your job, words on a page (or a screen) are like the lines on a blueprint—they define your design.

Professional writers know that writing well takes years of experience, and every professional writer knows that there is more to learn and understand about our language and how to communicate effectively.

Teaching you to write well is clearly beyond the scope of this book—there are many excellent books out there and a myriad of classes from learning extensions, colleges, or community colleges probably in your region, so we won't try to reinvent that wheel. Instead, let's look at some of the key aspects of writing that you'll need to master to be an effective game designer writer.

Mechanics

The first and most basic is, know the mechanics of writing. Remember high school or college English classes? If you are feeling a little rickety with your core mechanics, pick up a copy of Strunk and White's *The Elements of Style* (in fact, even if you are confident, get a copy of this book—it's a must for your professional bookshelf). This little book distills volumes of knowledge about writing effectively into just a few well-written and easy-to-read pages. You should plan to read that book at least once a year—each time, you'll emerge a slightly better writer.

Keep It Simple

Your next writing touch point is, keep it simple. Even if you have mastery of a large vocabulary, keep your writing simple and easy to understand. Your design document is a tool to be used by your development team—it is meant to be useful, not to show off how flowery you can craft a sentence or what complex words you can use.

Keep your sentences accurate, specific, and to the point, and use straightforward language. Don't be seduced by the desire to write overly complex sentences to capture the mood of the play:

> *As the party, now weary and wounded from their multiple battles, stumbles toward the oaken door, they do not know what to expect. The architecture is alien, and the area exudes a deep sense of foreboding. The thoughtful player will send a magically adept character to the ancient door to test for traps and will discover a devilish device they do not yet fully understand.*

Instead, write clearly, so the development team will understand the situation:

> *The final door the party encounters will be a different style than any of the previous doors. A CheckTrap spell will reveal that it is guarded by a trap, but the details will remain a mystery to the player.*

WRITING IN A WIKI WORLD

More and more, design documents are being authored in a Wiki environment, which works very well for large design documents. Wikis will often handle building tables of contents for you. They also allow you to write, edit, and revise right in a browser window using a very simple and easy-to-learn markup language. The real boon to using a Wiki is that it will track revisions, so it's very easy for someone on the team to hop onto the design document site and instantly see what you've just updated or revised. Wikis also provide an easy way for designers to collaborate together and for other team members to enter their own comments to the document (Figure 3.7).

While a Wiki can be a great tool, the editing window is often quite primitive, especially if you are used to all of the bells and whistles of a full-featured program like Word. For large chunks of design text, it's a good idea to author them first in something like Word, which will allow you to check the spelling (most Wiki editors don't have spell-checks) and revise the grammar easily. Once you have the text in good shape, go ahead and paste it into the Wiki editor to become part of the living design document. This extra step will make sure your writing is as polished and professional as possible.

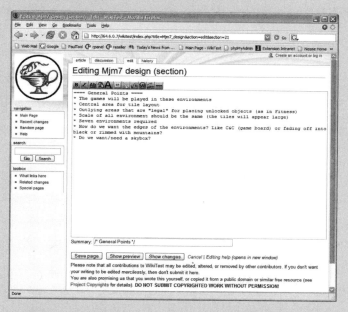

FIGURE 3.7   Editing content is easy using a Wiki's simplified markup language.

Write for Your Audience

Your next writing mantra is, "always remember your audience." Just as you communicate differently with different people in your life (imagine how you tell the story of your day to your seven-year-old son, your wife, or your grandmother), you will need to write differently to communicate effectively to your audience as a game designer.

More often than not, your audience will be the game's development team. This audience has very clear and simple goals for your design document:

- They want to understand the context of the game.
- They want to understand how the game plays.
- They want to understand the mechanics of the game, as it relates to their area of development.
- They don't want to read tons of prose that doesn't mean anything directly to them.

Often, the designer will also be called upon to present the design, high concept, or other design-related document to the publisher or the publisher's marketing team. That audience has a very different desire for your design writing:

- They want to be excited about the game.
- They want to understand the context of the game.
- They want to understand why the game will be fun and visually impressive.
- They want to understand why the game will be better than the competition.
- They want to know the cool key features of the game.
- They don't want to read tons of prose—they want to read writing that is short, sweet, and exciting.

Both audiences are very important, but have very different goals for your writing and very different agendas. Your job is to clearly understand the information your writing must deliver, and do your best job to service the audience.

A common trait is that no audience wants to simply read page after page of your design because the prose is flowery and interesting. Both audiences are comprised of busy people who work hard, and see your design writing as a tool they can use. Don't waste their time, so please remember our previous point: keep it simple.

The development team wants your writing to be clean, simple, and to the point. Your job is not to persuade them that the game is good or that you are a great writer. Your job is to provide them the vital gameplay information so they can implement the game in their area of expertise. Stay away from too many adjectives and adverbs—keep the prose simple and use good action verbs when you need them.

Don't be afraid of bulleted lists: the development team wants their information useful, and that's a great tool. Often, a short introduction paragraph and some bulleted text will convey all you need to convey.

The layout editor enables players to create their own custom tile layouts. The goal is to make the operation of this in-game tool as simple as possible, since the players will most likely be casual gamers. The key features of this tool are:

- *They can start with a blank playfield or load an existing layout.*
- *There will be no skybox or environment; the tiles will be simply floating in black space for visual simplicity.*
- *The cursor will be a translucent tile, highlighted green for a legal position and red for illegal; it will move with the mouse.*
- *A left click, if the cursor is green, will place a tile in the world, at the cursor location.*
- *Tapping the delete key, if there is a tile within the cursor, will remove the tile from the world.*
- *The player should be able to move the entire layout by clicking arrow buttons for the cardinal directions: a single click moves the whole layout in that direction.*
- *A counter on screen will indicate the number of tiles in the current layout.*
- *A valid layout must be a multiple of four (tile count). The tile counter will display red if it's not valid and green if it is valid.*
- *The player clicks the Save button to save the layout; the button only appears when the layout is valid.*

The preceding example is a partial but nearly complete design for an in-game tool to create custom mahjongg tile layouts. You can see that the section was introduced by some simple prose that presents the needed context. The bullet points cover the features of the tool simply and briefly. This section of the design could be handed off to an interface artist, who would be able to determine the interface needs and design goals. This design could also be handed off to a programmer for implementation, who would understand clearly what to do (and can use the bullets as a checklist for his work).

When you are writing to pitch a game or to get the "marketing machine" going for your current game, you still want to keep things as simple as possible, but you will want to energize your writing. You want your words to convey context and gameplay, but in an exciting manner that will get your audience excited about the game and get them visualizing the experience along with you.

The writing should be active (still avoid needless adjectives and adverbs), but no longer are you writing for an audience that wants "just the facts ma'am." You want to use energized prose, creative visualization, and dramatized gameplay to bring your ideas to life.

> *Movies are magic, baby, and someone needs to be the magician!*
>
> *You're young, talented, and you've just been handed the reins of your own movie studio. Have you done this before? Nope. But you have moxie, and saddlebags packed pull of your own Hollywood dreams.*
>
> *Success is your driving goal, but success is a lot like a club sandwich for you—lots of layers. You're going to make hit movies—maybe win an Oscar or two along the way. But that's not all—you want cash, a big house, a gorgeous spouse, and all the trappings and high-speed living you can fit in.*
>
> *You're a multimillion-dollar rainmaker—the more rain you can make for your studio, the more you can enjoy the good life. But remember that fame and fortune take hard work, and scandals lurk around every corner. Better keep a good lawyer on retainer!*
>
> *Hollywood Kahuna gives you the chance to dive into Hollywood in the late 1940s. You are given the reins of a large studio to run. Fail and you're out on the street, but succeed and you'll earn that big paycheck you crave and a chance to create for yourself a real Hollywood lifestyle.*
>
> *This game lets you have the thrill of running your own studio, but you'll also need to think on your feet, because challenges will abound and you'll be tested, both personally and professionally. Can you survive?*

Journalism as Your Model

There are two nearly foolproof ways to become a better writer: constantly write and constantly read. The more you write, the more you will understand language as a tool for communication. The same is true for reading: read every day, and you'll begin to pick up on the way professional writers use language to deliver information, create moods, and make points.

There are many, many styles of writing out there, but the one that most closely encapsulates the writing skill set you'll need as a designer is journalism. Reporters have written for papers for hundreds of years, and the style of simple, information-rich prose is perfect for design writing.

Get into the habit of reading newspapers every day. Read many types of writing, from hard news stories to interviews to feature articles. Each will show you various techniques for lean and nimble writing. The standard journalism approach uses a technique called the "inverted pyramid." In straight news stories, the journalist writes the most important, general information first (the base of the pyramid) and then begins to focus more and more on the smaller and smaller details. The idea for this type of writing is twofold. First, someone just giving the story a quick read will be able to glean the most important facts. Second, if an editor needs to cut a story to make it fit in the paper, he or she can simply cut from the bottom up, knowing that the main ideas of the stories are intact.

The journalistic "leanness of language" coupled with an inverted pyramid approach (used in sections of a game design document) provide a great foundation upon which to write your design and pitch documents.

Many great books can be found on journalistic writing. Begin with Strunk & White, and then peruse your local bookseller for another book or two of hard news writing techniques and you'll have the lessons at hand to hone your game design writing skills.

Point of View in Design Writing

When you write down a game design, you will have to refer to the player in some way during your writing. How do you do that? In fiction writing, a story has a point of view—a position from which the narrative voice is telling the story. The most common is third person:

> *The rain drove down hard, soaking any fool crazy enough to be out on the streets to the quick. Roberts pulled the collar of his trench coat tight and gripped it with a fist. He was 20 minutes late for the rendezvous, and that just might cost Jacqueline her left thumb. But somehow, all Roberts could think about was the drone of the driving rain and his cold, wet feet.*

Often, stories can be told in first person:

> *The rain drove down hard, soaking any fool crazy enough to be out on the streets to the quick. I was one of those fools. I yanked the collar of my trench coat tight and gripped it with a fist. Damn. I was 20 minutes late for the rendezvous, and that just might cost Jacqueline the use of her left thumb. But at that moment, I didn't care. All I could think about was the drone of the driving rain and my cold, wet feet.*

Occasionally, stories can be told in a second-person viewpoint. Many times, a second-person viewpoint requires the use of present tense to make it readable:

> *The rain drives down hard, soaking any fool crazy enough to be out on the streets to the quick. You are one of those fools. You yank the collar of your trench coat tight, gripping it with a white-knuckled fist. You are 20 minutes late for the rendezvous. That just might cost Jacqueline the use of her left thumb. But at that moment, you don't care. All you can think about is the drone of the driving rain and your cold, wet feet.*

In the preceding small examples, it's hard to tell which approach works the best; you need to think through the entire context of the story to make that determination. A third-person viewpoint gives you some distance from the characters and you can easily report on one character or another. The first-person approach places you within one character and locks you there, allowing you to explore that character more fully, but only interpret the world through that character's eyes. The second-person viewpoint is somewhat artificial, since it isn't how we generally converse or write. It also has the same limitations as the first-person viewpoint, but the use of present tense can energize the writing. This can often have an interesting effect, but can get tiring if you are reading hundreds and hundreds of pages of this point of view (while first- and third-person points of view are almost transparent for use as readers).

So, as a game designer, which point of view is most effective? That depends on your situation. If you are writing a piece that is meant to be energized, either for a pitch document or perhaps for a section of a design document that is illustrating the player experience, second-person is a great approach. Here is a short example:

> *You see your goal across the raging lava river: the suit of enchanted plate-mail. A quick scan of the environment shows no easy way across, and you know the gulf is too far to jump. The bridge above you has been destroyed and broken pieces of rubble litter the stone floor. If you test some of the smaller chunks of rubble, you will discover you can move them. You have an idea. You push a chunk over the edge and into the lava. The stone sticks up above the lava for a few seconds before it glows red and vanishes under the molten current. Your task is clear: push in a large chunk, then quickly jump on it, and leap to the rubble bank on the other side.*

This second-person point of view places you in the game, experiencing it as the player would, and provides a much energized way to describe a gameplay situation or puzzle. For more functional writing, however, the old standby of the third person is your best bet. You, as the writer, have the most control of the situation, and you can use clear and effective prose to describe player action:

> *The mini-map at the lower edge of the screen will show the entire scenario map. If a portion of the map has not yet been explored, it will be shown in gray. A red box will indicate the current view area. The player can left click on the map to slew the view to the new location. The player can also click on the cardinal direction buttons below the map to slide to view to the left or right.*

You'll want to watch out for the tendency to mix points of view in a single section of narrative. This tends to muddle the message and doesn't sound very professional, but it's surprisingly easy to do when you get into the excited "Zen" of writing and your words are coming fast and furious. Just be sure to keep a watchful eye, and always proof your work before you submit it to your team—don't just rely on your spell checker.

After the Homework

Once you've begun to explore these new skills, it's important to put them to work. There's no point in developing these abilities if they're not going to make you a better game designer, so it's a good idea to understand what you're going to be doing.

As a designer, it's often necessary to gather and report information. For example, you may be working on a medieval strategy game set in Europe during the Dark Ages. The appeal of your particular game is that it's grounded in historical fact, making accuracy all the more important to your development team. Your task is to research various aspects of the game to verify their authenticity. This requires you to gather information from various sources (books, magazines, documentaries) and present it to the other team members (slideshow presentations, meetings, documents). To properly describe ballistae and buttresses, you'll have to master the necessary vocabulary, and to communicate this information to your lead, you'll need to develop good communication skills, including talking and writing.

Or, you may be in charge of improving the scripting editor for your particular project. This task entails finding out what adjustments can be made, and then relaying this information to the lead programmer. First, you'll have to research scripting tools. This means gathering info about other tools, by installing and using them (since many scripting tools are bundled free with PC games). Of course, you'll be taking notes as you conduct your research. Next, you'll have to communicate this information to the lead programmer. First, you may have to submit your findings to your lead designer, which involves writing and/or talking about scripting. Alternatively, you may share this information with the lead programmer directly.

In all these cases, the important thing is that you're always thinking about the bottom line as you work on the development of these skills. Game design is a multifaceted job, and between meetings, brainstorming, documentation, project management, scripting, competitive analysis, and play testing, there is a wide range of abilities to master.

SUMMARY

In this chapter, we had our first boot camp session. To be an effective game designer, you are going to need some core skills and abilities upon which to build your future work and future game designs.

We first looked at the various ways we can gather and retain knowledge vital to our field of game design. To be a professional game designer means you'll always need to be learning, and so we spent some time looking at some core skills to increase your knowledge-gathering effectiveness.

We next looked at the core skills you'll need to share your information and designs with your development team and the world, from verbal skills to writing schools. As a designer, you are a conduit of information, and being able to communicate effectively is essential.

In the next chapter, we'll continue our boot camp as we examine ways in which we can work to enhance our creative muscles, since those are essential in our day-to-day quest to design addictive games.

CHAPTER EXERCISES

1. Make an appointment with an older family member or family friend and interview him or her about a time during his youth—perhaps the details of a first job. Don't take any notes—instead, listen carefully. When you are done, write your notes down and then transcribe them into a narrative and show them to your subject—how well did you listen?
2. Think back to the seminal rock concert Woodstock—what if you wanted to create an event like that? Using the technique of mind-mapping, explore all the different aspects of putting together a rock "event."
3. Pick one of the middleware technologies out there—perhaps Game Embryo or the havok physics system. Go to their Web site, read the white papers, and then try to write a one-page summary of their technology that you could use to instruct a nontechnical person—you never really know anything until you try to teach it!

4 Design Boot Camp: Creativity and Gray Matter

In This Chapter

- Care and Feeding of the Brain
- The Mind and Body Connection
- Enhancing Your Memory
- What Is Creativity?
- Creative Game Thinking
- Creativity Exercises

Working as a game designer is a job that relies on your intelligence, communication skills, wisdom, and creativity. Each and every day, you will be required to think effectively, to learn more and more about the game you are designing and the world around you—and you will be expected to communicate that new knowledge and your new discoveries to your development team.

As a game designer, you are a generalist—you will need to learn information on a myriad of topics, from technology to interface design to twelfth-century siege tactics. Moreover, your learning requirements will change drastically from game to game—in one game, you may study how to make effective poker bets, and in the next game, you will need to know the rules for competitive horse jumping.

Using your mind effectively is essential, and in this chapter we'll look into the ways you can take care of and enhance your mental faculties—and then learn how you can hone your creative skills to become a truly effective designer.

CARE AND FEEDING OF THE BRAIN

Probably the most vital piece of software you'll use in your entire game design career is your own mind. You'll use a pile of software packages during your career, and when that software gets old and outdated, there is generally an upgrade path to get you to the newest and most effective version. There is no automatic upgrade path for your own gray matter—it's up to you to upgrade and keep your brain operating at peak efficiency. There are a myriad resources out there that will guide you through many, many different approaches to enhance and invigorate your own mind, from Thai Chi to extensive mental and creative calisthenics. In this book, we'll simply address some key points that relate to your work as a game designer. Think of it as a starting point for your own mental upgrade rituals (Figure 4.1).

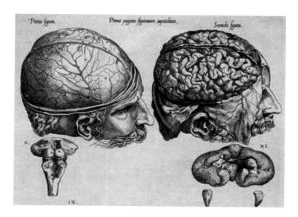

FIGURE 4.1   Your brain is your most important piece of software.

Mind and Body

The first key point, and it's one that no one disagrees with, is that your mind and body are connected—as one goes, so goes the other. Being sad and depressed causes you to ignore bodily health. Being in poor health hampers your mind's effectiveness. We're not going to preach a vegan diet and a ritual of six hours of daily yoga here, but rather some very basic elements to physical health that will pay you great dividends in the area of mental focus and performance.

Sleep Well

The first is simple: get enough sleep. While this may seem obvious, it is actually a point of concern in our industry, where crunch-time hours can quickly shred a developer's personal life. How much sleep you need is based on your own physiology, but there are some baselines, given the way a human body cycles into sleep through light sleep, dream sleep, and deep sleep. To have restorative sleep, you need to let your body move through all cycles naturally, and no matter who you are, that's a minimum of six hours and probably closer to seven or eight. Your body begins with deeper sleep, and most of the REM (rapid eye movement, or dreaming) sleep occurs during the final hours of sleep. For a balanced sleep that rejuvenates both the body and mind, you'll need a full dose of both types of sleep.

Your temptation may be to push through sleep and keep working, but in doing so, you are lessening your effectiveness and harming your mind and body—don't do it. Get your needed sleep.

Here are a couple of hints to help you get the most out of your sleeping time:

- Sleep in a darkened room, on a firm and comfortable mattress.
- De-stress and turn off your mind before you climb into bed (don't think about your worries or your day to come right before sleep).
- Don't eat for 90 minutes before bed.
- Don't read in bed—make bed for sleeping only. Read in a comfortable chair, preferably not in the bedroom.
- Stick to a regular sleep schedule as much as possible—sleep isn't something you can "catch up on" on weekends.

Breathe

The next touch point is oxygen. A brain deprived of oxygen doesn't work. Taken to the extreme, we're talking brain damage. However, not giving your body enough oxygen during your waking hours can also limit your mental acuity. Here are two goals:

Engage in some for of aerobic exercise. We're not talking Ironman triathlons here, but get your heart pumping on a regular basis. Walk to work or take an afternoon constitutional on the sidewalks around your office. Just get moving and get your heart beating for 10 to 20 minutes each day.

Breathe effectively. You'll also want to get in the habit of breathing more deeply. This isn't a constant thing, but you should take a break once or twice a day to take a little breathing break to do some relaxing breathing to oxygenate your mind. There are many techniques, but one of the simplest is to pause, sit still, and take in a deep, slow breath (through your nose, if possible) for a count of seven, hold for seven, and exhale for seven. The goal is to have your breathing be smooth and relaxed. The holding allows your lungs to pull the most oxygen possible out of the breath.

Eat Well

The final mind-body suggestion we'll give you is the one that fills up the most shelves at your local book superstore: eat well. We won't pretend to give you the end-all and be-all advice on this, since there are a million different approaches, and at least 15 or 20 of them are great programs. However, we'll get you started with a few simple pointers:

Cut down on the junk. Junk food is full of additives and processed oils and offers little to no health benefits. It's also the stuff that's most readily available at the office during those crunch-time sessions. Avoid it if you can, and bring in something a little more nourishing.

Watch your liquids. A balanced day's diet doesn't include 9 cups of coffee and 15 sodas. Just use your head. Recent research shows that a few cups of coffee a day is fine and even enhances the mind's functioning, but not cup after cup. And research nearly always shows that drinking water regularly is very, very good for you. Do it—toss in a slice of lemon if water bores you.

Eat reasonably well. This area is up to you, but avoid fast food when you can, eat some dark green vegetables, and make sure you get the right balance of vitamins in your day (especially Omega-3s, which are key in mental capacity building).

Here are some other short and sweet suggestions:

- Drink water whenever possible.
- Limit your sugar intake.
- Choose whole wheat products over refined flour products (and brown rice over white rice).
- Avoid hydrogenated oils.
- Limit your carb intake, but don't avoid carbs altogether.
- Protein is great for breakfast.
- Keep your animal fat (Omega-6 fats) intake moderate.
- Eat plenty of Omega-3-rich foods (such things as fish, herring, olive oil, avocadoes, and walnuts).
- Moderate caffeine intake; as long as it's below the "jitter" level, it's ok.
- A drink or two a day won't hurt and may help your cognitive abilities (it doesn't really matter what type of alcohol).
- Take a multivitamin (one with B-12 and folic acid).
- If you can help it, don't smoke.

These suggestions are a starting point, and will get your body working for and supporting your mind.

The Power of Being Bad

Think of the things at which you are good. Is it writing? Telling a great story? Painting water color? Fixing up old cars? Each of us has some unique skills and expertise that we've developed over the years. Unfortunately, what we are good at really won't help us grow our mind's capacity.

Now think for a moment about what you can't do . . . the list is much longer and often more interesting . . . can you figure skate? Are you a black belt? How are you on the violin? Can you drive a big rig? Spend some time thinking not about what you know nothing about, but about what you are pretty sure you would be terrible at if you tried. Maybe you are a good driver—then driving a semi wouldn't be such a leap with some training. However, if you are tone deaf and have no sense of rhythm, then playing the violin is a real stretch.

It's that distant, awful lack of skills that we want to focus on, because it's in the realm of the bad that we find the room to grow. Clinical research has shown that working hard on something you are utterly terrible at generates many, many positive physical and mental benefits. Putting your mind and body in a difficult situation and working hard on a skill will generate new muscle strengths, new muscle memories, and new neural connections in your mind.

Your most important piece of software, as a game designer, is your mind. This is a sure-fire upgrade path, so spend some time thinking about something that interests you but feels like it is a million miles away from your current skill set. Then, take the steps to start trudging those million miles—sign up for a lesson or two, block out some time and commit to you new endeavor. The going will be rough, but it won't be too long before you start to see the benefits in your regular working life—with sharper, clearer thoughts and a more nimble mind.

This author is the tone deaf fool with no sense of rhythm, and so has spent the last three years studying Depression-era blues guitar playing. It was an impossible task at first, and it's still not easy, but the benefits are tangible and the rewards well worth the effort.

Memory

One of the most useful skills to have is an effective memory. To do a great job designing a game, you'll need to have lots of information at the ready, from all of the books you have read, to the games you have played, to the key points the marketing team made during the kick-off meeting last week. There are two ways to store and recall. In the last chapter, we talked about the various ways to take notes to help you remember key concepts and ideas. Now we'll spend a little time talking about your internal storage device: your mind.

How many times have you read something or sat through a lecture and then were not be able to remember anything about it a week later? The human mind is very good at "auto pruning" information it thinks is useless for you (and in terms of biological survival, it probably is). Unfortunately, your mind's default settings don't reflect how important your new job as a game designer is. You'll need to do some training.

The first thing to know is that your memory—at least the throughput into your memory banks—is very limited. Your short-term memory is limited by what it can store—a mere seven discreet items at any given time (give or take one or two items). Your deeper memory and mind are very adept at dealing with abstract concepts and thoughts, but your short-term memory (think of it as the loading dock between your senses and your inner mind) isn't very good at the abstract at all. Since it's closer to your senses in the sequence, it is much more susceptible to sensory information, especially the visual.

If you approach memory with this in mind, you'll be in a great starting position. You'll want to couple things you are trying to memorize with visual images that are much easier to remember. Here are some basic tips to expanding the capacity of your memory:

Link objects together. This is a simple trick that uses associations. You remember the "Roy G. Biv" mnemonic from grade school—it was an association to help you remember the order of colors in the light spectrum (Figure 4.2). You associated an easy-to-remember word with the first letters of the colors, and therefore could remember them more easily. You link what you are trying to remember with something that's much easier to remember. For example, say you regularly deal with two brothers, Bob and Tim, but you just can't seem to remember which is which. However, you notice that Tim is larger and more portly. This makes you think of Tiny Tim from the Dickens story—certainly not large and portly, but rather the opposite. So, you link the idea of Tiny Tim with the brothers—remember, the opposite is easy. Therefore, if you need to know which brother is Tim, you think "Tiny Tim" and you know it's the portly one.

Visualize. Visualization is the cornerstone of good memory, and it comes naturally for some people and harder for others. The idea is to store a mental "picture" of what you are trying to remember. Image memory is more powerful and permanent than verbal memory. Some people come by this naturally—have you ever met someone who doesn't even know his own cell phone number, but can tell you the location of an old college yearbook in the myriad of boxes in the attic? That person has linked a visual and special memory to that object and has made the memory permanent. To use this technique, study the look and feel of an object, be it a face or a coffee mug. Visualize it in its current environment—think about the unique visual characteristics that make it stand out.

FIGURE 4.2   Mnemonics are often used to help us remember things, such as the phrase "Roy G. Biv" to remember the colors in a rainbow. Photo courtesy of NASA.

Make a story out of it.   Another great technique, especially useful when you are trying to memorize a list of very different objects, is to build a short story about the objects—something very vibrant and humorous. A technique like this could be used to memorize the names and faces of your development team, the order of the planets, the characteristics of a game's NPCs, and so on.

Think shape/color.   If you are trying to remember a series of objects, focus first on color, then shape, and then details. Your color memory is quite effective, since it's easy to internalize a color visualization.

Put them in a "physical mental space."   If you read the book *Hannibal* by Thomas Harris, you'll discover an amazing description of this memory technique (used by Hannibal Lecter). The idea is to create a "dream space"—say, an imaginary museum in your mind—and imagine objects you are trying to remember as exhibits in the museum. Imagine yourself in a physical place, wandering through the exhibits and seeing all the objects. This powerful and very visual imaginary structure will help to anchor the objects in your permanent memory.

Use the journey system. Another technique to memorize an assortment of disjointed objects is to imagine yourself in a journey from object to object. This is similar to the story technique, but with this approach, you imagine yourself physically moving from one object to another—you pick up a PEN to draw a picture of a WINDMILL that you then mail to the POLICE OFFICER . . . (and so on).

Chunking. Chunking will help you remember sequences of numbers or letters. Remember that you are limited in the throughput to your deeper memory by the limitations of your short-term memory. You can avoid this by chunking together items into a single meta item. Think of memorizing the sequence 6 4 3 2 9 8 4 5 2 6 5 1 3 4. This sequence is longer than short-term memory can process, but you can chunk it up into more manageable pieces, such as 643 298 452 65 134.

Memory skills are very much akin to physical athletic skills: they won't get better unless you work on them, and you'll need to keep up a certain level of memory fitness to keep your skills sharp. As a game designer, you don't need to break any kind of memory world record, but you would be well served to spend at least some conscious effort to hone your memory to a greater degree of efficacy.

Mastermind Group

Perhaps you've heard of the old-time definition of the term "salon"—a group of like-minded individuals getting together to discuss things, often the events in the world at that time. It's hard to underestimate the powerful effect of conversation with other intelligent individuals—you can learn from their discourse and also hone your own communication skills.

A mastermind group is like an old-world salon—it's a group of individuals who know a great deal (collectively) about a subject, and enjoy getting together to discuss and explore the topic (Figure 4.3).

As a game designer, putting together or participating in such a group of fellow designers is a great way to broaden your horizons and expose yourself to skills and wisdom beyond your own. Like an athlete who improves by playing against those with greater skills, you too will grow in your mental abilities by regularly putting your ideas on the line with more experienced designers.

In any situation like this, check your ego at the door and listen carefully. Don't be afraid to speak up, but don't spend so much time thinking about your discourse that you miss the conversation going on around you. Participate and concentrate fully, and you'll find that a Mastermind Group is a great professional development tool.

FIGURE 4.3   Long ago, salons were groups of intellectuals that came together to discuss the events of the day.

CREATIVITY

The human mind is capable of many things, and there are many types of intelligence we regularly use, from math intelligence to verbal intelligence to kinesthetic intelligence. We all have different skills "out of the box"—some may be great at sports, but not great orators. Some of us may excel in math, but shooting a basket is near impossible. Nearly all of our mental intelligences can be enhanced through practice and exercise. Creativity is one of those intelligences, and one of the most important to the game designer.

What Is Creativity?

So, what is creativity? Simply put, it is the ability to make new connections or associations between existing memories. If you don't have an active, engaged mind loaded with content, you can't be very creative. Technically speaking, a creative thought isn't creative because it's new and fresh to the entire world—it's a creative thought because it is a new connection in your own mind.

Think of small children who learn to pull themselves up to a coffee table and stand. They are making a new, creative connection between things they already know, such as "I can stand when Dad leans me against the coffee table" and "I can pull myself up when I pull on my jungle-gym toy" and "The edge of the table feels like my jungle-gym toy." The children have some knowledge, and the moment of creative thought is when the new idea is created, based on existing experience, to pull themselves up and stand. In the context of the larger world, it isn't really a new concept at all—but it's very new and exciting for the child.

Looking at it this way, we are all very creative individuals. For years, we have been making new associations that have helped us grow and evolve. However, the term "creative person" in our culture generally means a person who can make these associations, but make them in an innovative way most of us have not thought of. That's a tall order, indeed.

Game Design Creativity

All rewarding professions offer a degree of challenge, and meeting those challenges makes us grow, learn, stretch, and feel accomplishment. Often, challenges require the use of creativity to meet them—and nowhere is this truer than in the realm of game design. As a designer, you are a problem solver—your entire job is to meet a challenge and solve a problem with the application of creativity.

So, how well prepared are you? Are your creative muscles in top form?

Another vital arrow in the designer's quiver is wisdom, deep knowledge made real with experience. For a designer, this means a deep knowledge of games, in all forms and genres, from card games to role-playing games to first person shooters.

Beyond just knowledge of the gaming world, a designer must be like a movie critic and be able to deconstruct a game. What does this mean? It means that you must be able to break a game down into smaller component pieces—small enough to understand and analyze, and understand how they contribute to the whole of the game and what they are built upon.

A game begins as a simple idea. In the old days of solo game design, often that idea was a moment of inspiration that occurred to the creator—a simple "Aha!" that could then evolve into a game: "I want to fly a spaceship into a Martian cave."

More often than not these days, professionally created games come to life in a far less romantic manner. "We need a dungeon-based RTS to grab a niche in that growing market" might come from a publisher. "Our 3D engine is really only good at controlling floating objects and rendering water" might come from the technical director.

It's important to note that when ideas come forth in the form of constraints, this can often prove to be a very useful creative opportunity for a designer. It is then up to the designer to meet the constraints head on and be able to create a compelling idea for a game.

Idea Stress Test

When you are working on an idea, be sure to put it through some basic stress tests in the early stages. Ask yourself the following questions:

Does this idea touch or tap into something familiar to your game players? This question is key, because a wholly original idea might just fall flat if it doesn't tap into enough cultural knowledge of your players. There are reasons why alien spaceships in movies (on the inside) look like the inside of submarines—it's because we are familiar with that look and we can understand the environment more easily.

Are you reasonably confident the game idea can be "made real" with the tech you and your team will have at their disposal? At this juncture, you don't have to be overly precise about it, but just make sure you are keeping things within the realm of reality.

Is the game going to be hitting the target that's needed? If you are working within constraints or goals from a publisher, this is key. It just means that you have some solid awareness of what target you are trying to hit and you are at least shooting the arrow in the right direction—later, we'll work on sharpening the aim.

Does the concept have enough originality so it doesn't feel plagiarized? This is where your experience in existing games will come to bear—you have to know what has come before to know that you aren't about to pitch the same game that was a hit (or a flop) two years ago. This error in judgment often comes up to bite many novice science fiction writers, who write a story they think is wholly new and unique, only to discover that Robert Heinlien already knocked the same idea out of the park 40 years ago.

FORTS: GOING TOO FAR WITH CREATIVITY

Several years ago, our development team decided to make a totally innovative game—one that delivered gameplay that was completely new and a game concept no one had seen before. We began work on a game called Forts. For years (since the days of Video Easel on the Atari™ 800), we'd been fascinated with Conway's Life algorithm. It was a primitive attempt to use a grid-based computer field (represented by pixels that were on, or alive, and off, or dead) to simulate the life and death of cells based on simple rules of population density. The result, when run in real time, was often a beautiful organic kaleidoscope. We wanted to see if we could take that idea into three dimensions and add a fractal element to it to create living tree-like structures a player could control (Figure 4.4).

We worked hard to create a backstory for the game, the organic life components, and a gameplay dynamic (you grew your tree to touch a switch plate to open access to the next environment). We created a fully functional prototype

→

game, a great pitch presentation, and went knocking on publisher's doors. We were confident that when they saw how innovative and beautiful the game was, we'd have a signed deal in a heartbeat.

We went from meeting to meeting with the same results: quizzical looks from publishers, because they just couldn't understand what they were seeing. The game had no analog in the real world or in the game world to provide a point of conceptual entry. Frustrated, we tried to explain the game in terms they could understand. We told them the game was like "combat bonsai tree pruning." As I'm sure you can guess, that was the kiss of death. Who wants to play a game that's likened to the slowest hobby in the world?

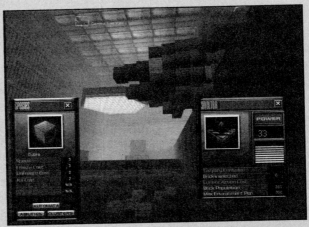

FIGURE 4.4   Forts was a creative game, but too different from a player's expectations to allow a publisher to sign on to produce the game.

We had created something wholly new, but we did so without providing any way for someone to easily understand the game, the world, or the mechanics. We "over creativitized" our game, to the point where it wasn't viable anymore.

Pairing Concepts Together

There are many ways to ponder the concept of an "interesting game idea." On one hand, it's thinking through a fresh and unique situation that will make a compelling game. This could be an original idea or perhaps a blending and combination of multiple ideas.

Consider the following list of rather mundane story and game nuggets (these are all items we've seen a hundred times before in games, movies, and stories).

First, some objects:

- Pirate treasure
- Princess
- An ancient calendar stone
- Fast vehicle
- Demon
- Starship
- A wagon full of goods
- Ring leader
- Huge robot warrior
- Magic sword
- Vampire
- Hover tank
- Decaying city

Now, some actions:

- Rescue
- Escort
- Destroy
- Win
- Avoid
- Capture
- Ride
- Find
- Hide
- Open
- Close
- Steal
- Return

From this list, you can see how we can construct a wide array of unoriginal, "seen it a thousand times before" games ideas, such as:

- "Find the pirate treasure."
- "Rescue the princess from the demon."
- "Find the ancient calendar stone to reveal the magical sword."

However, what if we take some of these rather mundane objects and combine them in a fresh way? Perhaps something like the following:

- "Steal the princess in a fast vehicle."
- "Hide the demon from the huge robot warrior."

On the other hand, the game idea may be tackling a familiar concept, but crafting it into a game. Think of something like a football game, a deer hunting game or a poker game. All those concepts have been wildly successful, but the ideas themselves are not new at all—in fact, it's the familiarity that makes the game concept compelling.

It's been said that one type of game that has the odds stacked in its favor is a game that simulates something everybody is familiar with but don't often get to do. Perfect examples are a professional football simulation and a deer hunting simulation.

The familiarity breaks down the barrier to access—everybody knows what the game is about. And the fact that the game can allow players to do something they never or rarely get to do in real life makes this type of game even more compelling.

Of course, it helps if the activity has some game-like aspects already built in and that there is a certain "hero aspect" to jumping in and entering that kind of simulation. Think of something like a skydiving game. It is certainly something everyone is familiar with, and very few people do it at all, much less often. There is even a sort of "hero-like" quality to the skydiver. However, the activity itself isn't that conducive, out of the box, for a game: fall, pull ripcord, float, and land.

Of course, we can always flex our creative muscles and try to make an idea that is "partly there" more suitable for a game. With our skydiving example, perhaps we focus on the control of the chute and guiding the avatar toward different scoring targets on the ground—sort of like a free-fall Lunar-lander game. It's not perfect, but we're closer to something that is workable.

Idea Depth

If you are fortunate enough to be able to think through a wholly original game, you have quite a task in front of you. As we've already discussed, the idea, whatever it is, must have some sort of "anchor" so the players will be able to understand what is going on and can get into the game.

However, game history is littered with original games that have been awful, mediocre, or just simply forgettable. Perhaps the idea was truly original and passed our initial litmus test of the questions we asked previously, but it was still lacking that something extra that allowed it to be a hit out of the park.

Of course, the blame could be the implementation—that 99% of work that follows the inspiration or birth of the original idea. This happens more often than anyone would like to admit.

But, let's assume, for a moment, that the implementation of the game will be spot on and every bit as good as it needs to be. Let's put the onus of responsibility on the initial idea for a game.

If the idea is solid, you should also strive to give the concept some depth. A concept may be a wonderful original idea or a compelling synthesis of familiar ideas arranged in a new way. However, you should also strive, whenever possible, to make your game concept strike a deeper chord—to feel like it is more than simply an idea, but something more than the sum of its component parts.

How do you do that? There are many approaches and no single path. Think through the deeply moving films you've seen or books you've read—what was it about them that stirred something deeper in you and made them an *experience to remember*?

Often, this resonance comes from that fact that the book or movie touched on a deeper human experience or emotion and somehow brought clarity or illumination to that emotion. Consider the movie *Lost in Translation*. If you ask a small sampling of people, you'll get some very polar responses, from "I don't get it" on one end to "That was one of the most moving films I've ever seen." We're not being overly scientific here, but more often than not, the "I don't get it" response will come from younger viewers, and the more mature viewers will be moved. Why? The film captures the ennui and adrift feeling many feel in later life, when we're not sure how all of our actions add up. Add to this feeling a ray of hope—a connection with another fellow human being who is struggling with the same issues, and together, there is a moment of deep connection . . . love even. While it can't last, it is a lighthouse casting a beacon for an adrift soul.

If you have felt those feelings later in life, the ray of hope offered by the film is beautiful and moving, even more so because it cannot last. If you have not yet struggled with your own ennui and self-meaning, the subtle emotions can be lost.

This story, which clearly doesn't work for all viewers, is powerful . . . resonant, because it captures something deeper in our human experience and psyche.

Let's consider one of our simple little game idea examples: "Hide the Demon from the Huge Robot Warrior."

How do we take this idea and add depth to it? If we think about tapping into human experience, what opportunity might exist? Demons are outcasts—negative reflections of what is right and proper. What if the Demon, who is being hunted mercilessly by a Huge Robot Warrior, is actually a byproduct of the hero's actions earlier in life—perhaps a brother shunned so severely by his "near perfect" brother that he devolved into the heinous creature that now stalks the dark forests? Perhaps the hero, in either a noble or misguided attempt to fix the wrongs of the past (a powerful motivation from the dawn of storytelling), seeks to hide and protect the Demon from his would-be assassin. In the meantime, the nonthinking Huge Robot Warrior is clear-cutting towns and villages, causing untold collateral damage, in his ceaseless quest to destroy the Demon.

Agreed, this may not be the best concept for a game, but the exercise here was to see how we could take a simple, serviceable, and slightly fresh game idea and add some depth to it by folding in the concepts of guilt, redemption, and blindness to repercussions. With a simple fleshing out of the concept, we were able to add significantly more to the idea itself and tap in to some powerful human emotions and experiences.

Brainstorming

Brainstorming is the process of trying to force creative associations out into the open during a specified time. It may be as simple as curling up on your couch with a cup of coffee and a legal pad, or as advanced as an organized team brainstorming meeting.

So, can you be creative on command? Often, the answer is yes, but at times, your mind may not be in the optimal state for brainstorming, so don't feel like you've failed if you tried to brainstorm and all you got was a drizzle.

If you are brainstorming solo, it's often a good idea to be in a distraction-free environment. At times, distractions may fuel the process, but more often than not, it's just more noise. You'll also want to have an idea of what you are brainstorming—what is your goal? Is it large or small? Even if your goal is large, don't make it too huge. Don't say, "I want to think of a game idea"—that's just too open ended. Generally, you are working with constraints that will help to guide you, such as "I need to think of a historical FPS that isn't another WWII clone."

If you can be more specific, that's great—perhaps your problem is something like "I need to think through the gameplay elements of the lizard warrior culture."

When you are brainstorming solo, you'll still want to take notes—you won't be able to feed off the energies of others, so start jotting down things you already know and see what happens when you pair them together, add, or take away. Soon, you'll get into a mental rhythm that puts you in tune with the problem you are trying to solve.

If you are going to be part of a team or group brainstorming session, you'll need to make sure you have a specific problem to address—the more minds involved, the more potential for creativity, but also the much greater potential to veer off course.

For team brainstorming, you need a central mediator—not to pass judgment on ideas, but to direct discussion, take notes, and guide the conversation down creative paths. You'll soon discover that development team members all have different "brainstorming personalities"—some are quiet and reserved while others shout loudly and get very excited. The mediator is there to make sure the maximum results are achieved, and that may mean drawing out the more reserved attendees and keeping a check on the "alpha" barnstormers.

So, how do you brainstorm in a group? Think of the definition of creativity again: making new associations between existing memories. In a group, you've just widened the pool of existing memories, and there are many minds working at making new associations. You need to document, on a whiteboard or flip chart, the ideas and observations that come to light, since those will serve as the "memory pool" for the group. Challenge the participants to find new and interesting associations that solve or support the problem at hand. As you warm up, you'll soon discover that the group, as when you solo brainstormed, will reach a point at which they are in rhythm with the problem at hand and the flow of the session—when that happens, buckle your seatbelt and take good notes.

BRAINSTORMING THOUGHTS

 ### *Designer: Steve Meretzky*

Several rules:
1. Have the right number of people. Too few people, and you don't get the critical mass that makes ideas fly. Too many, and people feel intimidated; it's too easy to let the vanilla "group consensus" quash great nascent ideas. I'd say four or five is ideal, but of course, that varies based on the personality and creativity of the people.
2. Try to get offsite. The change in scenery will help people to (as Apple™ says) "think different." Also, people won't be as distracted by the pull of their mundane tasks. Make everyone turn off their cell phones.
3. As everyone says, there are no bad ideas in brainstorming. But there are some that come pretty damn close, so try not to waste too much time putting them to rest when they do come up.
4. Serve margaritas.

Creativity Exercises

Training your creative mind is not only a good idea, it's a great amount of fun. Creativity exercises are like mental calisthenics; they train and grow your creative capacity. There are many great resources available to help you recharge your creative juices. We'll explore some exercises specifically designed to challenge your game design mind. These exercises are designed to do solo, but they also work well in a team environment.

Decode a Real-World Game

Play a "use your body" game and deconstruct it (go-karts, paintball, softball, Frisbee, golf, etc.). What are the rules of the game, both explicit and implicit? What skills are required? What do you do during play? What perceptions and senses do you use to gauge your progress? How do you know how well you are doing in the game? What risk and reward elements are part of the play? What aspects of the game make it fun and unique?

You'd be surprised how much you can get out of a deconstruction exercise of a game you've played for years—thinking through a game's systems, actions, and rules can give you a new understanding of how rule sets can create a framework for play.

Limited Story

Write a piece of "sudden fiction." This is a very, very short story (500 words maximum, or basically a single page). Focus on creating something compelling, but work to create the story quickly. Don't spend your time thinking through the ebb and flow of plot, since you'll end up writing in generalities. Dive in and be specific and detailed. Give yourself a 40-minute time limit.

Fiction into Game

Find a short story you are interested in or really enjoy. Give yourself one hour and write a short page on how that story could be turned into a compelling game. Focus on what the player will be doing, and see if you can capture the elements of the story that make it stand out for you.

Keep a Scrapbook

This is more a long-term project than a single session exercise. Keep a scrapbook of any news stories, pictures, stories . . . *anything* that catches your eye. These can be used later as an aid to creativity. Anything that inspires you but you can't use immediately should go in the scrapbook for later. Revisit the book from time to time—used colored markers to annotate your entries and jot down ideas you get flipping through the pages.

Miniature Worlds

Go on a walk and collect objects to make a "miniature world" diorama (inside a shoebox is great) and then put it away for a week, before you actually make anything. Now, revisit the found objects and use glue or whatever you like working with to construct a diorama of a miniature world, using just the objects you found on your walk. Put it away again for another week. When you come back, write a short essay on how the world functions and what makes it wondrous.

The "Andre Breton"

Andre Breton was one of the central architects of the surrealist movement in Europe in the 1920s. The more famous surrealists (such as Salvador Dali) were painters, but Breton used words to create his surreal, nonsensical art. He called it "automatic writing"—writing without thinking, allowing associations to flow from one to another. One of his most famous works was the nearly unreadable "Soluble Fish"—a surrealist "novel." While we wouldn't call automatic writing serious art, the act of writing without thought is a great and liberating exercise.

Pick an interesting line or character out of a story or game (to give yourself something to start with), and then do automatic writing on it for 10 minutes. Another approach is to cycle through a slideshow of images and write fluidly, allowing the images to inspire you. You are not looking to create plot, character, or even whole sentences, but rather a spontaneous flow of language.

Game into Fiction

Take one of your favorite games and write a fictional narrative of the adventure you had while playing. Don't worry about creating a complete story arc—just grab a section of gameplay or perhaps a single mission of scenario. Use action writing that engages the senses, and allow yourself to write about the sense you don't have while playing a game (touch and smell, for example).

Biography Snapshot

Take a picture from a newspaper, magazine, or poster—something interesting that focuses on a character that intrigues you in some way (for a great source of images of interesting people, check out the American Memory collection—part of the online offerings of the Library of Congress). Create an identity for the person (if someone famous, give them a new identity) and write a brief description of what was happening just before, just after, and just as the picture was taken.

Scroll Timeline

Get a roll of paper (10 feet should do) and create a "timeline" for your life so far. Mark on it every time you moved, where you lived, school, major events in the world, pets you had, concerts you've seen . . . the passing years—use these as the structure. Then, go back and fill in the details . . . tell the little, magical, and intense stories that define who you are. Use colored markers and allow yourself to sketch, doodle, or attach photographs. The act of recalling memories you haven't accessed in years is a great mental exercise, and the structure of a timeline will help you access and recover those memories.

SUMMARY

In this chapter, we took the next step in our preparation to think like a game designer—and to hone the tools we'll need for years of productive, creative work. First, we looked at how we can take some simple physiological steps to enhance our mind-body health.

We next explored one of our most vital skills as game designers: our ability to think creatively. We explored the definition of creative thought and then looked at some ways to think about core game ideas creatively. Finally, we reviewed some exercises that will allow us to stretch our creative muscles.

In the next step of our boot camp experience, we will dive in and explore the design document itself, and learn how we can write our own design documents, from the high concept to the scope of the overall game design and functional design documents.

CHAPTER EXERCISES

1. Create a short "thought ritual" for yourself at the end of the day—use one or more physical objects as a trigger to think about aspects or roles of your life during the day. After doing so, put the object or objects away to signify that you are done thinking and worrying and it's now time to rest and relax.
2. Pick one of the creativity exercises outlined previously and work through it to completion—what did you learn about your own creativity in the process?
3. Take a deck of cards and deal yourself a hand. Spend a few seconds trying to memorize the cards without first organizing them. Now, spend a few seconds arranging the cards as if you were playing a game and see if that makes it easier or harder to memorize. Continue this approach until you reach four hands of cards—can you memorize them all?

5 The Design Document

What is a design document? Think of it as the verbal blueprint for a game. As a game designer, your primary responsibility is to author all or part of a game design document, and then keep it current as development on the game progresses.

Design documents come in many forms, from short documents, to detailed Wikis, to voluminous tomes spanning hundreds of pages. No matter what the style or type of interpretation, effective game designs all share some similar components. These components may be separate documents, or may be combined into a holistic, single design.

In this chapter, we'll explore the key aspects of the foundational components of a complete game design, and look at examples that will help make the differences clearer. We'll conclude by getting started on the design document for the game we will craft in this book as our teaching tool.

DESIGN DOCUMENT COMPONENTS

As we touched on in the introduction, there are key components to an entire game design document. These components may be separate documents, or may be woven together into a meta game design document that touches on all aspects of the design.

Some game designs may only consist of several of these components—the type of project, scope, and needs of the development team will help the game designer and the project producer determine what is needed for a particular project.

All are components to a blueprint that will guide the development of a game, from the initial sales pitch all the way to the final project testing.

Process

Design documents are created by the design team in various stages. First, the core concept is outlined in a short overview document that explains the main principles of the game and some of the major features. If the game is a sequel, the overview doc may also cover any changes that differentiate this game from its predecessor. This document doesn't really apply to the scripter, but it's still important to review the document as a member of the team, to understand the focus of the game.

After the core overview documents are approved, work begins on the design documents, which outline all aspects of the game, including missions, features, characters, levels, and multiplayer. Once the design documents have gone through the approval process, the scripter can begin the work of implementing the design, using the design document as a blueprint.

For example, let's say that a studio is developing a first-person shooter in a Wild West setting. After the documents have been approved, the scripter and lead designer go over the documents and discuss the player experience in *Mission 3*. The artists have created the art assets, and the programmers have finished building the editor, so the scripter opens the *Mission 3* design document and reads that the first scenario is an encounter with three desperadoes. Two are carrying shotguns, and one wields a pair of revolvers. The scripter opens the editor, selects the *Mission 3* map, and places three enemies on the map. For two of them, he selects Shotgun from the drop-down menu; for the third, he selects *Dual Revolver*. Alternatively, if the editor doesn't employ drop-down menus, he types Shotgun.wpn in the Weapons field (or Shtgn.wep, or whatever else the program requires). In any case, the scripter assigns hostile behavior to the desperadoes, or indicates that they should try to flee at the first sign of trouble. Their behaviors are delineated in the design document, and the scripter's job is to execute that vision.

High Concept

A High Concept is a simple sentence or two describing the essence of a game. Often, this is the first place a game design starts—this can be the seed from which the game will grow. At times, a High Concept may actually be assigned from a publisher if you are going to be developing a game that will help them fill some necessary slot on their product matrix.

While most games are far more complex than a single sentence will allow, you need to be able to distill the essence of the game into just a single phrase. This helps when you are describing the game to a publisher or marketing team, and serves as the anchor against which you can test the focus of your game during the entire design process.

While the game design as a whole may be organic and changing, the High Concept is written in stone. If you change the High Concept of the game during development, you are changing the game in a fundamental way. The High Concept can be that test you compare all other additions or subtractions against, to see if you are still being true to the vision of your game.

Let's look at some potential High Concepts for some classic arcade games:

Asteroids® puts the player in a small spaceship in an asteroid belt. The player can turn and fly his ship and can fire projectiles that will break the wandering asteroids into smaller and smaller chunks. The player tries to survive as long as possible as more and more asteroids, and even some alien saucers, cross his path.

PacMan will challenge the player, represented as an abstract munching mouth, to clear a maze-like level of food pellets. The levels will be inhabited by creatures that roam the maze and will destroy the player if they touch him; the player can turn these creatures into "ghosts" for a time by gobbling up special food pellets. (Figure 5.1.)

FIGURE 5.1   Classic-style arcade games can often be easily described by a simple High Concept sentence or phrase.

These High Concepts are each only two sentences long, but they capture the core essence and gameplay approach to each game. It's important to note that a High Concept is not a "pitch"—it is not meant to get the blood pumping by selling the sizzle of the game—rather, it's meant to capture the game's core in as few words as possible to provide an effective starting point for the design work to come.

Pitch

The Pitch document is often separate from the standard design document because it addresses a different audience. While the primary audience of a "working" design document is the development team, the primary audience for a Pitch document is often a publisher or marketing team. The Pitch document, often accompanied with a small demo or proof-of-concept prototype, is the tool most used when pitching a game to a publisher to get the green light on a game project.

Several other key factors should be included in a Pitch document. One is a description of who the audience is for the game; the body of the document probably implies this, but you want to call it out clearly for the reader. Is the game aimed at hard-core gamers? Or is it aimed at girls between the ages of 6 and 12?

You also want to be clear about which platforms the game is intended for. In this age of multiple platforms, you need to address this issue—are you going to develop a downloadable PC game? Will it be a Flash game, played in-browser? Will you target all the major third-generation consoles?

Often, you will want to address the competitors in the genre of your game. Your goal is not to pretend there are no competitors, but to clearly identify them and address why your title will be unique. The lack of competitors can often mean a lack of a market. A rich field of competitors indicates an active market and provides a clear target to shoot for.

The Pitch may or may not be the place to describe the estimated schedule and budget for the game—check with your producer on this. Often, those discussions are separate, but often, a publisher will want to see everything together in one document to get a clear overview of the entire project.

As a designer, writing the Pitch document forces you to turn up the flowery, descriptive prose (which is to be avoided in the working documents) to make the most compelling verbal description of your game. While a Pitch document isn't often part of the formal design documents, writing it will force the designer to address core design issues, and expand on the essence of the game stated in the High Concept. Once a game has the green light, it's a good idea to share the Pitch document with the entire team, since it will paint a colorful picture of the game for the team and give them a more detailed glimpse into the type of experience they will be creating.

The following Pitch example was a document written for a game that nearly made it to the green light stage. You'll learn, as you grow in your design career, that the vast majority of Pitch documents never get past this stage. It doesn't mean the Pitch is bad or the design isn't valid (although certainly, that is the case at times); it may just mean that the project isn't right for a particular publisher or the timing is wrong.

In the case of our example, the idea was sound, but it would be going head to head with the work of Peter Mollyneux's team on *The Movies*. As good an idea as our Pitch was, the budget and team just couldn't realistically compete with a project that large.

HOLLYWOOD KAHUNAPITCH DOCUMENT

High Concept

Run a successful movie studio to churn out a string of blockbuster hits and earn enough cash to support your high-speed Hollywood lifestyle.

Let's Make Movies, Baby!

Movies are magic, baby, and someone needs to be the magician!

You're young, talented, and you've just been handed the reins of your own movie studio. Have you done this before? Nope. But you've got moxie and saddlebags packed full of your own Hollywood dreams.

Success is your driving goal, but success is a lot like a club sandwich—lots of layers. You're going to make hit movies—hell, maybe win an Oscar or two along the way. But that's not all—you want cash, a big house, a gorgeous wife, and all the trappings and high-speed living you can fit in.

You're a multimillion-dollar rainmaker—the more rain you can make for your studio, the more you can enjoy the good life. But remember that fame and fortune take hard work, and scandals lurk around every corner. Better keep a good lawyer on retainer!

Hollywood Kahuna gives you the chance to dive into Hollywood in the late 1940s. You are given the reins of a large studio to run. Fail and you're out on the street, but succeed and you'll earn that big paycheck you crave and a chance to create for yourself a real Hollywood lifestyle.

This game lets you have the thrill of running your own studio, but you'll also need to think on your feet, because challenges will abound and you'll be tested, both personally and professionally. Can you survive?

Your World

The game will take place in a fictional "Hollywood"—this Hollywood is made up of your movie studio grounds, the "flash" of downtown Hollywood (stores, restaurants, and clubs—a city block of expensive places to do deals, spend cash, and to "see and be seen"), and the Hollywood Hills, where the mansions of the movers and shakers are (and where you can buy or build your dream home).

The game world will be shown to the player via two "zoom levels" of maps. The larger world will show all three of these areas in a single environment, nestled in the Hollywood Hills. This will allow the player to quickly navigate and to see his empire at a glance. The more precise environments will focus on the

→

studio itself, the Hollywood strip (the Mini Hollywood of the game) and the player's own growing "Xanadu" of pleasure.

Movie Production

The "meat and potatoes" of this game is running a successful movie studio. You'll be given an initial budget for the studio (funds from some already committed investors), but the studio will begin as a bare-bones affair—one sound studio on the lot and that's it.

Your goal is simple: churn out blockbusters. Nothing else will do.

Your overarching tasks for the studio are the following:

Improve your studio physically (enhancing the capabilities)

Launch new projects

Oversee the progress on existing projects

Deal with "fires" as they crop up

Bring in investment dollars (to fund new projects)

Give yourself a salary that can support your very expensive lifestyle

Improving your studio is required if you want to really go places—right now, you can manage one low-budget film at a time, but to keep the green rolling in, you'll need to churn out 3–4 blockbusters a year. That means you need more sound studios, exterior sets, trailer blocks for the actors, special effects warehouses, and of course, a fleet of plucky little golf carts.

You'll have to shoot from the hip when you want to start a movie project—after all, you've never done this before, and no one trusts you . . . yet. But you've got your eyes set on Greta Garbo's old mansion and that takes cash. To get cash, you'll need a hit movie.

Start by buying the rights to an original screenplay, a book, a stage play, or even the latest hot video game. Or, try your luck and try to develop your own idea or pay some waiter down in the valley for his film treatment.

You'll need to sign on some investors, but to do that, you'll need to first bring in a top-notch director, actor, or actress. Of course, they'll want a complete script rewrite and control over the project. Bend, but don't break and feel free to lie if you have to—just keep your fingers crossed that you aren't found out.

Wine and dine your investors, start with a handshake and then bond your film and you're off to the races.

With the money in place, you've got to set up your production budget, hire the rest of the team, determine if your studio can handle what you need, and then push that fateful "green light."

$\rightarrow$

Of course, no production goes off without a hitch—as a movie is in production, you'll need to fine-tune the budget, fire the upstart actors, rewrite the script a half dozen times, and wine and dine your potential distributors.

If you've survived the process and the film is in the can, then you can take a deep breath while your tux is getting pressed. When opening night rolls around, you'll be there with the best escort money can buy and that million-dollar smile. Will the movie be a hit or will you need to leave town for a few weeks? If you've got the stomach for it, watch the returns coming in from the theaters and hope for a blockbuster. Who knows—come springtime, the Academy may come knocking.

Tired yet?—because you've got another movie to make. You may have bought the fancy house, but your new trophy bride needs a new mink and a lemon yellow Ferrari—is there no rest for the wicked?

The nuts and bolts of launching a production will be handled via an "office" interface, in addition to the zoomed-in studio map. The player's office will allow him to track multiple projects and handle all the deals and budgeting that are required to get a project up and rolling.

Once a project is underway, the player can use the office interface or the studio map to check on the progress of a movie. The office will present a more "business like" overview, allowing the player to manage the "numbers game" as well as calling meetings.

The player can also travel throughout the growing studio in his executive golf cart. Clicking on a building will present the player with an overview of what's going on for the current day and what's scheduled for the week. From this interface, the player can call impromptu meetings with gaffers, best boys, catering managers, and other "in the trenches" members of his movie empire.

The player can also travel to the Hollywood map to be seen or to call investor, actor, or director meetings over a double latte and a sprout burger.

Lifestyle

Sure, you are a movie producer, but that's only a means to an end. The true "glory" in this town is a fine woman on your elbow, a tony mansion packed to the gills with toys and furniture you never lose, a rep as an awesome party-giver, and of course, a fast car. Of course, to achieve those goals, you'll need to earn a lot of cash, and your only way to do that is by churning out a string of money-making movies.

Victory in this game is easy to understand, but difficult to achieve: satisfy the "three corners" of your life:

$\rightarrow$

Superego: Your practical side, represented by your "success ratio" (hits to flops) and your current income

Ego: Your material side, represented by your house, your cars, and the physical trappings of your wealth (butler, Steinway piano, etc.)

Id: Your "indulgences"—parties held, money spent on the strip, your "women friends," etc.

Of course, you also need to manage your reputation and you need to stay out of jail. You won't be able to lure in "cherry" investors for your movie studio if you're embroiled in some nasty legal tangles.

The map that displays the player's own home is the true visual indicator of success in the game. If strapped for cash, the player may need to sell off some assets (if the player is strapped for too long, he may get a visit from the repo team).

The player will have the option of building up his "stately pleasure dome" module by module, or he can (if he has the cash) purchase a Hollywood classic—a mansion once owned by a member of the old-guard of Tinsel Town.

From this environment, the player can manage his personal holdings, spend money on the trappings of success, host parties or informal rendezvous with his more beautiful actresses. He can also use his personal study as a partially functional office, but with the enhanced ability to hold more "discrete" meetings with investors or his own personal team of lawyers.

The Seamy Underbelly

Life would be easy if your personal life would just stay personal and if everyone at your studio just did what they were told . . . but what fun would that be?

As you work to satisfy your own personal need for success (in your own eyes, of course), you'll have to deal with irrational directors, prima donna actors, court injunctions, law suits from former wives, unexpected courtroom trials ("Why, exactly, did your investor wind up dead in his hotel room?"), lawsuits from investors, audits, the arrival of and unexpected "lovechild," lawsuits from whiney actresses, and more.

The More You Know

The game will also include a hyper-linked "cyclopedia" written by Magic Lantern's in-house writer and researcher. This cyclopedia will present a historical background for the game, exploring Hollywood and movie making

$\rightarrow$

from the 1950s until the modern day, and will provide real meat-and-potatoes insider information for the player who really wants to dive deep into the game's milieu.

Tone

The tone and feel of the game will be reminiscent of the classic "Leisure Suit Larry" style of humor—the game will present Hollywood in caricature and will enable the players to lose themselves in the debauchery of Tinsel Town.

The game will allow the player to step into the role of a smarmy, superficial Hollywood producer. Success will require the player to throw good taste to the wind and strive to hone the fast-talking, two-faced, often hilarious characteristics of their Hollywood alter-ego—a true Hollywood-style spin on the hapless (yet loveable) Leisure Suite Larry.

Team

The game will be created by Illinois developer Magic Lantern, Inc. (ML). The Magic Lantern team is comprised of senior game developers who understand how to deliver games on time and on budget. Magic Lantern has the capabilities to deliver a product of the highest quality (and fun to boot).

ML has been developing games as a team since late 1998, and to date they have completed 17 PC projects.

ML has a strong track record as an honest, talented, and hard-working team who works *with* publishers rather than against them. ML prides itself on exceeding publisher expectations.

In addition, Magic Lantern will bring veteran game designer Steve Meretzky onto the *Kahuna* team. Steve is one of the finest comedic game writers and designers in the industry (as well as a noted Hollywood history buff) and will ensure that the game will present an edgy yet hilarious tone.

Steve's Bio

Steve Meretzky is one of the most prolific authors of computer entertainment. His 14-year record of successful titles is unrivaled in the industry.

Steve was born and raised in Yonkers, NY, where he rooted for the NY Mets and against Richard Nixon. Meretzky moved on to MIT to pursue a career in architecture. MIT's department of Architecture convinced him that he should pursue a career in Construction Management. Several construction firms convinced Meretzky that he should pursue a career as a game tester for Infocom, where he moved onward and upward, producing some of the most successful titles in computer gaming.

Looking over this Pitch document, there are a few things to note. First, you can tell that the prose is energized and lively—much more so than for a traditional design document. The goal is to get readers excited about the game and what the player will be doing. You can also tell a great deal about the gameplay from this Pitch, but the details aren't specific, and that's the goal. Present a good overview of the actual play, without tying the design to certain approaches that may not yet be verified. The document also spends a few sentences on describing the team for the game—the goal is to make the publisher feel like they have the right folks for the job. Pitch documents may or may not have much technical information in them. If you are using a well-known engine for the game (such as the *Doom*® *3* technology), then of course you'll want to mention it. You want to make sure you avoid the "doomed by faint praise" misstep. Saying that you will base the game on technology that has powered two casual games in the last four years is an example—if you don't have something great to brag about, don't brag at all in the Pitch.

The companion CD-ROM includes another Pitch document for the game Combat that we developed for Infogrames several years ago. We thought it would be useful to see the Pitch document for a game that didn't make it (*Hollywood Kahuna*) and a Pitch document that worked and got us a game deal. (Figure 5.2.)

FIGURE 5.2   A screenshot from Combat, an arcade-style game. The original and successful pitch for this game is on the CD-ROM.

Scope

The Scope document is a first-step working document. Often, you'll create this at the same time you are creating a Pitch document. The Scope will expand on the High Concept and will touch on the main aspects of the game. Ideally, the Scope will serve as the jumping-off point for the major game design writing. Think of it as the *Cliff's Notes* version of the game design.

The following is an example Scope document from a game called Take Away that we developed for the Charles River Media book *Game Development with Lua*.

Title	Take Away
Platform	PC
Players	Single-player only
Genre	Action/arcade
High Concept	Take Away will pit the player, who controls a small ship, against an endless horde of enemies intent on stealing his supply crates. The player can fly and blast and must survive as long as possible—when his last crate is stolen, the game is over.
Goal	The goal is to accumulate as many points as possible. The player must protect eight supply crates from being dragged off screen by the enemy—when the last one is dragged off, the game ends.
Features	The game world is the screen area: the player cannot move out of the screen area.
	The player controls a ship—he can accelerate, turn, and shoot (there is no "gravity" in this game, so movement continues after a player thrusts).
	The game ends when the last crate is dragged off screen.
	The player earns points for each enemy he destroys.
	The enemies will try to steal the crates, shoot the player, and prehaps ram the player.
	The game will speed up through time.
	The player can save his game at any time.

As you can see from this example, we have gone much farther than just a High Concept, but the approach and tone are certainly not meant to "sell the sizzle" as with a Pitch document. The format for a Scope document can be whatever you would like. Over the years, we have gone to this table-based approach, because it forces us to keep our writing short and succinct. Using a document like this, the designer can then start to get a view of the areas that will need to be covered in the complete game design.

This is also a great document with which to begin an early design review process with your producer and team. You don't yet have a lot of time invested in the design as a whole, but a well-thought-out Scope will allow you and the team to catch any missteps (such as "did your remember to add multiplayer?") and enhance the framework before you roll up your sleeves and dive into the main game design.

Game Design

The Game Design document is the heart and soul of all the documents that swirl around a game under development. It is the true blueprint document, and its goal is to illustrate how the game is played and provide a comprehensive description of all aspects of the game so the development team can actually create the game.

When you are writing about objects, items, and characters in your game, don't simply describe them; go into detail about what they *do* in the game—what do they affect? How do they interact? How do they appear or disappear? What is their role and behavior?

The following outline will give you a basic structure for a solid Game Design document. Many successful designs have been created that use a far more complex outline, and many have succeeded with something much simpler. The complexity you will need will depend on the scale and scope of your project, and no one template will serve you across the board.

As you gain experience authoring Game Design documents, pay attention to the structure and organization that works for you as an author and for your team. Over time, you'll evolve several approaches to this document that will provide the structure you need to create a new Game Design document.

Take a few moments to look over the general outline, and then we'll look at what goes in each section in detail.

Game Design Document
I. Core Overview
   a. Summary
   b. Key Aspects
   c. Golden Nuggets
II. Game Context
   a. Game Story
   b. Backstory
   c. Primary Players
III. Core Game Objects
   a. Characters
   b. Weapons
   c. Structures
   d. Objects

Core Overview

The Core Overview section delivers a brief, but thorough, overview of the game. It's meant to get anyone up to speed quickly on the game, what will make it stand out—and play well.

Summary

The Summary is as you would expect—a short summary of the entire game experience. Much of this can be borrowed from the Scope or Pitch document, but remember that the Game Design document is meant for the development team—the prose should be lean and effective.

Key Aspects

The Key Aspects section of the document is meant to capture the essence of the game, but with a focus on gameplay and what the player is doing. This can simply be a short bulleted list or a simple paragraph. The goal for this section is to pull out the key components of the game that will be the central thread for a player's experience and enjoyment.

Golden Nuggets

The Golden Nuggets section has existed by many names by many different designers. Basically, this short section of the design lists the elements of the game that make it stand apart from the competition.

Game Context

The Game Context section of the document is where you describe the world that surrounds the game, be it the steppes of ancient Greece or the stadiums of today's NFL teams. Every game exists within some context (hopefully familiar to the player in some way) that is crucial to understanding what is happening in a game. In some games, this is a story based on the interaction of game characters. In another game, it may be the historical background to a battle or war.

Game Story

The Game Story section is where the designer explains and illuminates the story of the game, from the start of the game to the end. Of course, this section will contain "spoilers" on the game experience, but it is essential that the story of the game (from the player's perspective) be documented clearly.

Backstory

The Backstory section of the document explains "what has come before." It explains the context of the Game Story within the game universe as a whole. This section also describes (as much as needed) the game universe.

Primary Players

For games in which characters are key players, this section allows the designer to introduce and explain the main game characters, from the player's alter ego to his nemesis. For a large RPG game, this might be a very long section indeed. When describing a character, you may want to describe the character's backstory, his special abilities, his motivations, and anything else that will define how the character will act and what role it will play within the Game Story.

Core Game Objects

In the Core Game Objects section of the Game Design, the designer describes the various objects in the game (that is, those that affect the game experience. A piece of simple "eye candy" doesn't belong here.). For games that have many, many game objects, this section may be broken out into a Game Object document, or the two can operate in unison.

Characters

The Characters section describes game characters, from main characters involved in the game's story to lesser NPC allies and enemies. Again, this section can either stand alone or operate in unison with a larger Game Data document.

Weapons

The Weapons section of the document outlines any weapons or abilities that play an essential role in the game (that is, that they may be wielded by a player or other game entity).

Structures

The Structures section outlines any unique and game-play-significant structures found in the game. If you think of the various structures found in a grow-then-conquer RTS game, you'll have a clear sense of what information is recorded here.

Objects

The Objects section allows you to cover all relevant objects that don't fall into the aforementioned categories. These are objects such as inventory items and powerups; items that have a function in the game, but exist more in a supporting role or as a component to a larger quest, such as a puzzle.

Conflict and Resolution

The Conflict and Resolution section of the game is often very detailed if combat is one of the main challenges for the player. Every game has some form of conflict and resolution, and this area of the document is used to describe the conflict in detail.

So, what goes in this section? That depends on what you need to document, but for an example, let's consider a game in which giant, anthropomorphic robots do battle. The robots have missile launchers—the design of which would be covered in the Objects section. However, how are they used in a larger system? How does the player aim? How fast can the player fire? What happens when a missile hits an enemy robot? How does the firing player know he scored a hit? How does the unlucky receiver of the missile know he was hit? How did the missile affect the robot?

Those are the types of interactions you'll want to document in this section— basically, all the interaction systems that represent conflict between game entities.

Artificial Intelligence

Artificial intelligence is what controls and directs the computer opponents to offer challenge and provide assistance to the player. As we all know, computers, at their heart, aren't very intelligent at all. Neither are computer opponents, but the challenge is to design behavior that at least appears intelligent in the context of a given game situation.

In this section of the document, outline any of the behaviors that will define the actions of computer opponents, and any inputs (on the AI side) that will affect those behaviors.

Game Flow

The Game Flow section of the Game Design may be one of the longest, especially if you have a linear level-based game. In this section, address each gameplay area individually, whether it is a level or a mission. You'll want to include as much information here as possible, including what weapons or inventory items are found in each environment, what the victory conditions are, and what puzzles exist in any given environment.

The rule of thumb for this section is, don't include anything that wasn't first outlined in another section of the Game Design. This isn't the place to introduce new game objects, but rather to define the flow of play and the placement of defined game objects within game environments.

This is the place in the document to "anchor" the position of various puzzles and quests within the game. As mentioned above, you don't want to introduce anything new, but you do what to say when the various game situations will occur.

Remember that this section is a guide for programmers, artists, level designer and mission designers—after reading the description of a puzzle above and where it appears in the game in this section, they should come away with a clear idea of the how and why of implementation.

Controls

The Controls section of the Game Design document covers the user inputs and controls. You'll want to address any variations in control due to platform, and any approaches to flexible control mapping (such as the custom key mapping allowed in many PC-based FPS games). This section doesn't cover user interfaces (which is handled in the Functional Specification document), but the direct input by the player during the "in game" (as opposed to menu-based) portion of play.

Game Types

The Game Types section of the document covers any variations you will have in the gameplay experience. If you are only doing a single mode of play, this section is unnecessary; however, if you plan to have single-player, and various multiplayer modes, then explain those play modes here and the differences between them. Be sure to cover how the various game modes are initialized and how the various play sessions end. Also document, if any, play mode change or trump rules or behavior you explained earlier in the document.

You would also explain any saving and loading information in this section and how they might differ between game variations.

Definitions

You only need this section of the Game Design if you are either creating or using some nonobvious terms. Simply create your own glossary for key terms and references to make it easier for the development team to understand the prose found in the document.

References

The References section of the document contains information on any reference material that is essential to help capture the feel and flavor of the game. This section may list inspirational movies, competing games that are targets, or books that provide inspiration for the team. Use this section to provide answers to the "So you want more information?" questions the team will have. You may also want to put early concept sketches and prototype models in here as well, to show the origins of the early game development.

Game Data

Depending on what type of game you are designing, you may or may not have a Game Data document. If you think of our High Concept examples—*Asteroids* and *PacMan*—neither of those games feature a myriad of enemies, NPCs, or powerups, so a separate document isn't necessary.

Games with larger scopes, such as an RTS game with many buildings and units, or an RPG game, with a large cast of MPC characters, often require the addition of a separate Game Data document.

Game Data documents exist to provide a place to document all design and game specific information on specific items in a game. Often, this game data will be translated into something the computer can read—XML data, a script file, or some other database format. Many designers use programs such as Excel® for the Game Data document, since the data can be exported in a format that can easily be read directly into the game itself.

The format of a Game Data document depends on how you will be using the information. If the information covers the behavior of various weapon projects, each with wildly different implementations and effect, then a standard narrative might suffice, since a narrative approach will allow the designer to describe the weapon effects in detail so the art and technical teams can create them effectively.

On the other hand, perhaps you want to describe a large set of game objects, such as units available in an RTS. If all the units share some standard capabilities (movement speed, hit points, etc.), then a spreadsheet approach will allow you the most control, since you can easily see at a glance the spread of abilities and stats across ranges of multiple units. This is also useful if you need to make sure you have specific numbers of easy, medium, and challenging enemies.

The Game Data document is often part of the Game Design proper, but because it is often expressed in a form that can be read into the game directly, we have put it in its own category.

Technical Design

One of the most varied documents, from studio to studio and game to game, is the Technical Design document. This document is often written primarily by the technical lead of a project, generally with some input from the game designer. It is generally written once a first pass of a Game Design is complete.

What is the goal of the Technical Design? The purpose is to provide a technical blueprint for the team's programmers, at a down-deep level that allows them to dive in directly and get to work. Early in the games industry, Technical Design documents weren't really a formalized presence—a programmer (often the designer and producer as well) would write any game design documentation (if there was any), and along the way, he'd jot down notes on how he might implement Feature X or Feature Y.

In modern game development, there is a complex network of interdependencies, and often aspects of game technology must first be completed before other work can go forward. This document will cover what technical tasks need to be done, and the order in which they should be addressed to maximize the effectiveness of the entire team.

Technical Design documents, at the core, cover the primary areas of new development for the technical staff of a game, any tools that need to be developed internally, and any new hardware or software that will need to be acquired to facilitate development.

In our studio, we have used our own 3D engine for many, many games, incrementally adding to it in each project. As a result, the Technical Design isn't very long and is incorporated in our general Game Design document for a given project. For us, the Technical Design covers what new technical, programmer-added features we need to create and what new LuaGlue (see the next chapter for more information) functions need to be added.

Functional Specification

A Functional Specification looks at your game from the player's perspective. The design isn't concerned with what's going on under the hood, or what the internal game rules are, but rather what happens when the player does X or Y.

Generally, in the world of games, a Functional Specification doesn't say too much about the gameplay at all—it is more of an interface design document. What happens when the player presses the Option button on the main menu? What happens when the player presses the Escape key in the middle of the battle?

A Functional Specification document is a strange beast—it is often included within the Game Design document itself, either before or after the Controls section. Standing alone, it can be the most boring of documents, but it is also the most essential, since it describes the flow of the player through the various control interfaces of the game.

BE FUNNY

Designer: Joel Spolsky

Yep, rule number one in tricking people into reading your design is to make the experience enjoyable. Don't tell me you weren't born funny, I don't buy it. Everybody has funny ideas all the time, they just self-censor them because they think it's "unprofessional." Feh. Sometimes you have to break the rules.

Even though I'm not really that funny, I still try pretty hard, and even the act of flailing around *trying* to be funny is in itself amusing, in a sad-clown sort of way. When you're writing a design, an easy place to be funny is in the examples. Every time you need to tell a story about how a feature works, instead of saying

> *The user types Ctrl+N to create a new Employee table and starts entering the names of the employees.*

write something like

> *Miss Piggy, poking at the keyboard with a eyeliner stick because her chubby little fingers are too fat to press individual keys, types Ctrl+N to create a new Boyfriend table and types in the single record "Kermit."*

If you read a lot of Dave Barry, you'll discover that one of the easiest ways to be funny is to be *specific* when it's not called for. "Scrappy pugs" are funnier than "dogs. "Miss Piggy" is funnier than "the user." Instead of saying "special interests," say "left-handed avocado farmers." Instead of saying "People who refuse to clean up after their dogs should be punished," say that they should be "sent to prisons so lonely that the inmates have to pay spiders for sex."

Oh, and, by the way, if you think it's unprofessional to be funny, then we're sorry, but you just don't have a sense of humor. (Don't deny it. People without senses of humor always deny it. You can't fool us.) And, if you work in a company where people will respect you less because your specs are breezy, funny, and enjoyable to read, go find another company to work for, because life is just *too short* to spend your daylight hours in such a stern and miserable place.

The following is an example of using humor in a functional spec., taken from the Castles & Catapults function specification document:

Day-Time-Gold™

DTG as we call it around MLP . . . oh yeah. This little workhorse is always there, just plugging away. Upper right of the screen, tucked up and small as possible. The key info this displays is as follows:

Gold—that's right, gold. A numerical accounting of the gold in your coffers.

Soon-come gold. When you blast your enemy, you earn bounty gold, but you don't get to cash in until the next Build/Repair phase, so this little counter (only displayed during the Combat phase) just ticks off your upcoming earnings as you rape and pillage the landscape. Sweet.

Day. Remember, this is a phase-based game . . . and that means we're sort of f%$#ing with the whole notion of RTS versus turn-based play, but that's a soapbox for another day. We could call this "turn," but then folks would freak out . . . so we call it "day," as in "days into the battle" . . . which, basically, means "turns into the game" . . . yes, clever psychology at work, to be sure!

Time. Do we ever have enough? The time display harkens back to those old grandfather clocks of yore . . . showing the rising of the sun and the rising of the moon (not at the same time of course) in circular fashion. Daytime means fight and kill; nighttime means the armies roast weenies around the fire while you fix up your castle (as if dark and moonlight weren't visual indicators enough!).

Map

No clever name here—this is just a map. Top down, seen-it-before, view of the battlefield. Colored pixel-things represent the game units. A little rectangle represents the current view. Click and drag the box to slew the big 3D view wherever you want. Simple really. Oh, and this display will have a Help and a Minimize/Maximize tab.

Info Box™

Oh yes, oh yes . . . information is our friend! It wants to be free, really. The bottom left of the display hosts this general-purpose box aimed at fulfilling our info needs. The trick here is that we have three tabs along the bottom. Left-clicking a tab will change the context of this box.

The three tab thingies give us these results:

Info. This is the basic, nearly always-used use of this display. In this form, the Info box is subservient to what goes on in the Middle Thing (see below). Click on something in the Middle Thing, like a castle tile or military unit and you'll see details in this box (specifics below, of course).

Objectives. To win, you gotta do stuff. To do stuff, you gotta know what to do. Click on this tab and the Info box will display a list of mission objectives, color-coded for those achieved and those still just out of reach for the lame player. Mostly for those who forget things easily.

Menu. This one is pretty simple. The info box becomes host to some basic menu buttons (rather than cluttering and confusing things with a pop-up screen). The basic buttons (to date) are Save (saves the game—we'll need some other display for this, no doubt), and Quit Game (which will, after a confirmation click, throw the player back to the main menu).

Middle Thing

The specifics of this interface are outlined in the sections that follow. Suffice it to say that this is indeed the "middle thing" that exists in between the Map and the Info Box™. Its contents change with the context of the gameplay. The bottom line is that it'll take care of itself, when it comes to phase changes, and within a phase, the player controls the contents by clicking on little tabs. Weeee!

Message Box

At times, the game (clever AI!) or other players in MP mode will send a message to our fearless player. This message area will then pop up across the top of the screen and display the message and its sender. If our player comes out of his shell enough during an MP game, he can enter his own chat message and it too will be displayed in this screen area (like a banner across the top of the screen).

Flag Thing

Yup, it's just that—a flag thing. Upper-left corner of the screen. Each player picks a "color" or "team"—each has a flag associated with it. This flag displays the player's team, just in case he forgets (composition-wise, it also tosses some formalized color up in that corner of the screen, to make all those graphic artists who play the game happy with the freakin' Feng Shui of it all).

Tools Design

The Tools Design document covers the design and features of any game-specific tools that are required for the current game. This will vary from project to project. Some game projects use a third-party or middleware game engine, and all the tools may already be in hand. Some games may be simple enough that no external tools are needed.

So, what are game development tools? They can be almost anything from a simple tool that allows you to set the water level for a terrain map to a sophisticated tool that allows you to assign texture-mapping coordinates to a 3D model.

Today, many of the tasks once handled by tools are now handled by scripting languages (like the Lua language we'll learn about in the next chapter). Scripting languages give designers great control over the flow, function, and runtime data of the game, but often, scripting languages are not enough.

Games that present mission- or scenario-based play (such as an RTS campaign) often need to have some tool that allows a mission builder (which is often a game designer) to set up a mission, easily configuring options such as landscape, landscape models, enemy forces, and behavior and trigger points.

The Tool Design document is usually a collaborative document, partly written by the game design with the users of the tool (who may be artists, mission builders, or game designers) and the technical team involved to determine what the required and desired features should be.

Asset List

Again, based on the scope of your project, you may or may not have an Asset List document. Odds are, though, you will. Today's games are "asset rich," and keeping track of them is a major chore. So, what is an asset? Generally, it's a piece of content that needs to be created for a game. Some examples include an animated 3D model of a swordsman, a script for a narrator, an interface loading screen, a piece of music, a sound effect of coins dropping, or an animation of an explosion.

Generally, a game's Asset List is created together by the art lead, the lead designer, and the sound and music leads. More often than not, these lists take the form of an Excel spreadsheet. An Asset List is one of the most dynamic documents in this suite of design documents we have been discussing—it is generally used for tracking the status and filenames of any assets, and as a result, it is always being updated, cut, expanded, or augmented in some way or another.

As a designer, you need to be familiar with this document, even if you are not the author. The assets of a game are the visual (or aural) representation of game objects and entities, and correlate directly to entries in the Game Design document.

Marketing Plan

No matter what horror stories you have heard about the clashes between game developers and "marketing suits," each need each other. A marketing team needs a game to sell, and without those "suits," you'll never sell a single copy.

Some games have marketing plans (the larger, triple-A titles certainly do), while smaller titles are often managed more informally. We've worked on both, and if we had a choice, we'd prefer to have a marketing plan document from day one, so we can understand what our marketing obligations are.

A Marketing document generally covers the pre-launch and launch advertising push for the game, and most really aren't of direct interest to members of the game development team (other than their efforts to move games off the shelves!).

Of importance, however, are any items the marketing department may need from the development team, such as screen shots, gameplay videos, noninteractive and interactive demos. For many titles, the E3 trade show each May looms large, and many a team has struggled to deliver a playable demo for it. Knowing ahead of time what is required will make the deadlines much easier for the entire team.

Localization Plan

More and more, games are becoming international, and that means multiple versions of the same game, each customized to the language and cultural moirés of the selling countries.

At the most basic level, localization means translating game text from one language to another. As a designer, you want to know if your game will be sold internationally at the start, because it will affect how you organize the text for a given game.

Generally, games to be localized pull their in-game text from a central file, referenced by some index number. This file can then be translated. If a game has voice-overs, those need to be translated as well (often, these audio files will keep the same names from language to language, and will just pull the content from a language-specific folder).

Generally, the localization plan will be authored by the game producer, with input from you as the designer, the art lead, the sound director (for any voice-overs), and the game writer.

Target List

The Target List is the list of features you need to have in your game. Often, this list is initially populated with "must have" features that are a requirement from your publisher (things like 20 levels of gameplay, 2- 8-person multiplayer and such).

The Target List is often prioritized, and the publisher requests live at the top of the list. Also on the list are key features that you and/or the design team want to see in the game (these are probably already in the design document). The list of features is prioritized from essential features down to things that would be great to have in the game, but maybe not vital. The last items in the list are often nice little finishing touches, details, or Easter Eggs.

As the game progresses during development, you and the team will revisit this list often and resort the priorities of the items. You'll probably also have a bar on the list, indicating that items above the bar will most likely make it in the game, and items below will need to be cut or wait for the sequel. The producer will work with you to determine where the "slash or save" bar will go.

Where Do You Start?

At times, nothing is more intimidating than a blank computer screen. You've been given the go ahead to design a game. Where do you start?

Rarely will your options be so open ended. Often, you'll come in on a project already under way, or you will be given some guidance from either your producer or your publisher. You might be told, "We've got the Septuagenarian Mutant Tai-chi Toad license—we need a multiplatform FPS game design."

Your first job, of course, is to assess what you already have. Do you have a High Concept in place? Is there a Pitch or Scope document? Find out what you already have to work with and make that your starting point. More often than not, you'll find yourself with a Pitch document in place, but not Scope or High Concept (that experience has happened to us many, many times). If this is the case, read and study the Pitch document and then craft a High Concept that fits and captures the essence of the game. Share it with your producer to make sure you are on the right track.

WHERE TO START? AGATHA CHRISTIE'S *AND THEN THERE WERE NONE*

 Designer: Lee Sheldon

Respect the source material. I'll take an example from another medium. Hollywood has been in a frenzy the last few years to remake old television shows. One look at the big budget remakes of *The Avengers*, *Wild Wild West*, *Bewitched*, and so many more, makes it clear that winking, self-referential takes on the pop-culture of previous generations succeeds only in alienating the original fans, and baffling the younger audience. The same thing is true when adapting a novel written in 1939. It would have been so easy to make fun, and so wrong. Agatha Christie's *And Then There Were None* is the best-selling mystery novel of all time. I knew I had to remain faithful to the style and substance of the book.

$\rightarrow$

Research. Research. Research. A novelist gets to pick and choose what to include of a story's setting and history. A game designer is creating a virtual environment that comes alive for the player. It must feel real. There must be enough for the player to do. Almost the entire story takes place on a tiny, storm swept island. I took a single paragraph of "rumors" concerning the island from the book, and turned them into a chronological history of the island. This history and research of the south Devon coastline gave me a number of new locations and new features of the island. The ruins of a fishing village, an Admiralty testing site, an apiary, even wild goats all enjoy life due to the research; and make the island a much more interesting space to explore.

Decide what remains and what cannot. I added an eleventh character, because Dame Agatha wasn't concerned about player-characters. I changed the identity of the killer, so even if players had read the book there would still be a few surprises. I didn't change the time period. Not only did it add rich background, it gave me a chance to incorporate elements of the impending Second World War, things that Dame Agatha had no knowledge of when she wrote the original story. I didn't change the nursery rhyme that forms the backbone of the structure of the book. While this led to an inevitable linearity in the gameplay, it is the one feature everyone who reads the book remembers. Altering it would be like changing the rules of cricket. It just isn't . . . cricket, old boy.

If the High Concept is on the right track (so says your producer or design lead), your next step is the Scope document—work to keep it simple, but answer the majority of gameplay questions for the game. If a Scope is over five pages long, it's too long. With the Scope in hand, run it past the producer and perhaps the entire development team to get an initial read. Make sure you have everybody on the same page with the Scope document, because it will serve as your own blueprint for the larger game design document.

As you work on the design document, the scale and scope of the game will help you determine what other supporting documents you'll need to author. If you are new to the team, be sure to check with the producer and the tech lead to determine their process for the Technical Design and what your role in that document will be.

Once you get the ball rolling, it will be like the proverbial snowball—you won't be able to stop and the design tasks will keep coming. Just pay attention to the starting position and allow that to guide your initial design work.

What Medium?

Several years ago, "What medium do I write my design in?" wasn't even a question. You used a word processor to write the design and then printed out the documents for the team to read. Now, you can write collaboratively in a word processing document, you can author documents easily in HTML, and you can create fully dynamic documents by using a Wiki. So, which medium should you use?

This decision shouldn't be based on what's easiest for you, but rather what is the most effective for a team. If a game is small in scale and the design need not be very long to be effective, then old-school word processor and printouts may be the way to go. While having digital text is great, nothing beats having the blueprints for your work right there on your desk for you to look at as you use your computer to work on the game.

On the other hand, if you are talking about a large and complex game, then having a large stack of paper on everyone's desk is more of a distraction than a help. The development team doesn't want to have to flip through page after page to see what they want; instead, they want to just see the part of the design they are interested in. In that case, an electronic version such as a shared word processor document (with a dynamic linked table of contents) or an HTML page on your team's intranet may be the way to go.

More and more, though, large game designs are finding themselves written on internal Wikis. If you have a large and complex design, and the game design is mutable and changing frequently, or if you have multiple designers working on the same project, a Wiki is the way to go. Writing in a Wiki is the least intuitive, since each implementation of a Wiki has its own markup language, and you are writing in a browser window rather than a word processor. The good news is that it takes just a little while to learn the small set if Wiki markups you'll need (to define things like links, bulleted lists, and such). Most Wiki implementations also take care of making a table of contents for you, and you can't beat a system that allows anyone to easily edit the document at any time and an easy system to track who revised what in the document. For a large game, it's a lifesaver to have your art lead or tech lead be able to see in just a few seconds if the latest design revisions apply to them.

How Much Detail?

One key question for new designers is, how much detail do they need to go into in a set of game design documents? As you work through a number of games, this question will become more and more automatic to answer. The easy answer is, just as much detail as you need. So how much is that?

Your design documents are meant to be the blueprint from which game development professionals can build the game. If we think of the blueprint analogy, certain areas of the blueprint are general in scope, providing an overview of what pieces of the structure go where. Often, certain areas of a blueprint will be called out to provide a more detailed description and drawing of a specific area, such as a key joint. That analogy holds well for game designs as well. Cover the game across the board with a level of detail so nothing feels omitted, but the reader isn't drowned in details. Then, when you require an area of more detail, drill down deeper and explain things fully.

The goal is to make the game design autonomous—it should be able to convey the full sense of the game to the development team, even if you aren't around to answer questions. While at first blush, it may seem that this is writing yourself out of a job, don't worry. There is plenty for a game designer to do during the development of the game (just flip back to Chapter 2 to refresh your memory). You want your design documents to provide the support and direction to the development team without holding them up—you never want to force the team to always come to you for explanation or clarification.

OUR GAME

Following is an initial version of the basic Game Design for the game Eye Opener we will work to fully design, develop, and experiment with later in this book. It's often a great exercise to work quickly to put together a first pass at a nearly complete (at least at first blush) Game Design, and then set it aside for several days. When you come back to it, you will be able to read it afresh, and you will see all the areas in need of seriously enhanced details and design revision.

With that in mind, here is our first pass on our Game Design for our rather simple game,

Design Document — Eye Opener

```
document last modified: 12/12/05
author: Paul Schuytema
```

I. Core Overview
Summary
Eye Opener will put the player in control of an abandoned comic strip character: a disembodied eyeball. The player will play through both scrolling levels and adventure levels as he attempts to find the powerups and abilities to break into and star in a published comic strip.

Key Aspects
The player will be able to control the Eye as it rolls through horizontally scrolling levels. Throughout the game, the Eye will gain more abilities.

The Eye will be able to "raid" comic strip panels for powerups and inventory items.

Golden Nuggets

Eye Opener is set "inside" the world of black-and-white inked comic strips. The art will be hand drawn and the visual tone will be reminiscent of classic Sunday morning adventure comics.

The player will begin as a helpless eyeball, devoid of any abilities but rolling, yet full of attitude and moxie.

II. Game Context
Game Story

The Eye, hurt by his abandonment, strives to take over the Artist's current comic strip. The Eye discovers a hidden world between the panels of the comic that is fraught with danger, but as he makes his way from panel to panel, he is able to steal items from the comic strip that provide him with more and more abilities.

Along the way, he encounters a robot head that he discards as useless, but the head follows the Eye, eager to join in his adventure.

Eventually, the Eye has enough abilities to blast through the final traps set by the Robot Guard (who is protecting the strip) and challenge the Guard himself. If he wins, he will be able to replace the Guard in the comic strip, much to the surprise of the Artist.

Backstory

The Eye was a character in a failed comic strip by the Artist. The Artist crumples up and tosses away his silly design and begins working on a more interesting strip featuring robots in a faraway space station.

But the Eye will not be denied. When the Artist leaves his studio, the Eye pulls himself away from his crumpled paper and makes his way to the drawing table, determined to find a way into the comic.

Primary Players

Eye — The Eye is the main character and his quest is to break into the new comic strip. He begins with virtually no abilities and throughout the game, he steals items to give himself more power.

Robot Head — The Robot Head is an inventory item found by the Eye. The head is useless to the Eye, so when it is abandoned, it takes on a life of its own, following the Eye around and being both a help and a hindrance.

Robot Guard — The Robot Guard is one of the main characters in the comic strip that the Eye is trying to infiltrate. He learns of the Eye's efforts and attempts to set up traps to thwart the Eye's advance. The final conflict of the game will be between the Eye and the Guard.

III. Core Game Objects
Characters

Eye — The Eye is a rolling eye and is the player's alter ego. The Eye may be augmented with a Weapon and several Game Objects. The Eye can take X points of damage.

Robot Head — Once found and discarded, the Robot Head will follow the player around, making nonsense comments.

Robot Guard — The Robot Guard is the guardian of the comic panels. He will appear in several horizontal levels and in the final arena comic panel. The Robot Guard can take X points of damage.

Weapons

Bomb — The Bomb will detonate and destroy all surrounding objects. It will be triggered when the linked Detonator is activated.

Laser — The Laser can be equipped to the Treads. It will fire when the player taps the Enter key. The Laser adds X amount of damage points to the Eye.

Turret — The Turret cannot move. It will fire a modified laser slug and will deliver X points of damage to what it hits. If it hits a Bomb, it will detonate the Bomb. The Turret takes X points of damage.

Objects

Detonator

Image: Standard plunge type detonator

Where Found: In the scrolling levels—some will be already rigged to a bomb while others can be picked up.

Behavior: Each Detonator will be "wired" to a specific bomb. When activated by either the Eye falling on it or by the Eye using an action key on it, it will explode the bomb. The Detonator will then also disappear.

Treads

Image: Rolling robot treads

Where Found: In an early comic panel

Behavior: When activated, the Treads will fuse with the Eye to allow it more mobility and greater speed. The Treads are also needed to equip the Laser and the Claw. The Treads add X amount of damage points to the Eye.

Claw

Image: Robot claw gripper

Where found: Later comic panel

Behavior: This item will equip on the Treads and will allow the Eye to pick up other objects such as pen parts. This object also enables the "use" action. The Claw adds X amount of damage points to the Eye.

Pen Parts

Image: Various parts of a fountain pen (nib, pen body, ink)

Where Found: In various comic panels and in the horizontal levels

Behavior: The pen parts comprise the main quest of the game. When all the parts are found, the pen can then be used to activate access to the final comic panel to do battle with the Robot Guard.

IV. Conflict and Resolution

There are several types of conflict system in the game, with resolutions as follow:

Bomb — The Bomb will destroy all objects under and immediately surrounding it when it detonates.

Laser — The Laser will deliver X points of damage. Objects affected by the Laser: Eye, Robot Guard, Turrets.

V. Artificial Intelligence

Eye Opener will feature limited artificial intelligence, but the key behaviors are as follows:

Robot Head — This head will move with the player (once found and discarded). It will follow behind the player. It will occasionally utter a speech balloon of robot gibberish. It cannot be destroyed. The gibberish will actually provide the clues for a lock puzzle.

Turrets — The Turrets will realize when the Eye is on the same screen and will begin moving their barrels toward the Eye, but will stop at a random approximation. They will then fire a shot and will raise or lower the barrel depending on where the shot landed in relation to the Eye.

Robot Guard — In the early part of the game, the Robot Guard will appear at the top of the screen, peering down from a comic panel (uttering robot gibberish). He will slide back and forth within the panel in a pattern and will drop a bomb when near the Eye.

During the final battle, the Robot Guard will face the player with an arm-fired laser much like the Eye's own. He will move in the arena, seeking cover if a shot is fired and moving to the open to fire on the Eye. The Robot Guard will try to keep at least a distance of half the arena width away from the player.

VI. Game Flow

(to be expanded)
Introductory Animatic
Introduces the game story and backstory.

Horizontal Level One

This basic level will have the Eye with no abilities and he must discover that he can roll off ledges to trigger a detonator.

Comic Frame One

In these initial frames, we see the Robot Guard and the Eye will be able to pick up the Treads and the Pen Ink.

Horizontal Level Two

In this level, the Eye must use his treads to finish the level and the Robot Guard will begin dropping bombs on the Eye.

Comic Frame Two
In these frames, the Eye will find the Claw, the Pen Nib, and the Robot Head.

Horizontal Level Three
In this level, the Robot Guard will drop occasional bombs and the Eye will also encounter Turrets (dropped by the Guard?). The Eye will use the Claw to solve a switch puzzle to open the final door. He will be followed by the Robot Head.

Comic Frame Three
In these frames, the Eye will find the Laser and the final Pen component. The player must use the Pen to Exit the final frame.

Horizontal End Level
This level will feature a rewiring puzzle, with the clues provided by the Robot Head.

Comic Arena
In this frame, the Eye will do battle with the Robot Guard for ultimate control over the comic strip.

End Game Animatic
This will show when the player defeats the Robot Guard. It will show the Eye in the comic, the Artist returning, not liking the comic and crumpling it up and throwing the panels in the trash.

VII. Controls
The controls for Eye Opener will be very simple. There are as follows:

Horizontal levels:
Key control for level, right, and jump movement. Space bar to grab with Claw. Enter key to fire with Laser.

Comic Frames:
Mouse over will highlight inventory objects. Left click will place in inventory. Left click on object in inventory will use object. Right click will drop object.

Sample Doc

Now, let's go over the design document briefly. As you can see, the Summary outlines the core concept of the game in simple, straightforward terms. This section can be handed to anyone on the team, including programmers, testers, or marketing personnel, and you can be sure everyone will have a basic understanding of what the project entails. This is crucial, because over the development cycle, which can last for years, it's important to have a fundamental understanding of the game's central concept. Features, missions, and characters will come and go, but the concept must be both fixed and easily understood.

The second section, the Context, outlines the storyline and characters. Most games feature a protagonist of some sort, and a storyline that serves to contextualize player action. Some games, such as sports titles and puzzle games, don't employ a storyline or a central character. However, for games with a central narrative, it's important to define the major players in the story early on. In-depth discussion of personality or appearance can be saved for later documents. In the core Design Document, a summary of major points is sufficient.

The descriptions of weapons and artificial intelligence are simple, because Eye Opener is a pretty simple game. However, were this a World War II shooter, or a third-person action game, these sections would be much longer. Weapons design for a first-person shooter could be dozens of pages long, depending on the number of weapons, and artificial intelligence for games like *Half-Life 2* would require significant explanation in a design doc. On the other hand, for a puzzle game like *Polarium*, these sections would not be necessary. The structure and length of your design document is determined by the type of game you're working on.

The game flow describes the basic sequence of events in the game, and outlines the challenges the player will encounter in each section. Although later documents will flesh out this information with detail about game resources (like ammunition or health packs), enemies that must be defeated or avoided, and specific detail about the outcome of player choices, it's important to at least acknowledge the key points in the Design Document. For example, in a car combat game, the player may choose to avoid a duel when challenged by another character in the game. If the player has this option, what's the aftermath of rejecting a challenge? Is the player character going to be ridiculed by other characters? Or will it cost the character money? If it has no effect whatsoever, what's the player incentive to accept a challenge?

The Controls section may be accompanied by a diagram of the keyboard or game controller, depending on the platform. If the controls are complex, a spreadsheet indicating the various options and permutations may also be advisable. For example, when playing *The Elder Scrolls III: Morrowind,* the left thumbstick controls player movement. When pressed down, the left thumbstick also controls the Sneak option. A diagram can help communicate functions like this.

SUMMARY

In this chapter, we took a tour through the various documents, sections, and sub-documents that all come together to create the "meta" Design Document. Not every game requires all of these components—your experience and the type of game you are designing will dictate what documents you will need and the required detail level of each.

We then explored how to get started with your own design writing and looked at some questions you might have about the proper medium and detail level for your design work. Finally, we took an initial pass at our own Game Design for the game Eye Opener. We'll use this game, both in the book and in practice, to work through examples as we explore the many areas of game design.

In the next chapter, we'll wrap up our boot camp experience by taking a look at the scripting language we'll use to control both Eye Opener and the other examples in this book.

CHAPTER EXERCISES

1. Write a short High Concept for a game involving a Zen rock garden and timebomb ticking down to zero.
2. Write a short design treatment for how a console game controller (your choice of console) could be used to control a Foosball game.
3. Take a few moments and enhance the Eye Opener design document (it's on the companion CD-ROM). Add at least two more game entities and two more levels to the game design.

ON THE CD

6 Learning Our Tools

In This Chapter

- Scripting Languages in Game Development
- Introduction to Lua
- Lua Basics
- LuaGlue Functions

A t some point in any endeavor, it's time to dive into the water to see if you sink or swim. In this book, we'll let you dive into the world of game design and work through the analysis and experimentation of a complete game.

ON THE CD
You will find a fully functional 2D game engine on the companion CD-ROM. This is a tool that we developed to help you along your journey—think of it as a teaching tool you can use while reading this book and beyond to experience and enhance your game design skills.

One of the core skills we talked about in a previous chapter was the need to have some basic technical knowledge to better do your job. That's what this chapter is for: you'll need some basic technical skills to use our game engine. All aspects of the game engine are controlled via a scripting language called Lua. This is a simple, easy-to-use, yet powerful language perfectly suited for the world of game development and the task of game design and prototyping.

SCRIPTING LANGUAGES AND GAME DEVELOPMENT

A scripting language can allow artists to work directly on the GUI, bring designers and junior programmers (script programming is a great way to bring junior programmers "into the fold" of game development) to work directly on the game flow and logic, and allow level designers direct control over their environments and the play experience.

As a professional game designer, you will surely come across scripting languages on your game projects, from Lua to Python to the data definition language XML. Designers are not expected to be programmers, but they are expected to understand the basic concepts of programming and to feel comfortable in various scripting environments, be it scripting a mission sequence or prototyping an AI implementation.

Scripting languages are not high performance—they do not run at the speed of native code, and hence, are not the best tools for writing performance-heavy operations. However, a language such as Lua can be used as the controlling mechanism for calling high-performance native code functions and processes. C functions can be written to take advantage of that language's performance advantages, and then "glued" to Lua so a script programmer can use those functions.

INTRODUCTION TO LUA

Lua, on its own, is a simple yet powerful language that allows a game designer a great deal of control without the huge learning curve normally associated with programming. The language possesses powerful string and math functions, flexible data types, and the ability to define functions. (Listing 6.1.)

LISTING 6.1   The age-old "hello world" program in Lua.

```
—Lua's "hello world"
myString = "hello world"
print(myString)
```

When Lua is used in a game development project as a partner for a lower level, more powerful language, such as C++, it really comes into its own. Lua can allow game developers to rapidly prototype game situations or even complete games. It can allow game developers to craft the entire GUI for a game without any programmer intervention. It can be used to manage the saving and loading of save game files that can be easily read and debugged. Lua, in the world of game development, allows developers to create an environment that maximizes productivity and allows for easy experimentation (Figure 6.1).

Lua is its own language (syntax and comments that are pure Lua), yet it also consists of an API (application programming interface) that allows Lua to exchange data with an application your team might develop. Lua can also be extended by the creation of C functions called from within Lua (called "LuaGlue" functions). When used in partnership with an application development language (such as C or C++),

FIGURE 6.1   Lua is a scripting language that is gaining popularity among game developers.

Lua can be used as a framework for building a unique project-specific language, specially geared toward the task at hand. It's this extensibility that makes Lua so well suited for the game development environment. It's the ease of use that makes it great for game designers.

As mentioned before, our experimental game engine is a 2D (sprite-based) game engine for Windows (using Direct X). To provide us with the most flexibility (and the least technical hurdles to overcome), we have exposed all under-the-hood aspects of the technology to you via a set of LuaGlue functions. By combining Lua scripts (which are just text files) that use the Lua language and our custom LuaGlue functions, you will have easy and complete control over the entire game engine, without the need for a compiler or a programmer at your disposal.

If you are not familiar with the core concepts of programming, we suggest that you do at least a little homework, so you understand such concepts as functions, variables, strings, and control structures.

We'll now dive in and start looking at the Lua language in general and then at our engine-specific LuaGlue functions.

LUA BASICS

Lua is a simple language—its strength comes from the way it can be extended when used in partnership with C++—but it's still good to start at the beginning. In this section of the chapter, we'll explore the basic syntax of the language, to get your started. It's also a good idea to take a peek at some of the scripts included on the companion CD-ROM as your work through this chapter—they will give you an idea of how Lua looks in action.

If you run any of the game examples on the CD-ROM, you'll notice that two windows appear. The larger window is the main game window, and the smaller window is the Lua console. From here, you can directly enter Lua commands and see results if you use the print() function. This is a great tool to use as your learn about Lua (Figure 6.2).

FIGURE 6.2 You can enter Lua commands directly in the Lua console.

Language Semantics

Lua is a very flexible language with very little to get in your way or control you. This is either liberating or frightening, depending on your personality. To give us a basic sense of order, it's a good idea to have some guidelines for naming variables and such. We recommend using the following format for naming variables, constants, and function names.

```
MY_CONSTANT      —all caps with underscores for constants
myVariable       —initial lower case for variable names
gMyGlobal        —initial lowercase g to indicate a global variable
function MyFunction()    —first word caps for function names
```

In Lua, you can add a comment to a piece of text by adding two dashes (—) before the text (a line feed will end the comment). You can also do block comments.

```
— this is a comment in Lua that is on its own line
myValue = 7   —you can also add a comment to a line of script
—[[
— the [[ and closing ]] make this a block comment area
function Counting()
    for indx = 1,50000 do
        print(indx, "+", indx + 1, "=", indx + (indx + 1))
    end
end
—]]
```

VARIABLES

In Lua, you don't need to declare a variable before you use it, which sends up cheers from some camps and groans from others. The first time you use a variable, it is created. You also don't need to specify a type for the variable (string, number, etc.)—the type is inferred from the value you assign to the variable. This has the advantage of great flexibility, but also the disadvantage of creating a real debugging challenge if you aren't careful in your variable use.

To create, classify, and assign a value to a variable, simply use it within Lua:

```
myValue = 17
```

This creates a variable named myValue, and assigns the number value 17 to it.

A variable can change type by simply assigning it a value of another type. There are five variable types in Lua: nil, boolean, string, number, and table.

Nil

Nil is simply a single value type that is used to represent what variable has no value yet assigned to it. If you assign nil to a variable, you are actually deleting that variable.

```
myValue = nil    —this deletes the variable
local myValue    —this creates a local variable with an initial nil value
```

Boolean

Boolean variables can only have two values: true and false. Boolean variables are useful in conditional statements.

```
myValue = true   —creates a boolean variable with a value of true
```

String

Strings in Lua are relatively straightforward, but Lua does have a number of very powerful string manipulation functions that we'll explore a little later (in fact, fast string manipulation is one of the great strengths of Lua). Lua strings can be as small as a single character or contain over a million characters.

```
myValue = "hello world"   —a string variable
```

It should be noted that Lua will attempt to convert between numbers and strings if it makes sense within the context of a statement. Try these in the console:

```
Ready> print("8" + 8)
16
Ready> print("8 + 8")
```

```
8 + 8
Ready> print("hello world" + 8)
ERROR:[string "?"]:1: attempt to perform arithmetic on a string value
```

Number

Numbers in Lua are double-precision floating-point values. Lua does not contain an integer type (for values below 1e14, there are no rounding errors, so the integer type is not needed). Numbers can be represented as:

```
myNumber = 7
myNumber = 0.765
myNumber = 7.65e8
myNumber = 7.65e-2
```

Table

Tables in Lua are one of the language's most powerful aspects. There are many unique ways you can use tables that go beyond the scope of this book, but for now, let's keep things simple. If you are familiar with programming, you'll quickly see that tables are like arrays. If you are new to programming, think of a table as a list of items referred to by a single name. You can access individual items by using an index value.

For example:

```
myTable = {2,4,6,8,10}
print(myTable[3])
6 — the result of the print function
myTable[6] = 12
print(myTable[6])
12
```

In this context, the table functions just like a simple array to store a series of values. We use the square brackets to provide the index to get the value back out of the table.

OPERATORS

Operators are special symbols that allow you to have two values (such as variables) interact with each other. Arithmetic operators will produce an arithmetic result, while relational operators will produce a Boolean (true or false) result.

Arithmetic Operators

Lua supports the standard mathematical operators:

```
a + b = c   — addition
a — b = c   — subtraction
a * b = c   — multiplication
a / b = c   — division
```

Relational Operators

You can also use the following standard relational operators to compare values and/or statements:

```
if a == b then  — equal to
    print("a is equal to b")
end
if a ~= b then  — not equal to
    print("a is not equal to b")
end
if a < b then   — less than
    print("a is less than b")
end
if a > b then   — greater than
    print("a is greater than b")
end
if a <= b then  — less than or equal to
    print("a is less than or equal to b")
end
if a >= b then  — greater than or equal to
    print("a is greater than or equal to b")
end
```

Logical Operators

Logical operators perform a test on two arguments and will return a value based on their relationship. In Lua, the logical operators are always lowercase.

The and operator will compare two arguments. If the first argument is false, it will be returned; otherwise, the second argument will be returned.

```
a = 5
b = 10
c = 20
if (a < 10) and (b < 20) then
    print("this returns true — which is the value of the second argument")
end
if (a > c) and (b < 20) then
    Print("this returns false — which is the value of the first argument")
end
```

The or operator is the opposite of the and operator. It will return the first argument if it is not false. If that's not the case, it will return the second argument.

```
a = 5
b = 10
c = 20
if (a < 10) or (b < 20) then
    print("this returns true — which is the value of the first argument")
end
if (a > c) or (b < 20) then
    print("this returns true — which is the value of the first argument")
end
if (a > c) or (b < 5) then
    print("this returns false — which is the value of the second argument")
end
```

The not expression always returns a value of true or false. In Lua, false and nil are the only values considered "false" by the logical operators—any other value is considered true. The not operator will return the opposite value of the argument.

CONTROL STRUCTURES

Lua contains a small set of vital control structures that allow you to handle the lion's share of the decision-making within your scripts. All the control structures end their code blocks with the end keyword.

While you don't have to indent your control structures for your scripts to function properly, it's generally a good idea to get into the habit of indenting one tab stop (four spaces) for each "nested" control structure. As you'll see in later chapters, you'll be using many nested control structures in your game scripting, especially when you are writing your artificial intelligence functions.

If

The real workhorse is the ubiquitous if statement—if you are familiar with other programming or scripting languages, you've encountered this many times before. An if statement allows you to evaluate an argument, and if it evaluates to true, the script block will be executed. For example:

```
myValue = 7
if myValue < 10 then
    print("myValue is less than ten.")
end
if (myValue > 5) and (myValue < 10) then
    print("myValue is between five and ten.")
end
```

You can extend the functionality of the if statement by creating another block of script using the optional else keyword. The script block bracketed by the else-end terminators will be executed when the if argument tests false. For example:

```
myValue = 20
if myValue == 21 then
    print("the value is 21")
else
    print("the value is NOT 21")
end
```

In addition, you can string together a series of conditionals using the elseif keyword. You'll find this very useful during AI scripting, since Lua doesn't have a Case-style statement. For example:

```
myValue = 17
if myValue < 6 then
    print("myValue is between zero and five.")
elseif myValue < 11 then
    print("myValue is between six and ten.")
elseif myValue < 16 then
    print("myValue is between eleven and fifteen.")
elseif myValue < 21 then
    print("myValue is between sixteen and twenty.")
else
    print("myValue is greater than twenty.")
end
```

While and Repeat

The control structures based on while and repeat are similar in that they allow a block of script to be executed until some condition is met. The while structure evaluates an argument first, and if it evaluates to true, the block is executed (which means it might never be executed). The repeat structure tests the argument at the end of the block, guaranteeing at least one cycle through the script block.

The while structure uses the do keyword much in the same way as the if control structure uses the then keyword: to define the start of the conditional script block. An example of a while structure:

```
indx = 1
while indx < 10 do
    print("loop pass: ", indx)
    indx = indx + 1
end
```

In this example, if indx begins with a value of 10 or greater, the script block will never be executed.

In the `repeat` control structure, the `repeat` keyword begins the script block and it ends with the `until` keyword. The argument to the control structure immediately follows the `until` terminator, for example:

```
indx = 1
repeat
    print("loop pass: ", indx)
    indx = indx + 1
until indx < 10
```

In this example, if `indx` begins with a value of 1000, it will still move through the script block at least once. As you think through what structure to use, you'll need to determine if the code in the block must be run at least once—if so, you'll want to use the `repeat` structure.

You'll need to take special care that your argument will eventually return a `true` evaluation, or you'll find yourself trapped within the script block until you forcefully end your program.

For

Lua provides two types of `for` structures (numeric and generic), but we'll just cover the numeric structure here. We'll touch on the generic structure in the advanced section on tables in the next chapter.

The `for` structure allows you to execute a block of script a finite amount of time, based on the values of the expressions you provide. Here is a simple example:

```
for indx = 1,10 do
    print(indx)
end
```

After the `for` keyword, you provide a range of values for a variable you declare. The block of script will iterate once for each value in the range, with your variable changing in value each time through. The `do` keyword is used to begin the block, and `end` is used to terminate it.

You can use an optional third argument to define the "step" value of the looping. For example:

```
for indx = 10,1, -1 do --this counts backwards
    print(indx)
end
for indx = 1,100, 2 do --this counts forwards by 2s
    print(indx)
end
```

See Figure 6.3.

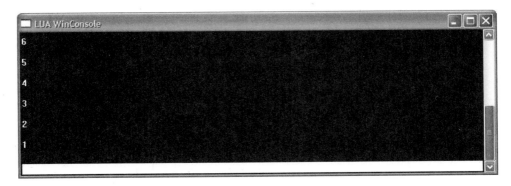

FIGURE 6.3   The console output of a loop counting backward from 10.

There are a few things to keep in mind when using the `for` structure. First, the expressions used to determine the parameters of the looping are only evaluated the first time through, so even if they change in the body of the script, that won't affect the number of iterations of the loop. Second, the variable that holds the iteration value is a local variable that is destroyed as soon as the looping is finished. To save that value outside the script block, you'll need to store it in some other global or higher level local variable.

FUNCTIONS

Functions are the primary tools for organizing the behavior of your game development scripts. Functions are blocks of Lua code that are called from a single identifier (actually a variable), and can perform a process, return a value, or both.

Here is a simple function definition:

```
function Wow()
    print(" ")
    print("Wow, that was awesome!")
print(" ")
end
```

To begin a function definition, you use the `function` statement, followed by the name of the function, and then a list of arguments that can be passed into the function. In this sample function, there are no arguments that can be passed into the function, but we still need to use the `()` to indicate an empty list. The block that defines a function is concluded by the `end` terminator.

Functions in script files are not executed when that file is loaded, but are loaded into memory and associated with the function name variable.

Single Arguments

Now, let's look at a function that takes a single variable as a parameter:

```
function SetName(myString)
print(" ")
print("Your name is:", myString)
print(" ")
end
```

In this function, `myString` is the argument that is passed into the function, and it used as within the function. In functions, these arguments are created as local variables that are discarded when the function completes executing.

Returning Values

In addition to using functions to perform isolated processes, functions can return values back to the calling script. To return a value, a function uses the `return` statement, followed by the value (often a variable name) to return. Here is a simple example:

```
function TimesTwo(myValue)
        myValue = myValue * 2
        return myValue
end
```

You can use a function that returns a value as an argument in a statement; for example:

```
a = 24 + TimesTwo(12)
print(a)
```

You can also have a function return multiple arguments, simply by separating them with a comma. Here is an example:

```
function ThreeDice()
        d1 = math.random(1,6)
        d2 = math.random(1,6)
        d3 = math.random(1,6)
        myTotal = d1 + d2 + d3
        return d1, d2, d3, myTotal
end
```

STANDARD LIBRARIES

Lua provides access to a number of standard function libraries that can allow you to perform some quite sophisticated tasks without the need for additional scripting.

Full details of the standard libraries included within the 5.0 version of Lua can be found in the language's online manual (*www.lua.org/manual/5.0/*).

Math Functions

Lua provides function-level access to the standard C library of math functions. The majority of these are simply Lua Glue interfaces to the corresponding functions in the C library. The functions are actually stored within a tabled called "math" that you can access with the following identifiers:

```
math.abs
math.acos
math.asin
math.atan
math.atan2
math.ceil
math.cos
math.deg
math.exp
math.floor
math.log
math.log10
math.max
math.min
math.mod
math.pow
math.rad
math.sin
math.sqrt
math.tan
math.frexp
math.ldexp
math.random
math.randomseed
```

The table also contains `math.pi`, which is a variable that holds the value of pi.

A few functions are of special interest to us in the realm of game development, as outlined in the following sections.

math.floor()

The `floor` function will round down a number to a whole value (remember, in Lua, there is no concept of floating point or integer). This function simply drops the decimal value. If you'd like to use this to round the number, simply add .5 to the number first:

```
a = 5.125
b = 5.75
```

```
a = a + 0.5
b = b + 0.5
a = math.floor(a) -- a will equal 5
b = math.floor(b) -- b will equal 6
```

math.random()

In the realm of game development, random numbers are everywhere. Lua's `math.random()` function will generate a pseudo-random number between 0 and 1 (like most other languages' random functions). What makes this Lua function work especially well for games is the ability to pass in a minimum and maximum value. The function will then generate whole number values between those arguments:

```
- 6 sided dice
myDie = math.random(1,6)
```

When you start your program, it's a good idea to seed the random number generator with a unique value, so you'll get the most random-seeming results. This is often done in the StartGui.lua file that initializes the game environment, on the script side of things. The easiest way to do this is by using the `os.date` function, so you get a unique time value for the seed:

```
math.randomseed(os.date("%d%H%M%S"))
```

For debugging, you might want to set the random seed to an integer value—this will assure that you'll get the same series of pseudo-random numbers each time you run the game.

math.min()

In the world of game development, it's often necessary to determine the lowest or highest value in a set of values (such as the highest stat of a hero character, or the state with the most electoral votes, etc.). The `math.min` and `math.max` functions will do this for you. Each function can take an arbitrary number of parameters, and it will return either the lowest value in the set (`math.min`) or the highest value in the set (`math.max`).

In Lua, much of our data will be in the form of tables, and this poses a bit of a challenge for using these functions, since you need to add each element of the table to the function call. Fortunately, we can build a Lua string and use the `RunString` LuaGlue function (which you'll learn about later) to perform the operation:

```
function GetMin(theTable)
    myString = "myValue = math.min("
    for index,value in ipairs(theTable) do
```

```
        myString = string.format("%s%d%s", myString, value, ",")
    end
    —remove final comma
    myString = string.sub (myString, 1, string.len(myString) - 1)
    —add final )
    myString = string.format("%s%s", myString, ")")
    —run the chunk
    RunString(myString)
    return myValue
end
```

This function will take a table as its arguments and will return the smallest value in that table.

MORE ON STRINGS

One of Lua's great strengths is its robust string handling capabilities. Lua has extensive pattern matching capabilities, and a set of solid string manipulation functions. In this section, we'll explore some of the most relevant string functions as they relate to game development. More information about all the Lua string manipulation functions can be found in the Lua online manual.

Type Conversion

Often, you'll need to convert a number into a string, and vice versa. To convert a string into a number, use the `tonumber()` function:

```
myString = "1234"
myNumber = tonumber(myString)
print(myNumber + 2) —- this will display 1236
You can also convert a number to a string using the tostring() function:
myNumber = 1234
myString = tostring(myNumber)
print(type(myString)) -— you will see "string"
```

string.char(n1, n2, ..)

This function will return a string based on the ASCII values of the numerical arguments passed in. This function isn't used very often, but it's useful to insert a line feed in a Lua save game file, to make the file more readable to human eyes. For example:

```
myFile:write(string.char (10)) — writes out a linefeed to the open file
```

string.len(myString)

Often, it's helpful to know the length of a string you wish to manipulate, and the string.len function will provide that information. It returns a number that represents the number of characters in the string that was passed as an argument. For example:

```
myString = "1234"
print(string.len(myString)) — will print 4
```

string.sub(myString, start, end)

This function will return a portion of the indicated string. The start value is where in the string you want to start grabbing characters, and the end value is where in the string the grab will stop. For example:

```
myString = "hello world"
newString = string.sub(myString, 1, 5)
print(newString) — this will print "hello"
```

You can use negative values for start and end—in that case, the positioning is based on the end of the string, rather than the beginning (–5 for a start value will position the start five characters from the end of the string). For example:

```
myString = "hello world"
newString = string.sub(myString, -5, 10)
print(newString) — this will print "worl"
```

You can also leave the end value off altogether. In this case, it will assume that it means the end of the string. In this way, you can grab a suffix of the desired string:

```
myString = "hello world"
newString = string.sub(myString, -5)
print(newString) — this will print "world"
```

string.format()

The string.format function allows you to format and build strings. You'll find yourself using this function constantly when you are outputting game text to a GUI Text object. The first use of this function, as we saw in a previous example, is to use it to append values to a string (since Lua doesn't allow you to simply add two strings together):

```
string1 = "hello"
string2 = "world"
for index = 1, 3 do
    string1 = string.format("%s%s", string1, string2)
```

```
end
print(string1)
```

See Figure 6.4.

FIGURE 6.4   The output of the "hello world" `string.format()` example.

In the preceding example, the first argument to the `string.format` function sets up the form the new string will take. The "%s" item means a string ("%d" means a digit), so the "%s%s" means the string will be constructed out of two string components.

The second primary use of `string.format` is to build a complex string out of component parts (many of which probably come from variables). For example:

```
myName = "Fred"
myStr = 16
myString = string.format("%s%s%d%s", myName, "'s strength is ", myStr, ".")
print(myString)
```

In this example, the pattern "%s%s%d%s" tells the function where to put in the component parts, so we get the result "Fred's strength is 16." In this approach, the arguments that follow the pattern simply fill out the pattern to create the result. We can also change the `string.format` approach to get the same results:

```
myString = string.format("%s's strength is %d.", myName, myStr)
```

In this case, we place the pattern and the fixed string elements together, and the variables at the end. Both work equally well.

Another use for `string.format` is to set up the display of digits to a desired number of significant figures. Look at this example:

```
myHealth = 17.34556
myString = string.format("%.2f%s", myHealth, "% of health remaining.")
print(myHealth) -- prints "17.34556"
print(myString) - prints "17.35% of health remaining."
```

In this example, the "%.2f" tells `string.format` to round the `myHealth` value to two decimal places.

BASIC I/O

In the context of this book, we are going to be using Lua to save and load vital game information. We'll learn more about this in Part III of the book, but the advantage of using Lua as a save/load system is that you don't have to parse the data at all—we can let Lua do that work for us, since all game data will be represented as valid Lua script files.

That being said, we still need to have a basic idea about writing out data to a file so we can create those valid Lua files, so we'll need to learn a little bit about how Lua handles file writing.

The first thing we have to do is open a file for writing, which we do with the `io.open()` function:

```
myFile = io.open("test_data.lua", "w")
```

This function takes two arguments: a string with the filename of the file you are going to create, and a string that indicates what type of control you will have for writing to the file. The "w" is for write mode—this will create a file, if one doesn't exist, and will write to the file as if it were new (all previous data will be lost). For our save game data, this is generally what we'll use, since we want to write a complete game state each time we save. We might also want to use "a" for append mode—this will preserve existing data and simply write new information from the end of the file.

If there is an error opening the file or creating it, the returned variable (in this case, `myFile`) will be `nil`. We can use that to check to make sure the file opened successfully before we write anything. Look at this example, which opens a file and writes out several lines:

```
myFile = io.open("test_data.lua", "w")
if myFile ~= nil then
    myFile:write("- Test lua file")
    myFile:write(string.char (10))
    myFile:write(string.char (10))
    myFile:write(string.format("%s%s", "- File created on: ", os.date()))
    myFile:write(string.char (10))
```

```
      myFile:write(string.char (10))
      myFile:write("print(\"hello world!\")")
      io.close(myFile)
  end
```

In this example, we open the file and use the `write()` function to write strings out to the file. The `string.char()` function writes out line feeds, so we have a file that's easy to read. We use the Lua escape character, "\", to enable us to insert quotation marks in the "hello world" line. Finally, we use the `io.close` function to close our file. If you run this script, you'll see that it will indeed generate a valid Lua file that you can then run using the `RunScript()` LuaGlue command.

LUAGLUE

LuaGlue functions are functions in Lua that are used to control under-the-hood functions created by a programmer in a low-level language like C++. In our game engine, we have created a number of functions that allow us, as designers, to have a wide degree of control over our game world. In fact, by using standard Lua, plus the following LuaGlue functions, we have all the tools to create a prototype game.

These functions allow us to set up examples, experiments, and actually build an entire game—all without requiring an additional programmer or deep programming skills.

Interfaces

In our game engine we'll be using through this book, we manage interaction (both user and game) within the context of a game interface. An interface is an abstract construct that consists of items on screen and script code to handle the various game inputs. An interface is defined by a Lua script file that defines all the interface elements, plus the event processing.

There is a special-case GUI (graphical user interface) file called "StartGUI.lua." This file will automatically run when the game engine is executed. We use this file to set up any initial values we want and to select the first visual interface we want the player to see.

RunGUI

This command starts a new interface by running the Lua file that defines the interface. The current interface will become inactive until it is restarted with this command.

```
RunGUI(ScriptName)
```

Event-Driven Scripting

In our examples and our upcoming game, we'll use the concept of event-driven control. That means that some event, be it a key press, a mouse click, or a time expiring, will be the mechanism we use to determine when some action may be taken. Today, more and more games are becoming event-driven, even when one of those events is the passage of time.

We use a function that will process our events. The game engine understands a small set of events and will call a specified function with a number representing the event that just occurred. We simply test for specific event and then do whatever action we need to.

SetEventHandler

This function selects the Lua function the system will call when a GUI event occurs.

```
SetEventHandler(Function)
```

"Function" must be a Lua script function in the form of:

```
function Function(id, eventCode)
  …
end
```

Sample Event

To illustrate this concept, consider the following example:

```
EVENT_SAMPLE = 1000
SetEventHandler("EventHandler")
function EventHandler(id, …)
if id == EVENT_SAMPLE then
    print("Sample Event!")
    end
end
```

Each interface file will have its own event function that will handle all the events for that interface. If you don't care about an event (such as a mouse click), the event will simply occur, but nothing will happen, because the event handler function doesn't capture it.

Events

The following outlines the events we can capture in our game engine. The events codes are numbers that were assigned by the engine programmer—the constants are defined to make the code easier to understand and read for us as designers. These definitions are found in the "StartGui.lua" file, which is loaded when the game runs.

While this may seem like a very limited number of events, we can do quite a bit with them. For example, the GUI_KEY_PRESS event also sends along the ASCII value of the key that was pressed, so with that single event, you can capture nearly all keyboard input.

```
— define constant values for all scripts
— Standard LuaGUI event codes
GUI_EVENT_BUTTON_UP = 0
GUI_EVENT_BUTTON_DOWN = 1
GUI_EVENT_SELECTION_CHANGED = 2
GUI_EVENT_TEXTFIELD_CLICKED = 3
GUI_KEY_PRESS = 4
GUI_REENTER_INTERFACE = 5
GUI_TIMER_EXPIRED = 6
GUI_ENTER_INTERFACE = 7
GUI_TEXT_SCROLL_END = 8
GUI_EVENT_TEXTFIELD_RETURN = 9
GUI_EVENT_HOVER_TIMED_START = 10
GUI_EVENT_HOVER_END = 11
GUI_MOUSE_BUTTON_DOWN = 12
GUI_MOUSE_BUTTON_UP = 13
```

Interface Functions

In the section that follows, we describe the game engine's built-in interface functions, which will allow you complete control over the game interface through the course of the book, from drawing a button on screen to controlling an animated explosion.

CreateItem

Creates a GUI item. The available items are listed later in the chapter. All items have an ID number that is assigned by the script author. As with all ID values, they must be unique within an interface. IDs can be reused in other interfaces to make a "standard" ID set for common items (buttons).

```
CreateItem(ID, ItemTypeString, …)
```

The ItemTypeString in the example is one of the defined item types, and the rest of the parameters are dependant on this item type.

DeleteItem

This function deletes an item from the interface. The item will no longer be drawn or react to user input.

```
DeleteItem(ID)
```

SetItemPosition

Use this function to position the item on the screen. The GUI command SetItem-Position also accepts "−1" as a valid width and height. If passed −1, the width/height will be the actual size of the texture translated to the current SetTransCoord. You can use this function to place buttons, text items, or to move and animate sprites around the screen.

```
SetItemPosition(ID, X, Y, W, H)
```

ItemCommand

Some interface items have commands that are specific to them. This is the function you use to use those capabilities. See Supported GUI Items later in the chapter for more information on these commands.

```
ItemCommand(ID, "CommandString", …)
```

SetFont

For items that use a font, this function will allow you to set the font type and size.

```
SetFont(ID, FontFamily, PointSize)
```

FontFamily is a string. It is the Windows name of the font, such as "Arial." Use the Windows font manager, found in the Control Panel, to see the names of the various fonts. PointSize is an approximation of the size desired.

See Figure 6.5.

FIGURE 6.5 An example of a game interface created entirely with the Lua commands described in this chapter.

EnableObject

All interface items are created enabled, but they can be disabled and re-enabled using this function. You can disable the rendering of an object, the function of an object (such as a button), or both.

```
EnableObject(ID, Enable, Draw)
```

If `Enable == 0`, then the item will be disabled; otherwise, it will be enabled. Disabled objects will continue to be visible, but not react to input, if `Draw` is not 0 (zero).

SetTexture

You can use this function to directly set the texture of any GUI object. The name is the string name of the texture. It is assumed to be in the "Textures" directory. You can use this button to swap in grayed-out art for a disabled button, to control an animated sprite, and so forth.

```
SetTexture(id, texturename)
```

SetTextureUV

This function sets the portion of a GUI object that's visible. It sets the background texture of any GUI object. The texture you specify will appear in the screen rectangle defined by the `SetItemPosition` command.

```
SetTextureUV(id, u0,v0,u1,v1,u2,v2,u3,v3)
```

Supported GUI Items

In the following section, you'll learn about the supported GUI objects and the Item Commands you can use to control them.

Sprite

A sprite is a static image, useful for backgrounds and other decorative elements.
To create:

```
CreateItem(ID, "Sprite", "Sprite.BMP")
```

Item Commands

```
ItemCommand(ID, "SetRotation", rotation)
```

This command will rotate the sprite (ID) to the passed rotation (in radians).

Button

A Button item is a three- or four-state button. The states are Normal, Hover, Selected, and Disabled. The only required state is "Normal." Any states that are undefined will be presented to the user as "Normal."

To create:

```
CreateItem(ID, "Button", "Normal.BMP", "Hover.BMP", "Selected.BMP",
"Disabled.BMP")
```

Item Commands

```
ItemCommand(ID, "HotSpot", x, y, w, h)
```

This sets the button's hotspot to the defined rectangle; the default is the entire rectangle of the graphic.

TextField

A TextField is a static text string that is displayed on screen. You can change the value of the string via script during the running of your game.

To create:

```
CreateItem(ID, "TextField")
```

Item Commands

```
ItemCommand(ID, "SetString", "String")
```

This command sets the displayed string to "string".

```
ItemCommand(ID, "SetColor", R,G,B,A)
```

This command sets the color for displayed string to specified color (A is the alpha optional).

```
myText = ItemCommand(ID, "GetString")
```

This command returns the current text displayed in the text object.

```
ItemCommand(ID, "Focus", on/off)
```

This command sets the input focus to the text object. When turned on, the text object will display a blinking cursor and will accept text input from the keyboard.

```
ItemCommand(ID, "SetEditability", 1)
```

If you create a TextField in Lua that you wish to be editable, you will need to issue the ItemCommand of `SetEditability` for any TextField objects you wish to be editable. Otherwise, the system will ignore the mouse and you will not be able to click in the field to select it. It is off by default, though, so you don't need to worry about turning it off if you didn't turn it on.

Other Functions

In the sections that follow, we'll cover the remaining built-in LuaGlue functions for the game engine we'll be working in with this book.

SetCoordTrans

This function sets the scale of the interface of the screen (it doesn't actually change the screen resolution). Set this to the value you wish to use for your default screen dimensions (in pixels) at the start of an interface file. Then, all of the positional numbers you provide will show up where you expect them on screen.

```
SetCoordTrans(800, 600)
```

RunScript

This function will run a Lua script and execute it immediately. This isn't like the RunGUI function, because it doesn't do the under-the-hood processing to register the interface. You would use this to load a script of functions, a saved game file, or something like that.

```
RunScript("ScriptName.lua")
```

StartTimer

This function will start an internal timer with the number of seconds you indicate (you can use decimals as well, such as 0.1 for a tenth of a second). When the timer expires, the GUI_TIMER_EXPIRED event will be triggered.

```
StartTimer(time)
```

PlayMusic

This function will start a music file playing (the file can be a wave, MP3, or Ogg Vorbis file). The number parameter indicates whether the music is to loop; a value of 1 means loop the files, and a value of zero means play once. The music is assumed to be in the "Music" folder.

```
PlayMusic(1, "PianoBlues.ogg")
```

StopMusic

This function will stop the currently playing music file indicated by the filename.

```
StopMusic("PianoBlues.ogg")
```

PlaySound

This will play a sound effect file (a wave file) from the "Sounds" directory. It will play the file immediately when the function is called and will play the file only once.

```
PlaySound("filename.wav")
```

QuitProgram

This function will quite the execution of the game engine and return you to the desktop.

```
QuitProgram()
```

GetMousePosition

This function will return the X and Y mouse positions (based on the resolution you set via the SetCoordTrans function). This is often used when processing a mouse button click event, to see where the mouse cursor was at that time.

```
x,y = GetMousePosition()
```

GetCollisions

This function will allow you to test for collisions between an indicated sprite and the other sprite objects in the world. The function will return a table (t), where t.n is the number of collisions and t[1]...t[n] are the IDs of the sprites that collide with the passed ID.

```
t = GetCollisions(SpriteID)
```

HitTest

This function is similar to GetCollisions, but it instead will test for collisions with an indicated x and y position (often provided by a GetMousePosition function call). This function returns a table with all GUI Items that occupy the passed location. t.n is the number of entries in the table starting at t[1] thru t[t.n].

```
t = HitTest(x,y)
```

RunString

This function will run a string as if it were a Lua command. This is useful if you are doing some internal processing to build some action script that can then be passed on to this function for execution.

```
RunString("myString")
```

SUMMARY

In this chapter, we concluded our game design boot camp. You first learned about game design and then what a game designer does. Then, we went to work to brush up and address the core skills you'll need to be a successful designer.

In this last chapter of Part I, we covered some basics of the Lua scripting language, since this is what we'll use going forward, to experiment and test out various game design concepts. Throughout the rest of this book, you'll work with a game engine that will enable you, as a designer, to test, create, and prototype various types of play experiences.

In the chapters that follow, we'll turn our attention to some of the more abstract concepts of game design, so we can understand, at the core, what we are doing when we are creating a new game. We'll then spend the final third of our book working through examples of key game design concepts as they are manifested in our own experimental game.

CHAPTER EXERCISES

1. Write a Lua "hello world" program in a text file, and use the Lua console and the `dofile()` function to load and run your program.
2. Write a simple Lua function in a file that will compute the Fibonacci sequence for the entered numbers, so that an entry like fib(4) will print the results 1*2*3*4. Use `dofile()` to load the function and call it from the console.
3. Write a function that will allow you to add a name to a table of strings, as in `AddName("John Doe")`. Write a function, such as `PrintNames()`, that will print all of the names to the console. Now, write a function, such as `WriteNames()`, that will write the names to a text file. Load the functions with a `dofile()` call and perform the operations from the console.

Part II

Game Design Theory

You've completed boot camp. You now have a solid understanding of the various roles a game designer plays during the development of a game, and a handle on the core skills you'll need to hone to deliver effective designs down the road.

Our next stop is the world of game design theory. We are going to spend some time delving into the core game design concepts and rules that apply to nearly every interactive game. This will give us a solid foundation on which to design our own games, and effectively analyze and learn from other games.

We then spend some time rattling around in the minds of our game players, seeing how they perceive and are affected by our games, to better understand the experience from their point of view.

From there, we move on to explore the concepts of creating player challenge within a game. How do we create a play experience that is fun and challenging, even as players grow in their skills and understanding of our game? We look closely at the concepts of challenge, risk, reward, and failure and derive some additional guidelines that will help us in our future game designs.

Get your thinking cap on, clear your mind, and let's begin our exploration of the atoms of gameplay.

7 The Atoms of a Game

In This Chapter

- Introduction to Game Atoms
- Catalog of Essential Atoms

There are many, many ways to deliver a compelling game to a player. You may create a scrolling arcade-style shooter or a photo-real simulation of rugby. No matter what type of game you create, there are core principles that hold true across the genres. In this chapter, we will look at a basic set of these gameplay "atoms" that will serve as the foundation for your design decisions as you move forward in your own game designs.

ATOMS

We've spend quite a bit of time thinking about how we define a game and learning how to think like a game designer. Now that we are diving into some of the more theoretical aspects of game design, it's time we start with the most basic elements, or atoms, if you will, of game design.

What is a game atom? It is a core design guideline or rule that applies to nearly every interactive game, no matter what the platform or genre. Of course, all rules are meant to be broken, and a clever game designer can always find opportunities to break, bend, or "split" these atoms, just like fiction writers have always found ways in which to break or bend the rules of grammar.

In the sections that follow, you will find an initial set of atoms we have used over the past dozen years to help create a solid foundation for game designs. Think of them as building blocks, rules, or as a series of checks and balances to make sure your game is on solid footing.

Clear Goal

A game should present a clear goal for the player.

As we saw in the early chapters, an end goal is part of what makes a game a game. As a designer, it makes good sense to let your players know what that goal is early on, so they can see their progress and understand their immediate actions in a larger context.

Certain games have this end goal built in and obvious. In football, the goal is to have the most points when the time expires (actually, this is true for many sports). In poker, you are trying to leave the table with the most money (or at least more money than you sat down with) (Figure 7.1).

FIGURE 7.1 In poker, the end goal is to leave the table with as much money as possible—hopefully more than you started with.

There has been a trend in interactive games to hide the meta goal from the player, for the sake of story development. This may often be the case in a novel, when the master goal isn't immediately clear to the reader for quite some time. However, our medium is different—it's all about action, interactivity, and challenge, and that player action should have a target. Great stories can be told when the end goal is in mind (think of a great mystery, when the goal of "find the killer" manifests itself in the first few pages).

Players like to see their target—it guides their actions and their perceptions. Think of it as the vanishing point in a perspective drawing—all lines lead to this vanishing point.

How do you present the goal to the player? That depends on the unique situations of your game, but it is desirable to present the goal to the player within the context of the game in some way, rather than just explain it in a manual or in an opening cinematic.

As a designer, you also want to remind players of the overarching goal from time to time, to keep them on track—don't hit them over the head with it, but don't let them forget. Think of Quake 2—the goal was to get to the large gun installation. During the game, you would often come to a window in the space station; out the window, you would see the large gun complex in the distance—this was a subtle way to remind the players of the goal, and a tool to allow them to gauge how close they were getting.

Nested Victories

Provide the opportunity for subvictories to the player.

While a player wants to have a clear idea of his overarching goal in a game, you don't want him to wait until the end of the game to feel a sense of accomplishment. A good game will provide many small challenges with opportunities for subvictories for the player. The player can then feel a sense of accomplishment and get that adrenaline rush and endorphin release many times during the play of the game.

A perfect example of "nested victories" can be found in the sport of football (American football, that is). The overarching goal is to have the most points when time expires. Time, however, is broken into quarters, providing four smaller subgames. Within this structure, a team with the ball has multiple subgoals: to score points (touchdown, field goal, etc.). However, to reach the subgoal of scoring points, a team must achieve multiple smaller goals, such as getting several first downs. Along the path to getting first downs, the team must run plays, and each play is its own little subgame, in which the defense may sack the quarterback or stuff the run (defensive subvictories), or the offense may hit a long pass or the running back may break out for a long run. Each snap of the ball provides the opportunity for a victory for each side, and these victories are nested several deep (Figure 7.2).

FIGURE 7.2 Football is a great example of a game with "nested victories."

For a spectator sport like football, this nested victory approach makes the game exciting to watch—even if your team isn't making progress toward the meta-goal, it can achieve small victories that will excite the crowd.

In a way, a computer game, even a single player one, is a spectator sport. The player is playing, and watching himself play, and providing opportunities for multiple victories along the way to a larger whole-game goal is essential for player fun.

Player as Agent of Change

Allow the player's actions to affect the game world.

Your player is a "prisoner" in your game world as long as he is playing the game. Imagine how frustrating it would be for players if they were trapped in their metaphorical cell and couldn't affect the world at all—no matter what they did, there was no change.

It's clear that this would be a frustrating situation, and it's one you should avoid. As players occupy the game world and act within that world, allow their actions to have consequences. These consequences should be both meaningful and visual.

An example of a nonmeaningful consequence, but one that helps to immerse the player in the world, is when the player's bullet holes mark up the wall of an environment and remain there. In this way, the player can see he is "making his mark" and his actions affect the game world. Of course, a clever player can make this meaningful as well, leaving marks as "breadcrumbs" that help him keep his bearings in a complex world.

Most of the time, the player's actions affect the other dynamic objects in the world. For example, in an RTS game, most of the effects seen by the player are in the actions and numbers of enemy troops. The base level of this atom is to allow player action to affect these dynamic elements—to provide continuous feedback that the player's presence matters in the world.

The next level is to allow the world itself to react to player actions. This can take many forms: allowing the player to chop down a tree, bullet holes that remain, paths that get worn in the dirt, structures built—almost any lasting change in the world that tells the player, "hey, I was here."

Allowing players to affect change in the world makes them feel important—that what they do matters. It also makes the world feel more alive and malleable and will help to pull the player even further into the experience.

Understandable Context

Make the context of the game and game world understandable to the player.

We touched on this atom in earlier chapters when we discussed creating a game that was familiar, in some way, to the player. When a player enters a game, ideally he wants to be swept away by a new and exciting player experience, but if he has to struggle with the context of the game world, the depth of immersion for the player will suffer.

Imagine a game in which you play a gaseous life form "swimming" in the atmosphere of Jupiter (this idea is not our own—it is the basis of one of Arthur C. Clarke's most famous stories). This context is so alien from our normal experience and understanding that the connection we make with the game will be fragile at best, since we are spending much of our mental energy attempting to understand just what the world of the game is about.

This certainly does not mean that the core idea for your game or game world needs to be stale and unoriginal. Rather, this atom is essential because you want the player to become immersed in the play of your game, and it is your job, as a designer, to create a structure and context that is clearly understood, so the player can spend his time playing, rather than wrestling with alien ideas and situations.

Understandable Rules

Make the rules of the game understandable by the player.

The next step beyond an understandable context for your game is that the game rules should be understandable as well. As a player plays the game, he will work out how his actions affect the game and what works and what doesn't. You will want to make the rules of the game logical and clear enough so the player can understand and use them (Figure 7.3).

FIGURE 7.3   Many classic arcade games featured controls that were so desperately simple every player understood them.

An extreme bad example would be a combat system based entirely on luck. In this case, there simply are no rules for the player to understand. Other examples would be rules that have no basis in logic, such as killing ant warriors spawns purple energy crystals used for spaceship fuel.

This atom is more about common sense than anything else: make your game rules logical and understandable. You don't want your players struggling with understanding how their actions affect the game—that isn't a satisfying challenge. They instead should be spending their time playing within the rules to achieve their victories and subvictories.

Skill Is Required

The player should use skill to progress in the game.

Again, this is another common sense rule, but it is also one of the most essential atoms in game design. For many games, skill is a hand-eye coordination skill, such as timing a jump over a lava river or aiming a rifle shot perfectly to hit a moving target. In other games, the skill is more a logical or problem-solving skill, such as, "how do I connect the wires to unlock the door?"

You want to avoid having success in your game based on a nonskill activity, such as merely clicking the mouse button when a player reaches a door or unlocking a dungeon door automatically once the player has opened all the treasure chests in the room. Progress based on nonskill feels empty and doesn't provide the opportunity for an adrenaline rush or a sense of accomplishment for a player. If you stage a huge boss battle against a ferocious creature, but have the player wear down the enemy by simply clicking to swing a sword, the victory will be hollow.

Engage your players' minds and dexterity in the game, and you will grab and hold their attention. We'll discuss repercussions of this atom a little later, such as giving the players a break (you don't want to wear them out by requiring nonstop skill) and ramping up the skill to increase challenge as their competency grows.

Success Feedback

The game should provide success feedback to the player.

As a player progresses in your game, he needs to know how he is doing. Is he getting closer to the end goal? Are his strategies paying off? Your game should provide feedback, both positive and negative, to let the player know how he is doing.

At times, this is obvious and built into the game system—in an RTS game, for example, the player can see directly if his attacks are cutting into the enemy forces or not. In a golf game, the player can see how close the ball he hit is to the pin.

The challenge, though, is to provide subtle feedback to the player that will help him determine the amount of success or failure he is achieving. In our golf example, if the player hits a ball with a high arc and the wind carries it off course, you can use a "double feedback" approach. The path of the ball's flight is one form of feedback. The golfer could exclaim something like, "Ugh! I hit that too high and let it get caught by the wind!" By doubling up the feedback, you provide vital information about what the player just did, and clues as to how the player can avoid the mistake in the future (in this case, by using a lower iron that won't loft the ball as much).

Consistent Interface

Provide a consistent approach to the user interface.

Every game has a learning curve, and one of the key jobs as a designer is to make sure that curve is smooth, easy to understand, and as fun as possible. One of the main points a player will learn when playing your game is how to control the game through the user interface, be it mouse clicks on buttons, keyboarding, or buttons on a game controller.

You'll want to make sure the user interface is clear and as simple as possible, but even more basic than that is that you'll want to make sure you are consistent in the way in which a player interacts with a game. You don't want to mix interface approaches unless you have a very good reason to do so. If you use left and right arrow buttons to scroll through horizontal lists of inventory items on one screen, don't switch to a vertical display on the next screen. If you use the Enter key to capture text input, don't also use that key to control the firing of a gun.

The rule is simple in concept, but you'll find yourself getting caught all the time, because as a designer, you'll be dealing with a myriad of interfaces, often thinking about them at different times and in different contexts. It's surprisingly easy to forget what approach you used earlier, so keep this atom at the forefront of your mind. Your goal for the players is simple: once they learn a way of doing something in a game—such as firing a weapon, moving, selecting an inventory item—use that same approach throughout the game, so they learn and understand the "grammar" of your game's interface and feel comfortable with new situations.

The AI Exists to Provide Challenge

Create artificial intelligence to challenge the players with their current skills.

Artificial intelligence (AI) is used to control entities in your game that will provide assistance and obstacles to your players as they progress toward the end goal. While "helping AI" is important, the bread and butter of AI is to control the opposition to the player.

Computer-controlled opponents do not have to be smart—they simply have to appear as if they are acting intelligently or appropriately within the context of the game. As a designer, one of your most important tasks is to design AI so it will match the players' skills and abilities at the point in the game in which they are encountered.

In general, computer opponents should not be easy to beat, but should provide a challenge that requires players to use skill and their current resources to defeat them. As the game progresses, the level of the player will increase and the resources available will probably also increase, so scale the computer opponents to match.

Give the Player a Break

Don't deliver intense action all the time; give the player a chance to rest.

Intense action is great, but a player will fatigue quickly if the gameplay is all action with no letup. Take a cue from the pacing in successful action movies—viewers need to have some rest between the action scenes to catch their breath, settle back into the characters, and prepare for the next sequence of action.

If you are delivering gameplay via missions, either build in some downtime within a mission or provide lighter, simpler missions between missions of high intensity. Generally, you don't want intense action to take up more than 75 percent of the playtime, and often, shooting for two-thirds action and one-third slower pacing is a good idea, especially if you have a story to tell to the player. The downtime in a game is a great place to deliver character development and exposition (in fact, cinematics are one tried and true way of doing this).

Randomness Can Be Good

Randomness can minimize predictability.

Two of the most boring types of experiences are ones that are either wholly predictable or governed completely by chance. Flipping a coin or playing rock-paper-scissors is great for deciding who will dive off the high dive first, but neither is a good basis for a game. Having your fate determined by a pure act of chance delivers no sense of accomplishment (Figure 7.4). In addition, playing a game in which the play unfolds the same way, time and time again, is an exercise in total boredom.

Fortunately, most games are at neither of these extremes, but some come close. Consider the child's game *Candyland®*. This game is nearly completely governed by chance—there are moments of strategy when players decide if they want to take a shortcut or not, but chance is the dominant controlling factor. It's a great game for small kids to learn the core dynamics of how a simple game works, but even a young child will find the victory rather empty when it is determined purely by the flip of a card.

In your games, you want to avoid the extremes, but you also want to use some randomness to make the game more interesting and less predictable. If you create a truly fun game, your players will log many, many hours playing it. If everything unfolds just the same, you will stop engaging the players' minds and they will become bored and find something else to do.

FIGURE 7.4   A game controlled completely by a "randomizer" like a pair of dice offers the player no real sense of accomplishment. At the other extreme is tic-tac-toe. The game requires some basic skill, but once the game is mastered, it becomes an unwinnable game, since every game will end in a draw if both players pay just the slightest bit of attention.

Two of the best ways to introduce randomness into a game are random encounters and stat variations. Random encounters are places or times in the game where there is a possibility of some opposition appearing, but randomness determines if the encounter occurs. This approach causes players to stay on their toes, because even if they have memorized the flow of a level, they won't be 100-percent sure of what is around the next corner.

Using variations in opposition stats is also a great way to use randomness to vary the gameplay in an interesting way. If a player comes across an enemy swordsman, don't have the swordsman always have 75 health points (the player will soon learn this), but rather have the swordsman appear with a health value in a range of points that matches the player skill (say a value between 50 and 100 points). In this way, the player may luck out and have an easy go of the encounter, or may be surprised to be tested by a seemingly innocuous foe. This keeps the game interesting and the player engaged.

Don't Let the Player Get Lost

Provide a world and interface that will always let players know where they are.

One might argue that finding your way out of an impossible maze is a great challenge, and that may be the case. However, it doesn't make it a fun game. Nothing frustrates a player more than feeling lost in your game. This can be physical (where am I?) or purpose based (what am I supposed to do now?), and should be avoided at all costs.

Players love to explore game worlds, but they also want to know how to get back on the proper path to progress in the game. If you are designing a game in which players are exploring a large world, provide interface tools that anchor them in space and tell them where they are. This can be a map, a guiding arrow, or some other tool (Figure 7.5).

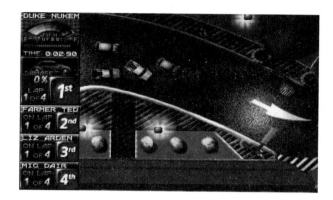

FIGURE 7.5 In Death Rally, guiding arrows were burned into the roadway, so the player always knew which way to go, even without a map. Used with permission. Copyright 3D Realms Entertainment 1996.

Crazy Taxi®, a great arcade and console game, allowed players to drive their cab throughout the streets of a large city, going nearly anywhere they wanted. The gameplay was frantic enough that the players couldn't take the time to study a map, but the game always provided a floating directional arrow that pointed toward their current goal. No matter where they were, they could always use the arrow to guide themselves back to their target .

The great console game *Metroid Prime®* used a map to anchor the player in space (actually, the game used a nested map system). The map would provide enough information to allow players to find their way back to a familiar spot if they became lost. In Metroid Prime, the map also became a questing tool. The layout of the game worlds also clearly implied where the next "point of interest" was, so the player never was at a loss to figure out where to go next.

Freeform exploration and large open-ended worlds can be great, but always provide some tool for the players to get them back into the main flow of your game.

Patterns Shouldn't Be Too Simple

Players can recognize patterns easily, so make your patterns challenging.

Human beings are very adept at determining patterns. We see images in clouds, faces in just a few lines, and musical note patterns after listening to a song just a few times. We automatically strive to find patterns and will often try to find order even when there is none to be found. Creating interesting play and challenge patterns is one of the most interesting and difficult tasks for a game designer.

Unfortunately, one problem many game designers encounter is that they design patterns of play that are too easy for a player to decode. As you develop patterns in your game (enemy movement, boss behaviors, level design, etc.), make sure they are challenging enough so a player won't glean the predictability immediately.

WHAT DOES A PLAYER DO?

 Designer: Ken Rolston

I interviewed for a position as lead designer on a big CRPG project that had been in production for many months. The acting project leads were artists. They proudly showed me colorful walls full of art illustrating the game's story and setting. It looked like production designs for a film.

These guys weren't idiots. They were talented, clever storytellers, trying to do the best they could without a designer.

But their work was completely wasted, because they could only imagine what the player would see as he went through the story . . . and not what he would do. They knew how to make a movie, but not a game. Like most of us, shaped by the TV and movies we've seen, they could only see the linear and spatial structures of the game experience, and not the underlying transactional and logical units a game designer must see . . . the economy of objects and doing.

A game design is a list of the objects in the world, and the ways the player can interact with them. He can move past them, or move them, or beat them up and take other objects out of them. Some objects he can take, some he can use, some he can look at. But everything is doing something with an object.

So don't think about what going on on the screen. That's a movie.

$\rightarrow$

> Think about what the player is thinking about doing, and how he is going to do it, and what with, and why.
>
> And when some excited person on the team comes to you and wants to put something cool in the game, ask him, "but what does the player *do* with it?"
>
> The game is not about what happens to the player. It is about what the player does.

"Just Barely" Victories Are Exciting

Provide ample opportunities for the player to snatch victory out of the jaws of defeat.

Nothing delivers the adrenaline rush of victory like a victory barely achieved. Sure, it can be fun to crush your opponent in Madden '06, but it's far more exciting to come from behind and score a touchdown on a 20-yard run as time expires.

Often, you can't control the moments when a player is against the ropes or near defeat, but you can create situations and mechanisms that will favor the creation of "just barely" victories.

Think, for example, of a boxing game. You will be able to know when the player is nearly knocked out. You can easily justify the idea of "desperation adrenaline" in that situation—a percentage chance that a player-thrown punch will arrive with more power than a standard punch (if it does indeed land). In a situation like this, you have tweaked the design to allow an opportunity for player victory of a spectacular fashion.

Often, tweaking the rules of the game to anticipate a near-losing solution isn't the answer—the answer more often lies in designing conflict so players are never in a situation that is mathematically hopeless for them to win. Give them the tools to pull out a victory, and from time to time, they'll pull out a squeaker—and those moments will be the ones they remember.

Provide a Range of Related Challenges

Provide the player with a range of related but varied challenges with a shared skill base.

As the player progresses in your game, he will be growing in the skills you have set out for him to master. As his skills grow, provide a variety of ways in which he can succeed with a single skill.

If one skill the player learns, for example, is a timing skill that enables him to swing on a rope across a chasm, don't lock him into simply swinging by a rope with that skill—it will grow boring and repetitive quite quickly. Instead, think of other gameplay situations that can use that same skill. For example, add that skill to a puzzle. Perhaps the player has to break a window, but he can't reach it. Maybe it's in a clock tower with a large pendulum swinging back and forth. Perhaps pulling on a rope that raises the window will allow him, if his timing is right, to have the pendulum smash the window.

The idea is simple: if you ask a player to learn a new skill for your game, provide multiple, but varied, opportunities for him to use that skill to achieve success (or at least continued survival) in your game.

Provide a Range of Abilities

Provide the player with a range of powers and abilities.

You players will be spending a lot of time in your game. To keep things interesting, provide them with the opportunities to develop multiple skills and reward them with a good variety and range of powerups (such as weapons) and abilities.

You don't want to give a player abilities that vary only in degree, such as an scaling arsenal of ranged weapons that all fire the same way but simply do more and more damage. If you look at some of the classic FPS games, the weapons, while nearly all ranged, were quite varied.

Consider a game like Quake 3. You had the very powerful (at point blank range) shotgun with very limited range. You had the slow-moving rocket launcher, but the rocket would do a large amount of damage in a radius around where it exploded. You also had the rail gun, which packed a devastating amount of damage, but only to a pinpoint, so aiming was key. All the weapons are ranged, but each requires some skill variation and some changes to how you play (Figure 7.6).

FIGURE 7.6   Variety is key to exciting and interesting play. An RTS game filled with nothing but swordsmen would be uninteresting. Blending a catapult and pikemen in with the swordsmen creates tactical variety.

Consider an RTS game. You wouldn't think of a medieval RTS game with nothing but variations of ranged weapons (archers, crossbowmen, catapults, etc.). To make the game exciting, you want a variety of units, from swordsmen to archers to horsemen to catapults. The variety creates many ways to play, opens the door for multiple strategies, and keeps enough variables in the mix so the player won't become easily bored.

Failure Should Have a Cost

Player failure should have a cost, but that cost shouldn't be frustration.

Most players will fail many more times than they succeed in a game. As a game designer, you are working to create a challenging experience that will allow the player to reach an end goal and win. To make the victory worthwhile, the play must be challenging so the final victory is satisfying for the player.

As the player strives for victory, he will fail. Perhaps he needs to make a long jump and times it wrong and plunges into a river of lava. Perhaps the player committed too many troops to the main castle gates and the enemy stormed the rear of the castle and killed the king. Failure is essential in building the value of the ultimate victory, and in teaching the player how to grow the skills he will need to succeed in the game.

As a game designer, you have a tricky balancing act to accomplish, because you must challenge the player, but you do not want to frustrate him if he fails repeatedly. A classic example is forcing the player to navigate through a long a dangerous dungeon before he reaches a boss creature. If the player dies battling the boss, he is respawned back to where he started and has to battle the level again and then the boss. After several failures, the player may be too frustrated and may simply give up.

Failure should have a cost, but the cost shouldn't be frustration or hamstringing the player so much that he can't compete in the game anymore. The cost to players can come in several flavors. They may lose points or lives. They may be forced to replay a section of the game. They may lose items of value. All of these are valid mechanics when used sparingly, but as a designer, be mindful of how you are penalizing the player and be benevolent rather than malevolent.

Another great tool is to build a "failure counter" into something like a boss battle. If the player fails several times, have the game provide the player with a hint or a powerup that will stack the odds more in his favor.

You want your players to earn victory, but don't make the cost so high that they bail out of your game entirely.

QUAKE 2 EXPERIMENT

Designer: Paul Schuytema

Many years ago, our development team tried an experiment with the classic game Quake 2. Quake 2 was a first person shooter with a clear goal (get to the large gun facility and destroy it) and clear subgoals (get to the end of each level alive). It featured a standard save game system that allowed the player to save the game at any time, and even provided a "quicksave" key.

We all played the game when it came out and enjoyed exploring the game world and battling the creatures, but we noticed something as we played—the game was fun, but it wasn't totally satisfying. We played, but we felt unfulfilled as we moved forward through the game. Then we noticed a play trait we all shared: before opening any new door or entering a new room, we would tap the "quick save" key to save the game. If we opened the door and died, we'd just tap the "quick restore" key and it was as if nothing had happened. We were learning the game, but we were playing in a context in which failure meant nothing.

We then tried an experiment: we all agreed to save the game only when we reached the time in which the game would load in new map data. This simple step totally transformed the game, since failure now had a real cost—our restore would take us back to the start of the level. Our play became quick and defensive, and grabbing health and ammo powerups was essential. Numerous times, we'd reach the end of the level with only a few points of health remaining—we were exhilarated and the value of our game experience increased a hundredfold.

Since that time, we've noticed many games, especially console games (often for technical reasons) allowing save games only at certain points. This approach can truly add value to the player "life" by providing a hefty cost for failure. The downside is that you can easily create player frustration if they have to work through too long of a play area or too much challenge each time.

Help the Player Prepare for Greater Challenge

A game gets more difficult the deeper a player gets into it;
help him prepare for the challenges ahead.

A well-balanced game will escalate in challenge and difficulty from easy to very challenging at the end. As the player gets deeper into the game, his core skills will be challenged more and more and your game will ask more from him before it rewards him with victory.

Your job as a designer is to prepare your players for the escalating challenges so they won't be hit by something out of left field that doesn't fit their current skill set or ability inventory.

The best way to do this is to introduce lesser but similar challenges earlier in the game, so players can "train" on those challenges. For example, if you have a boss monster that can only be hit in its one giant eye and only when the eyelid is open, introduce a lesser creature earlier in the game with a large, always-open eye that will only take damage when the eye is hit. In that way, you'll prepare the player for the larger challenge.

You don't want to introduce these lesser challenges right before you will give the players the main challenge—space out the proving ground from the crucible; otherwise, you'll be creating a pattern that is too easy for your player to deconstruct.

Story Serves the Game

Story is important to the game, but it should serve the gameplay, not the other way around.

Compelling stories can make for very compelling games, but only if the gameplay is solid on its own. Several years ago, there was a strong push for story-driven games, which lead to a host of games being created as vehicles for "large and interesting stories." Unfortunately, putting story first is like the old cliché of putting the cart before the horse. A game is not a story—a game is a play experience.

Fortunately, many designers have realized this and now work to blend story and gameplay in a way so the player gets a rich and immersive story while playing an interesting game.

Game branches should not exist merely as a vehicle for story exposition: every meaningful aspect of the game must have a gameplay element as well. The game should never pull control away from an engaged player to deliver a story element to the player. Cinematics can work well, but they must be placed at appropriate moments when exposition is called for, and not in the middle of play activity.

Think of your game, totally stripped of all story elements: is the game still fun to play? If so, you have the solid foundation you need to enhance the experience with a good story.

SUMMARY

In this chapter, we looked at some foundational elements of game design that we can use to create a solid and compelling play experience. We learned about goals, subvictories, and the need to offer variety and challenge to our players. We urge you to create your own list of atoms, phrased in your own terms, that you can use to build your own games going forward. As games move into new technologies and new genres, there will clearly be the need for new atoms upon which to build the next generation of games.

Our next step is to look inside your players' minds, to see what perceptions they will bring to bear on your game and how you can use this knowledge to help built the most effective and addictive gameplay possible.

CHAPTER EXERCISES

1. Think of a real-world game that doesn't seem to contain any, or many nested victories. Can you find those victories if you look closer? If not, how could you change the rules of the game to allow for nested victories?
2. Can you think of a particularly good example of a consistent interface in a game you've played recently? Can you think of an inconsistent interface in a game you've played?
3. Think of the general game design atoms discussed earlier—are there any you would add, based on your own design or play experience? Are there any you would cut?

8 Player Perceptions and Emotions

In This Chapter

- Player Perceptions
- Player Emotions

When a player sits down to play a game, there is a lot going on—on screen, but also in the player's gray matter. Information is coming at the player fast and furious, mostly visual and aural, and he is processing and reacting to that information in many ways.

In this chapter, we'll look at the stimulus a game sends out to the players and what they perceive and feel based on that stimulus. Exploring player perceptions and emotions will give us a deeper understanding of how the games we will design can affect and influence the player.

PERCEPTION

Not all people perceive things the same way, even when presented with the same information. Each person and each game player is unique. They arrive at a moment as a product of their past experiences, so what they see, hear, and generally perceive is colored by past information processing and their current state of mind. A tired person will perceive movement differently than a wide-awake player who just gulped down his fourth Mountain Dew. Understanding the perceptions of players is key to understanding their reactions and emotional involvement in your game.

Sound

We've placed sound first because it is one of the most immediate inputs players will receive from a game. Before they have focused their mind and their eyes on the screen, the interface, and their in-game avatar, players will perceive the sound and music of your game. Sound and music convey information, and are strongly linked to emotional reactions in game players. Aural input will rarely be the means of providing the majority of game information to a player, but used effectively, it can set the stage for the mood and tone of your game.

One aspect of sound to be aware of is that players have a great degree of control over how much sound and music they will receive in your game. When they are looking at your game screen to play, you can be generally confident that they will be seeing the game you envisioned. It's a different story on the sound end—the player has complete control over the volume of the audio output, and most games allow the option to toggle music playback on or off. That being the case, you never know how much effect the sound and music of your game will have on a specific player. Therefore, it often makes good design sense to think of sound effects and music as a supporting medium, adding information and mood to the game, but not delivering essential game information to the player.

Sound Effects

Sound effects are tactical aural output—they are specific, finite, and the result of some event in the game, such as the firing of a rocket, the explosion of a crate, the squealing of tires, or the clanking of football helmets. Sound effects exist to provide aural texture to the player (to make the world feel more real) and deliver information to the player. They are also effective at evoking a mood or emotion in a player, but this is linked more to the player's own interpretation of the sound effect (and the context of the game) rather than the sound effect itself.

When sound effects are used as texture (think of crickets chirping as your character walks through a field at night), they are perceived passively by the player. They work to contribute to the suspension of disbelief and the immersion of the player in the experience. During play, the player isn't directly conscious of these effects, although without them, the richness of the virtual world will suffer.

Event-driven sound effects provide an enhanced set of realism to the game, and vital feedback to the player. When events cause sound effects, it sends a subtle, subconscious message to the player that the world is working as it should. Of course, the sound effect has to match the event, or the effect will be quite the opposite. If a car slams into a brick wall and explodes, the sound of air being let out of a balloon will be very jarring for the player.

Player immersion is enhanced by event-driven effects because it sends a message to the player that his actions can affect the world. This pulls the player deeper into the game and creates a very important sense of power in the player—he can hear that what he does matters. The player's actions have meaning, and it serves to elevate his sense of power and urgency in the game.

Sound effects also deliver important information to the player. Event-driven sound effects often support something that is primarily indicated via something visual on screen. However, sound effects can also be used to provide information on what is happening beyond the screen space. Generally, these are still triggered by game events in some way, but they are not events occurring visually on screen—the sound of a door creaking open, for example. If the player is not looking at or opening a door at the moment, that sound effect sends the information that someone (or something) is opening a door he can't yet see.

In action games, especially first-person shooters (where the visual viewing area is quite limited), sound effects are a powerful informational tool, especially when they are positioned via stereo or three-dimensional sound. They can alert a player of the progress of an advancing opponent or what might be happening behind a closed door.

Music

For thousands of years, humans have had a strong emotional attachment to music. The flow of rhythm through time and the change from tone to tone create the sense of music as a moving, changing, and yet organized sensory perception. Our minds are hard-wired to react to rhythm and tone, and because of that, music is a powerful vehicle to deliver emotional responses (Figure 8.1).

FIGURE 8.1 Humans can be emotionally affected by music.

Play a fast rhythm and the heartbeat accelerates and the listener becomes anxious. Play a slow beat with a soothing melody and the heartbeat slows and the listener is calmed. Between these extremes lies a virtually infinite array of possibilities to evoke mood in a game player.

In the game world, music is one of the most powerful tools we have. The players will perceive music almost unconsciously, while they are engaged in the action of the game. Yet, while they are receiving the music, it is affecting their mood and their interpretation of the game tone and the current game situation. Music can be used to "set the tone" for a change in the game environment, and, as is in movies, to call attention to a certain moment in time.

It important to know that music, since it is often an "always on" type of output, will be perceived by the players while they are simultaneously receiving other input from your game. That means that the music has to "know" its role in the game at any given time—when the player should be concentrating on puzzle solving, character interaction, and when the player should be concentrating on music.

In general, music is an ambient perception—it is in the background and processed by the players passively while they are doing other things. The volume level should not overshadow effects or interface sounds, and the music should not have a rhythm or melody that distracts the player.

Movement

The next most obvious perception for a player, after sound, is the visual perception of movement. Even without full attention to what is going on on the screen, a player's eyes can pick up movement on and across the game screen. Our mental processing of visual input is hardwired to pay special attention to movement (since it may signify food or a threat).

It's no accident that instrument dials in cars have the face and the hands set in contrasting colors—that way, drivers can see a rapid change in an instrument out of the corner of their eye while their full attention is on the road.

Movement catches the attention of a game player and alerts him to some change in the game state, from either an action in the virtual world or some change in the interface. A game screen that remains static doesn't send the player any triggers or information telling him where to pay attention. A static screen quickly becomes an uninteresting screen and the player may lose interest in what is going on in the game.

Conversely, a screen that assaults the players with too much movement will only confuse the them and won't direct their attention in a meaningful way. Confused players quickly become frustrated and, again, lose interest.

For most games, the screen area is split between interface elements and a "window" into the game world. Both of these elements can use movement to alert the player to game situations that require his attention. As a designer, it's important to think of these elements separately (since they convey different information) but also together, since you don't want interface movement pulling the player's attention away from vital movement information happening in the game world or vice versa.

Generally, the primary area of player attention is the window into the game world, and the interfaces are of secondary (although vital) importance. Because of this, interface movement should generally be more subtle, not drawing the player's eyes from the area of primary attention. At times, though, you may want to pull the player's attention to an event on the interface. In that case, use of an exaggerated or eye-catching movement (or a flashing movement) coupled with a sound trigger can effectively grab the player's attention from the primary display.

QUAKE DONE SMALL

Designer: Paul Schuytema

Quite a few years ago, the first QuakeCon was held in Dallas, Texas. One of our 3D Realms fan Web site developers, who was also a gifted Quake® player, was coming down for the event and we invited him to our offices for a quick Deathmatch.

At that time, we had some of the hottest computers around: Pentium 150s with Rendition 3D cards. We could play with 3D acceleration (a very new thing in 1997!) and astounding frame rates (nearly 30 frames per second). We escorted our friend over to one of the new machines and set him up to play, but he immediately turned off the 3D acceleration and even though he was on a 21-inch monitor, he used the command to shrink the display area so it was about the size of a 3x5 index card. We thought he was nuts as we went to our machines and joined the game.

Over the next few hours, he pulverized us, racking up hundreds of frags. We weren't slouches, so the beating was painful. We stepped up behind him to watch him play. With the screen in software rendering mode and the display area so small, the screen just looked like a bunch of earth-toned pixels, yet as we watched, he picked off our team with ease.

We asked him what his secret was. He had the level memorized, so he always knew where he was, and the small screen size blotted out all detail

$\rightarrow$

except the change of a few pixels when an opponent was running past. That movement—that subtle change in the color field—is what he looked for. He could catch the movement easily, and aim, fire, and score a quick kill.

When playing *Quake*, part of the fun was imagining oneself in that alien world—to see the world in all its glory and become someone who truly inhabited that world. For our friend, the game wasn't about immersion, but rather racking up the points. He wasn't interested in being part of the world, but rather adjusting the world so it maximized his chance for success. His perception of movement was key, and nothing else mattered.

BATTLETECH PODS

Several years ago, Virtual World Entertainment ran a network of location-based entertainment centers that allowed players to step inside the cockpit of a giant anthropomorphic robot and battle other players in other robots. Of course, the robots were virtual, and the battlefields. Players actually sat in small, enclosed "pods" that simulated the cockpits of these robot warriors.

The final iteration of the pods was called "Teslsa Pods," and a player would sit in a flight-style chair, with joysticks for each hand and rudder pedals for the feet. What made the experience unique was the way in which the interface of the game was spread out over multiple screens and lighted controls (Figure 8.2).

FIGURE 8.2   The Battletech pod experience was all about overloading the player with too much information.

Straight ahead was the main view—our traditional game screen, but sans any interfaces. Below that were several green monochrome monitors that displayed system information. Surrounding the monitors were banks of lighted buttons and toggles used for engaging and configuring the weapon and defense systems of the battle robot.

During play, the main screen, the monochrome monitors, and the lighted buttons all flashed, moved, and displayed vital and constantly changing information. Everything else in the cockpit was black and the player was closed fully into the capsule. The cacophony of movement from the multi-instrument interface, coupled with the audio warnings and sound effects, created a sense of panic in the players. All around them were interfaces using movement and flashing lights to cry out for their attention and there was no way they could process all the information effectively.

For a computer or console game, this overuse of interface and screen movement would have been a disaster. In the context of the Battletech pods, it was exactly what the designers wanted. The chaos created by the interface created a sense of panic in new players, which was then followed by a rush of adrenaline as they worked feverishly to respond to the multifaceted controls. This process created a very effective primal emotional response in beginning players and provided a complex path toward mastery of the game. In this case, the overuse of interface movement created the desired effect.

Light and Color

The next most obvious perception for a game player is the reaction to the use of light and color in your game. With sound and movement, we're talking about something active that calls out to the player, demanding attention. The use of light and color is more passive—it is simply the makeup of the visual information on your screen.

Reacting to the specific content on the screen is a higher level function, and we'll discuss that in the section *Immersive Perceptions* later in the chapter. Now, we are merely talking about the interpretation of light and color by the player. One of the easiest ways to separate the content from the light and color is to blur your eyes and look at the screen of a game. When the specific objects disappear into merely areas of light and color, you are getting a rather pure perception.

Color itself is linked to many emotional responses, but the specific meanings of colors are often culturally specific. For example, in Western cultures, black is seen as the color of death, while in many Eastern cultures, white is associated with death. In our Western culture, white is associated with purity (hence the white wedding dress), while in India, red is the color of purity.

Levels of light and saturation of color, though, do have some universal reactions. Something that is made up of many bright, clear colors unusually conveys something optimistic and not dangerous. Conversely, a mixture of dark, muted colors and a dark environment reflect feelings of danger, fear, and oppression.

People also react to the grouping of colors—not in a specific emotional way, but rather reacting to the fit of the colors together. Colors that are combined from seemingly random locations in the color wheel can create a disjointed and dissonant message. Colors that fit together (such as complementary colors, or colors that are equally spaced out in terms of hue) create a sense of completeness to a scene.

As a designer, be aware of the player's perception of color and light, especially how the color of your interface elements blend together and how they fit with the primary colors seen in your game world.

Patterns

Like it or not, our brains are always working on something. We are always taking in sensory data and processing it in some way, either consciously or automatically. One of the most fascinating "automatic" operations of our brain is the act of detecting patterns in our visual and aural input.

Our mind is more comfortable with order and organization than with randomness and chaos. Looking at a painting by Jackson Pollack is an exercise in pattern recognition. As we view one of his classic drip paintings, our mind is looking for patterns in the shapes and colors—trying to work out an organized way to perceive the painting rather than as a myriad of chaotic squiggles of color.

One of the most basic pattern desires is for a simple source of order. We like to view or listen to things that feel like they are made up of discrete parts or components. We listen for recognizable note grouping in music. We look for repeating patterns in things such as architecture. We like to see elements that make sense and repeat when we watch a professional dance. At our core, we strive to deconstruct the world around us and to break it down into component parts.

A higher level but even more fascinating for pattern processing is our ability to see things that aren't there in seemingly chaotic or senseless visual information. Remember staring at the clouds as a child. At times, you would see a dragon, a castle, or a face. Our mind was searching to match components or parts of the chaotic cloudscape with similar components in our mental archive. If we see something that is a close match, we can "see" that object in the chaotic visual stimulus we are receiving.

As humans, some of the most important objects in our universe are other humans. As infants, we relied wholly on other humans to care for and protect us. As infants, we were very limited in our perceptions, and we could only "see" our important humans in a limited way, focused mostly on their faces. This is how we saw our mothers when nursing, and the components of a face were what we used to differentiate one person from the next. Because of this, one of our most refined forms of pattern recognition is the recognition of faces—in almost anything. A few lines scribbled on a paper, a fluffy cloud, wrinkles of fabric—anywhere we see a field of chaotic visual stimuli, our brain is searching for the components of a human face in it.

As game players, we also seek patterns. We look for movement patterns in the behavior of in-game enemies. We look for patterns in the layout of interfaces or environments. We look for patterns in the way we use game inputs to control our avatars.

Decoding a pattern in a game is a very satisfying experience for players, especially when the discovery of the pattern allows them to succeed and move on in the game on their quest for the end goal. At times, this pattern searching and recognition is unconscious, and at other times, it's very conscious. More often than not, the search for a play pattern in the game is unconscious—it is happening in the background as you play a game. However, the moment the pattern is discovered, it often snaps to conscious thought, and you are aware that you have just decoded something of importance. From there, you are aware and looking for the pattern as you attempt to move past the obstacle the pattern represents.

Immersive Perceptions

Immersive perceptions are the most complex, from an analytical point of view. In fact, it is merely what the player understands about what is going on in the game once he is immersed in the act of play.

Consider a player playing a first-person adventure game in which he is creeping through a medieval prison complex. His "in game" perceptions are complex, and act as if he has transported himself into the universe of the game. He notes the stone architecture. He notices a chest on the floor and steps over to it, hacks it open with a sword, and removes a small stash of gold coins. He hears a door creak open and a surprised shout—he reels around to see a guard carrying a battle-axe stepping into the room and advancing. He makes a quick decision: his sword is no match for the axe, so he turns and runs out the open door behind the table, hoping his speed will carry him to safety.

All of these perceptions are artificial—in truth, the player is sitting in a desk chair or on the couch and interacting with some form of game controller. However, when he is immersed in the game, he processes indirect, abstract perceptions into an experience of being somewhere else. This is a very powerful and fascinating phenomenon—blending both our innate ability to imagine ourselves in other places (as with daydreams or stories) with the very real perception of stimulus, but rather interpreting in such a way that it supports our "presence" in the artificial world.

Immersive perceptions, from a design point of view, are similar to real-world perceptions. If the player hears thunder and sees rain, he will understand it is raining. If the player sees a guard running at him with a battle-axe, he will perceive a threat and act accordingly.

The important difference is one of granularity. In our real and waking world, we perceive many, many small details, movements, and changes simultaneously. In a game, our perceptions are limited to generally two senses (sight and sound) and our resolution of experience is limited—we have no peripheral vision and we don't have enough visual detail to make out the dust in the corner of a room or a single strand of a cobweb.

Because of this, we need to strip the fictional world down to objects and events that matter in the context of the game (that is, they all have some meaning—in our waking life, most of our perceptions are meaningless). In addition, we want to have the objects, events, and actions of the game world be obvious enough to the player so he will notice them. Having a 3D model of a silent brown mouse hugging the wall and scurrying across the floor of a dark medieval room will do no good, since the odds are high that our player will not perceive it. However, by using exaggeration and contrast—such as a large rat, squeaking and with a contrasting color or obviously pink tail—the player will perceive the dynamic object and will be able to make a decision on how to interpret the entity and how to act.

EMOTIONS

In the previous section of the chapter, we explored the perceptions of a player in a game situation. We didn't explore how he reacts to those perceptions in a deeper way. When a player is playing a game, he is operating on two levels: on one level, he is working through the mechanics of the game using hand-eye coordination, problem solving, and pattern recognition skills. On another level, he is reacting to your game emotionally. The content of the game may be affecting him (the stories, the characters, and such), but also his involvement in the game itself will affect his emotions (he may experience frustration, excitement, a sense of failure or accomplishment). In this section, we will explore some ways in which a player will be emotionally affected by the game experiences you design.

Flow

Have you ever lost yourself in time? You started some activity and time just seemed to slip away completely—this experience is rare, but quite addictive. It's an experience that dedicated gamers long for—getting lost in a game for hours on end. To those around the gamers, they may seem like they are wasting their time, but for those experiencing the moment, it's something else entirely. It's the hallmark of a memorable, excellent game.

Author Mihaly Csikszentmihalyi, in his book *Flow: The Psychology of Optimal Experience,* has tagged this state with the name "flow." We've probably all called it by other names such as "lost in the moment," "dialed-in," "immersed," or simply "having fun." No matter what the label, we can all appreciate that moment of focus and concentration when the rest of the world seems to melt away and we are totally immersed in a given experience.

Csikszentmihalyi interviewed many individuals—from artists to musicians to laborers—and he found a common thread connecting the experience of "flow." When individuals were experiencing that mental state of flow, they were actively engaged in an interesting and difficult task. The state only occurred when an individual was actively engaged. Reading or watching a movie can capture the attention of a person, and pull him or her into the story, but those passive experiences do not create the state of "hyper focus" that is a hallmark of flow. When in that state, attention is so focused that the individual literally does not perceive any extraneous stimuli.

During our normal waking day, we are bombarded by stimuli and perception, and as we discussed earlier, most of this is meaningless. Yet our mind is very adept at processing data, so the processing of perceptions is ongoing, whether we are conscious or not. When we enter a state of flow, our attention is so focused that our mind literally stops all background processing of stimulus so that all attention can be paid to the task at hand. Because of that, we lose our sense of passing time, hunger, stresses, and worries. We are lost in the experience.

Csikszentmihalyi equates this state with the concept of "fun," but we think this is limiting the idea of fun quite a bit. As we explored in Chapter 1, there are many experiences we would call fun, and not all of them require us to be in the state of flow.

As game designers, though, this state of flow is the "Holy Grail" of game design. If you can create a compelling enough play experience that you draw in and engage the player so he enters a state of flow, you will have truly accomplished something wonderful.

Achievement

One of the most prevalent emotional responses from a game player is reacting to a sense of achievement or failure. During play, the player is aware of the goals he is trying to accomplish. These may be small, such as defeating a rogue infantry unit. They may be larger, such as winning a scenario or getting to the end of a level. When a player achieves something in a game, it generally generates a positive emotional response with an intensity related to the importance and the difficulty of achievement.

If you defeat an infantry unit by simply moving your own unit into attack range and dispatching them, you might react with a "Yes!" exclamation. If the enemy unit has been dogging your troops for the entire mission, and you are down to a single, badly wounded mortar team, and just before you are overrun, you launch a mortar that takes out the unit, the reaction may be more like "Take that! Who's your daddy now?"

The sense of achievement when you overcome great obstacles and finally achieve an important in-game goal is very powerful. Is very similar to the fist-pumping of a star soccer player as the announcer shrieks out "GOOOOOAAAAAAL!" (Figure 8.3.)

FIGURE 8.3   The moment of adrenaline-fueled success can be powerful indeed.

As a designer, you want to create multiple opportunities for this powerful positive reaction to achievement, but you also want to space those moments out, so the player also achieves the smaller but still satisfying moments of simple achievement.

Solving Problems

Humans love to solve problems. It grows out of our innate drive to recognize and decode patterns. Solving a problem or a puzzle can result in a feeling of achievement as we discussed earlier; however, the act of problem solving in and of itself is also very satisfying for a player.

When we engage our minds and attempt to work through an interesting puzzle or process, the simple act of discovery and deductive experience is often very pleasurable. It delivers a feeling of skill, mastery, and accomplishment along with the "Aha!" feeling of discovery. Problem solving also taps into our innate curiosity, because we need to explore the variables and components of a problem in a new way to unearth the solution.

Some players will work through problems or puzzles, but won't experience a deep satisfaction in the process (although they often will in the achievement of the goal: the solution). Other players may thrive on the process of puzzle solving in and of itself, and may even view your game as nothing more than a sequence to work through to get from one puzzle to the next.

Think of the groundbreaking puzzle *Rubik's Cube®*—the puzzle is fascinating and enthralling to some people and an absolute frustration to others. As a game designer, you will need to be cognizant of these two types of reactions to puzzle and problem solving, design the experience so frustration is minimized, but still provide the "meat" for the puzzle solvers in your audience (Figure 8.4).

FIGURE 8.4   Rubik's Cube is an addictive, fascinating, and often frustrating puzzle to solve.

Socializing

In the early days of electronic gaming, most of the socializing that went on was of the extro-game variety: it took place outside of the actual play of the game. Friends watched friends play on the arcade game, talked about high scores and shared the experiences through conversation.

That type of social experience is still vital today, both in the arcade and around the couch during a console gaming session. Now, that social interaction has expanded greatly. First was the introduction of multiplayer games, from taking turns to simultaneous play. Next, online games provided opportunities for people in disparate locations to get together into a single game session. Now, massive online persistent worlds will support thousands of simultaneous players with a persistence of game that spans many, many play sessions.

In this new context, social interactions are happening within a game world and structure, but the interaction may be purely social (two friends talking through their characters, but not necessarily "in" the game), or it may take place in the context of play (characters barking orders at each other as they attempt a squad level assault on another tribe's base). Social interaction is a very satisfying human experience, and many online game players cite that aspect of a game as the primary reason for playing. As humans, we are very comfortable with interacting with other humans through indirect means (letters, e-mails, telephone calls, telegrams, instant messaging, and such), so communicating with other humans through the vehicle of a game and game avatar isn't that alien.

As a designer, if you are creating a game in which multiple players can participate, be aware of both forms of communication: the game-related communication and the purely social communication. Make sure your game doesn't limit either of these so the experience can deliver a satisfying form of social interaction to the players, no matter what their goals are for communicating.

Responding to Character and Story

Stories can often trigger significant and complex emotional reactions. Since the dawn of the oral tradition, we've been reacting to the situations and characters presented in compelling stories. Most stories are presented in a linear form; that is, one event follows another and so on. Novels, plays, and movies all deliver their stories in a linear fashion.

Games are, by their nature, nonlinear experiences. The player's actions and interactions with the game guide the progress of the game. Yet games are a great vehicle to deliver stories to players. Done well, a story delivered through a game experience can generate powerful emotions in the player. The players are responding to all the perceptions and emotions of game play, but in addition, they are blending those emotions and responses with their reaction to the game story and the game characters.

Designers often ask the question, "can a game make you cry?" The answer is obviously yes. A well-crafted game affects the player significantly, and if we add to that mix a compelling story, we clearly have the ingredients to elicit tears from the player, or cheers or cries of rage.

The key, from a design perspective, is to seamlessly blend the reactions to the game and the reactions to the story so they feel, to the player, one in the same. We discussed in the last chapter that a story must serve the game (rather than the game existing as a vehicle for the story). In this context, we mean that the reactions of the player to the game should take precedence over the reactions relating to the story. A game story or character interaction shouldn't interfere with the player making the jump across the lava river.

Properly balanced, the reactions to story should take place during times when focused attention on the moment-by-moment game play is not essential. In this way, the designer can "weave" a tapestry of player reactions from both the game and the story, with story reactions delivering emotional punch and setting the emotional and expositional context of the game play elements to be forthcoming.

Unexpected Moments

As a game designer, one of your most important tasks is to think through all the possible combinations within a game and account for those in a meaningful way. That's called good, thorough design.

There are times, however, when players will discover things in your game that you never thought of. They may discover strategies or ways in which objects work together that weren't anticipated during development.

While gamers enjoy being immersed in the fictional context of a game, many gamers are also simultaneously aware that they are playing a game. And they are always looking for ways to "game the game"—to find shortcuts, cheats, and out-of-the-box solutions to game problems.

As a designer, this is either an exciting or a disturbing concept. On one hand, players may discover a way to "break" the reality of the game (perhaps they find out how to jump to an inaccessible ledge in a level that allows them to drop down into another room, but also see that the game world is just a visual façade), and hence become separated from the experience you have tried so hard to construct. On the other hand, players discovering new ways to play in the game world showcase the robustness of the game systems and celebrate the creativity of the players.

ZORK'S® MAGIC RAFT

Designer: Steve Meterzky

In Infocom's all-text adventure, *Zork I*, there was a rubber life raft, and an air pump you could use to inflate it. There were actually two raft objects: the uninflated raft (called, I think "pile of plastic") and the inflated raft (called, I think "rubber raft").

Zork (and many subsequent Infocom games) had a limit to how much "inventory" the player could carry. This was accomplished by giving each object a weight, and adding up the total weight of the objects in a player's inventory. If picking up an item put you over a weight limit, the attempt would fail.

$\rightarrow$

Some objects were containers; that is, you could put other objects inside them. The inventory weight check would take these nested items into account as well. The raft was, of course, a container.

Since the raft was two objects, if you were holding the inflated raft and deflated it, the inflated raft would be moved to nowheresville, and the deflated raft would be moved to your inventory.

Well, a player realized that he could load his raft with a bunch of stuff, and then deflate it, and the raft's contribution to his inventory limit wouldn't include all that stuff inside it, because it was all off in nowheresville. When he needed something in the raft, he'd just put down the deflated raft, inflate it, and there it was. Thus, he was able to effectively dodge the inventory limit.

At first, *Zork* implementor Marc Blank was horrified by this "bug," and started to fix it. But then he decided that it was so ingenious a way to get around the inventory limit, any player who thought of it ought to be able to use it!

Addictive Behavior

We've all heard our friends say, "Man, I'm addicted to that game!" What does that mean—to be addicted to a game? Addiction is, by definition, a drive so strong to do something (either good or bad) that we are almost powerless to stop it. Being addicted to a game means that we are compelled to go back and play the game again and again. We just can't help ourselves.

In gaming, addiction is the first byproduct of compelling game play. A game that isn't fun or compelling or doesn't provide interesting decisions won't be addictive at all. However, the addictive experience is also something more—it is the creation of a drive to get back into the game and try it again. This state is often created when a player sees progress toward a compelling goal, but does not reach that goal. Progress is essential, because a player who is "treading water" and not moving forward toward a goal won't see the benefit in the "just one more time" approach. If the player sees progress, but not yet full achievement, the drive will exist to pull the player back into the game.

The masters of addictive gaming were the early game developers at Atari. Games like *Asteroids*, *Battlezone*, and *Centipede* would suck untold quarters of out arcade players, and as soon as a game would end, they would drop in another quarter to play again. The design ideas behind these games were governed by the "crown jewels" of Atari (as they called them). These crown jewels of early game design were centered specifically on creating an addictive game experience. Simple game mechanics was rule one. An endless game with points as the meter of progress was rule two. And continued obvious progress (meaning more points earned) was rule three. The player could jump into the game, learn it in just a few seconds, and no matter how well he played, he could always do better. Because of the simple controls, the players always felt that more success was always just around the corner, and as they played, they could see their high scores growing. This created a fertile, addictive atmosphere that kept the quarters dropping. Of course, the on-machine display of the top-10 high scores was another tool—a lofty goal that immortalized a player for all to see—at least for a time.

Addictive gaming isn't always the goal, but creating those moments in your game when you can use the "carrot" of advancing achievement is a very important design skill.

Putting It Together

Now that we've talked about some of the ways people can be affected emotionally by games, the question is, how can a game designer learn to evoke these emotions? What can we do, as designers, to elicit an emotional response in the people who play our games? As a designer, you'll find yourself collaborating with other team members to create perceptions and emotions felt by players.

Emotional game play is a current buzzword in the games industry. Developers spend time trying to anticipate how a player is going to react to a particular stimulus on an emotional level. It's not just about resource management anymore; if a certain scene calls for the death of one of the player's teammates, it's important to ask about how that will affect the player emotionally. Was the deceased likable? Will the player be sad that he's lost a friend? Will the player laugh, because the teammate was despicable? If the player moves from a dark tunnel into a brightly lit forest, there is invariably some kind of emotional response, even if it's just a sense of relief.

As a designer, you may be tasked with documenting the emotional arc of a game, including stimuli intended to elicit specific responses. This may entail working with level artists, who will be involved in the process of establishing flow. If the game's supposed to create a sense of freedom, this needs to be reflected in the level design, perhaps using wide-open spaces to create that impression. If completing a mission is supposed to elicit a sense of seat-of-your-pants euphoria, then a series of puzzles or problems must be created for the player to feel victorious over something. This, too, must be reflected in the level design.

It's also important to work with sound designers and/or sound programmers when building a mood or perception. The visual impact of a dark room is considerably augmented by dead silence that's suddenly interrupted by the sound of breaking glass, as in the creepy Silent Hill games. The cheerful imagery of Animal Crossing is accompanied by childlike music and the use of a cartoony jibber-jabber sound when other animals talk to you.

It's impossible to predict exactly how someone is going to react to a stimulus or scenario, and we can't control the people who play our games. However, by giving careful thought to how people react to games, and by working closely with other developers (such as sound designers, composers, and level artists), you'll be able to design game play that's closer to the mark.

SUMMARY

In this chapter, we took a detailed look at the perceptions and reactions a player will experience when playing a game. We worked to order these perceptions as the layers in an onion, beginning with sound, then movement, and then the more detailed and complex perceptions. From there, we looked at the emotional responses of the player, which grow out of perceptions combined with the context of the game and the goals the player is trying to achieve.

The purpose of this chapter was to provide some insight into what's going on inside the heads of game players as they are playing your game. By understanding the perceptions and emotions of a player, you can better sculpt your design to achieve the player reactions you are looking for.

In our next chapter, we'll look at the concept of player challenge—how players deal with challenge in a game and how we can create challenging obstacles that match player skills and expectations.

CHAPTER EXERCISES

1. Consider a game play environment that uses three layers of sound to create a mood: ambient music, ambient sound effects (such as crickets in the background), and specific event-driven sound effects (such as the sound of footsteps approaching). What set of sounds would create the feeling of horror? How about a feeling of peace? How about anticipation?
2. Think of the last time you were "lost" in a game—can you articulate the specific aspects of the game that caused you to experience that moment of "Flow?"

9 ■ Player Challenge

In This Chapter

- Player Actions
- Game Flow
- Player Challenge

As we play a game, what holds our attention? What keeps us glued to the small screen? We remember things like gorgeous graphics, compelling stories, and richly textured sound tracks, but do those keep us coming back? The moment-by-moment "pull" to play a game is our desire to succeed over challenge. We enjoy encountering opposition and emerging victorious. We enjoy decoding patterns. We enjoy learning skills and then using those skills to clear the hurdles placed in front of us. As gamers, we long for challenge—sometimes difficult, sometimes easy, but it is the challenge of the game, the "pull back" effect, that keeps us playing.

PLAYER ACTIONS

Playing a game is called an "activity," because the player in engaged in doing something. A successful game doesn't have the players passively watching what is happening on-screen; rather, they are engaged in the ebb and flow of the game world in pursuit of both short- and long-term goals.

One of the essential rules of good game design is to make it painfully obvious what the player should be doing at any given time. Players should never have to question what they are supposed to be doing (unless, of course, they are currently in the middle of solving some sort of game puzzle). The challenge should come from attempting to achieve their goal, not in trying to find out what their goal is.

As a designer, you need to create an experience that is centered on the action of the player. The player should be actively engaged in the game at all times. Yes, that engagement will vary in intensity, but players should be engaged throughout their experience. Engagement pulls the players into the context of the game, and focuses their attention on the game situation rather than the real-life world around them. When you can grab and hold the players' attention, then you can begin to affect them with the experience of your game, from the skills needed for challenges to the emotions revealed through compelling storytelling.

To keep a player interested in a game, many variables have to come together. Some are clearly subjective: does the game appeal to their subjective likes (that's something that you, as a designer, can't control)? If so, does the game present a compelling situation and a series of goals that feel for striving toward? If the larger questions are answered, the player's involvement rests upon the moment-by-moment play of the game: does the game play feature the right amount of challenge (not too easy and not too hard)? Is the player actively engaged? Is the experience rewarding instead of frustrating?

When you think of everything that has to come together for a game to provide a compelling and memorable experience, it's no wonder that the truly "great" games are few and far between. In the last few chapters, we explored some atoms of good game design and spent some time considering the various perceptions and reactions a player has to the game and the game playing experience. In the coming pages, we'll explore the concept of player challenge, but the topic is moot if you first don't create a game experience that is based on player action, both mental and physical.

GAME FLOW

A game experience is something that occurs through time, and during the time of the game, be it a single sitting or a long game made up of many nights, the experience has a beginning, middle, and an end.

In many ways, a game experience is similar to a story experience (either as a novel or a movie)—the player moves forward toward a goal, overcomes many obstacles (that often tend to get increasingly challenging) until he reaches the final conflict in an attempt to achieve the final goal. In this way, movement through a game is very similar to the escalating plot diagram we've all seen so many times in our writing and literature courses.

If we were to chart it out, a game is actually more like a plot diagram for a novel, in which the overall movement is upward, but the path is broken up into smaller pieces, each with its own peak (the moment of most intense conflict or challenge) and valley.

Consider the venerable old arcade classic *Asteroids*® for a moment. The game begins very slowly, with only a few large asteroids slowly tumbling on screen. As you destroy the large asteroids, they break apart into smaller and faster moving pieces, creating a more intense challenge until you destroy the last chunk of rock—then you have a few seconds of respite and the screen comes alive again with even more large asteroids. This process continues until you lose all of your lives. What's the end goal? It's besting your last high score. As you move closer and closer to your score, the tension and excitement mounts until that last moment at which you see the Game Over screen and are rewarded with a high score or simply dismissed as an also-ran (Figure 9.1).

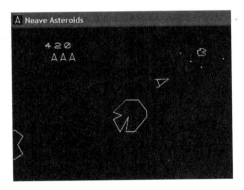

FIGURE 9.1 Game play in the style of Asteroids offers escalating challenge, but properly paced with periods of rest and lower intensity.

If Asteroids simply ramped up continuously with more asteroids and faster speeds, with no rest periods, the player would fatigue quickly, and cresting those recurring moments of intensity would be impossible. Asteroids is also a great example of a game in which the player is constantly doing something (moving the ship and firing), but the intensity varies through time. The player is always engaged, but the dramatic pacing of the game keeps the player refreshed and ready to play on toward the ultimate goal of a new high score.

CHALLENGE

The overt goal of any game is to overcome an obstacle. We call that "being challenged," since it requires some skill or luck or some combination of the two to clear the obstacle. A game is a progression of obstacles, from start to finish, woven together in the tapestry of a context that allows the whole thing to make sense for the player. Maybe it's a game about coming of age as a samurai warrior—perhaps it's a game of racing cobbled together cars in a post-apocalyptic future, or perhaps it's simply seeing how many red marbles you can shoot out of the advancing snake of marbles. No matter how you slice it, challenges abound.

Consider the game of darts for a moment. Do you remember trying to play as a child? Back then, it was a major feat just to get the dart to stick in the dartboard—that was a whopping challenge. Imagine if that's all there was to darts—just sticking a dart in the board. If you would pick up a set of darts now, hitting the board is child's play—you'll hit it every time, with minimal effort. The challenge is there, but you've mastered it, and so the game becomes rather silly (just like tic-tac-toe), and after a few tosses, you'll be done for good.

As players, we long for a variety of challenges in a single play experience and enjoy being tested as our skills grow. In darts, we test ourselves by going for the triple 20, or closing out an entire number with one round in the game variation called Cricket. In interactive games, we also long for a variety of challenges and multiple tests of our newfound skills as we work our way toward ultimate victory. In the pages that follow, we'll explore some ways in which we can create a compelling and challenging play environment for our players. (Figure 9.2.)

FIGURE 9.2 The darts game of Cricket allows the player to select the level of challenge and risk for each shot.

Escalating and Varied Challenges

Nobody wants to endlessly repeat a challenge he or she has fully mastered. In real-world sports, seemingly simple challenges like throwing a shot-put, running 400 meters, or driving a golf ball all have very many layers. Dedicated golfers work for years on perfecting their swings, and professionals have to work on their swings constantly, because there are so many variables at play that even a small change, like gaining or dropping five pounds, will have a profound effect. For these kinds of activity, the challenge comes in the pursuit of consistency and continuous improvement, and therefore the interest level can remain very high.

In a computer game, the level of the challenge is limited by the input a game can receive and the output we can deliver to a player. In a real-world golf swing, we have the setup consisting of club choice, the foot position, the grip, and the angle. During the swing, we have the changing in center of gravity, the use of the various arm muscles, the rotation of the club face, the speed of the club head, the stability of the golfer's head and shoulders, and on and on. We may have the same controls in computer golf for the setup (minus the grip, of course), but for the swing, we simply have the timing of some key or button taps. The level of control and feedback is far, far simpler, and because of that, the mastery of the simple timing task is not that difficult.

Because of this, players want different types of challenges in a game—they want variety and the chance to prove their acumen with existing skills through increasingly difficult challenges.

Because the variables in interactive game input are so limited, a single challenge rarely has the opportunity for constant and continuous interest and improvement, like the real-word analogues of the golf swing or the shot-put. New challenges need to be presented to the players that test their core skills and require greater and greater levels of proficiency.

If we evaluate the classic FPS shooter games from id software, such as *Wolfenstein, Doom,* or *Quake,* we see the escalation of challenge very clearly. Each game consists of a number of levels (the subgoal is to make it to the end of each level). The obstacles in the player's way are monsters or enemies, and the player will face monsters with more hit points, faster speed, and more deadly weapons as he moves forward in the game. Along the way, the player will grab weapons with more and more firepower and unique methods of attack. The core skills remain the same: moving in the game world and firing effectively at the targets (the enemies).

The variation in weapons and enemies creates varied challenges using the same core skill set, and the increasing power (both defensive and offensive) of the enemies creates an escalating challenge for the players. As they get more comfortable and adept at the core skills, the game will continuously throw at them challenges that will test the boundaries of their skill. In this way, the player can easily learn basic mastery of the game's core skills, but can remain entertained and interested in the game from level to level.

As a designer, you will always want to keep a strong conceptual handle on the core skills you are asking your player to learn. Throughout the players' time in the game, they will become quite adept at these skills (at the same time, they will also become comfortable and confident in their abilities in the game). It's your job to hold their interest by offering a variety of challenges that relate to the core skills, and to increase what you are asking from the players, in terms of proficiency, as they move deeper and deeper into the game. In this way, you will have your primary moment-by-moment hook to hold the players' attention.

Throwing new skill requirements at the player, especially if they are not related to each other, isn't generally an effective means to hold the player's interest, since a wide range of skill requirements diminishes the ability to develop mastery with a smaller skill subset. As humans, we generally are more satisfied with a situation that allows us to demonstrate our mastery than a situation that is simply different for difference's sake.

Risk and Reward

What feels sweeter, finding a trophy on the sidewalk or earning a trophy because you competed hard in the decathlon and bested all comers? Obviously, earning a reward carries with it the most sense of accomplishment. Now consider this: is it more sweet to have simply competed well in the decathlon and earned third place, or to have risked it all in the pole vault, trying to smash your own record (or fall terribly) and snatch first place?

As humans, we thrive on accomplishment, but we also enjoy feasting on the rewards of the risks we take. As game players, we are no different. It's no accident that nearly all of the red armor power-ups in *Quake* are located a long jump over some toxic substance. You didn't need the armor to continue, but it gave you a great advantage, *if* you were willing to risk the jump.

In game design, effectively challenging the players with numerous risk and reward opportunities is a great way to keep them engaged, and it's also a great way to provide numerous small subvictories within the play experience.

Stated simply, a risk and reward opportunity is a chance to earn something optional, but beneficial in a game. Succeed in the challenge to earn the object, and you will be better off than without it. Fail in the challenge and you will be worse off than you were before. It's a classic dilemma that can be represented very effectively in a game.

To effectively balance a game, often the reward, in terms of magnitude, is of lesser (although still important) value than the cost of failure. The reason for this is to keep the player's power balanced once he achieves the skill to snatch up a particular reward easily. If you allow the player to easily get too much of an advantage, the challenge of the game drops off drastically and you risk losing the player's interest.

Adaptive Challenge

One of the most interesting approaches to creating a challenging play experience for a player is to create a system that allows the game to adapt to the player's proficiency. This is called Adaptive Challenge, and it was first seen in some of the dog-fight and racing games of the early 1990s.

The classic example (and where this sprang from) is the racing game in which an unskilled player was lapped many times by the computer opponents, with no chance to ever win the game. Designers came up with the idea of putting a variable "governor" on the speeds of computer opponents, based on how far ahead of the player they were. The computer drivers may race past the player, but once they got a half lap or so ahead, the game mechanics would slow their average speed. In this way, they wouldn't gain a huge advantage over the player, and the human had a chance to catch up once they felt comfortable with the game. Once the human got close enough, the computer players would switch back to standard control again.

As a general concept, adaptive challenge mechanics are great tools to keep the player competitive, but you need to be careful so the player can't easily "see the man behind the curtain." You don't ever want the player to feel the artifice of a computer opponent losing and gaining skills. You will want to be as subtle as possible so the challenge posed by the game's computer opponents feels as natural as possible.

To design an adaptive challenge system, you will need to have some way of measuring player proficiency in a specific way. An example would be a percentage value for shots fired when dog fighting in a WWI biplane. This can very easily be calculated at runtime, and is a relatively accurate measurement of how well the player is doing (you will have to develop some baseline thresholds during the development process by play testing the game, so you will know what ranges are beginner, normal, and expert). In the case of a WWI dog-fighting game, when a player performs with a beginner rating, you may want to slightly slow the speed of enemy planes, or reduce the tightness of their turns or simply their selection of aerial maneuvers. If the player is in the expert range, you can do the opposite: increase the speed, tightness of turns, and maneuver variety to deliver a compelling challenge to a skilled player.

When you choose to modify computer opponent behavior to lessen or enhance the degree of challenge, always be sure to do so within a variable range, and one that isn't drastically out of whack with their normal behaviors. If you always cut the speed of the race car by 15 percent, the player will soon recognize the pattern, and it certainly isn't an interesting pattern at all—it will lead to frustration as the player realizes that you are "playing games" with his opponents. On the other hand, say if a computer opponent reduces his speed by 10–18 percent when he reaches a corner (at the normal level) and you are going to slow him down a bit, make the new range something like a 15–25 percent reduction in speed. In that way, it will be hard for the player to precisely determine any change in behavior, since "normal" and "easy" overlap nicely.

The real challenge isn't determining how to enhance or hamstring the computer opponents, but rather how to measure and evaluate player performance. In our dog-fighting example, the performance measurement was relatively straightforward. In other situations, it may require some study. Consider an example of a first-person shooter game. You have many weapon variations, and as players get skilled, they tend to prefer one weapon over another. A player may like a weapon that dispenses tons of shells to spray his opponent, because he likes to fire when running. If we look at a hit percentage, the numbers may call the player a beginner when in fact he may be quite skilled. Perhaps looking at something as average kills per minute, or average health rating, may be more applicable.

In open worlds with many, many interacting variables (such as an epic RPG game), assessing player performance can be quite challenging. Do you record the rate at which experience points are gained? The level and variety of weapons and treasure in his inventory? The number of quests, secrets, and encounters experienced? One of the most interesting challenges, as a designer, is to develop a system for monitoring performance that feels natural. Once you have that in place, or at least a first pass, test it out with many players on your team, to see if you are correctly assessing player proficiency. From there, it's a relatively easy next step to modify opponent performance to match the challenge with the player.

Boss Encounters

Many games used the tried-and-true approach of challenging a player with a "Boss" at the end of a portion of the game play. A boss is an opponent who stands apart from the vast majority of in-game opponents, in scale, ability, and behavior. A boss encounter is a test of the player's skills at that point and a chance for the player to prove skill mastery before continuing in the game. Often, the defeat of a boss will also reward the player with power-ups, weapons, and abilities that will be needed (and will help vary the challenge) in the next section of the game.

Since boss encounters have such a long history in game design, and are very effective tools to deliver those peaks of player challenge, they are encountered in many games. There are a number of battle-tested design rules and observations for creating a boss encounter, and we'll cover those here.

The boss should fit within the context of the game world. While the boss will stand out from the other "minions" the player has encountered in the game, the boss should feel like it is a natural part of the game world and context. In fact, boss encounters are also great story-telling moments.

The boss encounter is generally longer than a standard enemy encounter. Generally, a boss encounter lasts four to five times longer than an encounter with a standard enemy. The experience is meant to be a serious, long-lasting challenge for the player, so don't let it end too quickly. Play testing is the best way to gauge the duration of the encounter; you don't want the encounter lasting so long that you create player fatigue and frustrations.

The boss creature should dominate the player's attention. During a battle with the boss, the player should not be challenged by other entities in the game. Often, the best way to do this is to place the boss encounter in an "arena" environment—once the player enters, it's just the player and the boss, and only one can be left standing.

A boss battle should require constant player input. Beyond simply dominating the player's attention, a boss encounter should require the player to be continuously thinking and working. Generally, the players' strategy will begin by being evasive, as they try to decode the behavior of the boss, and will then switch to a combination of offensive and defensive activities as they hopefully chip away at the health of the boss on their way to victory. Keeping the players always doing something, for the short burst of the encounters, is a great way to get their heart pumping and to create that adrenaline rush that you hope to create during those moments of climax in a game. (Figure 9.3.)

FIGURE 9.3 Battling a boss is designed to be a more intense experience than regular game play and it is often comprised of several "acts."

The boss delivers a substantial offensive punch against the player. A boss encounter is special, and so should the risk and danger be for the player. Getting caught by the full offensive firepower of the boss should be very, very costly for the player. You have to deliver sufficient offense so that even the best-prepared player has to stay on the move and be defensive (and hence, more actively engaged in the encounter). It's also generally a good idea to make a boss' attack have a longer duration and be slower to track the opponent than he can move—in that way, the player can get "stung" by the boss's attack, but still have time to escape and survive within the same attack session.

There should be opportunity for the player to regain his advantage during the encounter. A boss encounter is long and the boss is deadly, so you need to provide a means for player recovery in the boss arena. Nothing is more frustrating for a player than to get whacked once by an attack and realize that he is doomed. Pepper the environment with health and ammo power-ups so the player can recharge. This will also enhance the player frenzy during the encounter and keep the energy level high.

The boss should exhibit a complex, but pattern-based form of behavior. To keep the player interested, a boss should exhibit a far more complex behavior than the enemies the player has met to date. This behavior should be pattern based, since one of the keys to defeating the far more powerful boss is the deconstruction of the pattern and the ability to use that knowledge. A well-done boss encounter is one of those great combinations of frenzy and puzzle solving, and that's why it has been such a successful design tool for so many years. Embrace the pattern aspect of boss behavior and use game play testing to refine it. The pattern should not be immediately obvious to the player, nor should it be too difficult. In addition, the hallmark of a quality boss encounter is when the player still has to work quite hard to defeat the boss, even when the pattern is decoded.

The boss often presents multiple targets to the player. While this is not always the case, the majority of boss encounters feature a creature or device that has multiple targets that need to be destroyed by the player in order to beat the boss. This generally allows for the creation of more complex behavior patterns, and creates some variety to the challenge the player faces.

Victory should deliver a moment of rest for the player. The boss encounter is intense, and clearly one of the peaks in the flow of a game, so when the player defeats a boss, the action should slow and allow the player time to catch his breath and gather the spoils of victory. Often, the arena itself will be the location of respite—perhaps there is a pause before the exit door unlocks or a simple danger-free puzzle for the player to solve before he exits. No matter what the mechanism—be sure to give the player the chance to take five before continuing.

The path to replay a boss should not be overly long. Because of the challenge inherent in a boss encounter, players will often be forced to battle the boss several times before they are victorious. Make sure the player doesn't have too far to trudge after being defeated by a boss and is forced to try again. Having them traipse through an entire level of your game before the encounter is only a recipe for frustration if they are defeated again.

Be aware of player frustration. Boss encounters are complex and ask a lot from the player. Therefore, be aware that the encounter is an opportunity to easily frustrate the player. Play test boss encounters relentlessly, especially against unskilled players, so you will be able to catch the burrs in the design that will lead to increased player frustration.

Other People

Hard-core game players have long lamented the predictability of artificial intelligence. They long for serious challenge, and after logging hours upon hours of play against artificial intelligence, they've seen it all. Several years ago, there were a few multiplayer games on the market that allowed real humans to play against each other over a LAN, and at times, the Internet.

Games like *Doom, Quake,* and *Duke Nukem 3D* all ushered in a new era of play, and the challenge was intense, since it was player against player. The experience was visceral, but it was still a new, rather esoteric way to play. All that changed in the late 1990s, when the beta of Counter Strike, a "mod" of the Half Life game, hit the Internet. Broadband and quick dialup connections were on the rise, and Counter Strike created a military first-person play environment based on the concept of player specialties. Players could play with different specialties, across a number of different scenarios. The game could also be set up to run autonomously on a server, and anyone could hop into a game and play at any time. By 2002, there were nearly 30,000 Counter Strike servers running on the Internet—the era of true Internet multiplayer gaming had begun.

In the years since then, we have seen the rise of the massive-multiplayer games, such as *EverQuest*®, *Star Wars Galaxies*®, and the *World of Warcraft*®. On the action front, we have immersive games like Battlefield 2 taking up where Counter Strike left off. While many of the persistent world games appeal to social gamers, there is also the element of challenge that comes with games that pit humans against each other. Players become engaged for a long period of time if they are presented with a series of interesting and varying challenges that pull from a related skill set, and players get frustrated when they can too easily decode the patterns and behaviors of the obstacles. (Figure 9.4.)

Multiplayer gaming presents a variety of challenges based on player skill sets, but the fact that the in-game avatars are controlled by other humans, rather than artificial intelligence, means that the encounters will be far more varied and interesting for the players. Players can talk with each other, scheme, and play off each other's strengths and weaknesses. Play often breaks out into team versus team, and the dynamics become even more complex and interesting for the participants.

FIGURE 9.4 Nothing offers more depth-of-challenge than battling another skilled human player online.

As a designer, creating an experience for multiple player challenge opens up many possibilities, but it also poses some limits on what you can realistically expect players to do. A multiplayer experience (we're talking challenge here, not specifically role playing or social gaming) features many, many variables interacting at once (the human players), and the complexity of the dynamic computer controlled entities in the world should necessarily be lessened, to keep the focus on the player experience. In addition, multiple players tend to want a quicker player experience. They may want to play for hours on end, but usually in a series of shorter missions. Multiplayer gaming tends to be more intense, moment by moment, so the short sessions are essential to fight player fatigue. The players usually rest and regroup as they prepare for the next mission or scenario.

One of the most challenging aspects of multiplayer game design is creating a play experience that presents interesting challenges to players of multiple skill levels. There are worlds of difference in skills and abilities between a seasoned player and a "newbie" online player for a particular game. Toss them together with no thought of balance and the experience will be sour for both parties.

One simple form of balancing is to create some sort of ladder or rating system outside of the game proper, to serve as a guide to place players of similar abilities together in games. This is a tried and true approach that can be the most direct means of skill-level balancing.

Another approach is to provide some sort of handicapping system in game (the approach taken by *Quake 3 Arena®*). You may want to enhance the damage done by lesser players or reduce the damage for the more skilled players. You'll need to be careful, whenever you are hamstringing a player's ability, that it "feels" right in the context of play. Only direct play testing (and lots of it) can really answer the question, "does this handicap system seem fair?"

No matter what the context, done well, a multiplayer game experience can provide a very compelling series of continuous challenges for players without the need for complex computer opponents or artificial intelligence.

Multiple Variables

What makes a game challenging? We've talked at length in this chapter about the concept of challenge and the various ways we can deliver dynamic obstacles to our players. However, what, in a challenging situation, makes it feel like it is a worthy obstacle?

Game obstacles feel too easy when we can quickly learn the skills needed to overcome them and see "what makes them tick." To escalate the level of challenge so it is interesting to the player, the obstacle needs to be defined by more than just a few dynamic variables. The more variables that define a given situation, challenge, or obstacle, the less likely it will be that the exact same obstacle will present itself again to the player. Variables interacting together create a fluid, alive-feeling game world to the player.

As a designer, when you are creating dynamic obstacles for the player, be sure to represent those obstacles, be they environmental or full-fledged computer opponents, by a number of variables, each generated by different world circumstances. This will create a blending effect that will make your world (and the challenges you create) more natural and organic.

You will want to avoid overloading your obstacles with too many variables—a situation that will be hard to debug, and hard to decipher by the player. While the players want variety, they also want to come to an understanding of how the game world works. If you have the behavior of a rogue Orc AI determined by 15 or 20 world variables, the player won't be able to determine what to do.

Casual Game Challenge

More and more players are flocking to casual games. While hard-core gamers often dismiss casual games as a small slice of the gaming pie, their numbers actually make up the largest population of games in the United States, with millions upon millions of players.

Casual games are often defined as having a short playtime (5 to 15 minutes), and a very easy-to-learn skill set. Most casual games offer a tutorial mode that will teach a new player the core skill set in just a few minutes. From there, play begins in earnest.

Progress is often measured in either points or levels solved or beaten, and the escalation of challenge follows the arcade model of more and more complex situations based solely on the core skill set mechanic. As the player is able to advance, he is able to process more variables and more variation in the puzzles and challenges encountered.

When designing a casual game, think carefully about the core skill set. This needs to be simple, yet interesting enough so it will hold a player's attention through many levels of play. Often, this skill set is based on pattern recognition—recognizing words, letters, or similar colored objects. To create an interesting challenge curve, consider a pattern-recognition skill that works both with simple and more complex and varied situations (Figure 9.5).

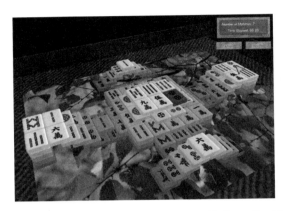

FIGURE 9.5 Pattern recognition skills fit well with casual games such as Mahjongg-style tile matching.

Simply escalating the variables in the same skill set can lead to a boring game experience, so the best casual games also introduce wrinkles in the game that make it more interesting as complexity increases. These are generally represented in terms of positive and negative power-ups that change how you search for and play out patterns. The idea is to keep the players active and interested and always looking for new ways in which to decode the next move in the game to give them the greatest impact.

Casual games may seem simple at first, but it's that simplicity that makes them a challenging and interesting design challenge. You have to accomplish a lot of play value with only a few skills and challenge variations, and you need to create an experience that is addictive rather than tiresome.

Challenging the Player

As a working designer, it will fall upon you to ensure the player feels suitably challenged by the interactive game experience. The sense of achievement that pulls the player along, the escalating tension that becomes the player's impetus to try the next mission—these are yours to create.

The process of developing challenges is an iterative one, dependent on feedback and objectivity. Often, the Quality Assurance department tests games for overall game play, and defects and bugs. QA reports may contain information about a game's difficulty, be it too easy or too hard. Individual missions may deviate from the overall difficulty curve in unacceptable ways, causing the player undue frustration. Imagine a first-person shooter with three levels of enemy artificial intelligence (for the sake of this example, easy/medium/hard). If the first few missions feature a gradually increasing number of enemies with "easy" AI, but the next mission features significantly more enemies, imbued with the next level of AI, the difficulty level has made a radical transition. Rather than easing the player into a new challenge, you have sharply increased the amount of work that must be done to complete the game. This specific decision has disrupted the game flow, and has created an escalation of challenge that creates more frustration than enjoyment.

When the QA testers report such findings to the design team, it's important to remain objective. There are always reasons for including a feature, or for making a particular design decision; however, if the result is not satisfying to the gamer, the rationale is of secondary importance. What matters is finding a way to keep the challenge fun and interesting.

Another factor with regard to the creation of player challenge is the structure of the game arena. For linear games with a clearly defined progression, it's much easier to control the player experience. A game like *Halo 2*, which pits the player against a series of ever-increasing threats, is an excellent example of well-developed player challenge. The game features a well-paced flow, moving the player from firefight to waypoint to firefight, enabling the player to feel tension and release, risk and reward. Boss encounters, such as the *Scarab* (the massive walking building), serve as transitions from one phase of the game to the next.

Now, consider these tools when creating a nonlinear game such as Grand Theft Auto 3, whose numerous mini-games (taxi driver, vigilante, street racer) can be played in any order. The game's designers managed to exert an impressive amount of control over the player, while offering a great deal of freedom to explore and interact. When the player passes through certain areas, rival gangs appear to be pretty oblivious at first. However, once the player has performed certain missions, the rival gang members become hostile. It's possible to play the mini-missions for hours without triggering this hostility, but once the player has executed that primary mission, the game's difficulty has escalated: when passing through rival territory, the player will always be fired on by an endless supply of enemy gang members. Even though GTA3 doesn't feature the linear and easily predicted game play, they managed to set parameters to define the user experience, guaranteeing a challenge that evolves with the player.

SUMMARY

In this chapter, we took a long and in-depth look at the challenges we present to the player. We examined how an active player is an interested player, and explored the need for escalating challenge to hold player interest, and the need to include some respite time for the player to recover.

We explored the need for players to be presented with risk and reward choices, to allow them to take a chance to earn that special power-up or ability. We also explored ways in which we can design player obstacles that respond to player performance, to better tune their experience with their ability. We also looked into some rules and approaches to developing compelling encounters with boss opponents as peak challenge moments in a game experience.

We then looked at ways in which other human game players can create constantly varied challenge opportunities. Finally, we looked at casual games to analyze the challenge in these deceptively simple but insanely popular types of games.

With this chapter, we wrap up Part II of the book. We now have a handle on the skills we need to be effective designers, and some of the abstract design issues we'll need to work with as we design actual games going forward. We'll now move on to Part III, where we dive in close to examine the various aspects of a game from a designer's perspective—and we'll do this within the context of our own game.

CHAPTER EXERCISES

1. Pick a common real-world game you are familiar with and play—maybe it's golf, darts, basketball. Imagine that you have total ability in this game; you are so good it's just not a challenge anymore. How would you augment the rules of the game to add challenges?

2. Imagine a computer game of Air Hockey. How would you design a computer opponent to provide adaptive challenge for the player? What performance parameters would the computer opponent log to know when it was time to ratchet up the challenge level? What variables would you adjust to provide a more vigorous challenge for a skilled player?

3. Look over the "Boss Atoms" and think through your own experiences battling boss entities in games—should any of the atoms be discarded? Are there any new items that should be added?

Part

III

Real-World Game Design

Okay, you've survived game theory. In the last section, we looked at some of the theatrical underpinnings of game design, challenge and player psychology. Now it's time to turn our attention to more practical, in-the-trenches game design issues.

In Part Three, we'll look at some of the major aspects of real-world design, from user interface design to puzzle design to creating a campaign structure and game story.

Along the way, we'll introduce more "atoms" of game design—little rules, suggestions and red flags to help you make the best design decisions. While our atoms may not cover every possible scenario or type of game, you'll come away with a good foundation of rules and tips that can be applied to a professional game design. Along they way, we'll look at design document examples and learn how we can incorporate the ideas into the documents we write in the future.

We'll also use our "sandbox" game, Eye Opener, to demonstrate the implementation of many of the ideas we discuss. Eye Opener will serve as a tool for you to peer "under the hood" and look at the continuum between game design, game scripting and actual implementation.

The examples are meant to introduce you to concepts, but they aren't meant to be static. Since we are working with a simple scripting language (Lua), you are encouraged to dive in and mess around. Change things—add things—use the tools to make your own game demo. Learn and have fun! (You'll also find additional resources for your under-the-hood tweaking on the CD-ROM.)

Time to roll up your sleeves, get that pencil sharpened and let's dive into some real world game design . . .

10 User Interface

In This Chapter

- Interface Atoms
- General Interface Design

Now it's time to dive in and get our feet wet with some very practical aspects of game design. We'll turn our attention in this chapter to the user interface in a game. The UI, as it's often called, is the vehicle in which the game communicates to the player, and vice versa. A UI can enhance a game experience or can frustrate players so much that they walk away from the game.

We'll begin by exploring some atoms for successful interface design, and then we'll roll up our sleeves and dive into our Eye Opener game and learn how to use our game engine and LuaScript to create our own interfaces. While we'll cover some specific examples in this chapter, and in the chapters that follow, feel free to dive in and try your own thing as well. The game engine provided with this book is a "sandbox" for you to play in—so let yourself have some fun while you are learning!

INTERFACE ATOMS

Game interfaces come in many shapes and styles, running the gamut from Windows®-like menus to fully 3D animated buttons and displays. No matter how an interface looks, the goal is the same: to provide vital information to the player. While there are many approaches to interface design, we can distill the principles of good design into a small set of atoms, or rules, which will help us design the best experiences for our players.

The interface should act as expected. This may seem obvious, but it is one of the foundational elements to good design. A game interface is primarily visual, and in these days of multilanguage localization, the visual use of iconographic elements is even more important (since you don't have to translate an icon, if it's done well). The elements of an interface should operate in an obvious manner for the player. A magnifying glass icon implies a zoom function; a disk or file folder implies a file operation, and so on. There is no need to force "creative" icons for obvious tasks, just to show off some unique art. Players will scan your interface, so make sure they come away with a clear idea of what the most obvious buttons and controls do. Also, don't forget that your players were raised in a world surrounded by Windows® icons, and they will come to your interface with expectations based on visual representation. You don't want to stray far from what they expect (Figure 10.1).

FIGURE 10.1 Windows toolbar icons are great when they behave as expected.

The interface should remain consistent. Humans are creatures of habit— once they figure out how something works, they want it to work that way all the time. Be aware of this in your interface designs: don't confuse the player by having different ways to do essentially the same thing in different parts of your game. If you use a horizontal scrolling queue of images to view swords to purchase, don't switch to a vertical queue when you enter the alchemist's shop. If the Enter key is the same as a mouse click on an Okay button, make sure it works that way throughout your game.

The interface shouldn't ask the player to remember. Computers are very good at recalling information; humans aren't. Complex interfaces should remember what the player did last, and present those values when the player re-enters the interface. Never ask a player to type in a value that was displayed on an earlier interface. If you are presenting the player with a complex interface task, make a help screen a single click away. For some games, like complex RTS or "god games," you may be asking the players to make decisions based on complex world data—if so, provide simple one-click avenues to access the relevant data they will need.

The interface should inform the player of the state of the game world. Game environments are very dynamic. Often, the player will be able to understand the state of the game world from the main screen area, but at times, that information may not be so obvious or easily represented by pure game world imagery. In those cases, the user interface can be used to inform the player about what is happening in the game world. The small green health bars above units in an RTS game are a perfect example: they are UI elements used to visually display vital information about the health of individual units in a way that just isn't practical to do through the main game display (sure, you can have an injured unit limp or crawl, but how visually informative is it when you have 20 limping units on screen?). The user interface is a tool to receive player input, and to report the goings-on in the virtual world to the player. The player should be able to quickly understand what is going on in the game world by a quick overview of the game interface.

The interface should provide layers of information. As mentioned previously, the interface should provide, at a quick glance, an overview of what is happening in the game world. What is the player's health? How close is he to a next level? What are your gold and stone reserves? What is the score? How much money do you have? All of this is vital, top-level information. A quality interface design also provides a drill-down option that will allow a player to, at his own choosing, view more detailed information concerning the state of the game world. Think of a quality RPG game you have played: top-level information on your avatar/character is at your fingertips, but with a few clicks, you can view inventory, spell lists, skill lists, and more. Think of the Age of Empires series—during play, you can always call up charts to see the status of your civilization in relation to the other in the scenario. Not vital for the moment-by-moment play of the game, but important for formulating longer-term strategies (Figure 10.2).

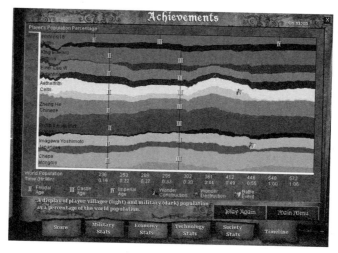

FIGURE 10.2   The Age of Empires games allow players to access detailed, although not essential, information when they want it. Used with permission. Copyright Microsoft Corporation 1999.

The interface should alert the player of vital changes. A game world is a dynamic system, and as the players overcome obstacles, they will be changing the game world and game state. They may have new mining units available for use, or their health may drop to a dangerous level during a battle with an ice demon. During play, vital pieces of information reflect the most urgent aspects of the changing game world, and these should be reported to the player in a dynamic manner. Important information that requires the player's immediate attention should "call" to the player. This may be an audio cue (like the "swords on shields" sound played in Age of Empires when a battle begins somewhere on the map), or a visual cue on the interface (such as a flashing health bar when the player's health drops below 10 percent). You will want to test out some different cues for the player, but once you determine an "alert approach" that works, be consistent and use it for all alerts, be it an audio cue, a flashing object, or an alert dialog box. Just be sure to have your interface communicate back to the players to help them take care of important decisions in the game.

PULLING THE PLAYER AWAY

Designer: Paul Schuytema

Sometimes, you learn more when you do the wrong thing when designing a game. When we were working on *Castles & Catapults*, a casual 3D RTS set in the Middle Ages, we struggled with how to alert the player when one of his armies entered into a battle. In the game, the player only had three armies, so a conflict was a big deal. Often, the player would be concentrating on commanding one army while another army, off screen, encountered the enemy. How should we let the player know?

A member of the development team came up with an approach that was simply the wrong way to go: when an army first started fighting, we took camera control away from the player and slid the camera over the terrain to the just-engaged army. At first blush, this sounded like a reasonable solution—after all, you would want to do something about your army that was just being engaged. In practice, it was awful—more often than not, you were paying attention to an army to get it ready for something important; and pulling the player away from his current activity, without his permission, was flat out

→

invasive. The feature received such flak that the publisher actually posted a page on the game's Web site saying that it was a feature, not a bug.

In hindsight, an aural cue or a flashing visual indicator would have been the way to go—we already had hot key controls to slew the camera to each army. The players could receive the cue and then act as they see fit, not as the development team decreed.

The interface should protect the player from errors. This may seem obvious, but it is also essential: don't let your player introduce errors into the game through the interface. The interface should check all input it receives and reject anything that will cause a game error. If the interface asks the player how many tanks to build, and the player inputs "gggg," the game shouldn't crumble. Players are notorious for clicking wildly and just exploring the interface, even when components of it are not being used at the given time. Don't let out-of-sequence player actions introduce errors. Also, if possible, segment your interface so only the relevant portions of an interface are displayed at any given time (the tabbed interface approach in Windows is a great example of this).

The interface should reflect and enhance the tone of the game. The most important role of your game interface is to deliver and receive input to and from the player. However, the interface is also a game component that will be on screen most of the time the game is being played. The game world may change dramatically during play, from winter mountains to a dank dungeon to an arid desert, but the interface will remain. Keep this in mind and allow the game interface to represent the visual style and tone of the game. If you are designing a medieval game, don't have an interface that looks like burnished aluminum—choose a stone or wood motif instead. Use the interface as a tool to shore up the tone and feel of the game, from the interface textures to the sound effects the interface will generate. (Figure 10.3.)

The interface should not overpower the game screen. Keep your interface small, but usable. Keep the vital information front and center, and don't overpower the data or screen real estate with fancy ornamentation or graphical elements. As a designer, it's always a good idea to collect screenshots of similar, successful games, and study the design of their interfaces. Look at how information is presented, and study the use of simple, elegant designs. You can have a visually exciting interface that does not overpower the screen—simple doesn't have to mean boring. Just remember that the players' eyes will be taking in

FIGURE 10.3   In Shadow Warrior, the simple interface used elements like the samurai sword and the yin/yang symbols to maintain the feel and tone of the game. Used with permission. Copyright 3D Realms Entertainment 1997.

many things simultaneously, and they will be constantly scanning the interface—do not make it confusing or overly complex. A tried and true approach is to mute the color range in the background interface elements (the parts of the interface that aren't presenting vital information) and to punch up the color and intensity of the areas of the screen that are delivering information to the player.

The interface elements should provide feedback if they are activated. A player will interact with many aspects of your screen. Some components will be purely visual and informational output, but interfaces also receive input from the player. This input may be a button click, a menu selection, text entry, or a key press. When players interact with the interface, provide feedback so they know they have done something. Have multiple states for a button (the general set is up, down, and hover), and link a button click to a sound effect. Highlight a cursor position in a list and make sure you have a visible flashing cursor where you are accepting text input. The players will be doing many things quickly during the play of a game—so be sure to let them know your game received their input, so they can move on to their next task.

KNOW YOUR USERS

Designer: Tom Hall

We did an interface for Commander Keen in "Keen Dreams," which was really a mouse-based interface. But at that time, a lot of people didn't necessarily have mice, plus the game wasn't a mouse-oriented game. So if you had a mouse, you had to switch over to it, then switch back to play, then switch back to save your game. If you didn't have one, you had to dorkily move the cursor around with your joystick. The point of this story, kiddies, is, just because you're excited about something doesn't mean it's appropriate for the game you are working on. Keep the end user in mind.

GENERAL INTERFACE DESIGN

You have a game interface to design and you feel comfortable with rules and guidelines, so where do you start? What's the next step?

Front-End Interfaces

When players load a game, they are rarely tossed into the fray immediately. Nearly every game experience gives players some choices to make before they embark fully upon the game experience. This may be as simple as starting a new game or loading a saved game, or it may be as complex as creating a full RPG character. No matter the genre of the game, the first interactive experience a player will have with your game will be the front-end interfaces.

Design

From a design standpoint, front-end interfaces are relatively easy to manage. There are certain questions that need to be answered before your game can fully launch, and the front-end interface is your tool to receive the initial decisions from your player.

Your first step is to determine what information you want to retrieve from the players before the game starts. Some is mandatory, such as do they want to start a new game or load a saved game? Other information may be optional, such as what bit-depth do they want for the color? What volume for the music? And so on. Optional information should not be placed in the players' way as they are getting ready to play the game—you should generally relegate those decisions to a different interface screen.

There are also other key actions for the player that are generally accomplished in the front-end interfaces, such as exiting the game, viewing development credits, and such.

Once you know what information is optional and what is mandatory, you can design the player's path through the front end. The general rule of thumb is to get the players into the game as quickly as possible—don't distract them with too much to read or look at—they bought your game to play it.

The front-end interface may be straightforward to design, function-wise, but it is very challenging visually. Often, a designer will work with an artist to fully design these interface screens. During most front-end interfaces, the entire screen is the interface (rather than a small portion of the screen when the player is in game). This provides a significant visual design challenge, and a significant artistic opportunity. These interfaces are the first stop in your players' journey, so they are a great place to begin to set the tone and feel of your game. If you are delivering a steampunk style of game, you can use large areas of screen real estate to showcase the pistons and gears of that genre.

The front-end interfaces do not ask too much from the player, concentration-wise, so you have an opportunity to further enhance the mood and feel of the game through music. In game, you'll want your music to be supportive and ambient, but in the front end, you can step the music up to front and center.

Eye Opener Implementation

Now it's finally time to roll up our collective sleeves and dive into some design issues with our very own game: Eye Opener. Eye Opener is a simple game, so our initial requests for player information are very simple indeed. We want them to choose between starting a new game, loading a saved game (we only have one save game "slot" for this game), exiting the game, or viewing the credits.

The first place to start is with pencil and paper—jotting down the information we need to have on that first front-end screen and making some quick sketches of what we might want the screen to look like. Since our tone is modeled off a black-and-white comic book, we want to first establish that in the main screen. A great approach is to have the buttons drawn in a comic book style—this will connect the tone with the form and function of the game. We also want to present the player with some visual sense of the main game character (our friend the Eyeball) (Figure 10.4).

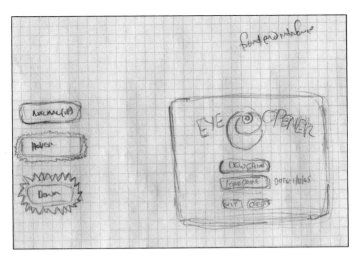

FIGURE 10.4   A rough first-pass sketch for the Eye Opener startup interface.

With the initial sketches done, our next step is to mock up the interface. For years, we've used Microsoft's Visio®, a chart-making program that allows a designer to put together a simple plain-Jane mockup of an interface in just a few minutes. With just a few objects, we have our mockup. A Visio mockup is a great image to present to an interface artist, because it clearly conveys the vital information and objects you want to present to the player, but doesn't impose any artistic style or interpretation, so the artist is free to do what he or she does best.

A Visio mockup can also do double duty as a prototype interface. You can simply export the Visio document as a bitmap, slice the components out of the image, and use them as a prototype interface object. That's what we'll do first, as we learn the Lua command to control our interface. (Figure 10.5.)

General Interface Control

ON THE CD

You'll find builds of our game on the companion CD-ROM. The builds are broken down to correspond with the chapters in Part III of the book. Each chapter may have one or more builds. Take a moment to locate the first build for Chapter 10. You can either run the build directly from the CD-ROM or copy it onto your hard drive and run it from there (you'll need to copy it to your hard drive if you want to edit and modify the Lua scripts).

When you run the build, the program will create two windows: the game window and the Lua console. The game window is what we are most interested in, but

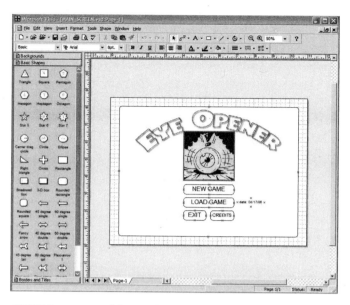

FIGURE 10.5 A Visio mockup is a first pass to lay out an interface.

the Lua console is where the game engine will report errors. We can also run command-line Lua from here, and examine or change game variables at runtime (we'll explore this in more depth later).

When the game first starts, it will run the StartGUI.lua file. Open this file and look inside. Near the end of the file, you will notice these two lines:

```
RunScript("Scripts\\LuaSupport.lua")
RunGUI("GUI_Main.lua")
```

The first line will run a script. In this case, we are running a script called "Lua Support," which contains many of the functions we will use in the game. The next line will run a GUI Lua file and will set that interface as the current interface. In this case, we are loading the Main GUI, which is the first screen we see in the game.

Whenever we wish to load a different complete interface, we will use this command to load the interface and make it the current interface, which means the game engine will respond to its items, such as buttons and text boxes.

The Main GUI Objects

Now, load the GUI_Main.lua file. This interface file contains the elements that make up the static and dynamic objects for the first interface screen of our game. If you look at the screen when it's running, we see that we have a white background, a game logo, several buttons, and some text (Figure 10.6).

FIGURE 10.6   The main interface running in our test engine.

Objects that don't directly take user input but display images on the screen are called *sprites*. Later in this section, we'll learn how we can manipulate sprites to make the active objects of our game, but for now, think of them as simply static objects. We generally define sprite objects at the start of an interface file, like this:

```
SetCoordTrans(800,600)
—100s Sprites
—white background
CreateItem(GUI_MAIN + 100, "Sprite", "white_box.jpg")
SetItemPosition(GUI_MAIN + 100, 0, 0, 800, 600)
—logo object
CreateItem(GUI_MAIN + 110, "Sprite", "game_logo.jpg")
SetItemPosition(GUI_MAIN + 110, 105, 0, 590, 300)
```

The first command is found at the start of every interface file of our game—it sets up the size of the game screen with which we are working. It doesn't actually change the resolution, but allows us to use numbers to define where objects will appear on the screen. For this game, we are working with a screen size of 800 pixels wide by 600 pixels tall.

We next define a sprite for the white background. By default, the game draws nothing and the screen is black. To have a white screen, we need to cover the screen with a white image. Since we are using a solid color here, we have a small, 32 × 32 pixels white image that we stretch to cover the entire screen. We start with a `CreateItem` call. We provide an ID number to identify the object. We use a constant (`GUI_MAIN`) and an ID number. The constants are defined in StartGUI.lua. We do this to ensure that all our objects in the game have unique ID values. This isn't such a big deal for a simple interface, but it will be very important when we have a lot more going on.

We then tell the `CreateItem` function that we wish to create a sprite and pass it the name of the image file (which must be in the Textures directory). We can use bitmaps, jpeg files, or even Targa files, if we wish to have an object with an alpha channel.

Next, we call the `SetItemPosition` function to place the object where we want it on the screen. We identify the object by the ID number we used when we first created the object. We give it the horizontal and vertical position (in an 800 × 600 screen) of the upper-left corner of the object; for the white background, that's 0,0. We then provide the size as width and height values; for the background, it's the full 800 × 600 screen. For the logo, it's a smaller 590 × 300 size. The game engine will stretch or compress the image to fit the size you give it. For the best visual results, you'll want the size in game to be the actual size, in pixels, of the source engine.

We'll next define an initial text item that will hold the date of the last save-game file. As we build our game, we'll eventually have this text object display information based on the save-game, but for now, we'll just enter a string ourselves. The text definition looks like this:

```
—200s Text objects
—date of last open
CreateItem(GUI_MAIN + 200,"TextField")
SetItemPosition(GUI_MAIN + 200, 550, 440, 550, 100)
SetFont(GUI_MAIN + 200, "Arial", 20)
ItemCommand(GUI_MAIN + 200, "SetColor", 0,0,0,255)
ItemCommand(GUI_MAIN + 200, "SetString", "date: 01/16/06")
```

For a text object, we create it and place it as we did with the sprites. We can then set the font. We use the text name of the font we wish to use that's found in the Fonts folder. This folder contains the bitmap that defines the font visually and the data file that tells the game engine how to draw the different letters (actually, the location and size of the letters in the image file).

We can then issue commands to our text object to define it even further. The first is `SetColor`, which allows us to specify RGBA attributes for the text we display. The RGB values range from 0 to 255. The A value is the alpha value, or transparency. A value of 0 is fully transparent, while 255 means fully opaque.

Our final items in this mockup interface are the four buttons. These are images we just pulled out of our Visio mockup, so we could get something up and working quickly. The button definitions look like this:

```
—300s Buttons
CreateItem(GUI_MAIN + 300, "Button", "uib_new_game_up.jpg",
   "uib_new_game_up.jpg", "uib_new_game_up.jpg")
SetItemPosition(GUI_MAIN + 300, 260, 350, 280, 64)
CreateItem(GUI_MAIN + 310, "Button", "uib_load_game_up.jpg",
   "uib_load_game_up.jpg", "uib_load_game_up.jpg")
SetItemPosition(GUI_MAIN + 310, 260, 420, 280, 64)
```

```
CreateItem(GUI_MAIN + 320, "Button", "uib_exit_up.jpg",
"uib_exit_up.jpg", "uib_exit_up.jpg")
SetItemPosition(GUI_MAIN + 320, 260, 490, 130, 64)
CreateItem(GUI_MAIN + 330, "Button", "uib_credits_up.jpg",
"uib_credits_up.jpg", "uib_credits_up.jpg")
SetItemPosition(GUI_MAIN + 330, 408, 490, 130, 64)
```

Again, we use the `CreateItem` function to create the interface object, We first assign an ID number and then tell the function that the object will be of the type "Button." We then provide the artwork for the buttons' states. The function takes three images for the up (which is the normal state), hover (when the mouse cursor is over the button, but no button is clicked), and down (when a mouse button, left or right, is clicked on the button). Since we are just doing a quick mockup, we will use the same image for all states—we won't see any visual change on screen, but the functionality will be there.

Handling Events

In the preceding section, we looked at how we created some basic GUI items in our game engine for the Main interface screen. While these objects will appear on screen just fine, we still need to script some means to receive input and act on that input. We do that by creating a special function called an "event handler" for each interface we create.

Events are sent by the game engine; they may be sent because of interface actions or actions in the game codes. The engine variation we are using is basic, so we have a small set of events that are listed in the StartGUI.lua file:

```
— Standard LuaGUI event codes
GUI_EVENT_BUTTON_UP = 0
GUI_EVENT_BUTTON_DOWN = 1
GUI_EVENT_SELECTION_CHANGED = 2
GUI_EVENT_TEXTFIELD_CLICKED = 3
GUI_KEY_PRESS = 4
GUI_REENTER_INTERFACE = 5
GUI_TIMER_EXPIRED = 6
GUI_ENTER_INTERFACE = 7
GUI_TEXT_SCROLL_END = 8
GUI_EVENT_TEXTFIELD_RETURN = 9
GUI_EVENT_HOVER_TIMED_START = 10
GUI_EVENT_HOVER_END = 11
GUI_MOUSE_BUTTON_DOWN = 12
GUI_MOUSE_BUTTON_UP = 13
```

The StartGUI.lua file just assigns constant names to the numbers that represent the various events, so the script will be easier to read.

To create an event handler function for an interface, first we have to declare the handler name in the GUI file (GUI_Main.lua) with this function:

```
SetEventHandler("MainMenuEvent")
```

This tells the game engine that the function MainMenuEvent should receive all GUI events when the Main interface is the active interface. Our next step is to define and configure the function to process the input. We won't cover everything now, but we'll add a few events to get us started with this interface:

```
function MainMenuEvent(id, eventCode)
    if eventCode == GUI_KEY_PRESS then
        if id == 27 then — Esc
            QuitProgram()
        end
    end
    if eventCode == GUI_EVENT_BUTTON_UP then
        —Exit button
        if id == GUI_MAIN + 320 then
            QuitProgram()
        end
        —Credits button
        if id == GUI_MAIN + 330 then
            RunGUI("GUI_Credits.lua")
        end
    end
end
```

We begin by defining the function itself using the function keyword. The end of the function is indicated by an end keyword. Everything in between is script that will run only when the function is called. You can see from the function that it processes two values: id and eventCode. The id is the ID of the interface object that is sending the event. The eventCode is the numerical value that represents what was sent from the engine (from the list at the top of the StartGUI.lua file).

To process events, we set up a small conditional for each major event (capturing the event first) and then identify the object that sent the event. Look at this section of script:

```
if eventCode == GUI_KEY_PRESS then
    if id == 27 then — Esc
        QuitProgram()
    end
end
```

Here, we enter the conditional if the event was GUI_KEY_PRESS, and then we can check to see if the key pressed was the Escape key (with an ASCII value of 27). If it was, the QuitProgram function is called and the game will exit. We do the same thing with a button click:

```
if eventCode == GUI_EVENT_BUTTON_UP then
    —Exit button
```

```
      if id == GUI_MAIN + 320 then
          QuitProgram()
      end
      —Credits button
      if id == GUI_MAIN + 330 then
          RunGUI("GUI_Credits.lua")
      end
  end
```

Here, we capture the button click event GUI_EVENT_BUTTON_UP (this event is triggered when the player releases a mouse button with the cursor within a GUI button object on screen). We can then issue different commands based on which button was clicked. In this case, the Exit button will call the QuitProgram function, while the Credits button will launch the Credits GUI, making it the active interface.

Enhancing the Button Art

Often, as you are working on a layout or interface design, you get an idea of how an interface element might look in the finished game. When a moment of inspiration hits you, grab a sheet of paper, sketch out your idea, and run it past your art director. Odds are, your art director will be able to see and understand the look and feel you are going for—even more so if you are discussing it with him or her as the idea is fresh in your mind. From there, they will be able to come up with a prototype or implementation that will bring your idea to life.

With our game, the idea came to create a button style for the interface that kept the rough pencil-drawn comic style the game will possess, rather than a clean and "formal" button approach. We quickly sketched the idea on a scrap of graph paper and showed it to Austin, our artist for this game. By looking at the rather lame sketch, discussing the idea with and seeing the prototype interface screen in action, he was able to understand the look we were after. Soon, he showed up with a set of wide and square button images for the three button states (up, down, and hover) that were better than we had imagined.

To implement the button, we will break it into two parts: the text, and the button itself. In this way, we can use the same art assets for all the interface buttons.

For this example, we'll only alter the New Game button. First, we need to get the art into a suitable format. Austin delivered the work hand-drawn, so we needed to scan it in and slice the images up so we could use them effectively. If we were doing a professional game, we'd have a 2D artist work on refining the digital images so they were totally spot on.

With our art for the three button states saved to the Textures folder, we are ready to modify the button script. We only need to edit two lines:

```
CreateItem(GUI_MAIN + 300, "Button", "uib_wide_button_up.jpg",
"uib_wide_button_hv.jpg", "uib_wide_button_dn.jpg")
SetItemPosition(GUI_MAIN + 300, 290, 310, 233, 106)
```

All we are doing here is swapping the "uib_new_game_up.jpg" filename (which we used for all three button states) for the three new images that represent each of the unique button states. We then edit the size of the button and the XY position to make it fit properly on the screen. (Figure 10.7.)

FIGURE 10.7 The main interface screen, now sporting a hand-drawn button.

At this point, we have a new button that responds visually. We move the mouse cursor over the button and the button will display the hover state. Click, and we see the down state of the button. The button isn't very useful, since it doesn't tell the user anything. We need to add a new text element to the button to tell the user it's for the New Game function:

```
CreateItem(GUI_MAIN + 200,"TextField")
SetItemPosition(GUI_MAIN + 200, 342, 350, 550, 100)
SetFont(GUI_MAIN + 200, "Arial", 30)
ItemCommand(GUI_MAIN + 200, "SetColor", 42,181,52,255)
ItemCommand(GUI_MAIN + 200, "SetString", "NEW GAME")
```

There is nothing tricky here at all: we are simply placing a text object within the bounds of the button so it looks to the user like the text is on the button. We colored the text so it matches the frame around the game logo (so the whole screen isn't black and white).

Informational Displays

Once a player gets into a game, he will leave behind the full-screen front-end interfaces, and his attention will turn instead to the moment-by-moment decisions that define the gameplay experience. During play, the player will require feedback and information, and this will be provided by dynamic user interface elements that must provide vital information but not stand in the way of his experience.

Design

The first step in designing in-game interfaces for the player is to take stock of what information you must share with the player. Begin with the most essential—what information the player *requires* to play at the most basic level.

Consider a basic RTS game in which you are controlling tanks on an open battlefield. What do you need to play the game? First, you need some sort of selection device, which is probably a mouse arrow. You also need to know if you have selected a tank—perhaps it's a tinting of the tank, a selection box, or perhaps the appearance of a health bar above the text. You also need to be able to tell the tank where to go—again, this is probably accomplished with some sort of mouse cursor or icon in the game world. Finally, you'll need to be able to tell the tank what to attack. Often, this is done in concert with a movement order—if the player indicates a section of ground with a mouse click, it is a movement order. If the player clicks on an enemy, it is a "move then attack" order.

Beyond this, nothing is essential to play the game. However, if you think through the overly simplified interface presented previously, it's not as trivial as it seems. The mouse controls need to be intuitive, and need to provide feedback (probably both visually and aurally) so the player is confident in his actions.

If we next think of important interface elements that support and enhance the player's ability to play the game effectively, we have some other information to consider with our example. The player would be well served to know the damage level of his tanks, so he doesn't send heavily damaged tanks into harm's way. The player also could use some information on the damage levels of his targets, whether absolute, like a health bar, or something more relative, such as black smoke pouring from a damaged target.

It is around these essential and important pieces of information that you should design your basic level in-game interfaces. The information should be presented in an intuitive manner, and ideally, the representation should be so obvious that the player doesn't need to read the manual to figure out what is going on.

When you are in the first stages of designing an in-game interface, you would be well served to spend some time looking at the interface designs and layouts of the best representatives of your game's genre. Explore the interfaces to look at things such as screen placement, size of interface elements, and how information is layered.

The interface during gameplay shows the vital information, and might also provide more in-depth optional information for advanced players or provide an input avenue for the player to perform some in-game functions. How you reveal and mask these elements to the player is key to the success of your interface. You clearly don't want to show the player all information all the time (will there be enough screen real estate left to show the game proper?), but you also don't want to make navigation to other elements of the interface an exercise in frustration.

As a designer, begin first with the most essential elements and then design access to the more detailed, optional, or operational elements the player will use during the game. Pay careful attention to grouping like information together, and allow your interface to prioritize information for the player, via size, color, and animation.

Reading some books on Web design and layout is a great way to begin to understand how a user's eye travels across an information-rich display. As you get a handle on what kind of look and feel you would like for your in-game interface, begin by sketching the information or using a program like Visio to lay out some first-pass attempts. Take those initial renderings and share them with your art director so the art department can begin to work on some first-pass implementations of your design.

It is a very good idea to prototype in-game interfaces as early as possible in the development process, so your development team can start using and testing them as soon as possible. You'll want to closely monitor how the interfaces are working—are they providing the correct information? Is the information clearly presented? Do the interfaces get in the way or enhance gameplay? Over many months, you can tweak and adjust the design, and your art team can refine the look so you can stack the odds in your favor for having a tried-and-true interface ready when your game is ready.

Eye Opener Implementation

The first step in designing our Eye Opener in game interfaces is to determine what essential information the players will need as they play the game.

First, the player will need to know the health of his in-game alter ego. Since our little rolling eyeball can augment his abilities with various powerups, we probably need some way to show that to the player. The player will also be able to interact with and select objects on the screen, so a mouse pointer is essential. From time to time, the player will have an opportunity to interact, via dialogue, with an NPC—

therefore, we need some way for the player to trigger that conversation. Finally, we need a way for the player to leave the game experience.

There are other important pieces of information we want the interface to convey, but we'll cover those later—for now, we have a handle on the most basic information that will allow our player to play the game effectively.

Let's consider the health of the eyeball for a moment—since this is a simple game, we won't be creating multiple "damage states" for our alter ego to show his health. Instead, we will show the health directly on screen via an interface element. Since we are dealing with a round object (an eyeball), why not reflect that idea in the interface element? After some initial sketching, we came up with the rather simple idea of a "gas tank-like" circular dial that is part eyeball and part instrument. The arrow works like the arrow on a gas gauge—it will move to the left as the health is drained from our hero.

We decided that we would place this object in the upper-right corner of the screen. We will be using the bottom of the screen as the ground plane for our action elements and for our inventory display for our adventure elements, so we want to keep that area free.

Let's look at how we set up the health interface. First, of course, was the creation of the art. In our front-end interfaces, we placed everything against a white background, so we could use pure rectangular images. In game, we don't know what will be behind the art, so we need to make our interface elements (the nonrectilinear ones) have an alpha channel so they will look proper against the background.

For this simple game engine, 32-bit targa files work best to display images with an alpha channel. We used Photoshop 7.0 to create the mask and export the targa so the square graphic would render as a circle on the screen. If you are creating your own art for some experiments with this technology, use whatever program with which you are most comfortable.

We placed the round background of the health meter with a familiar sprite script:

```
CreateItem(GUI_INGAME + 100, "Sprite", "uis_eye.tga")
SetItemPosition(GUI_INGAME + 100, 667, 30, 100, 100)
```

Our next element is the arrow. For this item, we created a simple hand-drawn arrow and placed it in a small image file butted against the left side of the image, since we will be rotating this object and sprites rotate about their middle. Again, we created a targa file with an alpha channel that hides everything but the arrow itself. We placed the object in the world, on top of the "eye meter" as follows:

```
ARROW_ID = GUI_INGAME + 110
arrowRot = 0
CreateItem(ARROW_ID, "Sprite", "uis_arrow.tga")
SetItemPosition(ARROW_ID, 663, 95, 100, 13)
```

You'll notice two differences right away. First, we created a constant to hold the ID value of the arrow object. We'll be referring to this object often in script, and this way we can more easily understand what we are controlling when we read back the script in several weeks time. We also create a variable called arrowRot that will hold the rotation of the arrow itself.

Before we dive into the other interface elements, let's take a quick look at how we handle the rotation of the arrow. Later, we'll blend this into the game logic, but this will give you a sense of what commands are controlling the object.

In our game engine, rotation is modeled in radians, so a complete circle represents the value of 2Π. Since we want our arrow to have an initial rotation, we will set this up during the GUI_ENTER_INTERFACE event with the following script:

```
arrowRot = 5.5
ItemCommand(ARROW_ID, "SetRotation", arrowRot)
```

This sets the initial rotation we want for the arrow with the SetRotation Item-Command. We can then set up the left and right rotation to a pair of keyboard inputs to test it out:

```
if eventCode == GUI_KEY_PRESS then
    if id == 91 then --[
        arrowRot = arrowRot + .1
        if arrowRot > 6.2 then
            arrowRot = 0
        end
        ItemCommand(ARROW_ID, "SetRotation", arrowRot)
    end
    if id == 93 then --]
        arrowRot = arrowRot - .1
        if arrowRot < 0 then
            arrowRot = 6.2
        end
        ItemCommand(ARROW_ID, "SetRotation", arrowRot)
    end
end
```

These small routines capture the [and] keys, add or subtract a .1 radian value from the current rotation, and then call the SetRotation ItemCommand. We put in checks if the rotation value drops below 0 or over 6.2, so we don't "overwind" the rotation. In this way, we ensure that the value is always within the value of 0 and 2Π.

Next, we'll add "out" buttons for jumping out of the in-game experience and for calling up a dialog with an NPC. These are hand-drawn buttons much like the New Game button we put in earlier. Again, we used Photoshop to turn the standard scanned-in images into targa files with an alpha channel. We then put the two buttons into the interface:

```
BUT_DISC = GUI_INGAME + 300
CreateItem(BUT_DISC, "Button", "uib_disc_up.tga", "uib_disc_hv.tga",
"uib_disc_dn.tga")
SetItemPosition(BUT_DISC, 636, 4, 50, 54)
BUT_SPEAK = GUI_INGAME + 310
CreateItem(BUT_SPEAK, "Button", "uib_speak_up.tga", "uib_speak_hv.tga",
"uib_speak_dn.tga")
SetItemPosition(BUT_SPEAK, 746, 4, 50, 54)
EnableObject(BUT_SPEAK, 0, 0)
```

For these buttons, we created constants with more easily readable names, so we can recall them easier deeper into the game scripting. Since the "speak" button isn't always relevant (it's only needed when an NPC is in range and can be talked to), we create the object, but set the `EnableObject` values to 0 to not render the object. Later, when we want to have the button appear, we use the command:

```
EnableObject(BUT_SPEAK, 1, 1)
```

Our final elements of this initial take on the interface are "slots" that will show the players, visually, what powerups and abilities they currently have. We'll begin by placing these as empty "holder" icons that we will then populate with icons for the collected powerups later:

```
—slot1
SLOT_1 = GUI_INGAME + 120
CreateItem(SLOT_1, "Sprite", "uis_slot.jpg")
SetItemPosition(SLOT_1, 640, 110, 30, 30)
—slot2
SLOT_2 = GUI_INGAME + 130
CreateItem(SLOT_2, "Sprite", "uis_slot.jpg")
SetItemPosition(SLOT_2, 675, 140, 30, 30)
—slot3
SLOT_3 = GUI_INGAME + 140
CreateItem(SLOT_3, "Sprite", "uis_slot.jpg")
SetItemPosition(SLOT_3, 725, 140, 30, 30)
—slot4
SLOT_4 = GUI_INGAME + 150
CreateItem(SLOT_4, "Sprite", "uis_slot.jpg")
SetItemPosition(SLOT_4, 760, 110, 30, 30)
```

See Figure 10.8.

SubGUI

In the next chapter, we'll look at managing inventory, but right now, it's clear that we will need some sort of "interface frame" from which we can manage our inventory, so we'll implement that now and introduce the concept of "subGUIs."

FIGURE 10.8   The Eye Opener in game display
we just set up.

In design terms, a subGUI is a user interface that "nests" within a larger interface. As a game player, you've seen them before; the interface that allows you to manage your equipment within the character screen of an RPG. The factory configuration screen within an RTS—basically, it's an interface that contains essential, but not always needed, information—can be hidden or called up as the player needs it.

Within our game engine, we can create a subGUI with Lua script. Let's look at the rather simple process. Think of a subGUI in our game as something that "lives within" one of our game interfaces. With some clever scripting, we can have almost total control.

First, in StartGUI.lua, we add another offset for our subGUI:

```
- Define GUI ID offsets
GUI_INGAME = 0
GUI_INVENTORY = 2000
GUI_MAIN = 10000
GUI_CREDITS = 11000
```

Here, we've defined GUI_INVENTORY as having an offset of 2000 for all the interface object IDs. We then create a new interface file for the inventory display, called GUI_Inventory.lua. For now, we'll simply have a container sprite (a visual frame we'll populate later) and a button to close the interface:

```
-100s Sprites
CreateItem(GUI_INVENTORY + 100, "Sprite", "uis_inventory.tga")
SetItemPosition(GUI_INVENTORY + 100, 0, 266, 800, 334)
-300s Buttons
BUT_EXIT_INV = GUI_INVENTORY + 300
```

```
CreateItem(BUT_EXIT_INV, "Button", "uib_inv_up.tga", "uib_inv_hv.tga",
"uib_inv_dn.tga")
SetItemPosition(BUT_EXIT_INV, 745, 306, 58, 58)
—Event handler
function InventoryEvent(id, eventCode)
    result = 0
    if eventCode == GUI_EVENT_BUTTON_UP then
        if id == BUT_EXIT_INV then
            ClearGUI(GUI_INVENTORY)
            result = 1
        end
    end
    return result
end
```

Most of this is pretty familiar fare—we use the new interface offset and create the sprite and single button element. There are a few key differences, though. First, you'll notice that we don't declare the event handler function—this interface is actually part of the GUI_Ingame interface, so it will use that even handler as the master control function. We do have an event handler, but it is just set up as a standard function.

Notice at the start of the handler, we have the line:

```
result = 0
```

This sets up the function to have no result by default. Notice that when we process the button click, we have the line:

```
result = 1
```

This sets the result variable to say that something happened in this subGUI. We then pass the result variable out of this function.

Let's look at our GUI_Ingame script now. We've added a line to the start of the script:

```
—dofile calls for sub-GUIs
dofile("Scripts\\GUI_Inventory.lua")
```

This calls and runs our new interface file from within Ingame, which is the active interface. We now add a simple control structure within the event handler (we add one of these for every sudGUI we have under a single master GUI):

```
if InventoryEvent(id, eventCode) ~= 1 then
—event handler goes here
end
```

This control structure first runs the special event handler for our subGUI, and then checks to see if anything was handled. If we pass back a value of 1 (which we do if the function actually does something), this structure will bypass the entire event handler for InGame. If InventoryEvent returns a 0, nothing happened in that subGUI, so the InGame handler works as normal.

The last two pieces of the puzzle are found in LuaSupport.lua:

```
function ClearGUI(id)
    for indx = 100, 999 do
        EnableObject(id + indx, 0, 0)
    end
end

function RestoreGUI(id)
    for indx = 100, 999 do
        EnableObject(id + indx, 1, 1)
    end
end
```

These two simple functions will take the offset for a subGUI as a parameter, such as ClearGUI(GUI_INVENTORY). In this case, the function will quickly loop though all possible IDs within a subGUI and disable the interface elements. Only the IDs with actual interface elements will be affected—otherwise, nothing happens (Figure 10.9).

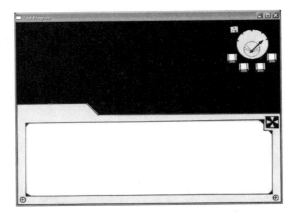

FIGURE 10.9 Our interface objects, this time showing the subGUI enabled.

With this approach, we can use ClearGUI() and RestoreGUI() to turn on and off whole subGUI interfaces with a single function call.

SUMMARY

We tackled a lot in this chapter, so take a deep breath and stretch your legs a bit. We started by looking at some of the design atoms for game interfaces. We explored a set of simple rules and guidelines that should help you hone in on and focus on creating the simplest and most effective interfaces possible.

We then looked at the front-end interfaces for a game and how they can set the tone and mood for the player experience. We dove in deep and started to look at our own game, Eye Opener, and how we set up the front-end interfaces for that game. If you are feeling a little lost with the Lua scripting, head back to Part I of the book and review the chapter on Lua, where all the functions we will use are covered.

Next, we talked about how to present the vital information to the player within the actual game experience. From there, we looked at Eye Opener again, set up some simple interface objects, and then looked at the concept of subGUI implementation within our game engine.

In the next chapter, we'll look more closely at designing an inventory and powerup management system, and then look at how we handle those within our Eye Opener game.

CHAPTER EXERCISES

1. You are designing a tycoon game that simulates running a successful urban nightclub. What elements of the nightclub's (and player's) financial position are essential to show continually on the in-game interface?
2. Using the included 2D game engine, create a "placeholder" front-end interface (the art doesn't have to be great—it can be "designer art") for the aforementioned nightclub tycoon game.
3. Using the included 2D game engine, create an in-game mockup interface that shows the information you outlined in exercise 1. Provide buttons to allow the player to "drill down" to more detailed information.

11 Inventory and Power-Up Management

While some great movies feature an unprepared hero battling to save himself or his family, very few feature a protagonist who battles forward using only his fists. Often, the resourceful hero cobbles together weapons from the environment around him as he battles his adversaries and makes them pay for their wrongs.

Likewise, in a game, players don't want to play through with nothing but their wits and their fists. *Duke Nukem 3D®* allowed you to battle with your fists, and you could be quite effective, but even a pumped-up hero like Duke needed to grab some weapons and ammo along the way.

Virtually every game features some sort of system for the player (or the player's minions) to collect items that will help him grow his ability in the game—from resources, to weapons, to magical rings, to golden keys. In this chapter, we explore the interesting challenge of managing a player's growing inventory and how we go about designing powerups and items that enhance our player's ability skills.

INVENTORY SYSTEM

An inventory system controls two things: how the player (and the game) manages the items in a player's inventory, and how those items work to influence the moment-by-moment gameplay. Managing player inventory is both a design and an under-interface issue, and requires careful thought so the system does not get in the way of the player as he becomes deeply involved in the gameplay. The interface must provide vital information, be intuitive to use, but stay out of the way. In the next few pages, we'll explore some design atoms that will help us craft the best UI approach to our inventory system, and then we'll dive into the actual design and implementation.

Inventory UI Atoms

In the following section, we'll expand our user interface design atoms to touch on points specifically aimed at user interfaces that represent inventory items for the player on screen. For many games, these rules will be overkill, because a player may only have one or two items, so not much management is needed. In other games, especially RPG games or adventure games in which player inventories can grow quite large, these rules will come in quite handy.

Only Show What You Need To

Don't confuse the player by displaying too much inventory information at once.

This really builds off our mantra in the last chapter, when we hammered home the need to keep a user interface simple and only show the player what he needs. When you think of inventory displays, first determine if your inventory items fall into natural categories, such as spells, weapons, and other items. If so, you can break your interface into several smaller displays to lessen the visual confusion for the player. You'll want to show what is vital and important to the players at the moment, so they understand their abilities with a quick glance at the interface. Items that are currently not having any direct effect on their performance should be moved into a subinterface that requires the players' action (such as a click) to access.

No Searching

Don't make the player search his inventory to find what he needs.

This is as much a general design atom as it is a user interface issue. First and foremost, you don't want to drown the player in inventory objects. Allowing a player to haul around dozens and dozens of items only means that the value of each item is diminished.

On the interface side of the coin, a large number of inventory items will be confusing to the player. First, these are often represented by iconographic or realistic images—having hundreds of available items means you won't realistically be able to differentiate between them visually. Having two items that look like swords won't give the player much information with a visual scan—he'll probably need to click or mouse over for more information, and that's an extra step he shouldn't have to take.

If you have many items for the player to manage, try to break them into categories, as we mentioned earlier. You don't want the player to have more inventory items than will fit on a single interface screen—scrolling through a list of items in an in-game interface is a sure-fire way to break the suspension of disbelief, not to mention confuse the player.

Provide Meaningful Information

Provide a simple means for the player to garner game effect information for inventory items.

Inventory items and powerups exist to augment a player's ability in a game. That said, we, as designers, need to remember to let the player know exactly what abilities, enhancements, or penalties an inventory object possesses. Having an icon of a magic ring simply isn't enough—we need to tell the player that the ring will add +1 to his sword fighting strikes and so on. True, some items a player may recover may be "mysterious" and the capabilities unknown, but once abilities are unveiled to the player, make them easy to review.

Approaches that have worked include a "tool tip" style pop-up that provides a short text explanation of the object. The information can also be built into the inventory to either be always visible next to the item (although this may chew up screen real estate and confuse the player), or appear in an information region when the object is clicked on. Some games have even used voice-over narratives to describe an object when more information is requested. The approach should fit your game and the interface tone—just make sure the player has the detailed information he requires about inventory objects when he requests it.

Show Capacity Easily

Players can only haul a limited amount of stuff—show that limit to the player clearly.

Players can't carry infinite items—you didn't design that many and it would be impossible for the player (or the code) to manage. In the real world, we can only carry so much in the packs on our backs—our trucks and trains can only haul so much. In the game, we need to be very clear to the player just how much he can carry and what his current encumbrance load is. In old-school *Dungeons & Dragons* games, this was based on weight, which was based on your character's strength. Each item had a weight and you could only carry so much.

Games have tried a number of different approaches, from a weight-based system to a spatial, grid-based system, to a simple limiting of the number of items you can carry, no matter how large or small.

Use an approach that works for your game, but be sure you are clear with the players so they understand their limits and their current load.

Avoid Inventory Tetris

Don't make the players play a nonessential organizing game with their inventory.

If you've played any RPG games at all, you've heard the term "Inventory Tetris." In the preceding atom, we made the point that the player should know his carrying capacity for "found objects." One clever solution was a grid that represented the sum total of the items the player could carry. Each item he found had a certain size and shape. By placing them on the grid, you could see exactly how much capacity an object used up. (Figure 11.1.)

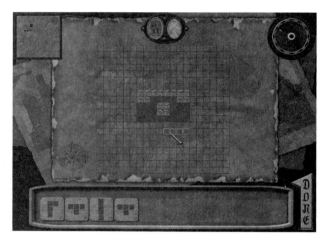

FIGURE 11.1   Inventory Tetris is a system which forces the player into arranging their items (all of which have a unique shape) into a limited grid space. Unless this is vital to game play, it's often a good idea to avoid this "meta game."

A great idea in principle, but it created an unexpected side effect: players would spend time (too much time) sliding objects around on the grid to maximize the available free space and ensure that they could carry as much as possible. Without meaning to, this design approach created a subgame that actually pulled the player's attention away from the game proper.

The core of this atom is that you don't want to make managing inventory limits so much work that you pull the players into a "management game" and away from the game you truly want them to play.

DESIGNING PLAYER USE ITEMS

What's the Difference Between an Item and a Powerup?

Throughout the course of a game, a player usually collects items that can enhance his performance in the game. He might get a magical sword that can cast a shield spell. He might get a communication enhancement that allows his tanks to communicate together over long distances. He might find a magical crystal that allows him to be invisible for a few seconds. All are items that change and enhance the player abilities in the game, providing play variety and often the abilities necessary to overcome some obstacle.

The concept of a "powerup" comes from the world of console gaming and was first seen as colorful little jewels the player could run over for additional bonus points. When the player ran over the jewel, he would be credited with points and the jewels would disappear. As game designs evolved, so did this type of item—they grew beyond just point bonuses and into items that could enhance or augment the player's alter ego. The common trait is that these items were used the moment they were picked up—either for an immediate point bonus or a short-term boost in ability, such as super-speed or a temporary shield. Sometimes, a powerup would last until you lost your life, and sometimes they would only last a few seconds.

So, we can make some clear distinctions—player items are objects found in the world that are taken by the player and added to some sort of inventory management system (either automatic or something the player manages). The items are generally made active by player choice and remain in force as long as the player has the item.

Powerups, by contrast, are enabled the moment they are picked up and only have a short-term or immediate effect. The player can't sock them away for later and has no direct control over managing them, other than striving to pick them up or trying to avoid them (Figure 11.2).

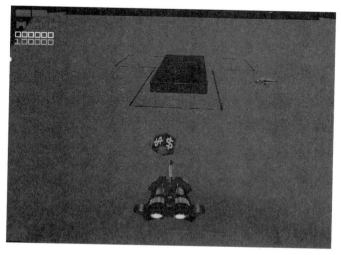

FIGURE 11.2   A powerup is "equipped" the moment it is picked up (or run over in this case). Often, powerups only function for a limited amount of time.

Of course, there are exceptions to these rules, but the general principles are sound: one approach puts control in the hands of the player, and the other puts control in the hands of the designer (with limited player control). At times, these systems can be used together, but to avoid player confusion, generally a game will adopt one approach or the other for those items that augment player abilities or points.

POWERUPS OR ITEMS?

Designer: Paul Schuytema

When we were designing the action game *Combat*, we thought long and hard about which path we should take: inventory items or powerups. Our game was meant to be a twentieth-century updating of a classic arcade game (*Tank*) and Atari 2600 console game (*Combat*). With the type of gameplay we envisioned, we could see both approaches working.

The answer came to us not as we sat down to write the design, but as we started to play the first crude levels of the game. The control of the hover-tanks was very involved—it wasn't complex at all, but it required a lot of player attention to manage turning, drifting, and strafing simultaneously. In short, we required a lot of action skills from our player—the reward was that you could make your tank do amazing things and you could be a very nimble robot assassin in the game—but you really didn't have time for much else.

Because of the level of player involvement, we decided on a powerup system—that way, the player could make the simple decision to run over a powerup or not—and didn't have to switch to an additional interface or hit any additional keys to make the powerup work. We settled on some very clear icons for the powerup objects, so that after just a few minutes of play, it was easy for a player to tell what a particular powerup would do.

The level designers could place the powerups from within the editor and match them to the challenges for the player to face. This had the unexpected (but cool) side effect of broadcasting to players when something big was going to happen, because of the powerups in that area of the level. When they came to an area of the level that had a shield powerup, a triple shot powerup, and a bounce powerup all in the same area, they knew something intense was going to occur.

Player Use Atoms

Earlier in the chapter, we looked at some design atoms for the interface aspect of inventory items. Now we'll turn our attention to the design and function of inventory items and powerups within the game. Items that enhance player abilities must be logical, easy to use, and provide some real benefit to the player; otherwise, they are just extra content that really has no impact on the game as a whole. As a designer, you need to make sure that inventory items and powerups matter; that they enhance the play experience and make it more interesting and fun for the player.

Alert Player of Powerup

Let the player know when a powerup up is active and what it's doing.

Ideally, you've designed powerups that are easy for the players to understand before they pick them up, so they can anticipate the effect it will have on their abilities. Once a player activates a powerup, though, you need to let him know that the powerup is active. Sometimes, this will be obvious—perhaps the powerup is a shield that makes a blue-glowing sphere around the player's ship—in that case, the powerup itself provides its own indication. Something like enhanced speed or strength, though, may not be as obvious, and you'll need to indicate something on the in-game interface to alert the player. It's also a good idea to remind the player of the limited duration of a powerup. Perhaps this is a progress bar that diminishes, or perhaps the powerup indicator on screen flashes as it's ready to expire.

Don't Give Too Much or Too Little

Don't overpower or underpower powerups or inventory items—keep them balanced.

You want your player to succeed in the game, but also be challenged. Make sure enhancement powerups and inventory items in your game provide the player with a balanced boost of performance. You don't want the enhancement so weak that it doesn't provide a visible enhancement to the player's abilities—that would be a letdown for the player and a waste of programming and art assets. On the other hand, you don't want enhancement items to provide so much of a boost that the player can just cruise through vast sections of your game unscathed—that's just as much of a letdown for the player.

Powerups should be matched to the challenges that lie ahead of the player. Without the powerups, the player should be underpowered (but perhaps can still succeed), and with the powerup, the challenge should feel just right.

Inventory items, such as magic armor or magical weapons—ones that remain with the player once equipped—should be considered part of the growing skill set of the player as the game grows more and more challenging. Without the inventory items, the player won't be prepared for what is ahead—make their use essential to your escalating difficulty curve.

Be Aware of Items Being Used Together

You never know how or when players may use inventory items, so be prepared to handle them in combination.

As a designer, you are always trying to balance challenge so the game always feels just a touch too hard for the player (but you know that success is clearly within the player's ability). With powerups, you control their placement and use is instant and temporary, so you'll have a solid idea of just what the player's capabilities might be at any given time.

With inventory enhancements that are under the player's control, you don't have such direct control. The player can equip any of the items at any time, and taken together, they may create an enhancement that is out of scale with the challenges the player is currently facing. As a designer, you need to know what the possibilities are and make sure that inventory items, when used together, don't amplify each other. Generally, it's better to allow a broader range of enhancements than a deeper level of enhancement at any given time. The player may be able to equip a protection ring and an enhanced sword, but not a "gauntlet of melee power" with a +5 broadsword, for example.

Easy to Use

Make it easy for the player to use or equip inventory items.

Usually, picking up an item is simple—the player walks over it. At times, he may have to tap a "Get" key of some sort. Either way, bulking up inventory is generally fast and easy. As a designer, you want to make using inventory items as easy as possible. If you have inventory set up so a player-character has equipping regions, equipping a sword may be as simple as dragging it into the left or right hand.

However, what if you have a rope that the player wants to use to tie together a bundle of sticks? How will you make using that item feel easy for the player? There are many approaches, but perhaps the most used and successful is the idea of "action slots"—inventory is broken into two areas: the "bucket" of stuff the player has (perhaps in his backpack) and those items associated with particular use points. That may be feet, hands, head, turret, portside—any means to anchor an item to a particular aspect of a dynamic game entity.

Equipping rollerblades to the feet of a character would have an intuitive effect— the player would roll and could move faster. Equipping them to the player's hands might not be so obvious, unless you have a "use" command that then allows the player to either put them down or give them to another character in the game that needs them more.

No matter the approach, make it clear to the players how they are able to use items in their inventory and what will get used if they invoke a general "use" command.

Make Use Obvious

For items that are meant to be used rather than equipped, make the use clear to the player.

Often, items in a player's inventory aren't for self-enhancement, like a magic ring, but for some other use in the game, perhaps a part of a puzzle. Having a wind chime in your inventory doesn't make you a more formidable fighter, but it can help you lull that 800-pound gorilla to sleep.

Many times, the key to a puzzle may be using an object in an unusual way, and it's up to the player to figure that out. However, the normal use of an object (whether it's used for that or not) should be obvious to the player and fit within the context of the game. A key is an example of an obvious object—it's used to unlock the door. Three salmon bones in a bowl are much more cryptic—too cryptic, probably. If something in the game is so strange, it almost shouts out: "pick me up—I'm used in a puzzle somewhere!"

Make Combination Intuitive

Often, players will need to combine inventory items—make this feel natural.

This is both an interface and design atom. From time to time, games often ask players to figure out that several items go together to create a new item (such as a knife, some twine, and a broomstick to make a spear). If this might be something you will use in your game, you should strive to have it be more than a single-time affair. If you are allowing the player to combine items, make that unique skill something the player would use several times. A cleaver design and tech team can even design a system of general combination, which would allow the player to make arbitrary combinations, even those the designer hadn't thought of.

If inventory combination is something in your game, make the act of combining items feel natural within the scope of your interface. You may have a small "make" interface that allows the player to drag inventory items together to see if they will combine. You may have an interface that simply allows you to drag one item on top of the other, or perhaps to be able to "use" an inventory item on another inventory item.

No matter what the mechanics are, you'll need to alert the player. You can do this in a very direct fashion (perhaps even in the manual, if anyone would ever read it), with perhaps an NPC bringing up the suggestion. A more subtle approach might be to have the player acquire an item that is already a combined item, and use of that object might "break" it into its component parts—that might fire off the "aha!" light bulb for the player and he can start to experiment with combining items.

Writing the Design

The actual writing of the design is quite simple for powerups and inventory items. The challenge is in conceptualizing just how they will fit into the game and if there be any kind of shared system across multiple objects. Powerup design is fairly simple, since you are often just enhancing existing abilities.

Inventory items that will become parts of in-game puzzles are also relatively simple, but you need to be clear about their roles, since they will most often exist in two places in the design doc—the items design and the puzzle design sections.

Inventory items that are enhancements to a player's in-game skills often require the most design work, since implementation is easier for the technical team if you can create a unified approach to all inventory items.

In the following sections, we'll look at some example design snippets of both powerup and inventory design to give you a feel on how you might want to get started.

Powerup Design

Powerups can often be designed just as we document and design other player-avatar abilities. Powerups are really just abilities that a dynamic entity possesses in a game, but are only activated once the "trigger" of the powerup is collected. Powerups tend to often be amplified abilities, but at times, they are wholly new abilities. Just document the powerups as you would any entity abilities, but be sure to indicate how they are placed in the world, spawn rules, and their duration. The following is an example from a fictional demo-derby style arena combat game between cars:

```
Powerups
  I. Placement
       Powerups are placed the same way as other obstacles in the arena data
       structure—as text codes that match the particular powerup:
       w,0,0,0,0,0,Pu7,0,0,0,w
 II. Powerups
       a. Speed
       ID: Pu1
       Duration: 5 sec
       In Game Asset: Pu1_icon.mdl
       Interface asset: uis_Pu1.bmp
       Behavior: This powerup provides a 1.5x increase in top speed and a 2.5x
       increase in acceleration while active.
       b. Triple-Fire
       ID: Pu4
       Duration: 10 sec
       In Game Asset: Pu4_icon.mdl
       Interface asset: uis_Pu4.bmp
       Behavior: This powerup will modify the firing of a gun, if the car is
       equipped with one. Instead of a single firing path, there will be
```

three: center, 30 degrees left, and 30 degrees right—three projectiles
will fire at once, one down each path.

Inventory Item Design

Designing inventory items for a puzzle is relatively simple, since their existence
only matters in the context of the puzzle. You'll still need to design in the management of their assets in the player's inventory. In Chapter 13, you'll learn about puzzle design in more depth.

Designing enhancement items generally requires you to think through inventory items as a general set of enhancements in your game, and to design a system
that allows for maximum flexibility, so your tech team can implement the system
and you can generate nearly all of your required items within that context. That will
require some thought as to how you can generalize those systems across your game.
For research, spend some time playing some classic RPG games, such as *Diablo®*.
Those games will give you some insight as to how inventory capabilities can be formalized across a larger system with individual items only reflecting a delta (change)
to some of the variables in the larger system.

In the following design example, we'll look at some inventory designs for a
fictional tank-combat game. The design snippet first covers some basics of the
inventory system as a whole and then outlines the specific behaviors of individual
enhancement items.

```
I. Item System Overview
    Before a player begins a mission, he must select his vehicle from the
    motor pool. That vehicle will then drive to the supply depot (in-engine
    cinematic) and will be the selected vehicle as the player outfits it
    for the mission.

    When a player wishes to equip an item from the supply depot, we first
    check to see if they match the class of vehicle the player would like
    to equip them to—if the class doesn't match, there will be no "equip"
    button when an item is selected.

    If the item can be equipped, then the player will add the item to his
    vehicle with the click to the "equip" button.

    All items will modify the existing parameters of the selected vehicle
    by a multiplier value. They can replace a component model of the
    vehicle. They can replace a texture "patch" on the vehicle surface.
II. Item Descriptions
    a. Bullet-proof Wheels
    Vehicle classes:
    sml_wh, med_wh
    Stats modified:
    lfw_damage: 1.75
    rfw_damage: 1.75
    lrw_damage: 1.75
    rrw_damage: 1.75
    max_speed: .9
```

```
acceleration: .75
Visuals Modified:
lfw_tex: whl_tex_bp.tga
rfw_tex: whl_tex_bp.tga
lrw_tex: whl_tex_bp.tga
rrw_tex: whl_tex_bp.tga
Description:
The bullet-proof wheels provide additional support for small and medium
wheeled vehicles. The wheels are not indestructible, but can take a lot
more damage. The incorporation of these hard-rubber wheels and bullet-
proof wheel guards will slow the vehicle slightly and will hamper
acceleration.
b. Gattling Gun
Vehicle classes:
sml_tur, med_tur
Stats modified:
tur_damage: 3.75
tur_rot_speed: .85
tur_proj_type: "hitscan"
tur_fire_type: "continuous"
tur_ammo_count: 100
tur_ammo_drain_rate: 4
tur_fire_viz_effect: fx_fire_gattling.cfg
tur_fire_sfx_effect: sfx_fire_gattling.ogg
Visuals Modified:
tur_mount_tex: tur_mount_gattling.bmp
tur_gun: tur_gun_gatling.mdl
Description:
The Gattling Gun can be equipped on small and medium turret class
vehicles (with treads or wheels). The gun is a continuous fire hitscan
weapon that will fire as long as the player holds down the fire key.
The gun delivers quite a punch when it fires on a target for any length
of time, but ammo use is four times normal.
```

Eye Opener Implementation

For the rest of the chapter, we'll dive into the implementation of the inventory UI in our Eye Opener game. The game uses a simple iconographic system. Inventory items are found when the player ventures into the "comic world"—here he can find and steal objects for use in the more dynamic parts of the game. In the sections that follow, we'll learn how the interface manages the player inventory objects.

General Concepts

Inventory.lua is a subGUI that is able to function in both level-scrolling and adventure scene settings. The file referenced by the gInventoryName resides in the Inventories folder on the companion CD-ROM, and is essentially a .lua document

ON THE CD

that is read by RunScript to create and load the Inventory table in all its glory (Figure 11.3).

FIGURE 11.3   The Inventory panel in Eye Opener.

By its very nature, Inventory.lua is centered on the custom-named inventory file (gInventoryName) that resides in the Inventories folder. That is, Inventory.lua is a subGUI, loaded by AdventureScene.lua or LevelScrolling.lua, which in turn loads its own content from the file defined in the gInventoryName variable. The Inventory.lua subGUI simply provides the proper screen placement and event handling components to make the gInventoryName inventory file meaningful.

Gameplay

LoadInventory() is called immediately after entering a gameplay file (AdventureScene.lua or LevelScrolling.lua). This function loads the player's gInventoryName file. If the file doesn't exist, this function creates it and sets values to default settings. This function is also called when the player advances to another scene. A simple check of the RunScriptNum variable determines the different functionality run in these two contexts.

```
function LoadInventory()
    if RunScriptNum == 0 then
        myFile =
io.open(string.format("%s%s%s","Inventories\\",gInventoryName,".lua"),"r")
        if myFile ~= nil then
            RunScript(string.format("%s%s%s","Inventories\\",
gInventoryName,".lua"))
            io.close(myFile)
        else
            Inventory = {}
            Inventory.TextX = 375
            Inventory.TextY = 356
            Inventory.TextSize = 20
            Inventory.TextColor = {255,255,255}
```

```
Inventory.TextFont = "Arial"
Inventory.Slot = {0,0,0,0,0,0,0,0,0,0,0,0,0,0,0,0}
gICount = 0
gMaxInventory = 0
end
RunScript("Scripts\\Inventory.lua")
if gInventoryOn == 0 then
    ClearGUI(GUI_INVENTORY,1,1000)
end
end
if (positionEditMode == OFF) and (levelEditMode == OFF) then
    for indx = 1,table.getn(Inventory.Slot) do
        -print(Inventory.Slot[indx])
        if Inventory.Slot[indx] ~= 0 then
            local y = 500 - (100 * (math.floor((indx-1)/8)))
            local x = 100 * (indx-1)
            if (indx-1) >= 8 then
                x = 100 * ((indx-1) - (8 * (math.floor((indx-1)/8))))
            end
            local ID = Inventory.Slot[indx]
            local i = ID - GUI_INVENTORY - 300
            local scene = Inventory[i].Scene
            local button = Inventory[i].Button
            local image1 = Inventory[i].Image1
            local image2 = Inventory[i].Image2
            local image3 = Inventory[i].Image3
            CreateItem(ID, "Button", image1,image2,image3)
            SetItemPosition(ID, x, y, 100, 100)
            if gInventoryOn == 0 then
                EnableObject(ID,0,0)
            end
        end
    end
end
end
```

The LoadInventory() function is simple. First, it checks to see if the requested inventory file exists. If not, it will populate the Inventory table with empty, default values. If the file exists, it is run, and then the inventory interface file is run, to make it the active GUI. Once it's the active GUI, the function loops through the valid, nonempty values in the Inventory table to create the inventory buttons and display them on screen.

The format of the inventory file is quite simple—it is simply a Lua file that lists the values in the Inventory table. It is generated via script, but is also a valid Lua file that you can open, view, and edit in a text editor (having an auto-generated save file be something a human, especially a designer, can read, is a lifesaver when it comes to debugging, tweaking and testing a game). The data in the file looks something like this, with the meta values for the table set up first and then the individual saved inventory items:

```
— Test.lua Inventory File
```

```
Inventory = {}
gICount = 0
function InventoryIncrement()
    gICount = gICount + 1
    Inventory[gICount] = {}
end
```

```
Inventory.TextX = 375
Inventory.TextY = 356
Inventory.TextSize = 20
Inventory.TextColor = {255,255,255}
Inventory.TextFont = "Arial"
Inventory.Slot = {8301,8302,8303,0,0,0,0,0,0,0,0,0,0,0,0,0}
```

```
InventoryIncrement()
```

```
— Item #1
Inventory[gICount].Scene = 1
Inventory[gICount].Button = 4
Inventory[gICount].Image1 = "uib_screwdriver_up.tga"
Inventory[gICount].Image2 = "uib_screwdriver_hv.tga"
Inventory[gICount].Image3 = "uib_screwdriver_dn.tga"
Inventory[gICount].Text = "Screwdriver"
```

AdventureScene.lua

When a player clicks on an object from the world, `AddToInventory(buttonID)` (which is found in LuaSupport.lua) is called. This function stores all necessary information about that item (its text description, button sprites, scene number where it was found, etc.). This info is stored in the Inventory table. A button is created to reference this object and placed in the inventory. Its ID is stored in `Inventory.Slot[i]` (where "i" is the first available unoccupied index in the `Inventory.Slot` table). By limiting the `Inventory.Slot` table to 16 indices, organization is simpler. (Figure 11.4.)

```
function AddToInventory(id)
    i = 0
    repeat
        i = i + 1
    until (Inventory.Slot[i] == 0) or (i == table.getn(Inventory.Slot))
    local y = 500 - (100 * (math.floor((i-1)/8)))
    local x = 100 * (i-1)
    if (i-1) >= 8 then
        x = 100 * ((i-1) - (8 * (math.floor((i-1)/8))))
    end
    gMaxInventory = gMaxInventory + 1
    local indx = id - (GUI_SCENE + 300)
    Inventory[gMaxInventory] = {}
    Inventory[gMaxInventory].Scene = gSCount
```

```
    Inventory[gMaxInventory].Button = indx
    Inventory[gMaxInventory].Image1 = Scene[gSCount][indx].Images[1]
    Inventory[gMaxInventory].Image2 = Scene[gSCount][indx].Images[2]
    Inventory[gMaxInventory].Image3 = Scene[gSCount][indx].Images[3]
    Inventory[gMaxInventory].Text = Scene[gSCount][indx].Text
    Inventory.Slot[i] = GUI_INVENTORY + 300 + gMaxInventory
    CreateItem(Inventory.Slot[i], "Button",
Inventory[gMaxInventory].Image1,Inventory[gMaxInventory].Image2,Inventory[g
MaxInventory].Image3)
    SetItemPosition(Inventory.Slot[i], x, y, 100, 100)
    if gInventoryOn == 0 then
        EnableObject(Inventory.Slot[i],0,0)
    end
    ItemCommand(GUI_INVENTORY +
298,"SetString",Inventory[gMaxInventory].Text)
    if Scene[gSCount].Sound ~= nil then
        gSoundID = PlaySound(1,Scene[gSCount].Sound)
    end
    StartTimer(3)
end
```

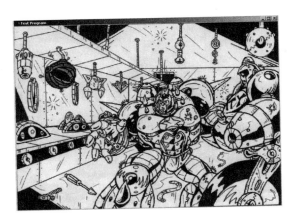

FIGURE 11.4 The "adventure scene" allows players
to pick up and add items to their inventory.

The first part of the function simply loops through values until it finds the first free inventory slot. It then calculates the X and Y screen position of the inventory object (on the inventory screen). We then enter the data in the table for the three images for an item (the up, down, and hover states), and the text tag we want to use. Finally, we create the button that represents, visually, the inventory object, on screen. If the inventory is not currently displayed, we still create the button, but disable it.

CheckInventory(scene,button) is used to make sure that items already collected do not appear in the scene upon reentry of that specific scene:

```
function CheckInventory(scene,button)
    result = "no"
    for indx = 1,gMaxInventory do
        if (Inventory[indx].Scene == scene) and (Inventory[indx].Button ==
button) then
            result = "yes"
        end
    end
    return result
end
```

SaveInventory() is run before exiting the AdventureScene.lua script:

```
function SaveInventory()
    myFile =
io.open(string.format("%s%s%s","Inventories\\",gInventoryName,".lua"),"w")
    if myFile ~= nil then
        myFile:write(string.format("%s%s%s%s%s","- ",gInventoryName,".lua
Inventory File","\n","\n"))
        myFile:write(string.format("%s%s","——————————","\n"))
        myFile:write(string.format("%s%s","Inventory = {}","\n"))
        myFile:write(string.format("%s%s","gICount = 0","\n"))
        myFile:write(string.format("%s%s","function
InventoryIncrement()","\n"))
        myFile:write(string.format("%s%s","    gICount = gICount +
1","\n"))
        myFile:write(string.format("%s%s","    Inventory[gICount] =
{}","\n"))
        myFile:write(string.format("%s%s","end","\n"))
        myFile:write(string.format("%s%s%s","——————————","\n","\n"))
        if Inventory.TextX ~= nil then
            myFile:write(string.format("%s%d%s","Inventory.TextX =
",Inventory.TextX,"\n"))
        end
        if Inventory.TextY ~= nil then
            myFile:write(string.format("%s%d%s","Inventory.TextY =
",Inventory.TextY,"\n"))
        end
        if Inventory.TextSize ~= nil then
            myFile:write(string.format("%s%d%s","Inventory.TextSize =
",Inventory.TextSize,"\n"))
        end
        if Inventory.TextColor ~= nil then
myFile:write(string.format("%s%d%s%d%s%d%s","Inventory.TextColor =
{",Inventory.TextColor[1],",",Inventory.TextColor[2],",",Inventory.TextColo
r[3],"}\n"))
        end
        if Inventory.TextFont ~= nil then
            myFile:write(string.format("%s%s%s%s%s","Inventory.TextFont =
",string.char (34),Inventory.TextFont,string.char (34),"\n"))
```

```
            end
        local myString = ""
        for indx = 1,16 do
            myString = string.format("%s%s%s", myString, ",",
Inventory.Slot[indx])
            end
        myString = string.gsub(myString,",","",1)
        myFile:write(string.format("%s%s%s%s%s","Inventory.Slot =
{",myString,"}","\n","\n"))
        for indx = 1,gMaxInventory do
            myFile:write(string.format("%s%s","——————","\n"))
            myFile:write(string.format("%s%s","InventoryIncrement()","\n"))
            myFile:write(string.format("%s%s%s","——————","\n","\n"))
            myFile:write(string.format("%s%d%s","- Item #",indx,"\n"))
            if Inventory[indx].Scene ~= nil then

myFile:write(string.format("%s%d%s","Inventory[gICount].Scene =
",Inventory[indx].Scene,"\n"))
            end
            if Inventory[indx].Button ~= nil then

myFile:write(string.format("%s%d%s","Inventory[gICount].Button =
",Inventory[indx].Button,"\n"))
            end
            if Inventory[indx].Image1 ~= nil then

myFile:write(string.format("%s%s%s%s%s","Inventory[gICount].Image1 =
",string.char (34),Inventory[indx].Image1,string.char (34),"\n"))
            end
            if Inventory[indx].Image2 ~= nil then

myFile:write(string.format("%s%s%s%s%s","Inventory[gICount].Image2 =
",string.char (34),Inventory[indx].Image2,string.char (34),"\n"))
            end
            if Inventory[indx].Image3 ~= nil then

myFile:write(string.format("%s%s%s%s%s","Inventory[gICount].Image3 =
",string.char (34),Inventory[indx].Image3,string.char (34),"\n"))
            end
            if Inventory[indx].Text ~= nil then

myFile:write(string.format("%s%s%s%s%s","Inventory[gICount].Text =
",string.char (34),Inventory[indx].Text,string.char (34),"\n"))
            end
            myFile:write(string.format("%s","\n"))
        end
        myFile:write(string.format("%s%s","——————","\n"))
        myFile:write(string.format("%s%s","gMaxInventory = gICount","\n"))
        myFile:write(string.format("%s%s","——————","\n","\n"))
    end
    io.close(myFile)
end
```

While this may be a rather complicated-looking function, it's actually quite simple. It first opens a file to write to on the disc, and then it will write out the initial parameters of the Inventory table to the file. We use the string.format() function we discussed in our chapter on Lua. This allows us to set up a string that is part text and part values taken from the actual game variables. The result is a string that is a valid line of Lua script.

We then walk through all of the elements in the table and write out their variables in the same way—when we are done, we simply close the file. The result is a human-readable text file that is 100-percent valid Lua script that we can reload simply by using a RunScript() command.

Inventory.lua

This script allows the user to peruse through inventory contents. The player can click items to view descriptions. They can also choose to delete items from the inventory using the SubtractFromInventory(id) function:

```
function SubtractFromInventory(id)
    for i = 1,table.getn(Inventory.Slot) do
        if Inventory.Slot[i] == id then
            DeleteItem(id)
            Inventory.Slot[i] = 0
        end
    end
    SortInventorySlots()
end
```

If an item needs to be deleted, only its tie via Inventory.Slot must be severed. It will no longer be loaded, and will subsequently be written over by other functions. The inventory information is then sorted via the SortInventorySlots() function:

```
function SortInventorySlots()
    table.sort(Inventory.Slot)
    h = 0
    for indx = 1,table.getn(Inventory.Slot) do
        if Inventory.Slot[indx] ~= 0 then
            h = h + 1
        end
    end
    for m = 1, h do
        for j = table.getn(Inventory.Slot), m+1, -1 do
            if Inventory.Slot[j] < Inventory.Slot[j-1] then
                —swap numbers
                t =  Inventory.Slot[j]
                Inventory.Slot[j] = Inventory.Slot[j-1]
                Inventory.Slot[j-1] = t
            end
        end
    end
```

```
        end
        for k = 1,h do
            Inventory.Slot[k] = Inventory.Slot[table.getn(Inventory.Slot)-h+k]
            Inventory.Slot[table.getn(Inventory.Slot)-h+k] = 0
        end
        for i = 1,table.getn(Inventory.Slot) do
            if Inventory.Slot[i] ~= 0 then
                local y = 500 - (100 * (math.floor((i-1)/8)))
                local x = 100 * (i-1)
                if (i-1) >= 8 then
                    x = 100 * ((i-1) - (8 * (math.floor((i-1)/8))))
                end
                SetItemPosition(Inventory.Slot[i],x,y,100,100)
            end
        end
    end
end
```

This function cleans up the player's inventory and reorders it neatly. It begins by using the built-in Lua function `table.sort()`. This orders the table so that all the zeros (the nonfilled slots) are at the front of the table. We then walk through the table and do a quick comparison of table values and swap them to place the filled slots at the front of the table. The final step is to walk through the table and reset all the position values for the items in the table and then issue the `SetItemPosition()` command for each item so it is drawn in its new location.

The Adventure Scene

In our sample game, the comic panels are called "Adventure Scenes," the locations in which the player can pick up and collect inventory items. The system is set up so a designer can set up and create his or her own adventure scenes, which might be something you want to explore as you work on your own sample game.

Basically, AdventureScene.lua is a shell that loads information from the Comic Frame One.lua adventure scene file (or any other user-defined adventure scene file). When AdventureScene.lua is run, it cycles through all of the aspects (buttons, background, music) of the first "slide" in the specified scene file (Comic Frame One.lua in this case).

Each scene file can hold more than one slide, and is accessed by pressing the "," or "." keys (for < and >). When the slide changes, AdventureScene.lua is re-run, loading the next slide.

Each adventure scene file is made to generate a table, whose values are set by the user (manually and/or in AdventureSceneEdit.lua).

Each slide has the following (Background & ButtonCount are the only essential items):

```
Scene[gSCount].Music = "PianoBlues.ogg" – Background music.
Scene[gSCount].Background = "Adventure Scene1 - 1.bmp"
```

```
Scene[gSCount].Sound = "sound1.wav" — Sound played when objects are
collected.
Scene[gSCount].ButtonCount = 5 — Number of buttons (inventory items) in the
slide.
```

Each item then has its own table, indexed by its scene and button number. The X and Y coordinates, height and width values (H & W), identifying text, and three states of button images (Images table) are required for each button.

The user must have the scene created and the items defined in the file before editing the locations of the objects in the program. When AdventureSceneEdit.lua is loaded with a file, the user can scroll through the available buttons using the left mouse button. When the player wants to "pick up" the active button, he clicks the right mouse button. It is then set in place when the player cycles to the next button. When the textfield reads "Done," the player can press the "." or "," buttons to go to another slide. Pressing Esc will save the scene file.

When a player is in AdventureScene.lua and left-clicks an item in the scene, the button is deleted and is added to the inventory via AddToInventory(id), discussed earlier. The button number (index for the Scene table) is determined by subtracting the GUI_SCENE and 300 constants from the passed ID. The Inventory table is then filled with the values from the Scene table, and further visits to this slide will not show the collected object (thanks to CheckInventory(scene,button)).

Currently, the changes made to the scene (namely, the deleting of items) are not saved to the scene file during AdventureScene.lua. This information is saved in the user's inventory Lua file and used with CheckInventory(scene,button). This keeps the scene uniform as a level, but allows the user's inventory to determine what does or does not appear in the level.

SUMMARY

In this chapter, we explored a topic vital to many games, yet often overlooked when we discuss game design in general: inventory systems. We first looked at some guidelines to help us craft the best inventory management user interfaces for our players.

From there, we took some time to explore the differences between game powerups and game items. We then looked at some design atoms that will help us create solid implementations of powerups and player-use items.

Our next stop found us looking at some design examples so we could see the differences between designing simple powerups and more in-depth inventory and item systems. We wrapped up by looking at how we could implement an inventory user interface system into our game Eye Opener.

In the next chapter, we'll explore the fascinating area of environment and world design, looking at how the game environment sets the tone for the game, visually, and guides and controls moment-by-moment gameplay.

CHAPTER EXERCISES

1. Think of an action game in which you, as the hero, must make your way, with only a sword, through an enemy-held castle to rescue a princess held hostage. What powerups might provide interesting play experiences for the player? What opposition could only be bested with a powerup (or two) enabled?
2. Take the inventory management system used in Eye Opener and see if you can adjust it so it shows up on the right side of the screen instead of at the bottom.
3. Advanced: Can you expand the inventory system used in Eye Opener so it could be used to "equip" a warrior in battle (that is, moving an item from general inventory to be in the left hand, right hand, etc.)?

12 Environment Design

In This Chapter

- Container for Interactivity
- Key Roles for Game Environments
- General Environment Design Atoms
- Level Design Atoms
- Eye Opener Implementation

Imagine diving into an exciting new game—the front-end interface looks great. You flare up a new game and see a cool, dynamic interface, allowing you to set up and equip your character for the strife to come. You launch the game in earnest and see nothing but a black screen filled with enemies, trinkets to pick up, and not much else—your character appears to be hovering over the void as you ready your sword for the fight with the floating giant rat . . . sound fun?

If you're like us, while the novelty of a floating giant rat will hold our attention for a few seconds, not much else will—the game seems bound to nothingness, and there is no "reality" to the game universe. A game without a compelling environment is much like that—a game without a foundation to stand on. The environment in which we plod, struggle, search, and strive plays a huge role in our overall game experience.

In this chapter, we are going to look in depth at game environments and the role they play in the fabric of our games. We'll also explore some key design atoms that will help us craft and design compelling spaces upon which to plan our adventures.

CONTAINER FOR INTERACTIVITY

No matter what sort of game you are playing, it's played within some type of container. We're not talking about a beige PC box or a slick black console box, but rather some sort of container space that defines the realm of the game. The game may be large in scope, and move from container to container, but the moment-by-moment play is always circumscribed by some type of boundary.

If we think of a board game, the concept becomes clear. The board game may be about the military rise of Charlemagne, but the game itself takes place within a 24-inch square board of painted landscape and overlaid movement areas. In a board game, the board is the limiting area of the game, and a visual support system for the tone and milieu of the game experience.

Because it is a "container," the game environment will necessarily have some boundaries. With technical advances in recent years, large environment games like MMOs can push those boundaries out so far (with continuous caching of terrain data) that the world can feel nearly infinite, but even in those cases, the world is still limited. Most games, though, have more reined-in boundaries that the player will encounter during the game. Part of the challenge for the designer and the development team is to make those boundaries feel natural within the constraint of the game, so the player won't even give a second thought to the fact that he can't proceed any further past the "edge" of your world.

Most seasoned players are well used to the concept of boundaries, and many earlier games had far more constrained boundaries, so they really don't notice them—there is no break in the suspension of disbelief when they reach the edge of your game world.

Working with the Team

Terminology varies from studio to studio, but there are two disciplines to cover in the area of environment design: vision and execution. Typically, the designer is responsible for the vision, and a level artist is responsible for the execution. At some studios, a single person handles both tasks, or the work is done by Level Builders or Map Designers. However, ultimately, one person must conceptualize and document the layout of space, and someone must use a 3D art program like 3DS Max or Maya to create the models and assets.

As a designer, you will most likely be involved in the process with an emphasis on environment design as a vehicle for a specific user experience. If you're designing a third-person exploration game like *Tomb Raider: Legend®*, you want the layout of the environment to facilitate climbing, jumping, and puzzle-solving, with the occasional combat encounter. When working with the level artist responsible for creating the environment, it's important to ensure that all of this has been communicated effectively in the design documentation. However you choose to organize and format your level design docs, you need to bear in mind the perspective of the coworker who will be implementing the vision.

KEY ROLES OF GAME ENVIRONMENTS

Your game environments are the "field" upon which the player will interact with your game. Environments may be active or static, but either way, they serve as the stage for the player's alter ego or agents to interact with the items, puzzles, and dynamic entities of your game. Taken from the highest conceptual level, the environment of your game has two primary roles: to deliver a sense of place and tone to the players, and to guide and direct their gameplay movement.

Capturing Tone and Feel

Perhaps the most important aspect of a game environment, even beyond its role in the dynamics of gameplay, is to serve as the foundational unit of the game universe. Earlier, we discussed how the game interface can support and enhance the tone, feel, and milieu of a game. The interface is, by its nature, an artificial construct overlaid on the game experience. It can reflect and support the feel of the game, but it isn't the game world itself. The environment *is* the game world and does more to cement (or break) the fiction of the game than anything else for the player.

Also remember that it's the environment of the game, more than any other single thing in a game, that will be in front of the player's eyes for the entire game experience. Robotic turrets may capture the player's attention, but may only appear in the first mission—the game world is the base for all missions. That means that you want to vary the look and feel of the environment to keep things visually interesting for the players (no one wants to play an entire game on uniform fields of green) and to alert them of changes within the game universe.

FLAMING TREES

Designer: Paul Schuytema

In *Castles & Catapults,* a medieval RTS we created, we wanted to show that the player was moving across Europe and into the Middle East, along the Crusaders' path. We didn't have a large world or a central map interface—all we had were the maps of our 16 missions in the campaign game.

We decided to use the game terrain itself as the tool to tell the story of the player's progress. The scenarios began on rolling hills in southeastern France

$\rightarrow$

and gradually grew rockier. As the player approached the Middle East, the grass was replaced by stones and scrub, and sand became more and more prevalent.

As the player entered the final scenarios of the game, when he was entering a dangerous and magical kingdom, the ground became more and more dominated by black rock formations and strange crystal veins. We also moved from large deciduous trees to palm tree clumps to gnarled and twisted trees with no leaves on them whatsoever. In the final setting, the ground was entirely black rock and the trees were alive with flickering green flames.

In this way, we used the foundation of the ground terrain and environmental details (such as rocks and trees) to signify player movement and to create a sense of foreboding and fear in the player (Figure 12.1).

FIGURE 12.1 In this prototype game, the environments helped define the player's location through the campaign world.

Guiding and Directing Play

Drop a human down into a sparse, sand-strewn desert and what will he do? Odds are, after he shakes his fist at you and curses you as you zip away in your helicopter—he'll turn in circles, wondering which direction to go. He may pick a direction and trudge off, but without some navigation sense, he'll probably be doomed to traipse in large-radius circles until he collapses from exhaustion.

Drop a human into a maze and what will he do? Fist brandishing aside, he'll start to follow the maze. If the human is clever, he'll drop a marker at his entry point, put his right hand against the right wall, and start walking, secure that if he simply follows the right wall, he'll either end up where he started or find the way out.

In both examples, the environment dictated the actions of the human. Both wanted to return to their "normal" world, but the poor soul stranded in the desert was thrown into an environment that provided no guidance at all, and hence the wanderer was just that—a wanderer. The maze environment provided some guidance to the human—there was a path to follow and a sense of purpose implied, the human wasn't helpless, and could work with the guidance supplied by the environment to eventually find his way out of the maze.

In a game, players thirst for challenge and direction. They want to know what to do next. While players want freedom of choice, they also want to understand what is expected of them and how and where to proceed. A game set in the sweeping expanse of the Sahara desert would provide an environment that would be very disturbing and frustrating to the player. That need for direction speaks to part of the success of FPS games, in which the player is a "rat in a maze" and is given a very limited path to follow as he works to overcome challenges and puzzles.

Ideally, a game environment feels "natural," whether it is rolling hills, a WWII map of Europe, or the plastic and fluorescent corridors of a future space station. The environment also directs play by providing structure to the player's actions. The rolling hills of a medieval RTS may have a "pinch point" canyon with walls of inaccessible limestone that guide the player toward an interesting battle. The countries on the WWII map may be in color for countries in which active battles may be engaged, and grayed-out when they are not yet "in the fray"—in that way, the map itself guides the player as he seeks to allocate his forces. The space station corridors may twist and turn, but when the player comes to a large warehouse, the presence of a single corridor leading off from the far side of the space indicates the direction for the player to travel.

As you consider the environments of your game, think of them as a platform for game interactivity, and as a design tool to direct the player forward in your game in a natural and almost transparent manner.

DESIGNING FOR GAMEPLAY

Game environments are more than just static levels filled with architectural details—they are the arena in which play happens—and often the environments themselves guide and direct gameplay. It's essential to keep this in mind as you design your own game worlds.

General Environment Design Atoms

In the sections that follow, we'll explore some design atoms that relate to the ways in which we can think about our game environments as dynamic entities contributing to the player's overall experience in our game.

Concept Art

Use concept art to help define the feel and flow of game environments.

When we think of concept art in the realm of games, we generally think of sketches that help us visualize characters and weaponry, but for years, skilled development teams have been using concepts artists much like movies do: to help define and create a sense of space and environment. Since game environments carry so much weight when delivering the "feel" of the game world to the player, it makes good sense to get a handle on the look and feel of environments early in the development process.

As soon as you have a sense of the key aspects of an environment (is it an abandoned Nike missile base or a fourteenth-century mill?), sit down with your team's concept artist to get him up to speed. Have him review the design documentation and discuss with him your vision for the game environments. Have him first do some quick pencil drawings to show you—that way, you can see if you are on the same page before he spends too much time. Once you have the right feel, have him work up some detailed drawings of key areas of your game—these will help you hammer home the tone of the game world, and will become a great tool for the team artists, level designers, and mission designers.

Sketch Your World

Even if you aren't a great artist, sketch first before implementation.

More often than not, your entire game will be made up of a number of environments, each of which will require its own design, assets, and implementation. Even if you aren't an artist, pick up a pencil and some graph paper and sketch out your game environments before you or any environment designers start working with the development tools to create them. Sketching the environment, the player flow through the space, and the expected puzzles, challenges, and obstacles will help you get a better handle on how the environment fits within the game. It will also provide a vital reference for whomever is actually creating the tool. Also, try not to sketch a single environment in isolation—work in connected units so that you get a sense of flow across multiple levels or missions—this will help you catch inconsistencies and problems earlier in the development cycle (Figure 12.2).

Ensure Continuity

Don't forget how a single environment fits into the whole.

You'll want to make sure that multiple environments, maps, or levels in your game all flow naturally together and feel as if they are part of a single, unified whole. If a single designer or artist is creating the game environments, this isn't generally an issue, since there will be some automatic continuity based on the creator. However, in that case, the developer needs to make sure the designer or artist follows the pacing and tone set forth in the design document.

FIGURE 12.2   Sketching out a map can help you get a handle on how to lay out the environment.

This becomes an issue when you have multiple artists or designers creating environmental content across many, many levels. In that case, it's easy for individual styles to clash, even when everyone is following the same style guide set out by the designer. It's also key to remember that each environment probably plays a key role in the larger whole-game story arc, and should work to contribute to that story—in setting, theme, and plot.

Style Guide

For large games, create an environment style guide for developers.

If you are working with a myriad of environments in your game, especially if they move from one region to another or set different tones for different areas of the game, you'll want to create a style guide. An environmental style guide doesn't have to be anything terribly detailed, but you should at least try to document some reference material for each environment, from colors to reference photographs to concept art sketches. Putting these materials together (this is ideal for a Wiki) will give all the developers a common starting point for each environment and will go a long way to ensure environmental continuity even across levels created by different developers.

PREY ENVIRONMENTS

Designer: Paul Schuytema

When we worked on the second iteration of *3D Realms™ Prey* game, we found ourselves creating environments across four different species: humanoid, saurian, insectoid, and a race of super intelligent "watchers" we called the Keepers.

We wanted a simple way to capture the feel of these environments so the level designers would feel confident that their work would reflect each species, but also allow them as much creative control as possible. We first began by assuming a list of "tone" words to define the sense of each species—these weren't linked to architecture, color, or anything concrete—they were meant to create an impression. Some examples:

Humanoid: Cannibals, deformed, dirty, madness, resourceful, grease, electronics, rust/corrosion, etc.

Keepers: Asexual, eternal, filigreed, hoary, prosthetic, secret, jealous, cold, etc.

From these initial lists, we were able to come up with a list of colors that represented each species (the dominant colors in the textures for the levels) and the colors of the lighting used in those levels. We then came up with a bulleted list of architectural feel phrases for each species, such as:

Humanoid

A lot of crap, stuff on top of stuff, things that aren't working and are just built over

- "Hospital grunge"
- Lots of scattered and sloppy tech
- Juxtaposition between dark earth-toned areas and hospital grunge bright areas
- Lots of horizontal and vertical lines—very geometric
- Save the curves for curved staircases, etc.
- Lots of layers and heights

→

> - Floor "tongue and groove" motif
> - Only real ornamentation are checkerboard patterns
> - Alphabet is letter-based, somewhat Arabic
>
> This approach, while not overly scientific or technical, gave us a great working platform to develop very creative environments that were consistent across species lines.

Signify Mood

Use the environments or levels to signify the mood of the game.

In addition to using environments to emphasize and support the tone and theme of a game, you can also use them to signify a change in mood for the play of the game at that moment. Think of some of the best horror movies you've seen—a good director will use the setting of the movie to set the mood of the story. Think of the classic movie, *The Exorcist*. When we were first learning about Reagan, the shots were well lighted and clean and full of colors, signifying an uplifting mood full of happiness and love. Contrast that with the first shots we saw of Father Karrass—bleak colors, sparse environments, and low ceilings—there was a pressure to these environments that made us uneasy—made us feel that something wasn't right with the father. As the movie progresses, Reagan's room morphs from a normal child's room to a dark and cold place and the walls and ceiling seem to close in, finally creating a terrifying and claustrophobic space.

The same effect can be achieved in game environments by the use of color, lighting, and ambient sound. Environments can create a sense of optimism or foreboding in the player. Darker colors, lower ceilings, and more patch lighting create a negative mode, while more uniform lighting and loftier ceilings can create a positive, even regal space.

Remember that your environments are your "canvas" to deliver a real sense of mood, and place, to your players.

The Façade of Freedom

Make the players feel like they have a choice, even when they don't.

Environments serve as tools for you to guide the player from one challenge to the next in your game—in a way, your game environments are leading a player through your game. Players like to feel they are in charge, even though giving them complete freedom in your game would simply frustrate and confuse them.

The challenge is to create the sense of freedom, while transparently directing and guiding the player. One of the best techniques to do so is to provide "Y" choices for the player . . . basically, a pair of paths for the players to explore that will provide some benefit or useful information, but not lead them to the end of the environment—they can choose to explore one path or both, in any order. Another technique is to provide a looping path to a point further on in the environment—the player can take either way and get to the same spot (one might be longer and easier, the other short and more treacherous). Off-road driving games have used this technique for years. The challenge is to provide a real sense of choice and freedom for the players while keeping them chugging along toward the end goal for the environment.

Resource Struggling

Always have the player struggling for resources.

A well-supplied player gets "fat and lazy." Always keep resources, from ammo boxes to stone mines, at a premium in your game environments. Keep your players hungry for more and never give them enough. That will drive them to action and keep them moving forward in your game. If they are always looking for that next box of ammo, they will seek out challenges and risk-reward opportunities and become more fully engaged in the game.

Resource management can be a learned skill for a player, so you may want to explore the idea of limiting resources even more for more advanced play levels. Playtest to get a feel for what the right resource levels are for a given skill level, and remember that your development team members are probably better players than gamers in the real world.

Level Design Atoms

In the previous section, we explored some design atoms that relate to game environments in general, whether you are creating outdoor terrain for an MMO, a city for an RPG, a mission map for an RTS, a side-scrolling environment for a platformer, or a level for an FPS (as gamers, we can get a lot of abbreviations into a single sentence!). So many of today's most popular games are level-based that it would be useful to spent some time looking at some design atoms that apply to level-based environments. These design guides are well suited for first-person games, but can also apply across a myriad of genres and play styles into any type of game environment that is defined by more compact spaces and the inclusion of architecture.

Focus on a Theme

Have a theme for each level you design.

If we are wearing a writer's hat and talk of "theme," we generally mean the "message" of our story, such as "prejudice is wrong" or "everybody needs friends."

If we are wearing our level-designer hat, theme could also refer to the message of our game, but it more likely refers to the central idea of a level. For a level to be believable, it needs to fit into the context of our larger game and feel contiguous to what has come before and what will come after. That said, level after level of interesting rooms and corridors will leave a flat, unremarkable impression on the player.

If you explore a real-world place that reminds you of a game level, you will notice one thing: there is a purpose for that space. If you visit an abandoned Nike missile base, you will find "levels" for the troops to live in and for their supplies. You will find places that house the electronics for control of the flight systems. You will find other areas that store the actual missiles and have the systems to move them into position in their launch tubes. Each space or region has a purpose, or theme.

When you are creating levels, make sure each level or region of a level has some sort of theme to keep it anchored—and make it something the players can deduce from their explorations. This will make the level "feel" more real.

Think through the level's place in the game universe, and derive an interesting theme or purpose for the space—one that offers interesting gameplay opportunities. Perhaps the level generates hydroelectric power. Perhaps it's a warehouse to store overseas shipping containers (some with deadly contents). Perhaps it's a research lab deep below the surface . . . decide on a theme and allow that theme and purpose to define the architecture and environmental flow through the region.

Purposeful Architecture

The architectural elements of a level should have purpose.

Interior level spaces are defined by their architecture, from the simple stone walls of a crude dungeon to walls fitted with steam pipes for a maintenance access tunnel. The architecture defines and encloses the space—even in exterior urban levels. As a level designer, you will want to give thought to the architecture you place in an environment to make sure it feels like it has a purpose being there.

In game environments, our game engine doesn't care about structure loads or proper floor joists. Support columns or load-bearing walls are nonexistent—to the engine, it's merely polygons to render and collision objects to process. As a designer, though, you should think as if these matter. Don't loft 4,000 square feet of ceiling with no visible means of support. Don't stick a large oak door on a brick wall without making a brick archway for the door opening. (Figure 12.3.)

Make your game levels feel like they have mass and were constructed by some intelligence, even if it is an alien intelligence. This will require some study of architecture, and you to go out into the real world and observe—explore old places like basements, old warehouses, attics—any place you can see the shell of the space and the support structures. Take a sketchbook, jot down ideas, start to learn how form follows function in architectural elements, and bring that knowledge into the levels you design.

FIGURE 12.3 The architecture in game levels should look like is has a structural purpose. The levels found in Max Payne 2 feature realistic and functional looking architecture. Used with permission. Copyright 3D Realms Entertainment 2003.

Know Your Technology

Even though you are not a programmer, get to know the technology.

Not much can tax a game engine more than a complex level. If you are designing level environments for your game, you will need to know the nuts and bolts of your game engine, especially the limits of the rendering system. Odds are the tech team will provide you with some debugging tools you will need to evaluate the performance of your levels. The most basic of these is a frame-rate counter, but you may also have access to data that shows rendered polygons, overdraw areas, texture management, and other key aspects of rendering that affect frame rate and game speed.

In the "old days" of FPS games, nearly every game environment had to be preprocessed in some way. The level often had to be broken down into a BSP-tree to speed rendering, and often lighting was calculated as well. Today's more advanced technology means that some engines don't require preprocessing, while other still do. Odds are, the more complex the potential level and the more detailed the lighting, the higher probability that it will require some processing.

While calculating character animation, bullet projectiles, and artificial intelligence can eat up computer cycles, the real governor on a game's speed is what is being rendered. As you create levels, talk with your tech team to see what they want you to avoid. Perhaps large, flat, open spaces are verboten. Perhaps long corridors where you can see for a quarter of a mile are a bad idea.

In general, you'll want to add maximum detail with a minimum of polygons and keep the player's distance view somewhat limited (which can easily be done via turns in corridors, L-shaped rooms, and such). You'll also want to work with a set of textures, not 100 different 2D textures, since each will need to be loaded onto the 3D card for rendering. You'll also want to keep the number of polygons visible to the player's field of view as consistent as possible, so the frame rate remains fluid.

Allow yourself to be a student of your technology and pride yourself on excellent gameplay, visual design, and high performance.

Embrace a Novel Idea

Take advantage of a novel idea or gadget as a focus for a level.

Creating a central gadget or novel idea in each level is a great way to hold player interest and offer some challenge for you as a designer. As you learn more and more about your game technology, you'll come up with interesting tricks you can deploy within the limits of the technology. Perhaps you can have a zero-gravity room, or a sequence of spaces that have sheet ice for the floor. Perhaps you devised a platform with a sequence of huge "Pit and the Pendulum" pendulums, swinging back and forth. Perhaps you created an interesting way to do collapsible and expandable circular tower stairs or the swiveling staircases from Hogwarts.

While you don't want to litter a level with gadget after gadget, using an interesting visual or interactive trick as a focal point for an environment can give the space real personality and make it stand out in the player's memory.

FORM AND FUNCTION

 ### *Designer: Matt Wood, Valve Software*

A beautiful environment is an integral part of a player's game experience. First-time mod makers and level designers tend to focus a bit too much on the aesthetics of the environment and treat gameplay as an afterthought. I think this is a natural process in developing skills as a level designer. At first, all you want to do is recreate your favorite movie set or last year's awesome vacation spot and make it look as accurate and realistic as possible; but get it out of your system quick because a map can't succeed on aesthetics alone.

→

Consider the in-game significance of what you're spending your time on: the value the player will get from it and how much it contributes to the overall goals of the level or game. The amount of detail something has should directly correlate to how important and relevant it will be to the player's experience. If you're spending days working on some tiny, awesome detail that the players can't use, blow up, or learn from, be prepared that it probably won't be appreciated, might confuse them, or worse, lead them astray or get them completely stuck.

Avoid Red Herrings

Don't send your player off on pointless jaunts into useless areas.

Creating a level gives a designer a great degree of power, since the layout and design influences and directs the player at every step. Experienced game players will assume that everything you put in the level is for some gameplay purpose, and will seek to explore every inch of the space your create, looking for all the treasure, enemies, powerups, secrets, and trinkets they can find. If you put a doorway in a wall, they will want to open it to see what's behind it.

With that in mind, you don't want to design "dead end" areas of your level that look as if they will provide some type of player reward only to dole out nothing in return for the player's time. Do that once, and you might get away with it, but try it a second time and the player will start to lose trust in you as a designer—and you will already be battling player frustration as they move deeper in the game. The general rule is, don't create useless areas in your game levels, and never, ever create an area that looks to be of vital importance but isn't anything more than a red herring.

Take Advantage of Revisiting

Revisiting the same place from another vantage point can be good design.

Nothing spurs on a player more than seeing something he wants but can't get. You'll fuel the drive for the player if you show him an area in your map he can't yet get to—especially if he can see something of value there. The player will work and strive to get to that location. Imagine if a player enters a large antechamber of a castle, with arched ceilings, and above the player is a doorway out onto a stone preacher's platform. The player can't get there now, but he'll strive to find the way there. Eventually, once he opens the secret stairs and climbs up the steps, he'll find himself standing on the platform and having picked up a magic ring or protection. From this new vantage point, the player can overlook the room where he once stood below and see it in a new light.

Setting visual goals for the players drives them on, and allows them to explore and experience your environments from multiple vantage points, which can also help to deepen their suspension of disbelief.

Avoid Cookie-Cutter Layouts

Don't allow your level to fall into a boring and repetitive pattern.

If you were one of the many thousands of kids who served as a dungeon master in the early hey-day of *Dungeons & Dragons™*, you understand boring dungeon maps. We're not talking about Advanced D&D, but rather the old-school set that came as three small booklets in a box. In those days, we weren't exposed to video games or dungeon designs—there were really no precursors. So, dungeon masters sharpened their pencils, grabbed some graph paper, and set out to design dungeons, and they all looked the same—they were either long corridors with rooms off either side (the "hotel approach"), or a series of rooms, connected by short corridors (the "snake approach"). Without inspiration, the designs were banal and boring and became quite repetitious—of course, we never noticed, because playing an RPG was such a new and wonderful thing.

It's still easy to fall into the trap of repetition when designing 3D levels, however, and you need to be conscious to make your levels more interesting than the layout of a hotel or a series of rooms just connected together. Laying out your level on graph paper first is a good way to get started—you don't need to capture every detail and nuance, since often, much of the creativity of level design occurs during the creation process. Using graph paper, though, gives you a chance to see the layout, and instead of just thinking of rooms and corridors, think of oddly shaped rooms, turning short corridors, and vary the size of the interior spaces—think of your level as a series of various-sized Tetris™ pieces all fit together rather than a snake of rooms connected by hallways.

Think Multiplayer or Single Player

When you are designing a level, think about how it will be used in the game.

Designing a map for a single player experience means that you are guiding the player through a space that he will, in all likelihood, only visit once. You will populate the areas with obstacles, both static and dynamic, and escalate the challenge from environment to environment as his action skills grow.

Multiplayer maps are regions that are often played through at a much higher speed (run away!), but areas of the map will be frequented again and again. Players will not simply move through your geometry looking for challenges, but rather they will seek out offensive and defensive opportunities in the environment itself.

Some multiplayer experiences are called Deathmatches, which means every player is for himself. In these situations, players often run at full speed all the time, and level designers should provide several "racetrack" like looping routes to allow player to traverse the level at full speed. These routes should intersect from time to time, ideally in open spaces that favor neither the sniper nor the "in your face" player.

Team multiplayer games often revolve around the "capture the flag" dynamic, with a team of players working together to defend a position and infiltrate an enemy position. Often, these are point-to-point maps with one or more central areas for larger scale skirmishes. The team sections of the maps don't have to be identical in layout, but they need to offer identical travel times and capabilities (both offensive and defensive) so neither side is at an advantage or disadvantage once they know the map.

LEVEL DESIGN RESOURCES

For the last several years, developers of level-based action games have often released versions of their level editors and game source code with the game. If the games have proven to be well designed and implemented and develop a large following, often an entire Internet community grows around those who "mod" the games by creating their own levels and code additions.

Matt Wood, a level designer at Valve who worked on many of the environments for Half-Life 2™, offers these online resource suggestions for those who would like to try their hand at level design or custom modding.

I'm biased since this is our engine, but the Source engine is a great engine to work with. I think we have some of the top mods on our engine as well. Here are some sites for working with Source:

- *http://developer.valvesoftware.com/wiki/Main_Page:* Valve's Wiki that covers all aspects of Source engine development, from triple-A title developers to level creation hobbyists.
- *http://gmod.garry.tv/:* The Web site for Garry's Mod, winner of PC Gamer's™ Best Mod of 2005.
- *http://www.empiresmod.com/:* The Web site for the Empires mod, a mod that blends FPS action with an RTS commander interface.
- *http://en.wikipedia.org/wiki/Half-Life_2_mods:* This WikiPedia article lists a large number of single player and multiplayer Half-Life 2 mods out in circulation, with links to their sites.

■ *http://halflife2.filefront.com/:* A huge repository of various Half-Life 2 files.

■ *http://collective.valve-erc.com/:* Another fine repository of custom Half-Life 2 levels, mods, and files.

Unreal is also a great engine to work with:

■ *http://udn.epicgames.com/Two/PublicModResource:* This is the official site to support users who are interested in creating custom mods or levels for Unreal Tournament 2005™.

■ *http://unreal.epicgames.com/UTMods.html:* A detailed guide for mod authoring in the Unreal™ engine.

EYE OPENER IMPLEMENTATION

In Eye Opener, we've created a system to allow for horizontal side-scrolling environments. The "platformer" environments are defined by a few simple items, including scrolling backgrounds, platform modules (which we call "crates"), elevator platforms, and such. The implementation is simple, but it allows you to see both the implementation and the creation of this type of game environment (Figure 12.4).

FIGURE 12.4 The horizontal scrolling environment in Eye Opener.

Under the Hood

To understand any part of LevelScrolling.lua, one must understand that the world is composed of 20px × 20px squares (30 tall and 40 wide define the screen).

Each square is indexed by its x and y location in the OnScreen table. This table is created in CreateWorld()(found in LuaSupport.lua), if the table has not already been created by a RunScript() call to an existing level Lua file:

```
function CreateWorld()
    gNPCToggleState = OFF
    gScreenEdgeR = 800
    gScreenEdgeL = 0
    cellID = 1
    if levelEditMode == ON then
        LevelEditCursor = {}
        LevelEditCursor.ID = GUI_PLATFORMS + 1999
        LevelEditCursor.X = 0
        LevelEditCursor.Y = 0
        CreateItem(LevelEditCursor.ID, "Sprite", "crate.bmp")
        SetItemPosition(LevelEditCursor.ID, LevelEditCursor.X,
LevelEditCursor.Y, 20, 20)
        gCurrentState = "Crate"
    end
    myFile =
io.open(string.format("%s%s%s","Levels\\",gLevelName,".lua"),"r")
    if myFile ~= nil then
        RunScript(string.format("%s%s%s","Levels\\",gLevelName,".lua"))
        io.close(myFile)
    else
        gLevelWidth = 40
        World = {}
        for x = 1,40 do
            World[x] = {}
            for y = 1,30 do
                World[x][y] = 0
            end
        end
        Detonator = {}
        Turret = {}
        Hover = {}
    end
    OnScreen = {}
    for x = 1,40 do
        OnScreen[x] = {}
        for y = 1,30 do
            OnScreen[x][y] = {}
            OnScreen[x][y].ID = GUI_PLATFORMS + cellID
            cellID = cellID + 1
        end
    end
    DrawWorld()
end
```

This function does some housekeeping if we are in edit mode (see Table 12.1), and sets up the World and OnScreen tables with empty, default values. OnScreen[x][y] is equal to the state of the square indexed by the x and y screen coordinates. The value determines what is displayed in the world with the DrawCell(x,y) function. OnScreen[x][y].ID is the GUI id for the interface object at that square.

TABLE 12.1   OnScreen Table

State	Displayed Entity
1	Crate
2	Powerup
3	Non-Player Character
4	Detonator Plunger
5	Detonator Box
6	Bomb
7	Hover Platform (the moving part)
8	Hover Base (the stationary bounds)
9	Turret

When the player advances through the level, AdvanceWorld(direction) is called, effectively recalibrating the onScreen table in relation to the World table (which actually holds all of the level information).

```
function AdvanceWorld(dir)
    if dir == "forward" then
        gScreenEdgeR = gScreenEdgeR + 20
        gScreenEdgeL = gScreenEdgeL + 20
        if levelEditMode == ON then
            if gScreenEdgeR > gLevelWidth*20 then
                gLevelWidth = gLevelWidth + 1
                World[gLevelWidth] = {}
                for y = 1,30 do
                    World[gLevelWidth][y] = 0
                end
            end
            ScrollBackground(GUI_BACKGROUND,"forward")
            ScrollParalaxBackground(GUI_BACKGROUND,"forward")
        else
            if gScreenEdgeR > gLevelWidth*20 then
                gScreenEdgeR = gLevelWidth*20
                gScreenEdgeL = gScreenEdgeR-800
            else
                ScrollBackground(GUI_BACKGROUND,"forward")
                ScrollParalaxBackground(GUI_BACKGROUND,"forward")
```

```
                    end
                end
        else
                gScreenEdgeR = gScreenEdgeR - 20
                gScreenEdgeL = gScreenEdgeL - 20
                if gScreenEdgeL < 0 then
                    gScreenEdgeR = 800
                    gScreenEdgeL = 0
                else
                    ScrollBackground(GUI_BACKGROUND,"backward")
                    ScrollParalaxBackground(GUI_BACKGROUND,"backward")
                end
        end
        DrawWorld()
end
```

In this way, the OnScreen portion "slides" along the World table and updates such values as gScreenEdgeR, gScreenEdgeL, and the WorldX and State values for each OnScreen square. gScreenEdgeR and gScreenEdgeL are measured in pixels; if a level is longer than the width of the screen, values greater than 800 are necessary. WorldX is the x coordinate of the World table the OnScreen x coordinate refers to, or is layered on top of.

At the end of AdvanceWorld(), DrawWorld() is called, walks through each square in the OnScreen table, and sets it equal to the new corresponding World table value. Depending on the states given above, different objects are rendered.

```
function DrawWorld()
    for y = 1,30 do
        worldX = (gScreenEdgeL/20)+1
        for x = 1,40 do
            OnScreen[x][y].State = World[worldX][y]
            OnScreen[x][y].WorldX = worldX
            DrawCell(x,y)
            worldX = worldX + 1
        end
    end
end
```

This function simply walks through every cell in the OnScreen table and calls the DrawCell() function for that cell:

```
function DrawCell(x,y)
    if OnScreen[x][y].State == 1 then
        CreateItem(OnScreen[x][y].ID, "Sprite", "crate.bmp")
        SetItemPosition(OnScreen[x][y].ID, (x-1) * 20, (y-1) * 20, 20, 20)
    elseif OnScreen[x][y].State == 2 then
        CreateItem(OnScreen[x][y].ID, "Sprite", "powerup.bmp")
        SetItemPosition(OnScreen[x][y].ID, (x-1) * 20, (y-1) * 20, 20, 20)
    elseif OnScreen[x][y].State == 3 then
```

```
        CreateItem(OnScreen[x][y].ID, "Sprite", "character.bmp")
        SetItemPosition(OnScreen[x][y].ID, (x-1) * 20, (y-1) * 20, 20, 20)
    elseif OnScreen[x][y].State == 4 then
        CreateItem(OnScreen[x][y].ID, "Sprite", "detonator_plunger1.tga")
        SetItemPosition(OnScreen[x][y].ID, (x-2) * 20, (y-1) * 20, 60, 20)
    elseif OnScreen[x][y].State == 5 then
        CreateItem(OnScreen[x][y].ID, "Sprite", "detonator_box4.tga")
        SetItemPosition(OnScreen[x][y].ID, (x-2) * 20, (y-1) * 20, 60, 60)
    elseif OnScreen[x][y].State == 6 then
        CreateItem(OnScreen[x][y].ID, "Sprite", "bomb.tga")
        SetItemPosition(OnScreen[x][y].ID, (x-1) * 20, (y-1) * 20, 20, 20)
    elseif OnScreen[x][y].State == 7 then
        CreateItem(OnScreen[x][y].ID, "Sprite", "hover_platform.tga")
        SetItemPosition(OnScreen[x][y].ID, (x-2) * 20, (y-1) * 20, 60, 40)
    elseif OnScreen[x][y].State == 8 then
        CreateItem(OnScreen[x][y].ID, "Sprite", "hover_base.bmp")
        SetItemPosition(OnScreen[x][y].ID, (x-2) * 20, (y-1) * 20, 60, 20)
    elseif OnScreen[x][y].State == 9 then
        CreateItem(OnScreen[x][y].ID, "Sprite", "turret.tga")
        SetItemPosition(OnScreen[x][y].ID, (x-5) * 20, (y-2) * 20, 180, 60)
         ItemCommand(OnScreen[x][y].ID, "SetRotation",
Turret[OnScreen[x][y].WorldX][y])
    else
        if levelEditMode == ON then
            if OnScreen[x][y].ID ~= LevelEditCursor.ID then
                DeleteItem(OnScreen[x][y].ID)
            end
        else
            DeleteItem(OnScreen[x][y].ID)
        end
    end
  end
end
```

`DrawCell()` actually created the GUI objects on screen. If there is no object at the specific cell location, the `DeleteItem()` function is called, just in case there was an object there previously. (Note: You can edit the names of the graphic files in this function and add your own images to the Textures folder to create your own look to the game. You can also swap in your own graphics for the two levels of background scrolling images.)

Hover platforms are handled by the `ManageHoverPlatforms()` function in LuaSupport.lua. This function scans the portion of the `World` table that is on the screen and finds the hover platforms (`OnScreen[x][y] == 7`).

```
function ManageHoverPlatforms()
    Skip = {}
    for y = 1,30 do
        worldX = (gScreenEdgeL/20)+1
        for x = 1,40 do
            if World[worldX][y] == 7 then
                adjustOK = YES
```

```
                    for indx = 1,table.getn(Skip) do
                        if Skip[indx] == worldX then
                            adjustOK = NO
                        end
                    end
                    if adjustOK == YES then
                        if Hover[worldX] == 1 then
                            if World[worldX][y-4] ~= 8 then
                                World[worldX][y] = 0
                                World[worldX][y-1] = 7
                                if gIsFalling == worldX then
                                    MegaTable["Eye"].Y = MegaTable["Eye"].Y - 20
                                    SetItemPosition(MegaTable["Eye"].ID,
MegaTable["Eye"].X, MegaTable["Eye"].Y, MegaTable["Eye"].Width,
MegaTable["Eye"].Height)
                                end
                            else
                                Hover[worldX] = -1
                            end
                        else
                            if World[worldX][y+2] ~= 8 then
                                World[worldX][y] = 0
                                World[worldX][y+1] = 7
                                if gIsFalling == worldX then
                                    MegaTable["Eye"].Y = MegaTable["Eye"].Y + 20
                                    SetItemPosition(MegaTable["Eye"].ID,
MegaTable["Eye"].X, MegaTable["Eye"].Y, MegaTable["Eye"].Width,
MegaTable["Eye"].Height)
                                end
                            else
                                Hover[worldX] = 1
                            end
                        end
                        table.insert(Skip,worldX)
                    end
                end
                worldX = worldX + 1
            end
        end
    DrawWorld()
end
```

This function then checks if the platform has been previously moved during
this turn (this can happen when the iteration across the World table occurs in a
downward motion across the entire screen). It then checks if the platform is going
up (Hover[worldX] = 1) or down (Hover[worldX] = -1). It adjusts accordingly, making sure the platform hasn't reached a hover base, and adds the World table x value
to the Skip table (eliminating it from further adjustment on this turn).

All other level scrolling-specific functions operate like DetonationCheck():

```
function DetonationCheck()
    local playerY = MegaTable["Eye"].Y + MegaTable["Eye"].Height
    local onScreenY = (playerY/20)+1
    if playerY <= 580 then
    local numX = (MegaTable["Eye"].Width/20)-1
        for indx = 0,numX do
            local playerX = MegaTable["Eye"].X + (indx*20)
            local onScreenX = (playerX/20)+1
            if (OnScreen[onScreenX][onScreenY].State == 4) then
                —Plunger
                local plungerWorldX = OnScreen[onScreenX][onScreenY].WorldX
                local plungerY = onScreenY
                World[plungerWorldX][plungerY] = 0
                —Bomb
                local bombWorldX =
Detonator[OnScreen[onScreenX][onScreenY+1].WorldX][onScreenY+1].BombX
                local bombWorldY =
Detonator[OnScreen[onScreenX][onScreenY+1].WorldX][onScreenY+1].BombY
                World[bombWorldX][bombWorldY] = 0
                —Crates
                local playerWorldX = OnScreen[onScreenX][onScreenY].WorldX
                for i =
1,table.getn(Detonator[playerWorldX][onScreenY+1].CrateX) do
                    local crateWorldX =
Detonator[playerWorldX][onScreenY+1].CrateX[i]
                    local crateWorldY =
Detonator[playerWorldX][onScreenY+1].CrateY[i]
                    World[crateWorldX][crateWorldY] = 0
                end
                DrawWorld()
                CreateItem(GUI_PLATFORMS + 1998, "Sprite", "kaboom_01.tga")
                local explosionX = (bombWorldX - ((gScreenEdgeL/20)+1)) *
20 - 9
                local explosionY = ((bombWorldY-1)*20) - 9
                SetItemPosition(GUI_PLATFORMS + 1998, explosionX,
explosionY, 38, 38)
                explosionFrame = 2
                gIsFalling = "no"
            end
        end
    end
end
```

They all find the location of specific squares (crates, characters, etc.) in relation to the player's character. This then triggers action. For this function, it triggers an action for the plunger and then the bomb, and then it will affect the crates immediately surrounding the bomb. This is the same basic logic as you will find in PositionCheck(), CollisionCheck(direction), and to a lesser extent AdvancePlayer(direction).

Creating and Editing Scrolling Levels

On the Main menu of the development sandbox build, click "Level Edit." Then, type the name of the level you want to edit (or the name you want to bestow upon the new level you are creating) when the blinking cursor appears. Then, press the button at the bottom of the screen to enter the level-editing interface.

When the scene appears, you will notice that a default set of scrolling middle ground and background appear. Your mouse also has become the Level Edit Cursor. A textbox describes your cursor as you cycle through the different items you can add to the level:

Crate: Basic level building block; the Eye can stand on it.

Power Up: Will change some of the Eye's traits. Makes a sound when picked up.

Character: When the Eye is near, it allows the Eye to initiate NPC conversation.

Erase: Allows the user to clear anything placed in the level.

Detonator Box: The Eye must land on it to detonate the linked bomb.

Bomb: Explodes when linked detonator is depressed; destroys items.

Hover Base: When placed, a Hover Platform appears above it. The user must place the upper platform in the same vertical plane to provide the vertical limits of the Hover Platform; the Eye can ride the Hover Platform.

Turret: The Turret will locate the Eye and attempt to eliminate it by shooting projectiles.

Finish Level: Left-clicking on this setting will save the level and exit the level editor.

Scrolling Backgrounds

The platformer environment features a scrolling background that creates the effect that the player is moving across a real landscape of some sort. This background can be changed and modified to allow you to experiment with different looks to the platform environment.

In ParalaxBackgroundScrolling.lua, `CreateScrollBackground(id,step,...)` is called (the function is defined in LuaSupport.lua). The `id` value is the GUI offset (`GUI_BACKGROUND` for instance). The `step` is the number of pixels that the background should move on each movement.

```
function CreateScrollBackground(id,step,...)
    BackgroundX = {}
    BackgroundX.Step = step
    gBackgroundCount = arg.n
```

```
    if gBackgroundCount == 1 then
        gBackgroundCount = 2
        arg[2] = arg[1]
    end
    for indx = 1,gBackgroundCount do
        CreateItem(id + 99 + indx, "Sprite", arg[indx])
        BackgroundX[indx] = 800*(indx-1)
        SetItemPosition(id + 99 + indx, BackgroundX[indx], 0, 800, 600)
    end
end
```

An unlimited amount of filename strings can be passed in as parameters. Each will be stretched to 800*600 and placed in the order in which they come, one right after the other, to create a long ribbon of background art. If only one is given (one must be given at least), the background will repeat that image as it scrolls.

ScrollBackground(id,dir) simply takes the passed GUI offset and moves the correlating background chain in the appropriate direction. If either end of the chain should appear on the screen, the other end of the chain attaches to it, forming a looping background.

```
function ScrollBackground(id,dir)
    if dir == "forward" then
        for indx = 1,gBackgroundCount do
            BackgroundX[indx] = BackgroundX[indx] - BackgroundX.Step
        end
        for indx = 1,gBackgroundCount do
            if BackgroundX[indx] <= -800 then
                dif = -800 - BackgroundX[indx]
                BackgroundX[indx] = 800*(gBackgroundCount-1) - dif
            end
        end
    else
        for indx = 1,gBackgroundCount do
            BackgroundX[indx] = BackgroundX[indx] + BackgroundX.Step
        end
        for indx = 1,gBackgroundCount do
            if BackgroundX[indx] >= 800*(gBackgroundCount-1) then
                dif = BackgroundX[indx] - 800*(gBackgroundCount-1)
                BackgroundX[indx] = -800 + dif
            end
        end
    end
    for indx = 1,gBackgroundCount do
        SetItemPosition(id + 99 + indx, BackgroundX[indx], 0, 800, 600)
    end
end
```

CreateParalaxBackground(id,step,yCoord,height,width,...) and Scroll-ParalaxBackground(id,dir) work the same way. The only difference is that the parallax background functions must handle the size of the parallax image and its height on the screen. The parallax background is the frontmost background image. In our example game, the background image is a planetary scene, while the parallax image is the pile of junk in the foreground. To create a realistic scrolling background effect, set the step value for the background lower than the step value for the parallax image—in that way, the distant background will scroll by slower than the foreground, creating a realistic movement effect.

SUMMARY

In this chapter, we looked at the role the environment plays as a container for the interactivity we present to the player. Environments support the milieu of a game, and act as a guide for the player, leading him from challenge to challenge.

We explored a short set of design atoms relating to environments and their general role in our game design, and then drilled a little deeper to explore some design opportunities and concerns within level- and architecture-based environments.

From there, we looked at the basic scrolling platform environment we implemented in Eye Opener, but from an under-the-hood viewpoint and as a tool to create new platforms and environments.

In the next chapter, we look at puzzle in the context of gameplay and how we can create unique and interesting mental challenges for our players.

CHAPTER EXERCISES

1. Think of a "period" or "other worldly" environment from a favorite movie you've seen recently. Write up a list of descriptive words and phrases you would use to "capture" the feel of the environment (as if you were working as a level designer for a game based on the movie).
2. Using the level editing mode for Eye Opener, create a new environment that offers a compelling challenge to the player and perhaps requires some thought to figure out.
3. Using either a collage of photo images or some hand-drawn images, create your own parallax scrolling background for the Eye Opener game environment.

13 Puzzle Design

In This Chapter

- What is a Puzzle?
- High-Level Puzzle Design
- Low-Level Puzzle Design
- Puzzle Types

Players love challenges, and they love to become immersed in a game that presents them with a wide array of challenges that test their abilities across the board. Players may learn hand-eye coordination skills, gunnery skills, tactical skills, and be tested in many ways by your game. You can increase the challenge and variety of player challenge by also incorporating puzzles for your players to solve during the game—giving them an opportunity to exercise their gray matter and their trigger fingers.

WHAT IS A PUZZLE?

A game experience is fun only when it delivers some challenge to the player. We like to be challenged and to overcome. We like to open a mysterious door only to be set upon by a horde of spider creatures—we hack, slash, and backpedal, and with some luck, we can dispatch the enemies, take a deep breath, and enter the room beyond. It would be no fun if the door merely opened.

Games present many types of challenges to a player. A first-person shooter can throw dozens of zombies at the player. A strategy game may serve up an opposing force of Panzer tanks prowling bombed-out city streets. A casual game may present you with a grid of letters and challenge you to find the words hidden within.

So, what differentiates an enemy from a puzzle? In many games, you have obstacles that require gameplay skill to overcome: timing a jump, firing a laser pistol accurately, sending a column of tanks to take out an enemy, using a freeze spell to halt the charge of a pack of werebears, and so forth. All these require the player to use learned game skills or acquired game abilities to overcome the challenge and move forward.

Other challenges require the player to perform some mental problem solving to get past a challenge—these are known as puzzles. At times, puzzles may be blended with normal obstacles, as in our previous freeze spell example. It may take the player some mental gymnastics to deduce that the freeze spell and not the "enrage" spell will work against the werebears. In an RTS game, often the tactics employed to successfully defeat a given mission require mental deduction and problem solving and then player action.

The hallmark of a puzzle is the requirement that the potential solver use his mental "thinking skills" to evaluate and determine a potential solution to a challenge, and not purely physical or mental "action skills."

A quality game will present a player with a variety of challenges and experiences. An action game with nothing but hordes of zombies to shoot and no problem-solving component will grow quickly boring. A game made up of nothing but puzzles with no other skill element or story thread to tie things together and immerse the player will present no interest for long-term play. A game that presents obstacles that require action skills, mixed with puzzles that require mental skills, will have the highest probability of success.

Beyond simply alternating between action skill challenges and puzzles, a designer can introduce even more play depth by blending the two, almost like a dovetail joint. By providing action skill obstacles for the players while they are in the middle of solving a mental skill puzzle, the players will be drawn into a deeper level of engagement in the game. This approach also helps to solidify the illusion that the game is presenting a rich and vibrant world to the players, since challenges overlap (as they do in our real lives), rather than simply follow each other like kids in a single-file line.

Some Examples

Before we discuss some rules for good puzzle design, let's look at a few examples of game puzzles, from a player's perspective.

You see a door. Not a plain door like all the others you've fought your way through—this door is ornately carved with a frame of elaborate hieroglyphics carved into the stone. A gold handle and keyhole adorn the door. You try it, but it's locked. You turn around and explore the room—nothing but some old crates and a stone ledge at the far end of the room. But wait! On the ledge, you see a faint orange glow. You back up and can clearly see a gold key atop the ledge. You run toward the ledge, jump, and slam right into the stonework—it's too high! Scanning the room again, you notice the crates. You get behind a crate and discover that you can push it. You push the crate over to the ledge. You can easily jump onto the crate, and from there you can reach the stone ledge and grab the key. You jump down, return to the door, and use the key to unlock it. The door swings open to reveal . . . (a classic from *Doom 2*, from the mind of John Romero—Figure 13.1)

You enter a large arena—in the center is a stage with two of the nastiest creatures you have ever seen. Across the arena is a door—the door you must leave through. Running frantically (to avoid the plasma bolts), you reach the door only to discover it is locked. As you turn to run away, you notice a small control panel on the stage with a switch on it. The creatures continue to fire at you as you run frantically around. Then, you get an idea—you run so that you place one of the large creatures between you and the other. The far creature can still see you and he hurls a plasma bolt at you, but it strikes the other creature instead. The second creature wails in pain and starts shooting at his partner. Soon, they are trading blows as sparks shower the arena. With both creatures occupied, you run to the stage, hop up (as the plasma sparks fill your vision), flip the switch, and hear the reassuring whoosh of the door opening. You hop down and sprint to the door, just make it to safety as the sole surviving creature turns his attention to you...

Rules of Puzzle Design

There are really two layers to puzzle design. The uppermost layer is concerned with the general type of puzzle and how it fits into your game. This isn't that dissimilar to the things we were thinking about with general interface design. The deeper level of puzzle design is the mechanics of the puzzle—how does the player solve the puzzle, and does it present a compelling challenge to the player?

In the pages that follow, we'll explore both levels of the puzzle design process to, again, arm ourselves with a series of "atoms" that will allow us to create the best puzzle possible.

High-Level Puzzle Design

There are several levels of puzzle design, from the in-the-trenches design of a "dismantle the bomb" puzzle to some higher level rules that will allow you to create more effective puzzles across the breadth of your game. In the sections that follow, we'll look at some of these higher level game design atoms.

Make the Puzzle Fit

A puzzle should feel natural within the game, as if it belongs there.

This is one of those common-sense rules that still needs to be stated. When you design a puzzle, make sure it fits neatly within the context of the game universe and story. If you have a game that's played at a frenetic pace, don't have a puzzle that features slowly sliding concrete blocks—it goes against the pacing of the game. If you are creating a military RTS game, don't toss in a jumping puzzle—it doesn't fit the game control scheme. Think of the classic puzzle game, *Seventh Guest*—in the old, nasty kitchen, the puzzle involved arranging old soup cans. In the library, there was a chess puzzle. Make your puzzle fit the environment.

Support the Story

A puzzle should amplify the story or theme of the game.

A puzzle should fit within the game universe and support and enhance the game experience, be it the game's story, the theme of the game, or the tone of the game. Think of a puzzle as an opportunity to connect with the players, interactively, and pull them even deeper into the universe and game experience. If your game focuses on the Knights Templar, a puzzle based on finding and placing the jewels in the stem of the Grail could work well—perhaps the knights hid them to render the Grail's recuperative powers useless. If you are designing an RPG and your meta quest revolves around finding a cure to a horrible plague, a puzzle to find the ingredients to concoct a potion of temporary immunity (so you can enter an infected village to hunt for clues) will further emphasize your story. Use the puzzle as a vehicle to bring the players into the struggles of the game world and allow them to use their mental skills to solve a problem or puzzle that has "real" weight to the inhabitants of the game universe.

Make the Puzzle Obvious

Make it obvious that an obstacle is indeed a puzzle to solve.

Letting players know that you are asking them to solve a puzzle isn't about breaking the suspension of their disbelief—instead, it's about letting them know what to do next. Nothing frustrates a player more than being confused as to what to do in a game. Don't add to this confusion by trying to "disguise" a puzzle so well that a player doesn't immediately understand what you are asking from him. It's not about making the puzzle easy or the solution obvious—it's about letting the players know what you expect from them.

A locked door with a keyhole is an obvious puzzle: find the key or find some other way to open the door. Having a dying NPC utter a cryptic word that's part of a multiword pass-phrase the player needs to know to open a magical chest on the far side of the world is a nonobvious puzzle, and only sets the stage for later player frustration.

Vary the Scope

Vary the scope and depth of puzzles within a game.

Puzzles test a player's mental abilities, but too many puzzles that are the same and test the same type of thinking will create either boredom or frustration for the player. If you are using puzzles in a game, don't stop at only one puzzle, since being a "lone wolf" will make it feel out of place. At least deliver several puzzles to the players, but vary the mental skills they require to keep them interested and the puzzles feeling fresh.

Don't have nothing but "hunt for the key" puzzles—if you are simply linking puzzles to door opening, add some combination-lock puzzles and perhaps a logic puzzle for a door that has no visible means of being locked. The variety will keep the players guessing and keep them interested in your game.

Focus on How

Don't make the player struggle with what to do, but rather how to do it.

This is a more puzzle-centric way of saying, "don't frustrate the player." As a designer, you can come up with all manner of wicked, difficult puzzles, but don't make them so obtuse that the player doesn't understand how to proceed. In our example of the gold key earlier, the player quickly understands what his goal is: to retrieve the gold key. The puzzle revolves around how he gets to the key—he isn't wasting his time at the door wondering, "What am I supposed to do?" It may be fun to devise a puzzle that's so fiendishly difficult that no one can solve, but the true art is to design a puzzle a player enjoys solving. Provide clues in the environment (both visual and aural) that will help the players understand that they are encountering a puzzle, and provide some clues as to what they are striving to do.

Keep a Puzzle Active

Don't allow the players to forget they are working to solve a puzzle.

Again, this may seem obvious, but often puzzles require the player to gather components to build a solution-widget or some device that is needed. This may take the players across large areas of the game, and they may be engaged in many other activities along the way. If this is the case, don't let them forget that they are also working to solve a puzzle—keep that focus and motivation front and center. The easiest way to do this is, don't spread your puzzles out too far across the game world or the gameplay timeline. If you must spread your puzzle out, then provide the players with reminders as they are engaged in other activities—with some reminder of what they are working toward (perhaps the castle tower on the horizon is belching green flames and black smoke—reminding the player that he is seeking the components that will gain him entrance to the tower).

Blend Player Activities

When possible, blend puzzles with action skill activities.

Players are more engaged in a game experience if they are doing many different things—if they have to keep assessing the game world and then overcoming both mental and action skill obstacles. Keeping their brain switching modes helps to fight fatigue and complacency and provides a more energized experience for the player. With this in mind, when possible, blend the mental skills of your puzzles with some of the action skills your game also requires. If a player has to leap atop a ledge to recover a key, have him hack and slash his way back to the door before he can open it. If a player is exploring the caverns of an ancient dungeon, attempting to recover the broken fragments of a long-lost magical sword, don't just let him freely walk the corridors—have him use his action skills to jump a crevasse and his magic skills to freeze several fire elements along the way.

Low-Level Puzzle Design

Earlier, we looked at some design atoms that helped us understand how to place puzzle challenges within the scope and context of the game. Now we'll turn out attention to the puzzles themselves and look at some design atoms that will help us create some interesting and compelling puzzle challenges for our players.

Avoid Artificial Pressure

Do not create artificial pressure for the players when they are solving a puzzle.

Ideally, your puzzle will provide enough mental challenge for your player so you won't need to throw external pressure on the player to solve the puzzle. At times, external pressure can be used to enhance the energy and pressure of the puzzle, such as solving a wiring puzzle to open an air vent before a room fills with water.

In the preceding example, the pressure was a way to force the player to think quickly when solving the puzzle, but the pressure of the room filling with water also fits into the context of the game and the very reason for the existence of the puzzle. What you want to avoid is throwing obstacles at the player that really have nothing to do with the puzzle, but are merely meant to occupy and stress out the player. Continuing to spawn chainsaw-wielding zombies as the player works to solve a key puzzle is simply a copout. The puzzle may be too simple, and you are just looking for an easy way to make the situation feel more stressful. As a rule of thumb, if pressure on the player doesn't have anything directly to do with the context or solution of a puzzle, avoid it.

Be Careful with Timed Puzzles

Be judicious when presenting the player with timed puzzles.

At times, nothing can be more exciting than attempting to defuse a bomb as the time to certain death ticks down in front of the player's eyes. Timed puzzles and challenges certainly have their place in game design, but be careful when deploying "burning fuse" puzzles. Timed puzzles can cause player panic and frustration easily—in general, a timed puzzle needs to be relatively easy to solve, and the player should understand that the puzzle does have a timer, even before he begins solving the puzzle. If you present a complex puzzle to players and then suddenly surprise them with a countdown timer, they will become flustered and may not know what to do next to solve the puzzle.

It's also a good idea not to employ too many timed puzzles in a single game experience, since they can be draining for the player, and if the player fails at a timed puzzle, the next appearance of a timed puzzle will lead to almost instant frustration.

Don't Kill the Player

Don't force player death as a requisite to learning to solve a puzzle.

It's perfectly valid to have death as a consequence of not solving a puzzle in a game, although this should only occur rarely. What should be avoided is forcing the player to die in order to learn how your puzzle works. Imagine a cavern over a molten lava river—there is a door on the other side. The player approaches and looks over the edge—he sees nothing but the side of the cliffs. He steps back and attempts a running jump to clear the gap and discovers, too late, that there is no way he can clear the jump. As the player falls, he sees an opening on the cliff face he was just on . . . as he falls to his death. The player then learns that if he just falls off the cliff (after he restores his last save game, that is), spins 180 degrees and pushes the controller forward, he can "catch" the ledge of the opening and get to a tunnel that will lead him to a retractable bridge that finally gets him to the other side.

An interesting puzzle, true, but one that forces the player to die at least once, but probably many times, in order to figure out what the game expects him to do. As designers, we are working to create a sense of "value" for the player's alter ego in the game, so that the simulated game actions feel like they have real consequences. However, by forcing the player to die in order to discover the solution of a puzzle, we immediately break the suspension of disbelief with our players.

Make the Solution Feel Possible

Make solving the puzzle feel possible for the player.

Perception is 95 percent of reality in the real world—in a game, it's 100 percent of the game's "reality." If you present players with what appears to be an impossible challenge, many will believe it's impossible, become frustrated, and simply quit the game. If you present a puzzle of amazing complexity, many players will believe that they simply can't solve it and will walk away from the challenge.

As a designer, your challenge is to create a puzzle that feels possible to solve, but doesn't present an immediately obvious solution to the majority of players (there are always some who will "get" your puzzle almost instantly). You want to create a puzzle presentation that feels manageable within the acquired skills of the player at that point in the game—ideally, the puzzle should feel "just out of reach" for the average player at first blush, but after some studying of the puzzle dynamics, the puzzle should feel accessible.

So, how do you, as a designer, do this? The first step is to be aware of the challenge level at the particular point in the game where you will be putting the puzzle. You will also want to make sure the puzzle "fits" into the context of the game so it feels natural. Finally, you'll want to incorporate something familiar into the puzzle as a "hook"—perhaps it's using hieroglyphics the player has encountered before, or part of a computer controller that's similar to something he's seen before. The goal is to make the players somewhat comfortable with the challenge, so they will feel that they can best it and will stick with it until they do.

Use Micro Puzzles

When possible, introduce "micro" puzzles that teach about larger puzzles deeper in the game.

This is a natural extension to the previous atom. To make players feel confident in their ability to solve a complex puzzle, introduce them to smaller, somewhat similar puzzles during earlier gameplay. If you are presenting them with a complex wiring puzzle to open a door, give them one or two small wiring puzzles early on—these "intro puzzles" shouldn't be considered major challenges in and of themselves; rather, they are precursors to the puzzle proper, teaching rather than offering too much in the way of challenge.

Consider a puzzle that requires a player to push different-shaped crates into a large pit, to stack them (in *Tetris* fashion) in such a way that you create a staircase so you can safely descend into the pit to explore a hidden room. The puzzle consists of several components: pushing the crates, dropping them, arranging them in the right order so they form the staircase, and pulling a tall stone out of the wall to use as a missing crate, to complete the puzzle. The puzzle has several layers, but the real "meat" of the puzzle is figuring out how the pieces fit together.

Earlier in the game, you can present a puzzle similar to our gold key example—pushing a crate to climb up to a ledge. This teaches the player that crates and objects can be pushed. Next, you can have an earlier puzzle in which the players must remove a part of the architecture and use it in a different manner—say removing a door to use it to lay across a chasm. Doing so, you teach them to look around the environment for alternate solutions.

In this way, you have provided several smaller challenges that expand the players' vocabulary of what can or can't be done in the game world, so when they come to your larger puzzle, they will be better prepared to overcome the challenge (and enjoy the process).

Don't Let the Player Miss Something Vital

Don't cripple the player's chance to solve a puzzle because he missed a clue or vital piece of inventory earlier in the game.

In short, don't hinge puzzle success on a single object if there is a chance a player won't have it. Nothing frustrates a player more than to realize that he is either dead in the water or has to backtrack through four levels of your game to retrieve a missing item.

The most sensible ways to avoid this problem are to either keep all items needed for a puzzle relatively close by, or provide some sort of "choke point" in the game in which you won't let the players continue unless they have item X or item Y. Say you need the player to have a scroll so he can read a secret word vital for solving a puzzle—perhaps this scroll is a "rite of passage" given to the player's party to safely leave a far-flung kingdom—the player won't be able to leave that portion of the game until he has the scroll, so you can be assured that he has it in his possession when he encounters your puzzle.

Failure Should Be Interesting

If the player is likely to fail when solving a puzzle, make the failure state interesting.

The players won't succeed every time—sometimes a puzzle will require several tries before they can successfully solve it. If they fail, don't make failure fall flat. If you are trying to wire a switch to open a door, and you get the wiring wrong, don't indicate failure by the lack of anything happening—perhaps the wrong wiring combination accidentally opens the cage that contains a rabid dog. The idea isn't to penalize the players, but to provide gameplay interest even if they don't succeed at first.

Reset the Puzzle

If a puzzle can be completed incorrectly, provide a reasonable way to reset the puzzle.

This follows from the preceding atom—if the puzzle is solved incorrectly, it should somehow get itself back into a neutral state for the player to have another go at it. Ideally, you'll do this in a "natural" way that feels like it fits in the game world. Of course, if your puzzle is to diffuse a bomb and the player fails—well, then the failure state will certainly be interesting, but resetting the puzzle will most likely be the player restoring the game. If the puzzle is more mundane—say a wiring puzzle—and the player fails, then perhaps the circuit erupts in sparks and all the wire segments fall to the floor and the player can start again.

Avoid Binary Puzzles

Don't present a puzzle to the player with an immediate "success or failure" result.

We've all seen it in the movies—the hero is working to diffuse the bomb. Seconds are ticking down and he is down to two wires—a red wire and a blue wire. Cut the right wire and the bomb is diffused—cut the wrong wire and BOOM!

While this may be exciting in movies, it doesn't work well to create a satisfying gameplay experience. It is the equivalent of clicking a button on the screen and maybe you'll win the game or maybe you'll lose. The lack of control and instant catastrophic result means the puzzle really isn't a puzzle at all—it's a coin flip. Puzzles are defined by their ability to offer a mental skills challenge for the player. If a player works hard and fails at a puzzle, he at least feels the value of his effort and hopefully has learned some skills to make the solution go better next time. A coin flip doesn't challenge the player at all, and hence provides no satisfaction—win or lose.

How to Document Puzzle Design

Earlier, we covered some atoms of good puzzle design and explored solid design approaches and landmines to avoid. With these in mind, and a sharp pencil in hand, how do you actually design a puzzle? How do you put that design into your design document?

Puzzles come in so many shapes, sizes, and approaches that we simply can't cover every variation here—later in this chapter, we'll look at some common types of puzzles to help you get started, but now we'll look at how to incorporate a general puzzle design into your design document.

First, you'll need to identify where in the game the puzzle will exist—this may be a place in an environment, or it may be a puzzle that is triggered by a set of conditions (perhaps it's triggered after a player recovers all five pieces of the "Spear of Destiny").

Your first job is to clearly call out where the puzzle will occur and what it will require of the player (as far as inventory, abilities, or such).

Next, you'll want to document the puzzle in narrative form. This won't be to the depth that you describe every detail and nuance of the puzzle, but rather to give a solid general understanding of the puzzle.

Your final job is to document the puzzle in detail, so it can actually be implemented. The level of detail will vary from puzzle to puzzle and designer to designer. Some designers will need to include pseudo-code indicating how the puzzle logic works, while other can simply explain the rules clearly. The best approach is to sit down with your tech lead and the general description of the puzzle. Have him or her look over the description and then provide the details of how you envision the puzzle working. You'll get some good feedback and ideas—what will work and what won't. Ask your tech lead what he or she needs from you, information-wise, to document the puzzle so a programmer can successfully implement it. Your job is *not* to do the programmers' job, but to help them do their job better. Use this meeting as your guide to what information is needed and what isn't.

Eye Opener Design Example

In the following example, we'll lay out the design of a puzzle we referenced in our design document back in Chapter 5:

PUZZLE DESIGN: WIRING PUZZLE

```
Location:
Next to the door at the end of Horizontal Level Three
Requirements:
Claw powerup, Robot Head minion, pile of wires inventory item
Description:
As the player approaches the door, he will notice it's locked. There is
a door controller next to it that looks to be broken and a pile of wires
on the ground. The "Talk" icon will appear and when the player clicks on
it, he will begin a dialogue with the Robot Head.

The Head will tell the player that a guard must have yanked out the
wires to stop their progress, so they must be close. He tells the player
that he thinks the player can rewire the switch. The red need to connect
to the red and the blue to the blue, it should be simple.
```

→

The player begins the puzzle and no matter how he tries with the wires he has, he can't solve the puzzle. He must pull one of the loose wires from the Robot Head to get an additional long wire (this will "shut down" the Robot Head). With the additional robot head, the player should be able to solve the puzzle.

When the connections are made, the player can click the Open button and the door will open.

Specifics:

Pile of wires:
  10 short wires, 1 long wire
  Robot Head:
  1 long wire

Cursor:

Change to claw cursor to signify that the player is using his claw controller.

Interface:

This is an alternate interface puzzle that will play as full screen.

Play Details:

The playfield is a 6 x 4 grid, with several grid points having terminals. One side of the field has red and blue terminals and on the other side is another set of terminals. A "path graphic" will appear between all terminals that can be connected. The layout of the terminals will be determined by a two-dimensional table structure in script.

The left side of the screen will show an inventory of what wires are unused. When the player uses a wire (by clicking on a path graphic), the path graphic will be replaced by a wire graphic and the inventory will be adjusted.

When the player clicks the Open button, the puzzle will check for a solution. If the solution is correct, then a small display will indicate "Door opening…" on screen and we will switch back to level view with the door open.

If the solution is not correct, the player will see a nonsense text message (like a system malfunction); the view will switch back to level view with the door still closed. The switch will span an explosion effect and the pile of wires inventory item will appear again below the switch.

Note: To keep processing as simple as possible, make sure the layout and wire inventory allows for one and only one solution of the puzzle.

In this design example, we outlined all the details of how the puzzle works, but did not describe how to implement it or just what the specific solution is (since that is determined by the layout of the terminals). We have given enough detail so a programmer or script coder can implement the puzzle correctly. In the following examples, we will see how the core of this puzzle was implemented in Lua.

LEVEL DESIGNERS

Designer: Paul Schuytema

While you may incorporate several hallmark puzzles into your game design, you may also "discover" puzzles along the way, during the development process. Never does this occur more frequently as when level designers are creating game environments. Level designers are part game designer, part 3D modeler, and part programmer—they are responsible for creating the actual play environment for nearly all first-person games and many RTS, adventure, and RPG games.

Level designers often work from a design document that outlines the requirements for their level (which we'll explore in more depth in a later chapter). Within those requirements, they are free to create interesting play situations, and often that will lead to impromptu environmental navigation puzzles, door access puzzles, and other interesting puzzle situations.

When I was designing the second iteration of Prey for 3D Realms, we created a flowchart system of "plot points" that we used to define the meta-flow through a game level. These charts defined the choke points in the level for cinematics and meta puzzles, and other key elements. The level designers would work from these and create their own interpretations of the level. Countless times, when I would sit down with level designers to review their progress, they would show me fascinating puzzles that they had implemented within their levels—often the inspiration for these would come to them as their were crafting the architecture or the flow of the level and they would have the inspiration of "wouldn't it be cool if we could . . ." and then they'd try it out.

It was a very clear example of how a team of creative individuals, all working toward a common goal, can infuse a game experience with far more inspiration that just a single designer working in a vacuum.

PUZZLE VARIATIONS

In the sections the follow, we'll quickly look at some general puzzle types you may encounter as a game player or may wish to implement as a designer. This is by no means an exhaustive list, since puzzles can come in so many shapes and sizes and many of them are unique. We'll also look at a few examples taken from our Eye Opener game, to see how we implemented them within the game itself.

The Key

The most basic form of an in-game puzzle is simply using an object as a "key" to enable something to happen. The classic example of this appeared in the very first adventure and action games: a door is locked and you must use a key to open the door. The general "puzzle aspect" of this type of puzzle isn't in using the key object, but rather in finding the key itself.

Often, many designers will enable an "automatic use" of the object if it is simply in their possession. Moving close to an unlocked door opens it. Moving close to a locked door with the proper key in your inventory also opens the door—there is no extra step to open the door.

The Unexpected Key

A variation of the Key puzzle is having the key itself be unexpected. It's obvious that a key opens a door. It's less obvious that the hairpin you found in an abandoned purse can be used as a lock pick to open the door. Sometimes this is called a "MacGuyver Puzzle" since it forces you to think like that old TV hero and come up with new ways in which to use familiar objects. Players are smart, and they will often assume that every object they find in a game has some use later. Often, they will be actively thinking of "unexpected key" uses of all their inventory objects when they come to an obstacle puzzle that isn't obvious in its solution.

As a designer, the trick is to have the unexpected key require some thought on the part of the player, but you want to avoid making the puzzle so nonobvious that only a fraction of your players get it. When a player "figures out" the unexpected key, you want the player to have a smug, "I feel good" reaction, and a sense that the unusual key makes perfect sense once it was figured out.

Eye Opener Implementation

In Eye Opener, we present the player with an Unexpected Key puzzle early on. When the player begins, he is simply a rolling eyeball with no real abilities at all. He will encounter an obstacle in the form of a wall that he simply can't get past. He will also see a bomb and a detonation plunger. It's obvious that the plunger will explode the bomb and clear the path, but how does the eye activate the plunger? He has no way (yet) to use anything in the game.

Detonation Puzzle

The puzzle is for the player to discover that the eyeball itself is the Unexpected Key. The player can follow a seemingly red herring path leading to nowhere, but when he reaches that position he can roll off and land on the plunger, thus triggering the bomb to explode (Figure 13.1).

Now, we'll dive into the Lua script and describe how we make this puzzle actually work, by describing the mechanics of detonation in our example game. Feel free to experiment with the Lua scripts to create your own variations to these behaviors and your own variations on this puzzle.

The file in which this action happens is called `LevelScrolling.lua`, and it is found in the scripts folder of the game build on the companion CD-ROM.

To understand any part of `LevelScrolling.lua`, one must understand that the world is composed of 20px × 20px squares (30 tall and 40 wide).

Each square is indexed by its x and y location in the `OnScreen` table (see `CreateWorld()` and `AdvanceWorld(dir)` functions in `LuaSupport.lua`). Each is complete with its own ID and State. The State can be changed (see `DrawCell(x,y)`) to display the proper entity at that location.

When the player advances through the level, `AdvanceWorld(dir)` is called, effectively recalibrating the `OnScreen` table in relation to the World table (which actually holds all of the level information). In this way, the `OnScreen` portion "slides" along the World table and updates such values as `gScreenEdgeR`, `gScreenEdgeL`, and the `WorldX` and `State` values for each `OnScreen` square. (Figure 13.2.)

FIGURE 13.1   The TNT plunger and the bomb in Eye Opener.

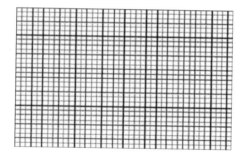

FIGURE 13.2   The world of Eye Opener is defined by a grid, with each cell being 20 × 20 pixels.

When a detonator appears in the level, it is actually composed of two distinct parts—the detonator and the plunger. The detonator is scripted for by setting `World[x][y] = 5` (and eventually `OnScreen[x][y] = 5`). The plunger is 4. The location of their defining square (which is saved in the `World` table of any level .lua file) is shown in the grayed-out area in Figure 13.3.

FIGURE 13.3 The detonation plunger is made of two parts.

The `DetonationCheck()` function (`LuaSupport.lua`) handles the detection of the presence of a plunger beneath the player's Eye image.

```
function DetonationCheck()
    local playerY = MegaTable["Eye"].Y + MegaTable["Eye"].Height
    local onScreenY = (playerY/20)+1
    if playerY <= 580 then
    local numX = (MegaTable["Eye"].Width/20)-1
        for indx = 0,numX do
            local playerX = MegaTable["Eye"].X + (indx*20)
            local onScreenX = (playerX/20)+1
            if (OnScreen[onScreenX][onScreenY].State == 4) then
                -Plunger
                local plungerWorldX = OnScreen[onScreenX][onScreenY].WorldX
                local plungerY = onScreenY
                World[plungerWorldX][plungerY] = 0
                -Bomb
                local bombWorldX =
Detonator[OnScreen[onScreenX][onScreenY+1].WorldX][onScreenY+1].BombX
                local bombWorldY =
Detonator[OnScreen[onScreenX][onScreenY+1].WorldX][onScreenY+1].BombY
                World[bombWorldX][bombWorldY] = 0
                -Crates
                local playerWorldX = OnScreen[onScreenX][onScreenY].WorldX
                for i =
1,table.getn(Detonator[playerWorldX][onScreenY+1].CrateX) do
                    local crateWorldX =
Detonator[playerWorldX][onScreenY+1].CrateX[i]
                    local crateWorldY =
Detonator[playerWorldX][onScreenY+1].CrateY[i]
                    World[crateWorldX][crateWorldY] = 0
                end
                DrawWorld()
                CreateItem(GUI_PLATFORMS + 1998, "Sprite", "kaboom_01.tga")
                local explosionX = (bombWorldX - ((gScreenEdgeL/20)+1)) *
20 - 9
                local explosionY = ((bombWorldY-1)*20) - 9
                SetItemPosition(GUI_PLATFORMS + 1998, explosionX,
explosionY, 38, 38)
```

```
                    explosionFrame = 2
                    gIsFalling = "no"
                end
            end
        end
    end
```

This function calculates the bottom of the Eye image (`MegaTable["Eye"].Y + MegaTable["Eye"].Height`) and determines what the appropriate y index would be for the `OnScreen` square. Then, it divides the `MegaTable["Eye"].Width` to find the number of squares that comprise the bottom of the image so their positions will all be checked in relation to a plunger.

The function then runs through a `for` loop, the `OnScreen` State of each square directly beneath each of the squares composing the bottom of the player's Eye image. If a plunger exists, its `World[x][y]` is set to 0 (which will delete it at the run of `DrawWorld()`).

Furthermore, the World table coordinates of the square below the plunger are plugged into the Detonator table (which is created during the placing of the detonator in LevelEdit.lua and housed in the specific level .lua file (see `LevelEditPlaceItem(x,y,state)`). The `BombX` and `BombY` indexes of the Detonator table reveal the World table coordinates of the attached bomb (allowing it to be deleted via `World[x][y] = 0`). The `CrateX` and `CrateY` tables (also created during LevelEdit and housed in the level .lua file) are iterated over, zeroing out their World states.

Finally, the world is redrawn, and an explosion sprite is set over the place where the bomb had been. Setting `explosionFrame = 2` triggers a continuous explosion in the `GUI_TIMER_EXPIRED` portion of LevelScrolling.lua.

All of this is made possible by the `PositionCheck()` function, which uses a similar setup to determine whether the player is falling through the air. `gIsFalling = PositionCheck()` is called at the beginning of `GUI_TIMER_EXPIRED` in LevelScrolling.lua and `DetonationCheck()` if `gIsFalling == "yes."`

Robot Head

Another example, on the design side, of the Unexpected Key puzzle type is the Robot Head minion we discussed in the puzzle design example previously. The Robot Head will follow the player for a section of the game, and provide some opportunity for NPC discussion, but its real function in the game is to serve as an Unexpected Key component to the larger door-wiring puzzle (Figure 13.4).

The player will not have enough long pieces of wire to solve the puzzle initially. It is up to the player to discover that the Robot Head, with its loose wires, is a source of the final needed piece of long wire. In that way, the head become a key to solving the larger puzzle.

FIGURE 13.4   The Robot Head is designed to be a key to a larger puzzle.

Risk-Reward

The concept of risk and reward has been part of game design for thousands of years. The idea is simple: players may have, at certain points in a game, an opportunity to take a "safer path" forward in the game, or to take a chance. If they take the chance and succeed, they will come away with some advantage in the game. If they fail, they will be worse off than if they had never tried.

This example comes up often in sports. Imagine the player in a championship NCAA basketball game—his team is down by two points and there are only a few seconds left. The "standard" path is to pass the ball inside to the big man for an easy lay-up to tie the game and force overtime. The risky path is to stop behind the three-point line and take a shot. The shot is harder and the chance of success is less. If the ball sinks, the game is won—if it dinks off the rim, the game is lost. These types of play opportunities are the stuff of legend in sports—those moments of remarkable victories (strange—the highlight reels don't often show the missed shots in this situation).

Think of the U.S. snowboarder during the 2006 Olympics—she was cruising to victory, with the gold medal hers for the taking. On the last jump, the safe approach was to simply minimize the jump and streak to the finish line for the victory. Instead, she chose to try a hotdog board grab. She lost her balance, fell on the landing, and watched as the second place boarder streaked past to grab the gold medal. In that case, she took the risk and failed and came out worse than if she had never tried. But her eyes were on the greater prize: the glory of a great hotdog move in the final jump of an amazing gold medal run—if she pulled it off, she would be in the history books for decades.

Games are ripe for these types of opportunities—of giving players a choice to try something difficult and spectacular and come out shining like a rose if they succeed. While not strictly a puzzle, the moment of player decision to accept or pass on a risk-reward opportunity is more akin to a puzzle-solving decision than an action-skill decision.

In addition, the "risk path" is often defined by the inclusion of either a puzzle element or an action-skill element. The player may decide to take a few precious extra seconds to solve a switch puzzle to open a door to retrieve the magical armor instead of simply blasting forward with his chain mail. In the time it takes to solve (or not solve) the puzzle, the hordes of were-rabbits are closing in on him. Or, the player may decide to take a risky jump over a lava stream to recover the red armor (an action-skill test from the classic game Quake). Succeed, and the player has the best armor in the game—fail, and he falls into the lava and has to restore the game.

Make It

A classic puzzle is one in which the player must make an object out of component parts. This type of puzzle comes in two key variations. In one variation, the puzzle is relatively simple: it's simply gathering the component objects. In this case, it's sort of like an expanded key puzzle, in which the key is made up of multiple objects, each of which must be retrieved.

The more complex variation blends in parts of the Unexpected Key puzzle, in which unlikely objects must be brought together to create the key object that neutralizes the obstacle the player was trying to overcome.

A classic simple variation of the Make It puzzle is when players must collect various items to create a magic weapon or other device that will provide them with the power they need to defeat or vanquish a significant foe or boss opponent. Perhaps the player has an ancient sword with a jeweled hilt, but some of the jewels are missing. As it stands, the sword is a pretty formidable broadsword, but for each of the original jewels found, it becomes more and more powerful, and when the final jewel is found, the sword can now cast the one spell that can vanquish the evil minotaur from the village.

A more complex example might be combining the basket you found (full of bread, which you gave to your party—now you just have the basket), a stick, and three sword belts. You can use the basket upside down, propped up with the stick, which is tied up with three belts in succession, to capture a wild white mink from the forest to present as a gift to the princess.

There are two keys to this type of puzzle: first is providing an easy interface mechanism for allowing a player to combine objects in a logical way (this was *much* simpler in the old days of text-based games!), and creating a "build" object that can be figured out from the player. You don't want to design some type of combination that's so esoteric that only you understand it, because you wrote the game design document. Having the player combine feathers plucked from his pet falcon with a broken off table leg, tied together with the gut taken from a crossbow in order to make a large paintbrush is getting rather esoteric, and designing a Make It puzzle that is that nonobvious will only frustrate and anger your players.

Eye Opener Implementation

In *Eye Opener,* we designed a simple variation of the Make It puzzle:

```
Puzzle Design: Pen Puzzle

Location: The door at the end of Horizontal End Level

Requirements: Pen cap (optional), pen body, pen nib, pen ink

Description: In the comic frames, the player has the opportunity to
recover various elements of the pen that the Artist was using when
creating the comic. With all the components in the inventory, the player
can combine the parts together to create a working pen.

When the player encounters the final door, it is locked and is missing
an opening switch or any form of handle—in fact, it looks like those
portions of the door simply haven't been drawn.

If the player uses the pen on the door, then he can "draw" a doorknob,
lock, and key, thereby making it a door he can simply open to reach the
final Comic Arena. (Figure 13.5.)
```

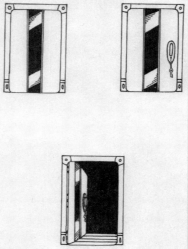

FIGURE 13.5 The images of the "undrawn" and drawn doors for the puzzle design.

Deduction Puzzle

A Deduction Puzzle tests the player's ability to solve a logic problem. Deduction Puzzles come in many flavors, from a simple riddle to a full-blown logic problem. The core element of a Deduction Puzzle is that you present the player with a series of clues that provide all the information he needs to solve the puzzle. Of course, part of the information is missing—it's the player's "outside of the game" ability to evaluate the facts and deduce a solution, often based on his understanding of knowledge or extra-textual knowledge.

There are no hard and fast rules for designing a Deduction Puzzle, just as there are no rules for creating a riddle. As a designer, this poses a challenge, and one you will need to overcome by running the puzzle past real-live people to make sure you aren't asking for too esoteric a knowledge set or deduction. Test out the puzzle on your development team and family and see if the puzzle is solvable and makes sense once the testers hear the solution (if they couldn't solve it themselves).

When writing out the design of the puzzle, begin with the information the player will have at his disposal from playing the game—the information he will need to solve the puzzle. Also list any knowledge the player must have outside of the game itself (this is where the real landmines exist), and then write out the puzzle, and see if it flows well from clues to mental skills to deduction. You may need to test out several variations before you get the logic and required information to feel just right for the context of your game.

Ordered List Puzzle

If you've ever given your child an unassembled present for Christmas, you understand this type of puzzle. With your child watching expectantly, you work through the assembly instructions, which are in the form of an ordered list, as you attempt to put the pieces together in the proper order to create the bicycle, robot, or whatever the object is. Of course, when you are finished, you are always left with a small handful of leftover parts that you surreptitiously drop into the box and hope they weren't *that* important.

In the world of games, we often encounter puzzles of this nature, in which we have to solve a series of small obstacles, often Key Puzzles, in a certain order, before we can clear the larger obstacle.

Rarely, in a game, are we given the entire list at once, however. We often get the larger obstacle first, but have no way to solve it. Perhaps you encounter a large brontosaurus near the edge of a crevasse. You need to get to the other side and you can climb atop the dinosaur, but it won't lower its head so you can use his neck as a bridge. The brontosaurus will lower its neck if you scratch its back, but you don't have a backscratcher. You explore the game world and find an anklasaurus with a backscratcher he can't use, but he wants some tender baby ferns to eat before he'll give you the backscratcher... and so on. Eventually, you'll have the entire list in front of you—perhaps five or six Key Puzzles, each of which will release the next item in your list until you reach the top of the list and get to clear the obstacle you wanted to clear in the first place.

These types of puzzles were the bread and butter of early adventure games, and provided players with untold hours of questing back and forth across game worlds. Nowadays, game worlds are so interactive, and so many other action skills can be tested, that we see these puzzles less often.

Be careful when employing these puzzles, because they can create the sense, in sophisticated game players, that you are simply "messing with them" to eek out more game time for them. These puzzles are still very effective, however, in juvenile games, when younger children love the idea of solving one problem after another in a related chain of events.

Game Puzzle

Often, a puzzle will take the form of a small game the player must win to best the obstacle. These types of puzzles come in many forms and often share gameplay approaches with old-time board or online casual games. If you are using a Game Puzzle, try to make sure the mini game fits within the context of the large game experience. In the wiring puzzle example we discussed (and will explore in detail later), it fits because we are "rewiring" a broken door controller to gain access to the next part of the game. The same game logic could have been used in a puzzle about the flow of water through irrigation ditches or finishing a safe path through a forest, but neither of those fits within the context of the game Eye Opener.

A classic example of this type of puzzle delivery was the classic game 7th Guest. In that game, you were trying to unravel the mystery of a haunted house, and each challenge you faced was actually a Game Puzzle. As we mentioned earlier, the puzzles "fit" neatly within the context of the game (soup can puzzle in the kitchen, chess puzzle in the library), but the puzzles themselves were actually complete games, rewarding to play in their own right .

These puzzles are the easiest to design, from the mechanical point of view, since a real-world example of the game logic already exists. The challenge is making sure the puzzle fits within the game itself so it feels natural for the players and provides them a challenge that matches their position within the flow of the game.

DESIGNING A PUZZLE

Designer: Bob Bates

There's something very satisfying about designing puzzles. It connects you to the player in ways that are unique. To me, it's almost a conversation. You present the player with a problem, he pokes around and tries to solve it. With each attempt, it's as if he's asking you a question, and with each game response, it's as if you're answering it.

The best puzzles are the ones that grow naturally from the environment of the game and draw the player deeper into the story while he is trying to solve it. The longer the player spends on a puzzle, the more he should learn about the world you have created and the characters that live there. Some people think that puzzles get in the way of the story, but I believe that good puzzles make the story better.

And of course, there's something uniquely satisfying about solving a puzzle as well. When that final piece clicks into place, there's an "Aha!" experience that you don't find anywhere else. It's like a seventh chord resolving to the tonic, or returning home after a long journey. There's just something *right* about it, some small bit of order in an otherwise chaotic world.

So, if you love solving puzzles, you'll probably enjoy designing them. Just remember that the solution has to make sense within the context of the game, and above all—play fair!

Eye Opener Implementation

Earlier in the chapter, we explored our wiring puzzle from a design standpoint. We will now look at it from the implementation standpoint. The puzzle exists as its own demo in the folder WiringPuzzle in the Chapter 13 folder on the companion CD-ROM.

ON THE CD

You will want to look at the file GUI_Puzzle.lua for this example. The puzzle mechanics are defined in three functions that set up the puzzle, set up the wires the player has, and check the player's solution.

We'll begin with the function that sets up the puzzle, both in data and on-screen: MakePuzzle(). First, the function defines the layout of the terminals:

```
terminals = {}
terminals[1] = {1,0,1,1}
terminals[2] = {1,1,0,2}
```

```
terminals[3] = {1,0,1,3}
terminals[4] = {0,1,1,1}
terminals[5] = {2,1,0,1}
terminals[6] = {3,0,1,1}
```

This table lays out the 6 × 4 grid and defines the objects that will be at each grid point. A value of 0 means nothing is there; 1 means a standard terminal; and 2 and 3 represent the red and blue lead terminals the player must collect. As this table is set up (you can try drawing it on graph paper—that's how we started this design), there is only one solution given 2 long wires and 10 short wires.

We next set up the solution of the puzzle:

```
—set up the solution table
solutionCount = 12
solution = {}
—path 1
solution[1] = {}
solution[1].startX = 6
solution[1].startY = 1
solution[1].endX = 6
solution[1].endY = 3
solution[2] = {}
solution[2].startX = 6
solution[2].startY = 3
solution[2].endX = 6
solution[2].endY = 4
solution[3] = {}
solution[3].startX = 5
solution[3].startY = 4
solution[3].endX = 6
solution[3].endY = 4
solution[4] = {}
solution[4].startX = 4
solution[4].startY = 4
solution[4].endX = 5
solution[4].endY = 4
solution[5] = {}
solution[5].startX = 3
solution[5].startY = 4
solution[5].endX = 4
solution[5].endY = 4
```

The solution begins with defining how many items, or wires, comprise the solution. We'll use this when we check for a player solution. The solution table is a multidimensional table that has one entry for each wire in the solution. The wire is represented by the value of the start position and the end position of the wires. We derived this from our graph paper example, and we'll use this to check against the wires the player places.

We then set up the table. This is a fairly complex looking operation that's really quite simple when we break it down. We walk through two loops that take us through every position in the table. We first check if terminal = 1, which means we are dealing with a standard terminal. If that's the case, we draw the terminal on screen as a sprite:

```
CreateItem(termID, "Sprite", "reg_lead.jpg")
SetItemPosition(termID, left + (indx2 * termSpacing), top + (indx *
termSpacing), termSize, termSize)
```

We next check to see if there is another terminal just below it for which we need to draw a terminal path:

```
if (indx < 6) then
                if (terminals[indx + 1][indx2] > 0) then
                    —wire goes here
                    CreateItem(wireID, "Button", "wire_up.jpg",
"wire_hv.jpg", "wire_dn.jpg")
                    SetItemPosition(wireID, left + (indx2 * termSpacing) +
termSize/3, top + (indx * termSpacing) + termSize/3, wireWidth,
termSpacing)
                    wires[wireID] = {}
                    wires[wireID].style = 1
                    wires[wireID].left = left + (indx2 * termSpacing) +
termSize/3
                    wires[wireID].top = top + (indx * termSpacing) +
termSize/3
                    wires[wireID].startX = indx
                    wires[wireID].startY = indx2
                    wires[wireID].endX = indx + 1
                    wires[wireID].endY = indx2
                    wireID = wireID + 1
                end
        end
```

We first look at the area directly below the current grid point (if we're not on the last row), and if the value is greater than zero, then some sort of terminal goes there, so we'll want to put a path object there. The path object is actually a button, which allows us to capture the player's input if he clicks to place a wire. We then add a record to the wires table, indicating the type of wire (1 for short, 2 for long) and the start and end positions of the wire (we'll use this when we check the solution).

We then continue, checking the spot to the right of the current grid points and then the spots below and to the right but two grid spaces away (for the long wires). Finally, we do the same thing if the current grid point is a lead terminal. When we are done walking through the table, we have drawn all the terminals of the right type, all the path objects (actually buttons) for every possible wire, and we've built a table of all the possible wire positions (Figure 13.6).

FIGURE 13.6 The terminals and wire paths are drawn for the wiring puzzle.

We next set up and draw the inventory of wire types in the function GiveWires():

```
function GiveWires(numLong)
    total = 0
    numShort = 10
    numShortUsed = 0
    shortID = 100
    numLongUsed = 0
    longID = 150
    top = 10
    left = 10
    spacing = 30
    for indx = 1,numShort do
        shortID = shortID + 1
        CreateItem(shortID, "Sprite", "wire_yellow_h_short.jpg")
        SetItemPosition(shortID, left, top + (total * spacing), 80, 20)
        total = total + 1
    end
    for indx = 1,numLong do
        longID = longID + 1
        CreateItem(longID, "Sprite", "wire_blue_h_long.jpg")
        SetItemPosition(longID, left, top + (total * spacing), 150, 20)
        total = total + 1
    end
end
```

This function is quite simple. We pass in the number of long wires to the function when we call it (that way, we can set it for whether the player has pulled the second long wire from the Robot Head). After setting up the basic variables, we simply walk through and draw a series of sprites, first the short wires and then the long. These aren't buttons, but rather a visual representation of what the player has in his "inventory."

When the player clicks on a wire path (remember, these are buttons), we process the placement of the wires in the event handler:

```
if wires[id].style == 1 then
    if numShortUsed < numShort then
        DeleteItem(id)
        CreateItem(id, "Sprite", "wire_yellow_v_short.jpg")
        SetItemPosition(id, wires[id].left, wires[id].top,
wireWidth, termSpacing)
        DeleteItem(shortID)
        shortID = shortID - 1
        numShortUsed = numShortUsed + 1
        wires[id].style = 0
    end
end
```

We process each type of wire (long or short, horizontal or vertical) separately. In the preceding example, we are looking at a short vertical wire. The player doesn't have to worry about whether he is using a short or long wire—all of that detection is automatic. We first see if the player has a wire of that type in his inventory left to use. If so, we delete the path button and replace it with a sprite that contains the wire image. We then remove one of the wires from the inventory (both by incrementing the counter of wires used and by deleting the wire sprite on the left side of the screen). Finally, we set the type value in the wires table to 0, which means that particular wire is now being used—we'll refer to this when we check for a solution.

When it's time to check the player solution, we do that in a single function:

```
function CheckSolution()
    numFound = 0
    print("checking....")
    for index, value in pairs(wires) do
        for index2 = 1, solutionCount do
            if (value.startX == solution[index2].startX) and (value.startY
== solution[index2].startY) and (value.endX == solution[index2].endX) and
(value.endY == solution[index2].endY) then
                --print("found one!")
                if value.style == 0 then
                    numFound = numFound + 1
                    print("found one!")
                end
            end
        end
    end
    if numFound == solutionCount then
        return true
```

```
        else
            return false
        end
    end
end
```

In this function, we begin by walking through the entire `wires` table. We do this using the `pairs()` function, which allows us to set up a loop that will hit every element of the `wires` table, no matter how many items are there.

For each element in the `wires` table, we walk through the entire `solutions` table, and check to see if we have an exact match for the starting and end positions of the wire. We then check to see if the type of the wire is 0, which means that it is indeed a wire placed by the player. If we have a match, we increment the number of matching wires variable, `numFound`. At the end of the loop, we compare that value with the `solutionCount` variable—if those numbers are the same, it means the player has placed a wire for every element of the solution and therefore the solution is valid, so we return a value of true, to indicate that the wiring puzzle was correctly solved (Figure 13.7).

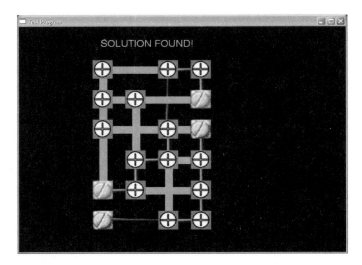

FIGURE 13.7   The wiring puzzle successfully solved.

Trial and Error

Asking players to solve a puzzle using trial and error is dubious, since we want to reward the players for their mastery of mental and action skills on our game. In the atoms section of this chapter, we warned against using player death as a precursor to solving a puzzle. If we avoid the idea of death as a repercussion for an "error" state, this type of puzzle may indeed provide a valid challenge for the player, albeit not as interesting as the puzzle types we explored earlier.

A simple form of this puzzle is presenting the player with three chests. One chest contains a treasure, while the other two will spawn a spirit that will attack the player. The player smacks at the chests with the sword to open them. If a spirit attacks, the player must dispatch the enemy first and then continue hacking at the chests to find the treasure. This type of puzzle was used extensively in the classic game Diablo®. The only problem, in the Diablo context, is that the player never knew what was in the chest, so if he found the treasure when he opened the first chest, he would still smack at the other chests, just in case there was more treasure to be found.

SUMMARY

In this chapter, we started out by exploring what defines a puzzle in terms of gameplay. We discovered that much of gameplay requires a player to use "action skills" he learns during the game, but a puzzle is different in that it tests a player's mental skills, which aren't necessarily learned in-game.

We then looked at several atoms of puzzle design and explored some design touch points of things we should strive for and avoid, both at the meta and micro levels, when we design puzzles for our games. We then explored several common types of puzzles, and looked at game examples and several examples with our "sandbox" game, Eye Opener.

Our goal was to come away with some ideas as to how we can effectively use puzzles within our game to create a variety of new and interesting challenges for our player. Next, we'll turn our attention to more "in your face" types of game obstacles and challenges and learn how to tune both static and dynamic obstacles for maximum player fun and challenge.

CHAPTER EXERCISES

1. Design a short "Unexpected Key" puzzle—the player is trapped in an Antarctic research station and his door is frozen shut. He has no food, no radio, and no torch or way to make fire—how does he get the door open?
2. Revise the wiring puzzle example presented earlier. Work to create a different layout of terminals and a different solution. Can you expand the field of terminals to make a larger puzzle? How would you handle a situation in which there are multiple solutions?

14 Conflict Design

In This Chapter

- Static Obstacles
- Artificial Intelligence Design Atoms
- Writing AI Designs
- AI Implementation Examples

In the previous chapter, we explored puzzles. Puzzles are obstacles you put in the players' way that they must solve to earn something or progress in your game. Puzzles are certainly challenges, but they aren't "aggressive"—they don't come after the player.

Most of the challenges a player faces in a game are often in the form of conflicts with game entities that either passively or actively oppose the player's existence or progress through the game. These moments of conflict are when players learn and use the action skills you require—they learn how to jump, fire a gun, organize units into a patrol group, or how to raid an enemy supply depot.

Static obstacles don't "bite back," but they still require the player to overcome them—perhaps it's a wall or a door or a pit that must be jumped. Dynamic obstacles are active and react to the players' actions—controlled by a form of "artificial intelligence"—these types of obstacles are the true enemies and the bread and butter of a dynamic and fun game experience. In the pages that follow, we'll explore these obstacles in more depth and learn more about how to design dynamic and seemingly intelligent obstacles for your players.

STATIC OBSTACLES

Nearly every game you play is filled with static obstacles, but you may not even notice them. Done correctly, static obstacles blend into the game environment and context so they feel entirely natural to the player. Flare up and play a first-person shooter, a platform game, or an RTS game and you'll be jumping, climbing, and avoiding all manner of things, from walls to trees to pits of quicksand. Often, these obstacles feel as if they are simply part of the world, existing there for no rhyme or reason.

As game designers, we know that nothing—absolutely nothing—appears in a game without some designer thinking of it, some artist creating the assets, and a programmer implementing it. Every hedgerow and tree exist in the game world by human intervention (yes, even when a "map" may be generated algorithmically, since the items still have to be designed and the rules for their placement determined).

Static obstacles, when they aren't puzzles (such as a locked door with a missing key), exist in the game world to provide opportunities for the players to learn or enhance their action skills. They also exist to guide the players through a game environment and to affect the placing of a player's progress through a game.

Static Obstacle Atoms

Just like any element in your game, you must think about how you place static obstacles in front of the player. While there isn't as much depth or detail to designing or implementing these types of obstacles, a few general rules of thumb will help you keep your game feeling fresh and natural to the player.

Fit the Obstacle to the Game

Make sure the obstacle feels natural in the game world.

This harkens back to several of the earlier design atoms we've discussed and simply means that you, as the designer, are responsible for populating your game world—the environment, the static obstacles, the puzzles, and the computer-controlled enemies, in such a way that they all feel like they fit together as smaller parts of a larger whole.

Vary the Obstacle

Don't place the same types of obstacle one after another.

This is a simple common-sense atom, but it just means that you want to pay attention to how you pace obstacles, both in terms of the skill you are asking for and the visual aspect of the challenge. Keep things mixed up and interesting for the players. This will also help to disguise the fact that you are presenting them with obstacles at all—if they are using different skills and seeing different types of impediments, they will be focusing on the game experience and not the meta "what is the designer trying to get me to do now" question.

Train the Skills

Remember that you are training your player—vary the skills and place them accordingly.

Static obstacles exist in the game primarily as a training ground for player skills that you will be asking them to use at a high level later. Keep this in mind and allow your static obstacles to challenge the players on all the action skills they will require in your game, be it shooting accuracy, the ability to climb a ladder, jump a chasm, or swing on a dangling chain.

Set up obstacles for them that help them grow their skills, but also keep the skills changing (don't put three "swinging on ropes" challenges in a row, as we discussed earlier) to keep the players' interest. You can also foreshadow (which may be a good thing or bad thing depending on your goals) what is coming up in a game by the types of skills you are asking your player to employ. Just make sure you provide enough static tests for their action skills before you throw a dynamic challenge at them.

Be Aware of Surprises

Anticipate if a player can "get around" an obstacle.

We all know what happened to Dorothy's innocence when she discovered that the mighty Oz was simply an old man behind a curtain. Her suspension of disbelief was broken and the world wasn't as magical anymore.

Don't let your inquisitive players fall into the same trap—players will use everything and try anything to fully explore a game environment and attempt to go where you do not want them to go. If you have static obstacles cordoning off sections of a map or level, play test the heck out of them to make sure an inventive player can't hurdle your impenetrable wall and discover that your game world is just a façade.

DYNAMIC "ARTIFICIALLY INTELLIGENT" OBSTACLES

The key to exciting dynamic obstacles is infusing them with behavior that appears "intelligent" to the player. For years, we've called this artificial intelligence, and while it isn't the most accurate term, it will suffice for now. Ever since the dawn of computers, researchers and science fiction writers have been looking for true digital intelligence.

In the 1950s, we were introduced to the Turing Test—a hypothetical test of a computer's intelligence. The idea was that a person could communicate with another person through a computer terminal—very much like a chat or instant message session. On the other side of the terminal could be a human being or a computer. A computer was said to truly be intelligent if it passed the Turing Test—that is, the humans couldn't tell that they were conversing with a machine rather than another human.

Truth be told, we're a long way from a successful Turing Test, but you can log on to MSN, messenger, chat with the SmarterChild bot, and find yourself shaking your head at just how far we've come from the first Eliza programs.

In the realm of games, we aren't really talking about true intelligence at all, but rather creating a dynamic challenge for a player that can take in some data from the game world and vary its behavior accordingly. Ideally, AI in a computer game is a challenge that reacts, in a meaningful way, to the actions the player is taking, to keep the level of the challenge high.

AI Atoms

In the section that follows, we'll explore a few atoms of good computer opponent and AI design. The goal isn't to create true intelligence, but to create the sense in the player that a challenge is reacting to him and that what he (the player) does really matters.

AI is a Façade

You don't need to simulate thought—just create enough reaction to make the challenge dynamic.

As designers, we all dream about designing a computer opponent that is so real that under the hood it percolates with emotion, drives, and desire and truly wants to win by defeating the player. While this is a noble dream, we have to be realistic and remember that computer intelligence is a façade to the player. Players who are engrossed in the moment-by-moment play of your game will attribute your challenges with all sorts of "intelligence" you never planned.

As a designer, you will need to take stock of exactly what a particular challenge or opponent is trying to accomplish, and then design the "intelligence" so it only processes variables that are necessary for proper behavior variations. You don't need to build more than you need—often, a "little less than you need" will be just perfect.

TOO MUCH THOUGHT

 Designer: Paul Schuytema

Several years ago, we were developing the sequel to one of the best shareware games ever: Scorched Earth. Our sequel was called Scorched Worlds and we wanted it to capture the feel of the original game, but do it in 3D. We also

→

wanted you to play against opponents who were genuinely smart. Our AI programmer at the time was taking a break in his pursuit of a Ph.D. in artificial intelligence and he was eager to take on the task.

His first pass at the AI was a masterwork of design—each opponent maintained something like a dozen personality variables, and they all pushed and pulled each other to create a very dynamic personality model that reacted to nearly every stimulus they could process, from the heat in their tank to the weather outside to the disappointment of a missed shot and the fire of a direct hit on the opponent. Looking at the console spewing out their AI parameters in real time, we couldn't help but marvel at how much was going on under the hood.

Unfortunately, the truth of the matter was that it really made no difference at all. The only thing the players could perceive of their opponents was how they moved their tank, how they fired their shot (and how they improved the next shot), and any pitch dialogue they spit out—that was it. True, their dialogue was tied to their internal mental state, but we did a test and simply randomized the dialogue—and it made no difference at all.

Our lesson is one that stuck with us for many games hence—if the player can't perceive, in a meaningful way that affects the game, what the AI is "thinking," then all of that thinking is just useless. We didn't need a dozen-point personality system to control an opponent that only affected the player in two or three ways.

FIGURE 14.1   Scorched Worlds didn't need the depth of AI we had programmed.

Minimize Cheating

Always try to minimize AI cheating.

Just what is AI cheating? Perhaps it's an FPS bot who "knows" that you don't have any weapons in your inventory that are effective at close range, so it charges and attacks close in. Perhaps it's a racing opponent that knows the top speed of your car is 180 mph, so it will vary its speed between 170 and 185 mph to make the game challenging.

Computer opponents have access to all the variables in the game, so they can easily "know" things about the player that the player couldn't possible know about them. Providing AI with this knowledge is called "cheating," and it's generally something you will want to avoid. Ideally, you will want your computer opponents to receive the same sorts of variables into their systems as the players receive in their feedback loop—and have them make their decisions based on the more limited set of knowledge.

Of course, there are times when "cheating" may be acceptable—in the racecar example, having the opponent understand the player's abilities and modify its performance to create a more exciting, competitive race may be a good design choice.

Keep It Simple

Allow simple parameters to influence the effectiveness of the artificial intelligence.

This is an expansion of our first atom—which tells us not to have the AI do more than it needs to. This atom refines that concept and says that the best computer opponents are those that are controlled by just a few variables. If you have a creature that is controlled by simply three variables (let's say its health, how many stones it has to throw, and how many magic users are in the player's party), then during the course of play, the player will be able to "pick up" on those variables and will be able to perceive the change in behavior in the creature when it is wounded or nearly out of rocks to throw. This knowledge will provide the clues the player needs to overcome the obstacle. Imagine, instead, if this creature was controlled by 50+ variables, including hunger, the weather, the time of day, and such. A change in a single variable in that complex of an equation will be insignificant and the player won't be able to perceive it, and hence won't learn the action skills needed to best the obstacle.

On the design side, having fewer variables means that it is much easier to test, tweak, and configure AI behaviors. You can keep several variables at a baseline level and simply tweak one and see the behavioral changes. You can then add some variation in them and still be able to understand how they work together—impossible if you are dealing with 50+ variables in real time.

Randomness Is Good

Introduce small amounts of randomness in AI behavior.

Computers are good at doing the same thing, over and over again. While this is great for number crunching, it isn't good when you have the same processes controlling your AI decision-making. In the previous atom, we argued that you want to keep the variables that control your AI simple and few in number. However, you don't want the limited scope of AI behavior to lead to a computer opponent that is wholly predicable.

Think of yourself—if you are a creature of habit, you'll still incorporate some randomness in your life from time to time. You may order something different at your usual restaurant or take a different street home. Most of the time, you are predictable, but from time to time you "depart the text."

This is a good technique for AI as well—when you are processing AI decisions, incorporate a little randomness so they will mostly make the right decision for the situation (and so the players can start to get a handle on their behavior), but from time to time, they will surprise the player.

Give Your AI Goals

Goal behavior can create more natural behavior in computer opponents.

Computer opponents are perfectly "happy" just living moment by moment and processing their decisions almost instantly—but often, that will lead to behavior that feels artificial and "computery." When we make a decision, it's really a goal—something we want to do, like 20 pushups in the morning or a stop by the store on the way home for milk and eggs. While certain things may distract us from our goals, we generally stay on task and then think of what to do next once we are done with our current job.

This design approach works very well to create realistic-feeling AI opponents. Instead of having them process their decisions multiple times a second and react accordingly (which, more often than not, will lead to herky-jerky behavior), design your AI actions to be goal based. When they evaluate the state of the world, give them a goal, which may consist of several actions. Perhaps the goal of an AI tank is to attack an enemy gun embankment. This goal requires a movement action and an attack action. During that time, the tank isn't really thinking about what is going on in the rest of the game world—it is simply dealing with its own goal that may take several seconds to a minute to accomplish. Of course, in this example, a human-controlled tank attacking it may break the AI tank from the goal and give it a new goal such as "defend yourself."

In general, computer opponents feel more natural to the player if they work from goal to goal, over time, rather than react to their immediate situation from second to second.

Writing AI Design

The previous list of AI atoms is purposefully short—because a good designer keeps AI designs as simple as possible. Simple designs are easier for the technical team to implement effectively and easier for the designer to tweak and for the eventual player to understand.

The first step is to determine if you are designing an AI system that will encompass many entities or simply something that will control a single entity. More complex, multi-opponent systems are generally the approach you'll want to take in larger games in which you will be presenting the player with many types of opponents. If that is the case, you'll need to first do some generalized design thinking before you dive in and design the individual enemies.

You will want to first list out what you want the result of the challenges for the players to be—what will they oppose and how will it react to them? What will the player see and perceive in the enemy behaviors? How will the enemy perceive the player and react to actions performed by the player? Think of this as writing out a laundry list.

From there, you will want to think through any states or behaviors you need for the enemies, such as "idle," "move," or "attack." These states will help you articulate the action of your enemies. Be sure to write out, as clearly as possible, just what defines each state or behavior.

Next, you'll want to determine the parameters that determine the behavior of your AI, such as hit points, sighting distance, movement speed, and such. This will help you break down your computer controlled opponents into stats that can be understood by the team programmers. Remember to err on the side of simplicity rather than complexity. Finally, you will want to write out, in either narrative or table form, the behaviors for a particular enemy or entity. Remember to clearly refer to any states, behaviors, or parameters you outlined earlier—this will make it easier for the programmer to match your intended behaviors with the behavioral systems you have outlined.

When you are designing multiple levels of AI skill, you can take two approaches. At times, it is easier to build the AI first for the most skilled opponent and then add some "noise" into the system to simulate a less effective opponent. At other times, as in something like Poker AI, it can be easier to design the basic skill level first and then add in more enhanced detail checking to simulate the more skilled opponents.

When designing your artificial intelligence, take some time to think of what will yield the best results and give you the most control over the process during development.

Design Example

The following example is pulled from the working design document for the Combat action game we designed several years back. The example covers some basic AI behaviors and the specifics of two enemies, a very feeble little hovering bomb, and a more deadly assassin robot. You'll notice from the design that the vocabulary to describe their behaviors is similar, since we were working to create a single system for enemy AI, with only basic behavioral changes, as opposed to system-wide changes, used to differentiate one from the other.

```
Enemy Design
I. Behaviors
Idle: remain in place and slowly turn left or right
Scan: turn to a heading and scan for player (not needed if vision is set to
360)
Move: move toward a target
Fire: fire at the player
II. Enemies
a. Bee Robot
Hitpoints: 1
Speed: 6
Attack type: ram
AttackSpeed: 0
Vision: 360
DamageDone: 10
VisionRange: 20 tiles
```

The Bee Bot will spawn into the world in idle mode. During the update it will scan for the player. If the player is in range, it will change its behavior to Move and move toward the player.

Each update cycle, it will quickly scan; if the player is still found, it will continue to move, otherwise it will switch to idle mode.

The Bot will move toward the player until it is destroyed by player fire or it rams the player and explodes.

```
b. Assassin Tank
Hitpoints: 250
Speed: 3
Attack type: laser
AttackSpeed: 3
Vision: 60
DamageDone: 100
VisionRange: 80 tiles
```

The Assassin Bot is meant to be slow, plodding, and deadly. It will spawn in idle state. Each update, if the state is idle, then it will either move (25%) or scan for the player.

If it selects the move behavior, it will select a random AI patrol node within range and make that its goal. If there are no patrol nodes in range, it will remain idle.

If it finds the player, it will fire at the player until the player is no longer in the scan range, then it will revert back to idle. (Figure 14.2.)

FIGURE 14.2 The simple-minded bee robot from Combat.

Examples

In this section, we'll look at some small examples of designer-created artificial intelligence in action, from three shipped games. All of these examples feature an AI that is primarily created via some sort of text-based script that uses the script (written by the designer) to call or set up code-controlled functions or behaviors.

These examples will let you see different ways to control and trigger AI decision points, and what kind of scripting might be required from a designer when implementing an AI design.

Frontrunner

In this first example, we'll look at a simple subset of the opponent AI in Frontrunner, a presidential election simulation. The player attempts to run a campaign against one or two computer-controlled opponents. In this example, we will look at the AI that controls how a campaign determines where to send their candidate for the next campaign and fund-raising stop. In this game, all of the AI was written in Lua, so it should be quite familiar by now (Figure 14.3).

In Frontrunner, there are three difficulty levels, and they affect the ability of the AI. A difficulty of level one means basically a random opponent, while a difficulty of three means a very effective campaign. Look at the following function:

FIGURE 14.3 Frontrunner used AI to control the opposing election campaigns.

```
function CampAITravel_Normal (Campaign, Person)
—determines how the AI travels
    if diffLevel == 1 then
        if GetCampaignData(Campaign, "LastAction") ~= "Travel" then
            Destination = DieRoll(50) + 1;
            if Destination ~= GetPersonLocation(Campaign, Person) then
                if Destination ~= 9 then
                    —no DC travel
                    Travel(Campaign, Person, Destination);
                    SetCampaignData(Campaign, "LastAction", "Travel");
                end
            end
        end
    elseif diffLevel == 2 then
        StateTravTable = {};
        for travelCount = 1,4 do
            tempVal = DieRoll(51) + 1;
            —no DC travel
            if tempVal == 9 then
                StateTravTable[travelCount] = 5
            else
                StateTravTable[travelCount] = tempVal;
            end
        end
        mostVotes = 0;
        mostVotesState = 0;
        for travelCount = 1,4 do
            if GetStateData(StateTravTable[travelCount],"ElectoralVotes") >
mostVotes then
                mostVotes =
GetStateData(StateTravTable[travelCount],"ElectoralVotes");
                mostVotesState =  StateTravTable[travelCount];
            end
```

```
                    end
             if mostVotesState ~= GetPersonLocation(Campaign, Person) then
                 if mostVotesState ~= 9 then
                 —no DC travel
                     Travel(Campaign, Person, mostVotesState);
                     SetCampaignData(Campaign, "LastAction", "Travel");
                 end
             end
         else
             —diffLevel == 3
             StateTravTable = {}
             stateCount = 1
             while stateCount < 6 do
                 pickState = math.random(1,51);
                 if GetStateData(pickState,"ElectoralVotes") > 12 then
                     StateTravTable[stateCount] = pickState;
                     stateCount = stateCount + 1;
                 end
             end
             lowSupport = 100;
             targetState = 1;
             for indx = 1,5 do
                 if TalleySupport(StateTravTable[indx], Campaign) < lowSupport
then
                     lowSupport = TalleySupport(StateTravTable[indx], Campaign);
                     targetState =  StateTravTable[indx];
                 end
             end
             Travel(Campaign, Person, targetState);
             SetCampaignData(Campaign, "LastAction", "Travel");
         end
     end
```

The function takes as its parameters the campaign and the person we are interested in (since often the presidential candidate and running mate campaign separately). We first handle the case of a difficulty level of one. In this case, the function first checks to see if they have just traveled (after you travel, you want to stay in one place for a while and do other things), and if not, it picks a random state, excludes DC, and then tells them to travel to that randomly selected state.

For difficulty level two, we add a little more "thinking." We first build a small table of random states. We then walk through that table to find the state in the random list that has the most electoral votes. If the person isn't already in that state, we send him off to the most "valuable" state in the bunch.

For difficulty level three, we add a little more to the mix. First, we build a table of six random states, but only states that have 12 or more electoral votes (the level three AI ignores the small states completely—unfortunately much like real-life politicians). We then walk through the six target states and find the state in which the candidate has the least support, and that becomes the next state to travel to.

In this example, we see how we can implement different difficulty levels by basically taking the same approach to making a travel decision (basically throwing a dart at a map) and then refining that to represent smarter AI levels. There isn't much to it, but the effect is noticeable by the player and the challenge level of the opponent ratchets up with each difficulty level.

Castles & Catapults

In this example, we'll look at a configuration file that defines the way in which an AI general controls general troop movement in a medieval RTS game called Castles & Catapults (Figure 14.4).

FIGURE 14.4 This prototype build used a set of situational commands, in script form, to control the behavior of the military units.

The goal in this mission-based game is to destroy the enemy keep—each battle only has two opponents, each with from one to three armies. Each side has one keep. The goal is to protect your keep and destroy the opponent's keep. For this game, the designer imagined various "world states" that defined the meta state of the world for the computer opponent. Those states were:

DANGER_NORMAL: Nothing special going on at all.

DANGER_ENEMY_VULNERABLE: There is a clear path to the enemy keep.

DANGER_SELF_VULNERABLE: There is a clear path to my keep (no defenders in place).

DANGER_WINNING: I have inflicted more damage to the enemy's keep.

DANGER_LOSING: My keep has taken more damage.

An army itself has several states of activity:

IDLE: The army has no orders and is simply "hanging out."

HOLDING: The army is holding a position.

MOVING: The army is moving to some target.

ATTACKING: The army is actively engaged in battle.

The computer-controlled opponent uses these states in a large probability table to determine how he should order his individual armies. Once every AI cycle (checked once every five seconds in the game), the table is referenced for each army to determine what they should do next. An example follows:

```
# my keep is accessible to the enemy
GROUP DANGER_SELF_VULNERABLE

        #
        # strike force as keep defender
        #
        # the army is idle
        GROUP IDLE
                NoChange                       0
                MoveToWaypoint_Rnd             0
                MoveToWaypoint_00              0
                MoveToWaypoint_01              0
                MoveToWaypoint_02              0
                MoveToWaypoint_03              0
                AttackArmy_ClosestToArmy1      0
                AttackArmy_ClosestToMe         10
                AttackArmy_ClosestToKeep       80
                AttackArmy_Weakest             10
                AttackArmy_Strongest           0
                AttackCastle_Rnd               0
                AttackCastle_ClosestToMe       0
                AttackCastle_ClosestToKeep     0
                AttackKeep                     0
                HoldPosition_Rnd               0
                HoldPosition_Keep              0
                SaveMyself                     0
        GROUP END
        # the army is holding position
        GROUP HOLDING
                NoChange                       10
                MoveToWaypoint_Rnd             0
                MoveToWaypoint_00              0
                MoveToWaypoint_01              0
                MoveToWaypoint_02              0
                MoveToWaypoint_03              0
                AttackArmy_ClosestToArmy1      5
                AttackArmy_ClosestToMe         5
```

```
                    AttackArmy_ClosestToKeep    50
                    AttackArmy_Weakest           5
                    AttackArmy_Strongest         5
                    AttackCastle_Rnd             0
                    AttackCastle_ClosestToMe     0
                    AttackCastle_ClosestToKeep 0
                    AttackKeep                   0
                    HoldPosition_Rnd             0
                    HoldPosition_Keep           20
                    SaveMyself                   0
          GROUP END
          # the army is in transit
          GROUP MOVING
                    NoChange                    70
                    MoveToWaypoint_Rnd           0
                    MoveToWaypoint_00            0
                    MoveToWaypoint_01            0
                    MoveToWaypoint_02            0
                    MoveToWaypoint_03            0
                    AttackArmy_ClosestToArmy1    0
                    AttackArmy_ClosestToMe      10
                    AttackArmy_ClosestToKeep    20
                    AttackArmy_Weakest           0
                    AttackArmy_Strongest         0
                    AttackCastle_Rnd             0
                    AttackCastle_ClosestToMe     0
                    AttackCastle_ClosestToKeep 0
                    AttackKeep                   0
                    HoldPosition_Rnd             0
                    HoldPosition_Keep            0
                    SaveMyself                   0
          GROUP END
          # the army is attacking something
          GROUP ATTACKING
                    NoChange                    90
                    MoveToWaypoint_Rnd           0
                    MoveToWaypoint_00            0
                    MoveToWaypoint_01            0
                    MoveToWaypoint_02            0
                    MoveToWaypoint_03            0
                    AttackArmy_ClosestToArmy1    0
                    AttackArmy_ClosestToMe       0
                    AttackArmy_ClosestToKeep     5
                    AttackArmy_Weakest           0
                    AttackArmy_Strongest         0
                    AttackCastle_Rnd             0
                    AttackCastle_ClosestToMe     0
                    AttackCastle_ClosestToKeep 0
                    AttackKeep                   0
                    HoldPosition_Rnd             0
                    HoldPosition_Keep            5
                    SaveMyself                   0
```

```
GROUP END
# the army has less than 3 units and is damaged
GROUP NEAR_DEAD
        NoChange                        0
        MoveToWaypoint_Rnd              0
        MoveToWaypoint_00               0
        MoveToWaypoint_01               0
        MoveToWaypoint_02               0
        MoveToWaypoint_03               0
        AttackArmy_ClosestToArmy1       0
        AttackArmy_ClosestToMe          0
        AttackArmy_ClosestToKeep        15
        AttackArmy_Weakest              0
        AttackArmy_Strongest            0
        AttackCastle_Rnd                0
        AttackCastle_ClosestToMe        0
        AttackCastle_ClosestToKeep      0
        AttackKeep                      0
        HoldPosition_Rnd                0
        HoldPosition_Keep               15
        SaveMyself                      70
    GROUP END
GROUP END
```

Each army has a full set of action probabilities, as outlined previously, for each of the world states. Some armies are set up to be defensive, and some are built to be siege armies, so each army can have different values. When it is time for the AI check to be made, the world state and the army state are referenced, to determine which probability list to use. Then, a 1D100 is rolled, and based on the values listed in the action table, the army's new orders are issued.

This example illustrates how a simple probability table can be used to allow a designer to set up and control the actions of on-field armies. The actual states and army actions are implemented in code, and this "config" file simply serves to determine which of the menu of actions will be taken at any given cycle.

While this may seem simple, this approach allows the designer to craft opponents who are defensive, aggressive, cautious, tactical, and flat-out insane (actually, insane is often the easiest intelligence to model!).

Poker

In this next example, we'll look at a short AI function that determines what a basic (not expert) computer opponent will do, bet-wise on its turn when playing Five Card Draw. This function does not handle the decision whether it will draw new cards—that is handled in another function—rather, this determines if it will check, raise, or fold given its current hand (Figure 14.5).

FIGURE 14.5   The AI for computer opponents for All In Poker were written in Lua.

```lua
function DrawEasyBet(playerNum, myPressure)
    local myHand = GetHandScore(playerNum)
    local myRaise = 0
    local cash = GetPlayerCash(playerNum)
    local myBet = 1
    if myPressure > 0 then
        - I can call, raise or fold
        if myHand < SCORE_PAIR then
            myRoll = math.random(1,100)
            if myRoll > 65 then
                myAction = CALL
            else
                myAction = FOLD
            end
        elseif myHand < SCORE_STRAIGHT then
            myRoll = math.random(1,100)
            if myRoll < 25 then
                myAction = FOLD
            elseif myRoll < 66 then
                myAction = CALL
            else
                myAction = RAISE
                if gTableMaximum == -1 then
                    if cash < gTableMinimum then
                        cash = gTableMinimum
                    end
                    myRaise = math.random(gTableMinimum, cash)
                else
                    myRaise = math.random(gTableMinimum, gTableMaximum)
                end
            end
        elseif myHand < SCORE_4_KIND then
            myRoll = math.random(1,100)
```

```
            if myRoll < 25 then
                myAction = CALL
            else
                myAction = RAISE
                if gTableMaximum == -1 then
                    if cash < gTableMinimum then
                        cash = gTableMinimum
                    end
                    myRaise = math.random(gTableMinimum, cash)
                else
                    myRaise = math.random(gTableMinimum, gTableMaximum)
                end
            end
        else
            myAction = RAISE
            if gTableMaximum == -1 then
                if cash < (gTableMinimum*3) then
                    cash = (gTableMinimum * 3)
                end
                myRaise = math.random(gTableMinimum*3, cash)
            else
                myRaise = math.random(gTableMinimum*3, gTableMaximum)
            end
        end
    else
        — I can raise or check
        if myHand < SCORE_PAIR then
            myRoll = math.random(1,100)
            if myRoll > 65 then
                myAction = RAISE
                myRaise = math.random(gTableMinimum, gTableMinimum*2)
                —myRaise = myRaise + myPressure
            else
                myAction = CHECK
            end
        elseif myHand < SCORE_STRAIGHT then
            myRoll = math.random(1,100)
            if myRoll > 35 then
                myAction = RAISE
                myRaise = math.random(gTableMinimum, gTableMinimum*3)
            else
                myAction = CHECK
            end
        elseif myHand < SCORE_4_KIND then
            myRoll = math.random(1,100)
            if myRoll < 35 then
                myAction = CHECK
            else
                myAction = RAISE
                if gTableMaximum == -1 then
                    if cash < gTableMinimum then
                        cash = gTableMinimum
                    end
```

```
                        myRaise = math.random(gTableMinimum, cash)
                    else
                        myRaise = math.random(gTableMinimum, gTableMaximum)
                    end
            end
        else
            myRoll = math.random(1,100)
            if myRoll < 10 then
                myAction = CHECK
            else
                myAction = RAISE
                if gTableMaximum == -1 then
                    if cash < (gTableMinimum*3) then
                        cash = (gTableMinimum*3)
                    end
                    myRaise = math.random(gTableMinimum*3, cash)
                else
                    myRaise = math.random(gTableMinimum*3, gTableMaximum)
                end
            end
        end
    end
end
end
```

The function passes in the player number (which identifies which computer-controlled player it is) and the "pressure" value. In Poker, pressure is when someone before you on a turn places a bet or raises a previous bet. If the player to your left bet $5, then your pressure would be $5—you'll either have to bet that amount, raise, or fold (quitting the turn and losing any money you already have in the pot).

We then poll the values for the player's hand and how much cash he still has in his bank. We then handle the player's decision-making based on whether he has pressure on him for the turn (a player with no pressure can't fold).

We base the decisions on the score of the player's current hand. If he has less than a pair, he will most likely fold (65-percent chance) or call (35-percent chance). Even a basic player knows enough not to raise if he doesn't even have a pair in his hand.

We then march up the hand scores, and the better the hand gets, the higher the chance the player will raise. We determine actions based on a 1D100 roll and have the actions weighted by percentages. This ensures that most of the time, the computer opponent will "do the right thing," but also insures that it won't appear as a robot to the human player—there will at least be some variety and ambiguity in its actions, making the play feel more natural and interesting.

If the computer opponent's score is between SCORE_STRAIGHT and SCORE_4_KIND, there is a 75-percent chance it will raise, because it's clear it has a very solid hand. If it does indeed have four of a kind, there is no randomness or bluffing at all—the computer player will raise the bet some value between the table minimum and the table maximum.

After we deal with the possible decisions if the player has pressure on him, we walk through similar conditional statements for no pressure. For the basic player, these are basically the same decisions, except that the player will check instead of fold, which means he will make no bet and the next person in line will take his turn.

At the higher levels of computer opponent (this particular game, All In Poker®, has three levels of AI: normal, skilled and expert), the AI looks at its hand scoring in more detail, looks at how much money is currently in the pot, and what percentage of its own bank is currently in the pot (an expert player with most of his money already in the pot is less likely to fold and simply lose the money without a fight).

Eye Opener Implementation—Turret

In Eye Opener we want the opportunity to challenge the players by presenting them with some wall-mounted turrets that swivel and fire upon their eyeball as they attempt to pass. Turrets are managed by the GUI_TIMER_EXPIRED of Level-Scrolling.lua (Figure 14.6).

FIGURE 14.6 The simple "aim and fire" turrets in Eye Opener.

Their behavior consists of "processing" and "done." When `MegaTable["Turret"].State` is processing, `ManageTurrets()` is run (LuaSupport.lua). This function is the basis for the Turret AI:

```
function ManageTurrets()
    for y = 1,30 do
        worldX = (gScreenEdgeL/20)+1
        for x = 1,40 do
            if World[worldX][y] == 9 then
                tarX = MegaTable["Eye"].X +
(math.floor(MegaTable["Eye"].Width/2))
```

```
                    tarY = MegaTable["Eye"].Y +
(math.floor(MegaTable["Eye"].Height/2))
                    turRot = Turret[worldX][y]
                    turX = ((x-1)*20) + 10
                    turY = ((y-1)*20) + 10
                    CreateItem(OnScreen[x][y].ID, "Sprite", "turret.tga")
                    SetItemPosition(OnScreen[x][y].ID, (x-5) * 20, (y-2) * 20,
180, 60)

                    FaceTarget("turret", turX, turY, turRot, tarX, tarY,
worldX, x, y)
                end
                worldX = worldX + 1
        end
    end
    DrawWorld()
end
```

This function simply scans every 20 × 20 block for the ones that are turrets (when `World[worldX][y] == 9`) (for more information on how the World table works, see the `DrawCell(x,y)` and `DrawWorld()` functions). When it locates a turret, it uses the `FaceTarget("turret", turX, turY, turRot, tarX, tarY, worldX, x, y)` function to align itself with the line of sight to the eyeball:

```
function FaceTarget(object, curX, curY, curRot, tarX, tarY, worldX, x, y)
    —first, figure out the sides of the triangle:
    a = curY - tarY
    b = curX - tarX
    c = math.sqrt((a*a)+(b*b))
    —now, find the angle to the target:
    angle = math.acos(b/c)
    —now, determine the presence of negatives:
    if a > 0 then
        if b > 0 then
            angle = math.pi + angle    — Upper-Left
        elseif b == 0 then
            angle = 1.5 * math.pi    — Directly Up
        else
            angle = math.pi + angle    — Upper-Right)
        end
    elseif a == 0 then
        if b > 0 then
            angle = math.pi            — Directly Left
        else
            angle = 2 * math.pi        — Directly Right
        end
    else
        if b > 0 then
            angle = math.pi - angle    — Lower-Left
        elseif b == 0 then
            angle = .5 * math.pi       — Directly Down
        else
```

```
            angle = math.pi - angle    — Lower-Right
        end
    end
    if curRot > angle then
        angleDif = curRot - angle
        if angleDif < math.pi then
            angleDif = "ccwise"
        else
            angleDif = "cwise"
        end
    else
        angleDif = angle - curRot
        if angleDif < math.pi then
            angleDif = "cwise"
        else
            angleDif = "ccwise"
        end
    end
    if angleDif == "ccwise" then
        curRot = curRot - .1
        if curRot < .1 then
            curRot = 6.2
        end
    else
        curRot = curRot + .1
        if curRot > 6.2 then
            curRot = 0
        end
    end
    if object == "turret" then
        Turret[worldX][y] = curRot
    end
end
```

This function really doesn't have much more logic going on than some simple trigonometry (which can often send shivers of fear down a game designer's spine—designers don't need to be super-skilled at math, but they certainly do need to know how to manage some simple math if duty calls). We basically create a triangle where the endpoints of the hypotenuse are the turret and the target (the Eyeball). By doing this, the hypotenuse becomes the line that we can sight from the turret to the eye. We can then calculate that angle and use it to rotate our turret sprite.

Of course, it's not that easy. We need to handle the special case of the cardinal directions, and then we need to determine our direction of rotation and reset the rotation value if it falls below zero or greater than 2Π.

In the GUI_TIMER_EXPIRED section of LevelScrolling.lua, ManageTurrets() is only run for three cycles (at the end of which it runs TurretFire() and the State is set to "done"), and it rests for 15. The TurretFire() function looks like this:

```
function TurretFire()
    for y = 1,30 do
        worldX = (gScreenEdgeL/20)+1
        for x = 1,40 do
            if World[worldX][y] == 9 then
                pIndx = pIndx + 1
                MegaTable["Projectile"][pIndx].ID = GUI_INGAME + pIndx +
899 —Starts IDs at 900 (not including offset)
                MegaTable["Projectile"][pIndx].Origin = "bad" —Shooter
("good" or "bad")
                MegaTable["Projectile"][pIndx].Damage = 10 —Damage (#)
                MegaTable["Projectile"][pIndx].Rot = Turret[worldX][y]
                turRot = Turret[worldX][y]
                MegaTable["Projectile"][pIndx].X = ((x-1)*20+10) +
50*(math.cos(turRot)) —X coordinate (#)
                if turRot > math.pi then
                    MegaTable["Projectile"][pIndx].Y = ((y-1)*20+10) -
math.sqrt(50^2-(50*(math.cos(turRot)))^2) —Y coordinate (#)
                else
                    MegaTable["Projectile"][pIndx].Y = ((y-1)*20+10) +
math.sqrt(50^2-(50*(math.cos(turRot)))^2) —Y coordinate (#)
                end
                MegaTable["Projectile"][pIndx].XTh = 20*(math.cos(turRot))
—Thrust along the x-axis (#)
                if turRot > math.pi then
                    MegaTable["Projectile"][pIndx].YTh = -1 *
math.sqrt(20^2-(20*(math.cos(turRot)))^2) —Thrust along the y-axis (#)
                else
                    MegaTable["Projectile"][pIndx].YTh = math.sqrt(20^2-
(20*(math.cos(turRot)))^2) —Thrust along the y-axis (#)
                end
                CreateItem(MegaTable["Projectile"][pIndx].ID, "Sprite",
"enemyfire.jpg")
                SetItemPosition(MegaTable["Projectile"][pIndx].ID,
MegaTable["Projectile"][pIndx].X, MegaTable["Projectile"][pIndx].Y, 10, 5)
                ItemCommand(MegaTable["Projectile"][pIndx].ID,
"SetRotation", MegaTable["Projectile"][pIndx].Rot)
                if pIndx == 30 then
                    pIndx = 0
                end
            end
            worldX = worldX + 1
        end
    end
end
```

While this function seems complex, most of it is trigonometry again. We scan the world, and if we find a turret, we add a Projectile item to the world's MetaTable. We set this up with the X and Y coordinates, the type of shooter (good or bad), the rotation of the projectile sprite (which will never change once it's fired), and the X and Y Theta values, which will determine where the projectile is drawn the next update cycle (so it follows the path that represents the rotation of the turret at the moment of firing). We then physically create the projectile sprite, set its rotation, and record the ID number of the sprite in the MetaTable so it can be updated during the next draw update.

The "intelligence" of a turret is very simple—it rotates to face the eye (the player) and then fires. The turret will always rotate correctly, since we haven't introduced any "noise" into the rotation calculations. We only fire the turret every four update cycles so it doesn't inundate the player with projectiles—the spacing provides enough time for the player to recognize the projectile and take evasive action, thus providing an interesting challenge to the player.

To increase the effectiveness of the turret (and the appearance of its intelligence), we could do several things:

■ We could make it sit stationary, as if in "idle state" until the player comes within a certain range, and then run the turret rotation function—this would make it seem like it "wakes up" when it notices the player—no real upgrade in intelligence, but rather in its appearance of intelligence.
■ We could increase either the rate at which it fires or the speed of the projectiles. We could also create the effect of burst fire by having it not fire for five cycles, and then fire every cycle for three cycles and so on.
■ We could have it take into account the direction of the movement of the player and adjust its rotation so that when it fires, it's leading the player slightly (which should make it more accurate unless the player quickly checks direction). This is called "deflection shooting."
■ If we wanted to "dumb down" the turret, we could try:
■ Adding some randomness to the rotation calculation so it won't rotate to face the player exactly every time.
■ Having it rotate seemingly randomly for several cycles and then process a "genuine" rotation—this would make it look confused, like it lost the lock on the player.
■ We could slow the rate of fire and the speed of the projectiles.

As you can see, even with a very simple form of intelligence we can alter the behavior in both directions to provide a varied challenge for the player, and one that can be scaled for his position and action-skill level in the game.

Eye Opener Implementation—Arena

In the final battle of our fictional Eye Opener game, our hero enters an arena, set within an empty frame of a yet-to-be-drawn comic, to do battle with his nemesis, the Robot Guard. Both are armed with projectile "pulse laser" weapons. In this battle, we want the Robot Guard to exhibit more intelligent behavior than our simple turrets—we want him to feel more like an actual opponent rather than a simple machine (Figure 14.7).

FIGURE 14.7   The final arena battle in Eye Opener.

The Arena AI relies heavily on the MegaTable (which houses values relevant to both the player's character and the Robot Guard). The table is created in the CreateMegaTable() function (in LuaSupport.lua). The key parts of that function we are interested in create our two opponents and set us up for managing the projectiles:

```
MegaTable = {}
—Eye
MegaTable["Eye"] = {}
MegaTable["Eye"].ID = GUI_PLAYER + 1
MegaTable["Eye"].X = 40
MegaTable["Eye"].Y = 500
MegaTable["Eye"].Rot = 0
MegaTable["Eye"].Sprite = "OpticAl Aerial.tga"
MegaTable["Eye"].Width = 100
MegaTable["Eye"].Height = 60
MegaTable["Eye"].Treads = 0 —Replaces gTreads
MegaTable["Eye"].Damage = 0
MegaTable["Eye"].DamageMax = 200
MegaTable["Eye"].TreadsOn = 0 —Equipped? (0-No, 1-Yes)
MegaTable["Eye"].LaserOn = 0
MegaTable["Eye"].ClawOn = 0
MegaTable["Eye"].TarX = -1
MegaTable["Eye"].TarY = -1
MegaTable["Eye"].Speed = 3
MegaTable["Eye"].State = "done"
—Robot Guard - Arena
MegaTable["RobotGuardArena"] = {}
MegaTable["RobotGuardArena"].ID = GUI_PLAYER + 3
MegaTable["RobotGuardArena"].Rot = 0
MegaTable["RobotGuardArena"].X = 400
```

```
MegaTable["RobotGuardArena"].Y = 100
MegaTable["RobotGuardArena"].TarX = 0
MegaTable["RobotGuardArena"].TarY = 0
MegaTable["RobotGuardArena"].Speed = 3
MegaTable["RobotGuardArena"].Behavior = "normal"
MegaTable["RobotGuardArena"].State = "done"
MegaTable["RobotGuardArena"].Damage = 0
MegaTable["RobotGuardArena"].DamageMax = 500
—Projectiles
pIndx = 0 —Index of projectiles in the MegaTable table
MegaTable["Projectile"] = {}
for indx = 1,30 do
    MegaTable["Projectile"][indx] = {}
    MegaTable["Projectile"][indx].ID = 0—GUI identification number (#)
    MegaTable["Projectile"][indx].XTh = 0 —Thrust along the x-axis (#)
    MegaTable["Projectile"][indx].YTh = 0 —Thrust along the y-axis (#)
    MegaTable["Projectile"][indx].X = 0 —X coordinate (#)
    MegaTable["Projectile"][indx].Y = 0 —Y coordinate (#)
    MegaTable["Projectile"][indx].TarX = 0 —X coordinate of the target
(#)
    MegaTable["Projectile"][indx].TarY = 0 —Y coordinate target (#)
    MegaTable["Projectile"][indx].Origin = 0 —Shooter ("good" or "bad")
    MegaTable["Projectile"][indx].Damage = 0 —Damage (#)
    MegaTable["Projectile"][indx].Rot = 0 —Sprite Rotation (radians)
    MegaTable["Projectile"][indx].Speed = 20 —Moving Speed (#)
end
```

By putting all the relevant data we need within a single, multidimensional table, we have everything at our fingertips, and it will become much easier to debug or determine what is going on under the hood.

The GUI_TIMER_EXPIRED section of ArenaBattle.lua triggers the ManageRobot-GuardArena() function (which is in LuaSupport.lua), which houses the meat of the Arena version of the Robot Guard's AI. MegaTable["RobotGuardArena"].Behavior holds a string (either "normal" or "avoid") which refers to the specific pattern of action the Robot Guard will take. These are the States in each behavior:

Normal

"processing": Turning toward player

"approaching": Moving toward player

"firing": Firing three projectiles

"resting": Period of inaction

"done": Ready to reevaluate behavior type

Avoid

"processing": Turning from nearest threat
"approaching": Fleeing from nearest threat
"resting": Period of inaction
"done": Ready to reevaluate behavior type

`MegaTable["RobotGuardArena"].State` is the state of the behavior the Robot AI is in. The first chunk of script in `ManageRobotGuardArena()` determines the behavior type of the AI (if the State is "done," we are ready for reevaluation). The script checks for the distance between the projectiles and the Robot Guard, and the distance between the player and the Robot Guard. When the guard is in the state of "done," we set the state to "normal" and then run a check against the player or any projectiles to see if we need to change the state to "avoid":

```
if MegaTable["RobotGuardArena"].State == "done" then
     —Set defaults
     alertDistance = 200 —radius within which an object will cause
"avoid" behavior
     MegaTable["RobotGuardArena"].TarX = MegaTable["Eye"].X
     MegaTable["RobotGuardArena"].TarY = MegaTable["Eye"].Y
     MegaTable["RobotGuardArena"].State = "processing"
     MegaTable["RobotGuardArena"].Behavior = "normal"
        —Is the player too close?
     tempAlertDistance = math.sqrt(((MegaTable["RobotGuardArena"].X +
90) - (MegaTable["Eye"].X + 50))^2 + ((MegaTable["RobotGuardArena"].Y + 80)
- (MegaTable["Eye"].Y + 30))^2)
        if tempAlertDistance < alertDistance then
            alertDistance = tempAlertDistance
            local Xdistance = (MegaTable["RobotGuardArena"].X + 90) -
(MegaTable["Eye"].X + 50)
            local Ydistance = (MegaTable["RobotGuardArena"].Y + 80) -
(MegaTable["Eye"].Y + 30)
            MegaTable["RobotGuardArena"].TarX =
(MegaTable["RobotGuardArena"].X + 90) + 100*Xdistance
            MegaTable["RobotGuardArena"].TarY =
(MegaTable["RobotGuardArena"].Y + 80) + 100*Ydistance
            MegaTable["RobotGuardArena"].Behavior = "avoid"
        end
     —Is one of the player's projectiles too close?
     for indx = 1, 30 do
        if (MegaTable["Projectile"][indx].ID ~= 0) and
(MegaTable["Projectile"][indx].Origin == "good") then —Projectile exists
            —Determine distance from closest target
            tempAlertDistance =
math.sqrt(((MegaTable["RobotGuardArena"].X + 90) -
(MegaTable["Projectile"][indx].X + 10))^2 +
```

```
((MegaTable["RobotGuardArena"].Y + 80) - (MegaTable["Projectile"][indx].Y +
2))^2)
                    if tempAlertDistance < alertDistance then
                        alertDistance = tempAlertDistance
                        local Xdistance = (MegaTable["RobotGuardArena"].X + 90)
 - (MegaTable["Projectile"][indx].X + 2)
                        local Ydistance = (MegaTable["RobotGuardArena"].Y + 80)
 - (MegaTable["Projectile"][indx].Y + 10)
                        MegaTable["RobotGuardArena"].TarX =
(MegaTable["RobotGuardArena"].X + 90) + 100*Xdistance
                        MegaTable["RobotGuardArena"].TarY =
(MegaTable["RobotGuardArena"].Y + 80) + 100*Ydistance
                        MegaTable["RobotGuardArena"].Behavior = "avoid"
                    end
                end
            end
        end
```

If either of these distances is less than a radius of 200 pixels, the Robot Guard sets its destination to a point located away from the threat by setting MegaTable ["RobotGuardArena"].TarX and MegaTable["RobotGuardArena"].TarX accordingly. This difference in TarX and TarY is the only difference between "normal" and "avoid" behaviors, other than the lack of the "firing" state.

So, when the State is "processing", FaceTarget(object, curX, curY, curRot, tarX, tarY, worldX, x, y) is called. For this function call, object is robotguard and the last three parameters are ignored (they are only used in Level Scrolling). This function incrementally adjusts the Robot Guard's Rotation (MegaTable["Robot-GuardArena"].Rot) so that the Guard is oriented toward its TarX and TarY. When this process is complete, the State is set to "approaching."

When the State is "approaching," ApproachTarget(object, curX, curY, tarX, tarY, moveSpeed) is called. For this function call, "object" is robotguard and moveSpeed is MegaTable["RobotGuardArena"].Speed. This function moves the character's sprite along a trigonometrically determined path toward its target. The ManageRobotGuardArena() function monitors the progress, advancing to the next State when the Guard has taken 30 steps, or when it has reached its target.

When the State is "firing," ArenaFire(origin, curX, curY, curRot) is run every five cycles of GUI_TIMER_EXPIRED. For this function call, "origin" is "bad" (since it is the enemy's projectile). After three projectiles have been fired, the State is set to "resting." When the State is "resting," the Robot Guard does nothing for 20 cycles of GUI_TIMER_EXPIRED. At the end of this, the State is set to "done" and the behavior-determining process begins again.

If, at any time, the Robot Guard is outside the bounds of the arena, the Boolean function ArenaBoundsCheck(entity) (where entity is robotguard) will return true, and the State will immediately be set to "done." This way, the behavior will be reevaluated, and the TarX and TarY will hopefully be determined to be within the bounds of the arena.

When all of this is put together, we get the effect of an opponent who is aggressive, but only to a point. If the player approaches too close or too many projectiles are homing in, the guard becomes defensive, turns, and moves away, putting distance between himself and the opponent.

To increase the appearance of intelligence for the Robot Guard, there are a few things we might want to explore:

■ We could add obstacles in the world, and the avoiding guard could seek cover behind the obstacles.

■ We could add an additional behavior "sidestep" that would be activated if a projectile is getting too close—the guard could then try to sidestep away from the projectile.

■ We could alter the guard's firing rate depending on the distance of the player— if the player gets too close, the guard could step up and fire more rapidly, with the hopes of driving the player backward.

This example demonstrated how just a few states and behaviors can create quite a complex and flowing challenge for the player. The guard isn't following a pattern, but rather is moving through an organic set of states and their related actions, always reacting to the world around him (which is defined by player action).

To create a compelling and challenging computer opponent, you don't have to go overboard—just a few behaviors that take into account player action can deliver much of what you are looking for as a designer.

SUMMARY

In this chapter, we looked at the types of obstacles you will throw at your player during the course of a game. We first explored static obstacles and how those can serve as training tools to help your players learn the skills they'll need to tackle the dynamic obstacles they'll encounter in your game.

We explored artificial intelligence and looked at some core, simple design atoms that will help us keep our AI designs simple and effective. We then learned how we can describe artificial intelligence in our design documents, and finally, we walked through a number of examples in which scripts were used by a designer to actually implement computer opponent behavior.

In our next chapter, we'll look at designing the ebb and flow of play across your entire game, so the experience pulls the players along and guides them toward their final end goal.

CHAPTER EXERCISES

1. Write an AI design that describes a general commander overseeing the field of battle for a major Civil War conflict. What aspects of the battle influence his decisions? What decisions can he make? How could you make this AI have multiple levels of difficulty?
2. In Eye Opener, see if you can implement some of the suggestions to make the turret more effective. Do the same thing to "dumb it down."
3. Look at the final arena battle AI—how could you add additional behaviors to the AI to enhance the challenge and intelligence of the robot guard? Can you implement those ideas?

15 Game Flow Design

In This Chapter

- What Is Game Flow?
- Missions and Scenarios
- Mission Design Atoms
- Writing Mission Designs
- Campaigns
- Static versus Dynamic Campaigns
- Campaign Design Atoms
- Writing Campaign Designs

Gamers want to be heroes—they want to slay the dragon, win the girl, and bring peace to the kingdom—not to mention a nasty plague to the enemy kingdom across the river! However, gamers don't want to be heroes instantly—they want to earn their badges and work their way up to that moment of total victory where they can live happily ever after. They want to snatch victory from the jaws of defeat many times, perhaps even lose a close one only to come back better than before.

In short, gamers want a continuous heroic experience through challenge after challenge, each providing a satisfying resolution and inspiring them to continue. They want to feel like they matter in the game world—like it wouldn't survive without them. They want to experience the ebb and flow of a great story in which they are the star . . .

WHAT IS GAME FLOW?

Let's travel back to the early days of computer game development. Arcade games were all the rage, but games on the Apple II and Atari 800 were still coming into their own. Most games were small affairs, and extended play borrowed from some of the design concepts of the arcade games: more enemies and faster speed, the further you got into the game until eventually you lost.

During those early days, some of the most popular games on the Apple II were sports games, and several of the best sellers were centered on track and field events. While other games gave players the same play experience, only ramped up in difficulty, these early sports games presented the player with multiple sports and tested the player on multiple action skills such as speed keyboard mashing and rapid angle determination.

While these games captivated players, much of the interest came from the novelty of gaming in the first place and the fact that we could now see animated 2D graphics on screen. Replay of the game meant going for higher scores, since a single pass through the game was maybe 20 minutes tops. For these games, there really wasn't the concept of game flow—the games were just too short (Figure 15.1).

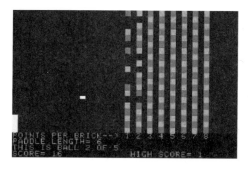

FIGURE 15.1   Early computer games didn't need to rely on any kind of game flow—the fact that they existed intrigued the players enough.

Fast forward to today's console and high-end PC games—gameplay for a single run through of the game ranges from 6 hours on the short end to 100+ hours on the long end. The player expects an experience that is fulfilling and takes him on an entertaining ride as he strives to best the game and meet the final meta-victory condition.

Since today's games are longer and more complex, we often break them down into smaller parts, much like a novelist breaks a book into chapters. One long continuous flow would be hard to develop and test, and would become tedious for the players, as they are hungry for subvictories and a more accessible ebb and flow of the game's dramatic plot.

The flow of the game from one section to the next, be it a mission or a level, is game flow. Game flow also encompasses the design of mission-based objectives (to provide subvictories), larger campaign issues, and most importantly, seeks to address a game that escalates in challenge and reacts to player performance as the player moves deeper and deeper into the game.

MISSIONS AND SCENARIOS

In Chapter 12, we spent a good deal of time thinking about levels within a game— as game environments that can direct player motion forward through the game. Levels, from a design sense, are about location, and more often than not, they exist as a framework to present challenges to the players as they move forward in space, with the meta-goal of the level being reaching the end.

In missions or scenarios (and in this chapter, we'll use the term *mission*), the goal isn't necessarily reaching a physical location in the game world, but rather fulfilling a set of criteria that represents success. You may need to hold a location for a given amount of time, or destroy a structure or escort a valuable treasure— these activities take place within a game environment, but aren't necessarily defined by the environment. The player may be able to hold position without moving in the game world at all.

Mission-based games have been around since the start of interactive gaming— the ability to break a larger quest into smaller portions allowed for the creation of full-fledged campaigns and allowed designers to explore the world of story across play that spanned many play sessions and many, many hours.

Missions come in many flavors and styles, but one distinction worth mentioning is the difference between static, or set-piece missions and dynamic missions. Set-piece missions are play experiences in which the obstacles have all been carefully selected and placed in the game environment by the game or mission designer. There may be exactly three mages, two trolls, a large furry ape, and nothing more. The challenges remain the same from play to play and the units in the mission are designed to provide a precise and balanced challenge for a player. Often, campaign missions make use of set-piece missions to recreate a historical event or battle. The Age of Empires series features campaigns that make strong use of set-piece scenarios.

Dynamic missions are missions that may have some existing set-pieces, but the lion's share of the opposing units are "spawned" during the play of the mission. This may occur as a computer-controlled opponent works through the unit creation process of an RTS game, or perhaps the scenario simply spawns in units of a certain type until the mission is won or lost. These types of missions can throw varying degrees of challenge at a player, since it's never the same mission twice. Classic RTS games like Starcraft use a dynamic mission approach.

Mission Design Atoms

In the pages that follow, we'll take some time to explore some design atoms that will help us craft solid missions that challenge players but avoid some of the traps that may frustrate them. Missions can be seen as their own discrete unit of play, or they can participate as merely a part of a larger whole—either way, the gameplay circumscribed within a mission structure provides an encapsulated play experience for the player filled with challenges and, hopefully, the opportunity for player victory, and, more importantly, player fun.

A Single Key to Each Mission

Each mission should focus on a single key tactical element.

It's easy to pack a lot into a single mission, but the more you pack into a concentrated game experience, the more you dilute the importance of each element. When designing a mission, focus on a single tactical element and build the mission around that. A mission element might be "Escort the caravan to Dacca" or "Destroy the enemy's keep" or "Hold the mountain pass until reinforcements arrive." The single tactical premise will keep the player engaged, but not confused. There can be plenty of intrigue and challenge in a single escort mission if the players' units are besieged by nomadic raiders at multiple choke points along their escort path. A simple tactical core to the mission will make the experience clear for the player, and make the mission easier to design and test, since you are limiting the number of variables active during a single play session.

You should also make sure that you vary the tactical "key" from mission to mission to keep the play interesting and challenging for the players. You don't want them to say, "Oh, this is just like the last mission, I can beat this with my eyes closed."

Keep Mission Goals Simple

Don't make the victory goals for a single mission overly complex.

This atom works in concert with the previous atom. Missions should concentrate on a single tactical element to allow the player to focus on solving a single complex problem. Within a mission, however, there may be multiple victory conditions, such as "Escort caravan; Gather 1,000 units of wood; Advance to Iron Age," and so on. The goals should not introduce any additional tactical elements, and any additional, ancillary goals should follow naturally with the pursuit of the primary tactical goal.

In fact, multiple victory conditions are not really a test for the player; rather, they are a guide to help the player progress toward the most important victory element: the tactical goal. The gathering of resources may be needed to construct wagons for the caravan. The technology advancement may allow the player to train and equip mounted archers, which may be essential to fend off the raiding nomads.

Inform the Player

Let the player know the victory conditions for a mission.

This may seem obvious, but it is worth stating: be *very* clear when you let the players know what they must do to succeed in a mission. Under the hood, you will be checking for the fulfillment of certain conditions (often checking the variables of certain values, such as how much wood they have or has "caravan unit X reached trigger Y?"). Be sure that you can articulate all of these checks via a mission overview that fits the tone and feel of the game. For example, Ghost Recon 2 featured a series of cinematic briefings that were delivered in the form of a historical documentary, establishing a military look and feel. They also informed the player of all key objectives, which were also available during gameplay in the player's heads-up display.

Also be sure to allow the player to revisit the mission objectives at any time during play, and if you have multiple objectives for a single mission, indicate on the objectives list which ones are accomplished and which are not.

Introduce Tactics

If needed, introduce tactical concepts to the player through mission play.

Many mission-based games rely on the player making sound tactical decisions to meet the victory decisions. If this is the case, don't assume your player understands the first thing about tactics. Tactical decisions are basically dynamic resource management decisions: the deployment and ordering of dynamic units to oppose dynamic obstacles. The simplest tactical decision is that "I have more strength than you and so I order my charges to simply advance and meet the obstacle head on" (hopefully, I was right and after a skirmish, more of my units are left standing).

More complex tactical decisions revolve around using movement and surprise to create an advantage. This may be a feint or distraction or it may simply mean taking your fastest units around to the rear of your enemy and hitting them where they are weakest.

You, as a designer, will probably understand the best tactical decisions a player can make for a given scenario. If that's the case, you may need to introduce those concepts to the player directly, perhaps through the story vehicle of an adviser, or just in the mission overview. You may have some training missions or campaigns, or you may build it directly into the flow of the game. However you do it, if you require tactical acumen from your player, be sure to introduce and teach the basic concepts through simple directed missions.

Alert the Player to Changing Goals

It's okay to change goals to simulate a dynamic world—just let the player know.

Often, you may want to create the impression of a real-life world in your game by changing the goals of a mission midway through. Perhaps the player is charged with escorting the crown jewels to the king in his northern palace. Midway through the mission, a rider approaches the player's party and tells him the throne has just been usurped and the pretender to the throne is sending elite guards after them to recover the jewels. The player must now head for the eastern fortification, where loyal troops still control the fortress.

While the preceding situation is created by the designer during development, it creates a sense for the player that the world is alive and dynamic and that he is participating in something that is malleable instead of fixed—it also causes him to think on his feet and pumps up the adrenaline quite a bit.

If you do change the objectives during a mission, be clear about letting the player know—ideally, it would be within the context of the game, rather than a dialog box popping up. Also remember to update the mission objectives that the players can reference during the mission to provide them with the new information.

Ramp Up Difficulty

Make the missions more challenging as the player progresses through the game.

A constant level of challenge is no fun once a player has mastered it. No matter how challenging your missions, the players will figure out a way to beat them (if the game is interesting enough, that is) and once they do that, it becomes boring.

Mission-based play provides a natural way for you to ratchet up the difficulty. Each mission can introduce a new tactical concept and new units and more aggressive AI. As you increase the challenge level from mission to mission, make sure you ramp up smoothly. Generally, try to avoid increasing difficulty on multiple fronts at the same time. Perhaps one mission introduces a new tactical wrinkle, the next introduces new and challenging units, and the next introduces a commander who is far more adept at resource management. In this example, difficulty is increased a step at a time, so the player can notice the areas in which the challenge has increased and focus his attention there. Throwing everything at players all at once will create confusion, and they won't know where to concentrate their efforts and may walk away frustrated.

Create a Story Arc

Each mission should act like a chapter to a book, with its own story arc.

Novels are so satisfying because you generally have a large, sweeping tale, but that tale is broken down into smaller chunks, and each acts as its own story. A well-written chapter will ramp up tension to a moment of climax and provide a resolution for the reader—not to the entire book, but to the elements within the chapter.

Think of your missions in the same way, even if they aren't part of a large and grand campaign story. Players feel most satisfied when they can achieve subvictories in a game, and those victories resonate more when the players struggled through an escalating arc of challenge with the mission. To complete the mission story arc, you'll want to have some sort of wrap-up for the victory, and not simply cut away to the main game interface with the word "Victory!" emblazoned on the screen. If your mission is part of a larger campaign, take some time to explain how the victory affected the world as a whole and how the participants (winners and losers) were affected. For example, in *Halo 2*, each time the player clears an area or resolves an objective, there's a brief sequence in which the supporting cast congratulates the player on a job well done. The consequences of these actions are relayed to the player through conversations, radio chatter, video feeds, and other in-game devices. This provides a reward, but also enhances the game flow by further immersing the player in the game world.

If your mission is standalone, spend at least a few seconds in game for a resolving camera shot of the battlefield or situation—perhaps with the winners pumping their fists and the losers heading back to camp—just some to provide that moment of rest, relief, and contemplation that comes after a climax in a story arc.

Used "Forced Defeat" Sparingly

Don't force the player to lose too often in your game.

There may be times when your larger campaign design will call for a mission that the player *will* lose. You may want to make a dramatic point or set up a series of comeback missions. Just be aware that players don't like to lose, and you don't want to pull this trick more than once in your game. A seasoned player will understand what you are trying to do, but novice players may become frustrated and angry once they realize that the game designers set up a no-win situation for them.

A forced loss mission should *only* be used as part of a larger campaign structure—never force the player to lose a mission if the mission is standalone—you'll only anger and frustrate the player (and you'll become known as a cruel designer!).

Equally Balanced Equals Boring

Don't set up mission obstacles that are equal on both sides of the fence.

Don't misunderstand—your missions must be balanced so they play well and feel fair. However, a balanced mission, play-wise, is not the same thing as playing a mission in which the forces on both sides of the conflict are identical.

Imagine a Roman-era skirmish mission about two conflicting generals battling with their forces. Each side marshals 50 legionnaires of identical ability, both offensive and defensive. How exciting would the battle be? Both sides would charge each other, and odds are that one side would end up with a single footman remaining, and who that is would be basically based on a coin flip.

Going up against an identical force is just plain boring. Imagine our previous example with one side having 20 archers (who can fire from a distance but are slow and have no defensive shielding) and 20 legionaries, and the other with the 50 footmen. Now you have a recipe for something interesting, because each side must play to its strengths and exploit the weaknesses of the other side. It's in balanced inequality that a player will find a truly challenging and fun experience.

Keep Replayability in Mind

Missions often take multiple play-throughs for a player to succeed, so plan for it.

When a player is working through a level-based game, he often will revisit a single level only once during the play-through of a game. Mission-based games will often find players tackling the same mission several times before they can figure out how to achieve the victory conditions.

When a player revisits a mission that just defeated him, he wants to see two things: familiarity *and* something new. If the mission is wholly new, the player can't draw on the experience of his recent defeat. If the mission is exactly the same, the player can easily predict what's going to happen and the makeup of the opposing forces, so the victory the second time around feels somewhat hollow.

Allow your missions to play out with a small amount of randomness—perhaps there is a variance in the location of the resources, or the exact number or location of enemy troops. A slight amount of randomness will keep the experience fresh yet familiar as your player tries again.

Writing Mission Designs

So, how do you document the design for a mission? It can vary greatly from project to project, but no matter what tools or technology are used to create a mission, there are several key steps.

First, you'll want to outline the major touch points of the mission—that is, what is the mission doing within the scope of the entire game? Is the point of the mission to introduce archery units to the player? Is the mission designed to introduce the concept of a flanking attack? Is the mission designed as a mechanism to bring the player to the alien base? Figure out what the essential purpose of the mission is, because that will be the guiding light that will focus the rest of the design.

Your next step will be to determine the tactical key to the mission—what is the tactical approach that will yield the best results for the player. What type of tactical mission is it?

From there, you will want to describe the environment for the mission, documenting any essential features. Often, the designer will put together a sketch of the mission as well, highlighting the layout of the environment and the general placement of objects in the mission-space.

Next, outline the resources available to all sides that will be involved in the mission, either as starting units, set-piece units, world resources, and such. Finally, write up a short narrative that describes the ideal flow of the scenario and the challenges the player must face, figure out, and beat.

Missions are usually created via some sort of tool, either off the shelf or custom-created by the tech team. The goal of the written design is to provide just enough guidance for the mission creator (who may very well be the designer) to put together the mission. The real art and craft of mission creation occurs in the development tool—that is when the mission can be tweaked, tested, retested, and tweaked again. It's not uncommon for a production game mission to have undergone dozens and dozens of revisions to balance the play and provide just the right amount of challenge.

The following example is a rough design for a mission in a fictional fantasy RTS campaign game, where the player is attempting to break through a mountain pass held by rock trolls.

```
I. Mission Design: The Merridian Pass
a. Core purpose:
Introduction of Pegasus archer units
b. Tactical key:
Use superior mobility to attack the enemy from behind
c. Environment:
Hilly steppes, with the center area of the map dominated by a rocky ridge
with a narrow pass near the center.
d. Player forces:
The player begins with a squad of longbowmen, two squads of swordsmen, and
four mounted archers. At the three-minute mark, Ralston will appear from
the south with four Pegasus archer units.
e. Opposition:
Set piece army from the Kingdom of Merridia, featuring a front line of rock
trolls, a pair of mounted commanders, and a company of goblin spearmen.
f. Victory condition:
The player forces reaching the stone road at the north side of the map.
g. Description:
```

In this mission, Merridia's forces are halting the advance of the small human strike force. They have positioned rock trolls to hold the ridge pass, and are supported in front and behind by goblin spearmen. Two commanders patrol the rear to stop any breakthrough and to provide a combat and morale bonus for the goblins.

The player will attempt to punch through with his small force, since he is trying to reach the road to the north. Given the limited force, it will be hard for the player to break past the trolls (who will not advance through the pass). At the three-minute mark, Ralston (commander unit) will arrive on the map at the south edge with four newly recruited Pegasus archer units.

The archers can fly over the mountains and can take out the enemy commanders and the rear-guard goblins. The reduction in force should allow the players to target and destroy the trolls and make their way through the pass.

Note: while the trolls won't advance south through the pass, they will head north to follow and attack the Pegasus units, so the player could theoretically punch through without dispatching the trolls.

CAMPAIGNS

Campaigns are large structures that link smaller game-play experiences together, creating a unified game flow. Campaigns can link levels, missions, or even adventure game or platform environments. The experiences are linked together to form a larger story arc that guides the player from the start of the experience to the ultimate win-lose-draw end state.

Campaigns offer an opportunity for your players to become deeply immersed in your game, and properly designed, the campaign will reward the players with missions or levels of growing complexity and sophistication (to match their growing skills) along with the larger story arc and game context.

If you are considering a long campaign game, you will want to consider the addition of either tutorial missions at the start of the campaign or a smaller tutorial campaign itself, to teach the player how to interact with the game. Both approaches have been used with great success, and the high water mark was probably the William Wallace tutorial campaign for Age of Empires II: The Age of Kings. The tutorial campaign was played out like an actual historical campaign, so the players learned what to expect from the game, the narrative, and the historical immersion as they were learning the basic mechanics of the game.

Static and Dynamic Campaigns

Campaigns can be either static or dynamic. Static campaigns are simply a collection of play experiences (such as missions) organized in a meaningful way. The results of one mission have no bearing on the results of the next mission (often, in these campaigns, a player must win a mission to unlock the next mission). The ebb and flow of the game universe is presented through the content of the missions and any story-based exposition presented to the player via mission briefings or campaign cinematic.

Dynamic campaigns maintain some data "under the hood" that will modify and affect future missions based on the previous player results. Perhaps it's as simple as the player being able to keep any loot earned in one mission and bring it into the next. More detailed systems might affect the availability of enemy forces or player units and may even guide the flow of narrative text or cinematics.

Both approaches can create the feeling that the larger world and game story is dynamic and reacting to player action. The dynamic campaign actually does react to the efforts of the player, which at first blush can seem like a great idea. The word of caution here is that if you do decide to implement a dynamic campaign, make sure the dynamic variables don't have too large an effect on the components of a single mission, since it can be easy to lose the game balance you have worked so hard for. In addition, it's possible, if the effects are cumulative, that you can drive the players into a state in which they cannot win or one in which they are invincible—neither of which is very fun.

Campaign Design Atoms

In the section that follows, we'll explore some game design atoms related to campaign design. The goal is to create a seamless game flow that immerses the player in a world that feels vibrant, alive, and larger than the player's actions at a given moment. Properly implemented, a campaign structure can serve as the backbone for your game story (see Chapter 16) and the conceptual thread that will link all your missions together into a single meaningful quest for the player.

Research

Campaigns imply a larger world that should be supported by research.

If you are creating a sweeping campaign, be sure to do your homework first. Even a fantasy or science fiction campaign will be well served by research. You first need to think through the central premise of your campaign—is it about a war for freedom? Is it about rescuing a scientist trapped deep in an underground research facility? With the central focus of your campaign in mind, you can begin some research that will help you breathe live and details into your campaign. Even though a campaign may sweep across 30 missions, the attention to detail in your story-telling and mission continuity will resonate to your player.

If you are designing a campaign based around military action, research the great battles of history that took place with similar technology (even if it is fantasy)—the lessons of history will no doubt spark some inspirational ideas that you can bring into the campaign flow and mission design of your game.

THE MYTH OF PRESTER JOHN

Designer: Paul Schuytema

When we were working to create the campaign that would link together the missions of our medieval RTS, we read a lot of history. We knew that the game would be set in the twelfth century, because the types of units and technology fit with our interests and gameplay goals. We also knew that we wanted to bring in some fantasy elements—not too heavy-handed, but enough to make the game feel unique.

During our research, we came across a numbers of stories referring to the letter of "Prester John." Prester John was supposedly a priest who had made a pilgrimage to the holy land and had found the proverbial "land of milk and honey." He set up a kingdom there in a magical land with wealth beyond anyone's wildest imagination. The letter told of this magical land, but also that Prester John's kingdom was under siege by the infidels. He was requesting

$\rightarrow$

brave knights to come to his aid—if they came, they would be rewarded with riches beyond belief.

Of course, the letter was a fake—it was distributed around Europe as one of the many "hooks" to get knights to commit themselves and their men at arms to the Crusades.

For us, though, it was perfect. We used the letter and the allure of Prester John's kingdom as the motivation force that drove our player across Europe and into the Middle East. Of course, in our game, we added a twist. There indeed was a Prester John, but he was not a goodly priest—instead, he was an evil magician who lured his victims to him, since he was bound to his magical lands. Too late the player realizes he's been lured into a trap, and must battle magical minions and weaponry just to survive.

In our game, we used historical research to get a feel for the time, but we also discovered a historical element that later became the seed that allowed us to grow a complete campaign.

Nested Victories

Populate your campaign with many opportunities for player victory.

The fact that a campaign is made up of discrete gameplay elements makes this an easy goal to achieve. As in our earlier discussions of the nested victories inherent in a game like basketball, a player likes to feel like a winner, and no matter how interesting the struggle, he wants to win and win often. A campaign game gives you an opportunity to provide the player with opportunities to feel heroic.

As you begin to think of your campaign as a larger story arc, don't forget to pepper the campaign missions with close calls and maybe even a defeat. While players enjoy multiple victories, they enjoy close victories many times more than an endless series of easy wins.

Meta Story Arc

Allow your campaign to tell a larger story.

Earlier, we discussed how a mission should have its own small story arc encapsulated within it, like a chapter in a novel. If a mission is a chapter, then a campaign is a novel, and should present the player with a large story arc.

If we graph out the story arc for a novel, we see that it isn't a smooth escalation up to the moment of climax, but rather something more like the teeth of a saw blade. Allow the missions to provide the victories, but use the campaign structure to create those narrative dips that represent setbacks and larger obstacles.

As the players work through the missions of a well-crafted campaign, they will enjoy the moment-by-moment gameplay and the challenges it provides, and will feel the fire of heroism through their mission victories. They will also get to understand their actions within a larger story in which not everything is rosy. Eventually, they'll reach the climax point where their efforts will achieve the victory.

Allow Strategic Decisions

Strategic decisions in a campaign allow the player to feel in control.

Missions are all about tactical problem solving, in which the player makes specific decisions for the deployment of individual units. If it fits your campaign and you can manage it, allow the player to make strategic decisions from a higher-level campaign interface. Strategic systems are large scale and don't involve the specific moment-by-moment control of units, but rather the allocation of large-scale resources.

This can be done simply by allowing the player to select the next mission from several potential choices, and allocating troops units or points to the mission (think of a turn in the classic, all-strategic board game Risk).

Strategic choices will allow the player to feel more in control of the entire game world. With some simple design, you can implement an approach that won't play havoc with the play balancing at the mission level.

Writing Campaign Designs

If you will be using a campaign structure to create the game flow through your game, where do you begin? First and foremost, you'll want to determine the meta story arc for the campaign—is it the Allied invasion of France? Is it about a party of outcasts who finally find and deliver a cure for a deadly plague?

Once you have the conceptual thread, you can begin to document your design. For a static campaign, you don't need to go into too much detail, since the real detail is in the individual mission designs. Your goal is to lay out the sequence of missions, the unfolding of the larger story and how the missions fit together (the role of the individual missions).

Remember that part of the campaign design is actually interface design: how are you going to present the sequence of missions to the player? Will you be using a map to show the lay of the land? Will you be simply providing mission briefings? Will the player be able to manipulate objects or forces in the campaign view? Think about the way in which you will be presenting the campaign structure, visually, to the player. The campaign will need to be introduced, but you will probably also need to present information to the player between missions or levels—how will you do that?

If you are designing a dynamic campaign structure, you will need to document just what variables will be dynamic, and in the mission designs, you'll need to reflect those variables in the design. Remember that for dynamic campaigns, you will want to inform the player of any changes in the game world due to his actions (or the opponent's actions) so the player understands that the rules have changes slightly.

Figure 15.2 is a simple design example for the first act of the campaign in Castles & Catapults. The details of the individual missions are handled in the mission designs and the editor files, but this campaign design snippet shows how you can lay out the game flow to understand how the various missions will all fit together.

FIGURE 15.2   This prototype campaign screen attempts to anchor the missions by placing them on a map of medieval Europe.

```
I. Campaign Overview

Premise:

Prester John sends a letter the hero runs across during the 2nd half of Act
I. The hero decides to follow the directions given in the letter, in the
hopes of finding Prester John and his wondrous kingdom. The letter,
however, is an elaborate ruse intended to lure and deplete mighty warrior-
kings — those who might someday oppose Prester John — so that he might
destroy them on his own turf.

Note: In nearly every mission, the player will have the ability to build a
castle, control a castle, or gain control of a castle.

Mission 1: easy European mission—tutorial

Mission 2: normal European mission—first mention of Prester John (indirect)

Mission 3: Germanic/Alps—possession of letter of PJ

Mission 4: toasted by "Black Army"

Mission 5: running away from "Black Army"

Act I:

The player views a pre-game animatic, giving the player a context for his
character, the battle that lays ahead, and so forth. During this part, the
Opening Chant plays. In this case, the first two missions are centered on
```

the player's goal of reclaiming a couple of castles, one in Brittany and the other in Alsace-Lorraine. The player is assumed to be British royalty. This is most likely the closest to history the game actually gets.

Mission 1:

This is the tutorial mission. The player is given a small keep and a small army, with the goal of reclaiming a weakly held castle in Brittany from an upstart French lord who wants to reclaim this section of France from England. The player receives help from an advisor throughout the mission (could be in the form of text messages without fancy graphics or voice-over). The player's keep is on the high ground and has the advantage. The player will also receive reinforcements after a certain length of play, in the case that the player is having a little trouble and doesn't achieve a quick and stunning victory. However, the player should be able to win without the reinforcements.

Mission 2:

This is a semi-tutorial mission. The player must liberate another keep that the Holy Roman Emperor has attempted to take on the borders of Alsace-Lorraine. The player receives a modicum of guidance from the advisor. The player has loose armies (up to 3) and can build a keep. The player, upon conquering the castle held by the enemy, obtains the Prester John letter.

This cues another animatic, detailing the story of Prester John. This also causes the player's character to go into a brief reverie during the animatic, showing the player's longing for a paradise on earth. It is during this time the Hero's Theme is played. Minimal voice over leads into the music (voice should sound old, wizened).

Mission 3:

The player moves with his army toward Prester John. He encounters his first obstacle, a petty lord who will not let him pass his castle without a fight. The player must lay siege to the castle and conquer the lord before moving on.

Mission 4:

The player, in possession of the castle, must fight a legendary force — The Black Army, alleged to be a roving band of marauders who are highly organized, very wealthy, and extraordinarily powerful. The player will lose the castle he gained in this fight and will be directed by his forces to abandon the keep — losing the battle, but not losing the war.

Mission 5:

The player is running away from the keep in Mission 4 and toward Prester John. If the Black Army is moving in closer to the British lands in France, then they pose an immediate threat to the player's homeland. They need Prester John's help. The player must fight a couple of loose armies of Huns for the control of an abandoned keep in the southeast, near Saracen territory.

Sample Doc

In this document, you can see the progression of missions. First, an establishment of the world through animatic sequences. Second, the tutorial, which comes with a safety net in the form of reinforcements. This allows the player to experiment with gameplay, becoming acclimated to the controls and responses. After this, the player engages the enemy on more even ground, and is rewarded with a letter from Prester John, which sets up later encounters and provides the player character with a motivation.

The fourth and fifth missions drive up the tension by forcing the player to abandon the keep and keeping the player on the run. There is a clear goal, however: contact with Prester John, who can help the player turn the tide. This was foreshadowed in the second mission, when the player found the letter.

CREATING GAME FLOW

The creation of mission flow is a collaborative effort between game designers and scripters, along with other members of the development team. The goal is to create a series of objectives that pull the player through an interactive experience in the same way that each scene draws an audience member through a movie or play.

The difference is that the player is a participant, not a spectator, so the designer must learn to approach game flow from the perspective of the player. Unlike the developers, a player experiences the game for the first time on its release date; by this point, the developers have played parts of the game hundreds of times, if not thousands. To keep the experience meaningful and enjoyable, the designer must constantly approach each individual goal as though for the first time.

Each mission will probably go through a series of approvals, including leads, producers, and management. Along the way, it's likely that missions will be altered or even cut, requiring the designer to revise the campaign and mission flow. Art assets will be revised, depending on manpower or scheduling issues—often, it's just not possible to create everything the team had hoped for. This, too, necessitates a revision of the overall game flow.

Due to these factors, it's important for the designer to be able to identify the goals and tactics inherent in each segment of gameplay, from the small scale (individual encounters) to the large scale (overall campaign flow and storyline). If every element is justified in some way—this particular encounter is interesting for this reason, and propels the storyline in this fashion—then changes during the production process will not impede the game flow.

SUMMARY

In this chapter, we first explored the concept of game flow, and how structures such as levels, missions, and campaigns can define the path the player takes through the game. We then looked at the concept of a game mission or scenario and how objective-based missions differ from location-based levels.

Thinking as a mission designer, we reviewed some core design elements to keep in mind when designing missions for our game, and then reviewed some touch points for writing successful mission designs.

We then turned our attention to campaigns and learned how they support a larger story arc and can define the game flow of the play experience. We discussed the differences between static campaigns and dynamic campaigns, which can affect later missions. After examining some campaign game design atoms, we looked at some tips to better help us write the design and flow of a campaign structure and looked at a real-world example.

In our next chapter, we'll turn our attention to the world of story and learn how we can craft and deliver a compelling story that supports and enhances the player's moment-by-moment gameplay.

CHAPTER EXERCISES

1. Imagine a modern-era military RTS game and you are the mission designer. Write a short mission design key that requires the player to open and ignite one or more oil wells.

2. Imagine that you are creating a historical medieval scenario, and currently, the set-piece scenario you are designing pits two identical forces together. Each has 25 short-swordsmen, 15 pikemen, and 10 crossbowmen. Do some quick historical research and see how you could adjust the units on one side to a similar but different type to create a more interesting battle (one in which each side could have the advantage if they understand their strengths and weaknesses).

3. Find an interesting event or series of events in history that could be co-opted for an interesting campaign game. Write a short description of the missions or scenarios that would comprise this campaign.

16 Storytelling

In This Chapter

- What is a Story?
- Storytelling Atoms
- Writing as Game Design
- How Do You Deliver a Story in a Game?
- *Eye Opener* Implementation

Have you ever listened to a friend excitedly tell you about what happened in a game he played—as if it actually happened to him? The game experience can be so engrossing that it can deliver a compelling story to a player, and the play experience itself can become the source of an oral story shared between friends. "Hey, did I tell you about the time I threw the winning touchdown in the Super Bowl with only three seconds left?"

WHAT IS A STORY?

An age-old question, really—what is a story? A tale of heroes and deeds done well. That's one possible answer. More to the point, a story is an explanation—it explains a conflict between a character, called the protagonist, and some obstacle. The protagonist works to overcome the obstacle and either succeeds or fails. It's as simple as that. Of course, a protagonist doesn't have to be a hero, or a person. In the realm of games, the protagonist could be the entire planet of Zufta-Prime, or perhaps the country of France or a blue whale named Cindy . . .

The core concept is that a story is about a conflict and how it is resolved. We've been telling each other stories for as long as we could talk—maybe even longer. We've told stories about a hunting party's conflict with an enraged wooly mammoth.

We've told stories about how our great grandparents made their way to Ellis Island. We've told stories about how some friend we know . . . yes, a friend, found his way home in a snowstorm after having too many watermelon-pucker shots on Saturday night. Conflict and resolution is all around us, and it fascinates us today just as much as it did when the stories were immortalized on cave walls 10,000 years ago.

How Does a Story Fit into a Game?

If a story is about a conflict, then what is a game about? A game is about a conflict as well—an attempt to overcome challenges to finally win. Boiled down to their bare essentials, there isn't much difference between the core components of a story and a game. However, a story is an explanation—it is told to us. A game (like life) is something we do. There *is* a difference.

But the two can come together quite nicely—what if you could participate in a story, if you could become the hero battling obstacles, and what if, instead of a story teller telling you what happened, you could control what happened, you could be responsible for the resolution?

It's a natural fit, and that's why games and stories have been intertwined for thousands of years—games like Go are stories of military conflict—*Monopoly* is a story about a rise from modest beginnings to wealth (or perhaps poverty!).

Interactive games—the kind we are interested in designing—have been wedded to story since the very first arcade games surfaced some 35 years ago. If you have followed the ebb and flow of game design theory over the last 10 years or so, the importance of story has cropped up again and again, from being essential to the game experience to flat-out getting in the way. The sensible viewpoint these days is that moment-by-moment gameplay trumps story, but story is a vital ingredient to add depth, emotion, and context to the game experience.

As designers, crafting a compelling game in today's market means also crafting a compelling story and wedding the two together seamlessly. To do that, we must first dive in and learn about some of the core components of just what makes a story tick.

Storytelling Atoms

In the pages that follow, we're going to take a crash course in story writing. As a designer, you may not be responsible for the in-the-trenches detail of your game's story—that task may go to a writer. More likely than not, however, the story will first evolve out of the work of a designer as he or she seeks to find the threads to bind the game experience together. Regardless of who writes the final story, a designer needs to understand the key touch points involved in story writing, so he or she can effectively create at least the story skeleton that will support the game.

Identify the Hero

Create the protagonist, who will become the alter ego of the player.

Every tale needs a hero, and the same is true for many games. Some titles, such as *Elder Scrolls IV: Oblivion* or *Animal Crossing: Wild World*, allow the player to build a hero from scratch. Others, such as Ghost Recon and Battlefield 1942, don't feature a central character at all. However, for those games featuring a clearly defined main character, it's important to give some thought to the nature of your protagonist. In the world of a game, that hero may be a dashing young knight, or may be an entire alien civilization, or perhaps a country at war—no matter the scope, define the hero. Get to know your heroes—what makes them tick? What are they hoping for? What would they fight for? A well-rounded hero isn't always about strength and power, but some weakness, too. What are your hero's greatest strengths and abilities? What is your hero's greatest weakness? What secret is he hiding from everybody? Take notes—imagine the past, the defining events, the victories and defeats that made your hero who he is today.

Define a Problem

A good story isn't about smooth going, it's about friction.

Imagine your hero has a problem, a real big juicy problem, something that won't just go way. Is it a situation? Is it another character (the protagonist)? Is it an itch that just can't be scratched? Is it a situation that requires escape? Think through the problem your hero has and define as many aspects of it as you can. Has another country invaded your "hero county?" Is your hero riddled with self-doubt because his father's dying words were, "I wish you had made me proud"? Imagine a problem that hits the hero where he hurts most—at his weakest points—imagine a problem your hero can't imagine overcoming. That's when you have created an interesting situation.

Strive to Overcome the Problem

The meat of a story is the narrative of the hero's efforts to overcome his problem.

Your hero wants to solve his problem, but obstacles stand in his way. He has much to learn and far to go, and for every two steps forward he takes, he stumbles back three. Imagine the problem getting worse and direr as the hero struggles—not better, like quicksand. Imagine your hero growing stronger in the face of adversity, but wondering, "Will it be enough?" Imagine your hero reaching his breaking point, that point at which he is ready to give up.

Last Chance

From the jaws of defeat, your hero claws out a narrow victory.

The chips are down…the bases are loaded at the bottom of the ninth . . . time is running out . . . air is running out—think of any cliché you can. Your hero is ready to take his last gasp. He has battled and fought, but he has not won the war. He has looked deep into himself and found strength, but the odds grow greater and greater as his nemesis can be heard offstage laughing. Before he can strike the final blow, he recalls his purpose, his drive, and what he is fighting for . . . he slashes with the last energy he has and . . . drops his nemesis. He is exhausted, but victorious.

Have your hero snatch away a narrow victory—it will be one that will resonate with power, since nothing is more heroic than victory grabbed at the last moment against all odds.

The Hero Gets the Girl

With the nemesis defeated, they can live happily ever after.

After the release of the final deathblow and narrow victory, the hero is propped up by his forbidden love. Together, hand in hand, they walk toward the sunset, ready to rule the kingdom together with a fair hand.

The moment of climax in a story is exhausting, both for the hero and those hearing the story. To allow the climax, and all the struggles leading up to that point to sink in, the story must have a resolution in which we see the results of the battle—not in too much detail, just enough so we feel secure that, at least for the moment, the world is right and good.

Understand the Plot Arc

An effective story builds to a climax and then resolves.

In our earlier over-the-top examples, we touched on the key aspects of the plot arc of a traditional story. It begins with a character and a problem and the potential for some tension, and the tension mounts a little bit each time the hero attempts to solve his problem. He may be victorious in a battle, but the foe gains strength and the war rages on. No matter what type of game story you are writing, you can probably boil it down into our corny examples and see how they fit into the arc, ramping up toward crisis and then offering the release that is the resolution.

Outline

Outline the plot arc of your story before you write it.

In the previous atoms, we looked at the elements of a compelling story, but in a very general way. A story, even for a game, will have more depth to the conflicts, the characters, and the final crisis. Jot those down in outline form, from one plot point to the next, from the moment the problem is identified to the final gasp of resolution. Look over your outline—change it around and adjust it until you feel like the heading in your outline fits neatly within the escalating plot arc you are striving for.

Write

With the outline in hand, write the narrative for your story.

You now have the notes in hand and the plot outline to guide you—it's time to put fingers to keyboard and start writing your story. For a first pass, don't worry too much about your use of language or turning a witty phrase—simply be clear, concise, and accurate (remember when we talked about writing like a journalist?—this is the perfect time). Just get a draft of your story out—keep it short and simple. Your game may eventually offer up 30 hours of playtime, but a game that long rarely needs a story over five pages long.

Revise

Once you have the story in place, revise it.

Ask any working writer what the most important skill of a writer is, and it's a five-to-one bet that he or she will say, "the ability to edit and revise my own work." Don't think of your story as art—think of it as craft—more akin to making a sturdy chair than the Mona Lisa. You want the chair to look good, true, but you also want it to be sturdy, well made, and perform the functions of a chair admirably.

Don't get hung up on your own words—go back and make them better, clearer, and easier to read. As an experiment, go ahead and cut out your first sentence or two—odds are you don't need them. Cut, primp, and tidy up your story until it feels just right—then share it with members of your development team. Get their feedback and then revise again. Figure three revisions minimum before you'll have something that will work for you.

Have a Theme

Give your story a message that's worth sharing.

Good stories are based on universal themes of human experience, and good game stories are no different, even if the protagonist is Great Britain and the antagonist is Germany. What is the message of your story? You don't have to hammer us over the head with it—you don't even have to state it literally anywhere in the story (in fact, it's better if you don't), but have a theme at your core. Is the theme about redemption? The hollow feeling of revenge? Are you saying, "don't judge people until you know them better?" "Defend those you care about?" Whatever the theme, make it your job to know it, understand it, and use it to guide your conflicts, plotting, and writing.

Keep Your Focus Narrow

Don't' write too big of a story.

The more zoomed in you can keep your story, the better. Even sweeping tales like Isaac Asimov's *Foundation Trilogy* zoomed in to focus on characters and their struggles. Don't write a story about the three millennium galactic ebb and flow of a rogue star-faring civilization—rather, focus in on how a band of rebels is trying to break away from the rules in a single backwater base. The larger your story, the harder it will be to convey during the play of your game. Keep the scope simple and the focus based on the struggles of your heroes, however you have defined them.

Work with a Writer

For professional polish, work with a professional writer.

Odds are that you'll have to tackle story writing at some time during your design career, and you should embrace the challenge—nothing is more exciting than to see your story come alive in the dynamics of gameplay. Often, the story will be delivered in the game as exposition (perhaps by a narrator as voice over for a cinematic) or dialogue—for those "commercial grade" deliveries of your story, work with a professional writer if you can. You job is to design the game—the challenges, the flow, and the interactivity. Professional writers know how to use language and can take the framework of your story and turn just the right phrases to make it compelling for your player. Remember that the game story isn't art—it's craft. Revisiting the chair analogy, a good designer story is like a well-made dining room chair. Bringing in a professional writer will turn that chair into a Louis XIV fainting couch.

Writing as Game Design

Earlier, we took a crash course in story writing, with an eye on the minimum elements we need to tell an effective game story. With a story in hand, there are many ways we can use that story—it can be presented to the player as cinematics or through other in-game delivery methods. The story itself can be a useful design tool. Some designers may feel liberated or more comfortable expressing game design through the vehicle of story. For games that are ruled by a central quest or struggle, a story may be a great first step, before even a design document, to get you thinking about what you want to see in the game and what elements you might want to pull into the realm of interactivity.

DESIGN STORY

Designer: Paul Schuytema

When we first started designing the second iteration of the game Prey at 3D Realms, we spent a lot of time thinking about character and how we could create an interesting opening to the game that would clearly define the character, and illuminate the internal and external struggles that would drive the game forward. The natural choice was to write the story of the game, to allow us to learn about the character and how he interfaced with his world. It turned out to be a great first step and the story allowed us to more easily get a handle on the core design elements and made creating the first working set of design documents much easier.

Look back along your path, my Brave Son. It is not as you expected, is it? Now turn your heart to the future . . . what do you see? Ah, like all who have come before, you too see nothing but the unknown. But for you, this path will be an even greater unknown . . .

In the darkness beyond the reservation, the dark outline of the Mongollon Rim recalled the arched back of a puma, waiting to strike. Sparks danced toward the sky, painting the rim in a weave of yellow gold. The central fire, freshly piled with aged pine, crackled and popped. But none of this interested Talon Brave. He preferred instead to keep to the shadows, away from the disapproving glances of the clan elders. Once again, the moon had vanished from the sky, signaling the time for a fire dance. The Gans, masked dancers representing the mountain spirits, danced in a quadrangle between the seated elders and the fire.

Talon took a final drag from a dwindling cigarette and flicked it to the ground—the ember blazed for an instant as it ignited a patch of dried grass, but soon there was nothing. Another pull from his bottle of Soda Jack bourbon, the final sip really, and he let the bottle fall from his fingers as he turned his back on the ceremony and walked back through the shadows of the motor pool.

The elders did not notice Talon's departure—they never even saw him there in the shadows. Instead, they focused, as they had every 30th day for a long as their clan had memories, on the Fire Dance and the rhythmic chants that served to tempt the Gans. Tradition demanded a precise intonation to the chants, and the masked dancers, who represented the four mountain spirits, would react to the chant, moving into the fire as the spirits were said to have moved in from the mountains and touched the clans, so very long ago.

Heads bent, none noticed the crackling blue latticework that appeared across the clouds over the reservation—only moments ago, the sky had been a clear dusting of stars. The chanting continued as the electrical blue glow widened, and the newly formed cloud seemed to part in the middle, to pull apart like a vapor dissipating.

The light illuminated the clan circle, and the elders turned their heads skyward, and for a moment, the chanting and the dancing stopped. But then an elder began his chant again, louder now as he pushed himself to his feet. The others joined in, careful to keep to the sacred rhythm, as they too stood. All raised their arms to the sky, as the true mountain spirits converged upon their circle.

In a hissing of rapidly ionized atmosphere, a column of bluish-white energy burst from the cloud and engulfed the clan circle. For an instant, the circle of tribal elders could be seen in silhouette, first in human form, and then only their bones visible as their flesh vaporized. In a flash, there was nothing but a settling cloud of desert dust. Seconds counted off in silence, and then the alien ship began its final descent.

HOW DO YOU DELIVER A STORY IN A GAME?

How do you deliver a story to the player in a game? The old writing rule is a great place to start: "Show, don't tell." In the best of all possible worlds, the key aspects of the story will be delivered to the player via the moment-by-moment gameplay experience. The environment can help to create the setting. The obstacles the player encounters can define the conflict and the hero's striving against the larger conflict. Details dropped into the game world, from objects found scrawled on the environment walls to inventory items picked up by the player can all help to tell the tale.

In reality, you can't deliver all aspects of a deep story in this way. The in-game experience of the story is best suited to deliver the details of the story that bring richness to the world and depth to the story.

The easiest way to deliver story to the players is to present it to them, either in the form of cinematics or perhaps as mission briefings as they work through a campaign. During this time, you have the player's full attention and you can fully control the experience. Lavishly produced cinematics can impart story and mood with careful musical scoring, dramatic lighting, and the performance of virtual actors.

Classic games like *Command & Conquer*™ and *Diablo II*™ employed professionally produced cinematics to deliver the more complex portions of the story. For the RTS game, these were delivered as contextual mission briefings to set the stage for the next gameplay element in the campaign game. In *Diablo II*, the cinematics were set up almost as player rewards—when the players finished a chapter, they were rewarded with a powerful cinematic that would help to explain the game even further.

With the increasing power of technology, more and more of the expositor "cinematics" can now be handled not as rendered movies but as scripted sequences within the game engine (Figure 16.1). The landmark example of this was the opening sequence for the original Half-Life, in which we see through the eyes of hero Gordon Freeman as he arrives at the research facility. The stunning opening set the stage for the story, gave the players an unprecedented sense of place, and made them feel as if they were truly part of the story. Many a game developer and player gasped the first time they saw that landmark opening (your author among them) .

FIGURE 16.1   The visual fidelity of today's games allows storytelling directly in the game engine. In Prey, we meet the hero's grandfather not in a rendered cinematic, but through storytelling within the game itself. Used with permission. Copyright 2006 3D Realms Entertainment.

Another primary way to deliver story to the player is through the mouths of the characters the player encounters in the game. In the early text adventures, these were short narratives displayed on screen. Later, RPGs added some simple graphical portraits of the speaker, but text was king for many years. With the advent of the CD-ROM, game developers started playing with using voice-overs to deliver character dialogue and story.

With the ability to script sequences in the game itself, we can now deliver interactions with other characters directly through the primary game interface, and not some secondary talking interface. In games such as *Half-Life 2* and *Doom 3*, the player receives the story just as if he were an individual in the world—seeing it for himself and hearing it from the mouths of the characters inhabiting the world.

Of course, the designer had a hand in creating those moments when the player happened to be in the right place at the right time, overhearing those vital little tidbits of information that in all likelihood he would have missed.

Narrative and Level Design

Level design, the construction of the game world, has a profound impact on the narrative structure of a game. For example, the structure of *Halo 2* is such that the player is frequently moving from an enclosed space into a larger area, where allied forces are fighting with aliens. This enables the player to stride into the area, at which point the soldiers all begin to address the player. Because the protagonist is Master Chief, they're all respectful and deferential; because he's new on the scene, they all provide information.

The conversations are not crucial to the game experience, because the player knows what the situation is, and is primarily looking for enemies to shoot. However, this has the effect of establishing a strong narrative in the game, creating lifelike characters who respond to stimuli, and making the player feel like the star of the show. The level design was created to facilitate this experience.

A game like *Animal Crossing: Wild World*, which presents the player with a nonlinear arena to explore, creates the opportunity for a different kind of narrative, in which the player instigates the flow of information. Instead of cut scenes and scripted voice cues, *Wild World* allows the player to determine the timing and amount of interaction with the characters in the game. This makes it more difficult to tell a story according to the traditional rules of narrative (the three-act structure of rising action, climax, and denouement), but allows the player to have more control over the game's storyline.

In addition to the sequence of events, level design can also impact the mood of a narrative. For example, *Quake 4* and *Doom 3* employ dim, claustrophobic level design. Combined with the dark subject matter, this creates a sense of tension and morbidity as the player moves through the level, waiting for the next enemy to jump out and attack. Were the game to take place in a more open environment, like *Battlefield 2*, the player might feel more in control of the scenarios—the player could run forward to engage the enemy, or retreat and take cover behind this bunker. While that might make for interesting gameplay, it would rob those games of the paranoia that drives the experience forward.

HUMOR IN GAMES

Designer: Al Lowe (creator of Leisure Suit Larry)

What did I know? I'd never written humor. Hell, I barely passed college freshman composition. What was I doing trying to make people laugh? How did I get myself into this?

On the other hand, I loved comedy films, TV shows, albums, writing, cartoons, and every other form of humor. I had told and collected jokes all my life. Being the youngest, smallest, weakest, and least athletic student in my class turned my sense of humor into a survival skill.

So I tried to make my games different. Where other games made you their hero, I made you the goat. Where other games used violence, I used awkwardness, humiliation, titillation, and sexual innuendo. Because I lacked confidence in my programming skills, I found beta-testers and implemented a system that recorded to floppy every input they typed that the game couldn't handle. I then took those files, sorted them, and, because I didn't have the resources to extend the game to handle their ideas properly, wrote a smart-ass response instead, because text costs nothing.

In later games, after coming up with an idea that seemed funny, it took us months to implement it, and nothing stays funny for that long. So, as we neared shipping, I would get depressed. What was I thinking? This isn't funny! Yet, when I showed it to outsiders, they would laugh and soon my confidence would be restored. Hey, maybe this isn't so bad after all . . .

In short, it's hard work to be funny. Maybe that's why it's done so little. So how do I teach you to do it? Be true to yourself. Write what you think is funny. Test it. Refine it. Edit the hell out of it. And then hope that someone else agrees with you!

Eye Opener Implementation

In *Eye Opener*, we can deliver the game story to the player through some "old school" techniques: the animatic and the text dialogue. No matter how complexly or simply you deliver the story to the player, you want to keep the delivery simple and the information clear. Remember our atom about narrow focus? Keep the story focused on what matters to the players; otherwise, you'll risk disconnecting them with the game experience.

Story Animatic

The opening story of our sample game is told through a technique known as an animatic, which is basically a slideshow of images that tells the story. The classic 3D science fiction RTS Homeworld used an animatic to tell the story of the destruction and subsequent search for the human home world, and while it was simple in execution, the images conveyed a powerful story. (Figure 16.2.)

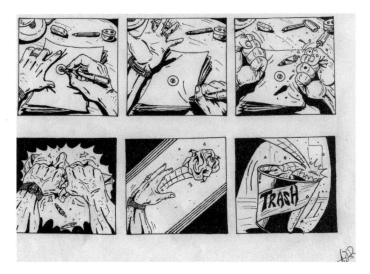

FIGURE 16.2   The original comic panel that we adapted into the opening animatic for *Eye Opener.*

Our opening animatic, which you can play from the "animatic" link of the sandbox build, presents a series of comic-style images that tells the story of how our plucky Eyeball refused to be tossed in the trash.

The slides themselves are defined in a Lua script that is designed so a designer can easily set up and create the individual slides.

Editing the Animatic

Cinematic editing is similar to Adventure Scene editing in that every entity that is to be edited must first exist in the script of the cinematic file. Editing is only useful for changing the position of an entity, and setting the timing of the slide changes, which are the elements you really want hands-on control over.

Cinematic Lua files are created by the designer to create and fill a Slide table. It has the following indexes:

Background: Slide background sprite.

Music: The string of the file to be played (an Ogg Vorbis file, located in the Music folder within the game build folder on the companion CD-ROM).

Sprite: The sprite displayed on the slide (there can be only one per slide).

SpriteX, SpriteY, SpriteWidth, SpriteHeight: Define the size and position of the sprite image.

Text: Text to be displayed on the slide (there can be only one per slide).

TextX, TextY, TextSize: Define the size and position of the text on screen.

TextColor: Table of R, G, B values for text color.

TextFont: String identifying the font, which must exist in the Fonts folder (also in the game build folder on the companion CD-ROM). ("Arial" for instance.)

Timer: Amount of time the current slide is displayed.

Sprite, Text, Timer, and Music are all optional items for each slide. An example of a slide entry looks like this in the file:

```
— Slide #1
Slide[gSCount].Music = "OpeningCinematic.ogg"
Slide[gSCount].Background = "ui_bg_ingame_frame.tga"
Slide[gSCount].Text = "Eye Opener"
Slide[gSCount].TextX = 240
Slide[gSCount].TextY = 275
Slide[gSCount].TextSize = 60
Slide[gSCount].TextColor = {98,182,240}
Slide[gSCount].TextFont = "Sui"
Slide[gSCount].Timer = 3.0
```

To create a new cinematic file, it's easiest to open the "Master.lua" file in the Cinematics folder (in the game build folder found on the companion CD-ROM) and rename it. You can then edit, add, or remove slide definitions. At the bottom of each Cinematic file are the options `timerToggle` and `positionEditMode`.

The variable `positionEditMode` can be ON or OFF. This determines whether the cinematic will be loaded for viewing or editing. The variable `timerToggle` can be ON, OFF, or EDIT. ON means that the timer will automatically advance through the slides, creating a viewing experience. OFF means that the user must manually advance the slides. EDIT means that when the user loads the current cinematic file, the time each slide is shown is recorded in the script, effectively allowing the user to set the timer by "feel" rather than by number in the script.

In the position editing state, the user can cycle through each entity in the slide and alter its position using the arrow keys superimposed on the number pad (2, 4, 6, and 8). The number 5 cycles the user through the entities. When the status textfield reads, "Done," the user may advance the slides forward or backward with "." (>) or "," (<), respectively.

When Esc is pressed, the settings are saved back to the cinematic Lua file.

Experiment with this tool and a sequence of images and text to get an idea of just how much story you can tell via an animatic.

NPC Conversation

We have created a little Lua tool that will allow you to create simple interactive NPC dialogues, which you can use to reveal puzzle information, or deliver key aspects of a game story to the player. We'll first look at how the system works.

NPC Talk Function

TalkCheck() is continually run during the GUI_TIMER_EXPIRED portion of Lua-Scrolling.lua. If a character exists in the space directly surrounding the player, the Speak button will appear in the upper-right corner of the screen.

```
function TalkCheck()
    talk = "no"
    if (MegaTable["Eye"].X >= 20) and (MegaTable["Eye"].X <= (780-
MegaTable["Eye"].Width)) then
        local numX = MegaTable["Eye"].Width/20
        for i = -1,numX do
            local x = ((MegaTable["Eye"].X + (i*20))/20)+1
            for j = 0,2 do
                local y = ((MegaTable["Eye"].Y + (j*20))/20)+1
                if OnScreen[x][y].State == 3 then
                    talk = "yes"
                end
            end
        end
    else
        talk = "no"
    end
    if talk == "yes" then
        EnableObject(BUT_SPEAK, 1, 1)
    else
        EnableObject(BUT_SPEAK, 0, 0)
    end
end
```

Whether the player can converse with an NPC is controlled by a state variable. gNPCToggleState can be only the constants ON or OFF. gNPCState is the primary variable used in the NPC process, and can take the values "Done," "Intro," or "StatementDisp."

When the speak button is pressed, gNPCToggleState = NPCInterfaceToggle(gN-PCToggleState) is run (LuaSupport.lua). This function enables or disables the GUI objects needed for the NPC. It also will call gNPCState = NPCProcessState("Intro").

```
function NPCProcessState(state)
    if state == "Intro" then
        GrabStatement(2)
        return "StatementDisp"
    elseif state == "StatementDisp" then
        return EvaluateResponse()
    else
        gNPCToggleState = NPCInterfaceToggle(ON)
    end
end
```

NPCProcessState(state) is a simple version of a finite state machine, and determines the next step in the dialogue. If the state is "Intro," it calls GrabStatement(2) and sets gNPCState to "StatementDisp." If the state is "StatementDisp," it sets gNPCState to the returned value of EvaluateResponse(). If the state is "Done," it clears the NPC GUI by calling gNPCToggleState = NPCInterfaceToggle(ON).

```
function EvaluateResponse()
    if NPC[gStatementNum][gResponseIndx] ~= 1 and
NPC[gStatementNum][gResponseIndx] ~= 0 then
        gStatementNum = NPC[NPC[gStatementNum][gResponseIndx]][2]
        GrabStatement(gStatementNum)
        return "StatementDisp"
    else
        gNPCState = "Done"
        gNPCToggleState = NPCInterfaceToggle(ON)
        return "Done"
    end
end
```

GrabStatement(num) displays the proper nonplayer statement with the four possible responses for the player.

```
function GrabStatement(num)
    gStatementNum = num
    if gStatementNum == 1 then
        ItemCommand(GUI_INGAME + 205, "SetString", NPC[gStatementNum][1])
        ItemCommand(GUI_INGAME + 201, "SetString", "See ya.")
        ItemCommand(GUI_INGAME + 202, "SetString", "Later.")
        ItemCommand(GUI_INGAME + 203, "SetString", "Bye.")
        ItemCommand(GUI_INGAME + 204, "SetString", "Have a good one.")
        gNPCState = "Done"
    else
        ItemCommand(GUI_INGAME + 205, "SetString", NPC[gStatementNum][1])
        ItemCommand(GUI_INGAME + 201, "SetString",
NPC[NPC[gStatementNum][2]][1])
```

```
        ItemCommand(GUI_INGAME + 202, "SetString",
NPC[NPC[gStatementNum][3]][1])
        ItemCommand(GUI_INGAME + 203, "SetString",
NPC[NPC[gStatementNum][4]][1])
        ItemCommand(GUI_INGAME + 204, "SetString",
NPC[NPC[gStatementNum][5]][1])
    end
end
```

In NPC.lua, there exists a table of tables. Each table contains a statement or question at its first index. The four subsequent indexes hold the indexes of relevant responses to that question or statement. Here is an example of a statement:

```
NPC[3] = {"How are you?",4,5,6,7}
```

If num ~= 1 (if the statement is not a "Goodbye" statement), the function displays the statement at num index as the NPC's dialogue. The possible responses are displayed for the player to choose. If the num == 1, that would be the signal to wrap up the conversation (thus the gNPCState = "Done" portion).

When the player selects a response, NPCProcessState(state) will call Evaluate Response(). If the response is not a "Goodbye" response, the function calls Grab-Statement(num) using the 2nd index from the table containing the player's response (that is, the computer responds with the first available response to the player's input).

When a player wants to end the conversation, he simply selects the "Goodbye" response.

NPC Dialog User Information

ON THE CD

To create your own dialogue scripts, open NPC.lua from the Scripts folder (found under the root game folder on the companion CD-ROM).Right now, the file looks like this:

```
NPC = {}
NPC[1] = {"Goodbye.",0,0,0,0}
NPC[2] = {"Hello.",3,8,9,10}
NPC[3] = {"How are you?",4,5,6,7}
NPC[4] = {"Fine.",3,8,9,1}
NPC[5] = {"Just peachy.",8,3,9,1}
NPC[6] = {"Horrible.",10,8,9,1}
NPC[7] = {"Excellent!",9,10,8,1}
NPC[8] = {"Are you okay?",5,6,7,4}
NPC[9] = {"How's this weather, eh?",6,7,4,5}
NPC[10] = {"How is my driving?",7,4,5,6}
```

To the left are several rows of NPC[number]. The number contained in each of these rows is the index in the NPC table for the material in quotation marks to its right. That number is directly associated with this statement or question.

The four numbers following the statement or question are the indexes of the appropriate responses to the material in quotes. A 0 in the responses tells the program to end the conversation. Thus, if we were to spell out the second line:

```
NPC[2] = {"Hello.",3,8,9,10}
It means this to the program:
```

Statement	Possible Responses
"Hello"	"Are you okay?"
	"How's this weather, eh?"
	"How is my driving?"

To alter the NPC dialogue, simply add or subtract indexes to the NPC table, making sure that each entry consists of five comma-separated values contained in {}. The statement or question must be in quotes and followed by the valid indexes of responses. Keep in mind that the NPC will respond with the first available response of any entry in the table.

The "Goodbye" statement can be changed to any other farewell statement, but its responses must remain 0,0,0,0 for the program to function. If you want the computer to say the "Goodbye" statement, just place 1 as the first response of an entry in the NPC table. That way, the computer will respond with it, if given the opportunity.

To test your NPC creation, load LevelScrolling.lua with the Talk level.

SUMMARY

In this chapter, we tried to define what a story is and how it relates to what a game is. Both share some very similar traits and can dovetail quite nicely if we remember that the key element of a game is the player and his agency in the world (as opposed to being a passive receptacle for story).

We then explored the fundamental atoms of what makes a story a story and how we can work to craft vital yet simple game stories that can serve as backbones for our games. From there, we explored the idea of storytelling itself being used as a tool to help us design games with more depth and resonance.

We then turned our attention to how we can deliver a story to a player within a game, from the low-tech text box to the advanced in-engine scripted sequences. We then looked at some low-tech examples of animatics and NPC dialogue systems within our *Eye Opener* test game.

And now, we've nearly come to the end of our journey. In our next and final chapter, we'll take a few minutes to explore your next steps as you look to embark on the exciting adventure of designing your own games.

CHAPTER EXERCISES

1. Imagine what sort of super-hero you would like to be—what powers would you like to have? What amazing mental or physical abilities would you have? Jot down your list of amazing powers that would allow you to be the greatest super-hero ever. Now imagine a weakness that trumps all of your powers—is it physical, like kryptonite, or is it a secret? Heroes become far more interesting when they must battle to overcome a significant weakness.

ON THE CD

2. Using photos grabbed from an Internet image search (and the game sandbox provided on the companion CD-ROM), put together your own animatic that tells a story—see if you can imply a deeper and more intense story than the words and images themselves supply.
3. Using the NPC system discussed earlier, write out an NPC script for a character who is holding a "ring of power" and knows he should give it to you, but is driven to keep it (as a scripting enhancement to this exercise—can you modify the Lua code to create even more flexibility in the NPC dialogue system?).

17 Next Steps

In This Chapter

- Practice Your Skills
- Create a Demo Portfolio
- Breaking into the Business

ast-forward five years into the future. Imagine the clean desk we first saw way back at the start of the book—but it's clean no more. Legal pads and graph paper litter the desk, ringed with coffee stains. An empty can of Mountain Dew™ stands in the corner. Pencils of every length litter the surface near the keyboard. On the monitor, a once-clear desktop is now strewn with shortcuts and temporary files. The empty bookcase near the desk is now packed with eclectic books—books on pirates, poker, and architecture. Books on the history of video games and the fractal geometry of nature. Books on writing and editing and character creation. On the top shelf—not yet full, but getting there—are copies of the boxes of three games—games you've helped to design. And you're just getting started.

Does that sound compelling? Many a designer's desk looks like that—littered with the clues of work well done and long hours spent crafting play experiences. You may not be there yet, but hopefully you have gotten a sense of the skills you'll need for this career path, and some helpful design advice that will help you get started down the right path. We've shared a long journey of learning together and now it's time to ask the question: "What next?"

PRACTICE YOUR SKILLS

First and foremost, you will want to practice your skills. In this book, you were presented with a rather in-depth look at the skills you'll need to succeed as a professional game designer. Game design is an exciting profession, and it's one in which your primary skills are your wisdom, your intelligence, and your ability to think creatively. In a way, you *are* your own tool.

The best advice we can give you is that you should realize how important your mind is to your job, and you should do everything possible to pack it full of new knowledge, exercise it like crazy, and take care of that lanky and awkward support system connected to your neck (also known as your body). Take care of your mind and it will serve you well for years to come (Figure 17.1).

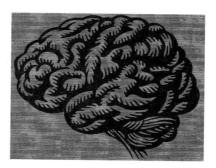

FIGURE 17.1   Your mind is your most essential piece of software—take care of it!

ON THE CD

In addition to taking care of your internal software, you will grow your skills by thinking and acting like a game designer. Play the best and worst games from the list on the companion CD-ROM and evaluate them as a film critic would review a film. Get to know what works and what doesn't, and start to grow your own vocabulary of game design understanding and techniques that work in a game. In addition, start you own list on what to avoid in the games you design—learning what doesn't work and what to avoid is essential in your role as a designer.

CREATE A DEMO PORTFOLIO

As you practice and hone your skills, you should also develop a portfolio of your work. This can include reviews and critiques of games, sample game design scope documents, full design documents, and even snippets of sample games in which you try a technique or approach you are interested in.

Look at some of the tools out there that you can use to create demo game experiences. Learn level design skills—even if you aren't interested in being a level designer—because the crafting levels in some of today's most popular games can get you used to working with professional tools and technology. In addition, the act of level design encapsulates many of the aspects of game design as a whole, and you can really show off and demonstrate some of your design abilities.

If you do learn to design levels, get involved in the Internet community. Get to be part of an online modding team, so you can learn about collaboration and can work on some larger projects. If you create levels, post them on fan sites that critique custom levels and start paying attention to player feedback and learn from that feedback, revising and improving your work.

ON THE CD

Use the tools on this book's CD-ROM—you've been provided with a complete 2D game engine and a scripting language (Lua) that will allow you to create complete games. The *Eye Opener* demo provides much of the structure you need to get started creating your own games. You might also want to pick up a copy of *Game Development with Lua*, also from Charles River Media. That book will take you deeper into Lua and provides even more "sandbox" tools that you can use to craft your own demo games (the script examples in both books are 100-percent compatible).

BREAKING INTO THE BUSINESS

If you've decided to break into the industry and pursue your dream of being a game designer, how do you do it? Where do you start? The first step is getting the education you need to learn the skills that will allow you to perform. That can come from schools, books like this, professional organizations, mod groups—almost any source.

The next step is learning about the industry, so you understand the current trends, the ebb and flow of publishers and developers, and where development will be heading for the next five years. Learning about the industry is more than just playing games and studying them—it's learning about the business of making and selling games.

Finally, it's about getting out there and trying to land your first job. You'll need a positive attitude, the ability to handle rejection, some clean clothes, and the ability to communicate effectively with your potential employers.

What Education Do You Need?

The game development industry is skill based—that is, your value is derived from your skills, not necessarily any pieces of framed paper you have hanging on your wall. We've hired programmers with graduate degrees, and ones who dropped out of high school. We've hired level designers away from aerospace firms, and away from pizza delivery. It really doesn't matter what your educational credentials are, as long as you have the skills (and a way to prove those skills) to do a great job.

That being said, a few skills aren't directly related to your education, but are essential—maturity, responsibility, and dedication. If you apply for a job with a four-year college degree in hand, you will have indirectly already proven these skills, since you can't earn the sheepskin without a healthy dose of at least basic levels of those skills. If you apply for a job and your resume lists "pizza delivery" as your last job, you better have some way of proving those "I am a grown-up" skills, and having a list of service jobs with only three months at each won't cut it. If you are green or don't have much on your resume to back up your work, find some references that can tell a prospective employer about your skills, and your ability to be counted on, communicate, and handle responsibility.

If you want to get into game design and wonder what educational path to take, there are several to consider. We wouldn't recommend the "no school at all" path unless you are a true savant with years of experience, deep technical and research knowledge, and tons of demos to back up your self learning. When we hired the programmer who didn't finish high school, he already had years of programming skills under his belt and was raking in some nice royalties on a DOS extender he wrote years earlier. In short, he had the chops and could prove it.

There are two primary education paths to take these days once you get out of high school: a four-year college program or a technical training program.

In recent years, more and more technical and vocational schools have taken up the gauntlet of training young students to be ready for the games industry. The majority of these technical schools are professional art vocational schools that have enhanced their curriculum to add game development courses and programs of focus. While many of them focus more on 2D and 3D art skills, many are also offering programs in game development and design.

There are also schools dedicated to preparing you for a career in game development, such as Full Sail or DigiPen. These vocational schools have built curriculums from the ground up to prepare students for the industry and have faculties who have been in the trenches and understand how the industry works.

The following is a short selection of some of the vocational schools that offer programs in game design and development:

The Art Institutes (many locations): *www.aii.edu*
DigiPen Institute of Technology: *www.digipen.edu*
Full Sail: *www.fulsail.com*
Vancouver Film School: *www.vfs.com*

Four-year colleges offer bachelor's degrees either directly related to the games industry or more general degrees that will give you a great start. If you are interested in a more "classic" major, what would be good for a game designer? I had a student ask that once of the great "grand old man" of computer game design, Chris Crawford, during a lecture he was giving at a college where I was on the faculty. Chris' answer was simple and heart-felt: "Anything but computer science!" While I'm not as opposed to computer science as a major as Chris is, I understand his point: as designers, we need a breadth of knowledge, and computer science curriculums tend to isolate students from the larger world, rather than allowing them to explore it. I would recommend majors such as History, English, Biology, Sociology, and Psychology—any of the majors that teach you about the challenges of the human condition, because that's where great stories and great games emerge. Also, I would recommend a liberal arts school over a standard university curriculum, since as a designer, you are interested in absorbing as much breadth as you can, and that's the basic approach of a liberal arts degree.

A number of four-year accredited college programs and graduate programs are now cropping up with a specific focus on the games industry, and offer the best of both worlds: industry-related vocational training with the rigors of a standard college curriculum. Several of the colleges and programs are listed here:

Carnegie Mellon Entertainment Technology Center (graduate program): *www.etc.cmu.edu*

Florida Interactive Entertainment Academy (graduate program): *www.fiea.ucf.edu*

The "Guildhall" at SMU: *www.guildhall.smu.edu*

Savannah College of Art and Design: *www.scad.edu*

So, which approach holds the most promise? It's really up to the individual to stand out and shine, not the educational program. Since this industry is based on skills, it really boils down to which approach will build the better skill set.

All things being equal, I do have my preferences (but remember, these are just the opinions of one man). I've been hiring developers and designers to work in the games industry for the last 10 years, and I tend to favor students with a four-year degree who have a portfolio beyond their core schoolwork to show me. Next down the list would be the vocational schools, since those require a basic mastery of core game development skills. If I'm evaluating a candidate without a degree, I had better see something spectacular and I will check their references very closely.

A word of warning: no matter what anyone tells you, for you to stand out from the crowded field of other job applicants, you'll need to do some work outside of your standard coursework—some work related directly to the games industry and done wholly on your own. This demonstrates dedication, ingenuity, and a real desire to succeed. It also shows that you can pick up core skills on your own. A game demo or a level portfolio, done outside of school coursework, is a great approach.

Learning the Industry

To get a job in any industry, it's a good idea to learn as much about it as you can, even before that first interview. The games industry is a "digital" industry with a very dedicated following of consumers, from the casual to the fervent. As a result, there is a wealth of online sources that can help you learn about the industry and keep up with the ebb and flow of sales, development, technology, and new game platforms.

To get you started, here are some essential industry-wide sites you'll want to bookmark and keep in touch with, at least once a week:

Blues News: *www.bluesnews.com*

Gamasutra: *www.gamasutra.com*

IGDA: *www.igda.org*

Game Daily Biz newsletter: *biz.gamedaily.com*

You should also try to get involved. See if there is an IGDA (International Game Developers Association) chapter nearby—join and attend the meetings and get to know the movers ands shakers in your local area.

If you can, try to make it to the Game Developer's Conference (*www.gdconf. com*) held each spring. The conference brings together developers from all across the industry and the world. You can attend sessions, learn about tools and techniques, network, and even attend a job fair where you can get your resume and demo CD-ROM in front of dozens of prospective employers. You can even volunteer to be a conference associate—you'll work a few hours each day for the conference in exchange for the ability to attend the entire session—it's a great place to learn, meet, and greet (Figure 17.2).

Networking

If you're serious about finding work as a video game designer, you need to establish and cultivate a network of professional contacts. Before you begin, it's important to think of this from the perspective of the developer. If a prospective coworker approaches you, and appears to be both knowledgeable and professional, you'll probably be much more likely to offer your help. So, when presenting yourself, be sure you've done your research. Study the companies you're interested in working for. If you're going to be talking to developers, learn about the companies they work for, and the games they develop. You'll be better equipped to hold up your end of the conversation. Also, make sure your presentation is appropriate. Dress appropriately; the industry standard is T-shirts and jeans, but that's after you're hired, not before.

FIGURE 17.2 The Game Developer's Conference, held every spring, is *the* place to meet and network with other game designers.

As for establishing your network, there are a number of ways to do so. First, the International Game Developers Association meets regularly in cities all across the country. Even if you must travel, try to make it to a few meetings. You'll meet industry professionals, each of whom knows dozens of other developers. Don't be afraid to say that you're looking for work. If you know what you're talking about, have something to offer, and present yourself well, you'll make solid contacts. Also look into attending conferences and expos in your area. These are also attended by developers, and give you an opportunity to attend seminars and lectures. Although the big events (GDC and E3) are in California, there are others to choose from. Visit Web sites like *Gamasutra.com* for more information about industry events.

Finally, consider creating professional resources like business cards and Web sites. A set of business cards can be purchased fairly cheaply. Even with hosting fees, an online portfolio can be obtained for less than $100, making it a worthwhile investment. Look at the Web sites of developers in your field of interest, and see what they've done with their Web pages. You can find such Web sites linked from other industry sites, like corporate Web pages or places like *Gamasutra.com*.

Going for the First Job

Okay, you have your skills honed, a demo CD-ROM at the ready, an education that will serve your well, and a polished resume. You're ready to get your first job—so what do you do now? First and foremost, you'll need to refine your "self sales pitch"—what about you makes you unique, skilled, and a valuable addition to a game development team? You don't want to come off pompous and full of yourself (quietly confident and humble always trumps pompous), but you need to figure out the tune you'll play when you blow your own horn.

There are many resources to find job openings. A good place to get a feel of what's out there across the industry is an aggregate site such as GameJobs (*www.gamejobs.com*). On these sites, you'll find multiple listings across the board. You can also check out the job fair at the Game Developers Conference. This is a good place to start, but perhaps not the best—hundreds (if not thousands) of applicants will be taking this approach, and being a tiny fish in a pond packed with Koi is not a great way to stand out.

The best approach is to find out what kind of games you are interested in designing and what aspect of design most interests you (as a new designer, odds are you will be working under a senior designer and will be working on a portion of a game design, not the whole ball of wax). Find developers who make those kinds of games and visit their sites. Nearly every development studio hosts an employment page of current job openings—look at what's available, and when you find something you like, contact them directly.

Be sure to pay attention to their application guidelines, because your resume will be dragged over to the trash icon if you don't follow their procedures. Always strive to include a well-written, but short (no more than a page or page and a half) cover letter that shows the development studio that you know their work and their development style.

Be prepared for rejection and don't take it personally—if you get a response and a request for an interview from 5 percent of the applications you send out, you are ahead of the bell curve. When you do get that interview, be professional, be clean and well dressed, but most importantly, be yourself (but an outgoing, conversational you). It'll take some time, but if you've done your homework and have the mental chops it takes, you'll find your first home in the industry and will find yourself stepping up to that new and empty desk, ready to begin your adventure.

Resources

There are many places where you can find more information about game design. Numerous articles on the subject are available for free online. Visit Gamasutra (*www.gamasutra.com*) and GameDev.net (*www.gamedev.net*) for articles on game design, working in the industry, and news about publishers and developers.

For information about the International Game Developers Association, visit *www.igda.org*. Be sure to visit their forums, particularly the Breaking Into the Industry section. For more games industry news, visit Next Generation (*www.next-gen.biz*) and Games Industry (*www.gamesindustry.biz*).

All of the aforementioned Web sites feature job postings, and they all link to other sites that offer even more information about the industry. The more you learn about this field, the better equipped you'll be when you're called in for a job interview.

SUMMARY

In this chapter, we looked at what your world might be like in several years. The work will be hard and intense, but challenging, exciting, and rewarding. We then looked at what you can do next to hone your skills, produce some quality demos, and get the education you need to be a competitive candidate for a job as a game designer.

We then explored some steps to take to prepare for that first job. It'll take time, patience, and a thick skin, but if you work hard, the future will be bright. Interactive games aren't going away—it's truly a growth industry, and over the next few years, consoles will grow to an even larger position of dominance, and the idea of gaming will become more and more mainstream.

And now, our time together is done. I hope you enjoyed our journey and I hope you learned some things along the way. As I look back on these 17 chapters, I can see that I've only scratched the surface of what it means to be a game designer. It's a wonderful profession, and one I'm proud to be involved in (on one way or another, I've been designing games for nearly 30 years so far—and I'm not done yet).

As a game designer, always thirst for new knowledge, both about the craft of game design and the world around you. Inspiration is everywhere—open yourself up to it. Take notes, make doodles, and then design the best games you can. Enjoy the results, but also revel in the processes.

I hope this book helped, in some small way, to get you started down your own path. Thanks for spending your valuable time, and please let me know about your adventure (you can reach me at *paul@schuytema.com*). Now, the next move is up to you!

About the CD-ROM

This book features a companion CD that provides support materials, the sample game, plus a number of useful tools, utilities and goodies.

SYSTEM REQUIREMENTS

- P450 or better processor
- Windows 2000/XP
- 32MB of RAM

For the game and "sandbox" demos:

- DirectX 8.1 or higher (see README_DirectX.rtf for link to download))
- DX-compatible 3D video accelerator

Folders

The files on this disc are organized into folders as follows:

- *Figures*: All of the figures from the book, organized in folders by chapter.
- *Game*: this folder contains the *Eye Opener* game referenced in the book
- *Demos*: this folder contains sub-folders that have various demos and script examples (plus those found in the game)—there is also a support document explaining several of the demos that are beyond the scope of the book, but should be of interest to those who want to use the 2D game engine and Lua to experiment with their own games.
- *Documents*: this folder contains the *Eye Opener* design document, a Lua scripting style guide, sample game design documents and a list of the best games.

- *License:* This folder contains the distribution license documents for both Lua and Ogg Vorbis.
- *Lua:* This contains the Lua console and the Lua manual.
- *Take Away:* A bonus retro-style arcade game and design document using the same game engine. *http://www.lanterngames.com/*
- *VSLua:* for the programmer/designers out there—this beta program integrates Lua programming and debugging into Microsoft's Visual Studio
- *Zeus:* This is the shareware version of the Zeus program editor—a great tool for editing Lua scripts.

Software

The following software products have been included on the CD-ROM:

Lua

Tecgraf, PUC-Rio
http://www.lua.org

VSLua

Suite 307, Evacuee Trust Complex
Aga Khan Road, F-5/1
Islamabad, Pakistan
http://www.itrango.com/

ZEUS

Xidiconc P/L
P.O. Box 697
Lanccove, NSW Australia 2066
http://zeus.objectweb.org/

Index